It's Alive!

It's Alive!

THE CLASSIC CINEMA SAGA OF FRANKENSTEIN

Gregory William Mank

San Diego • New York
A. S. Barnes & Company, Inc.
In London:
The Tantivy Press

For my beautiful Barbara
My Greatest Blessing

First Paper Edition
Manufactured in the United States of America

For information write to:
Oak Tree Publications, Inc.
P.O. Box 3051
La Jolla, California 92038

The Tantivy Press
Magdalen House
136–148 Tooley Street
London, SE1 2TT, England

Library of Congress Cataloging in Publication Data
Mank, Gregory W
It's alive!

Includes material on eight Frankenstein films produced by Universal Pictures.
Bibliography: p.
1. Frankenstein films. I. Universal Pictures Corporation. II. Title.
PN1995.9.F36M3 791.43'75 80-26625
ISBN 0-498-02473-3

1 2 3 4 5 6 7 8 9 84 83 82

Contents

Acknowledgments vii
Introduction ix
Frankenstein (1931) 1
Bride of Frankenstein (1935) 43
Son of Frankenstein (1939) 67
The Ghost of Frankenstein (1942) 89
Frankenstein Meets the Wolf Man (1943) 107
House of Frankenstein (1944) 125
House of Dracula (1945) 141
Abbott and Costello Meet Frankenstein (1948) 151
Denouement 167
Further Frankensteins 175
Biographical Appendix 181
Notes 193

Acknowledgments

This book had many allies: The Academy of Motion Picture Arts and Sciences in Los Angeles, where Anthony Slide, head of the Academy's National Film Information Service, provided me with copies of studio records, period reviews, publicity data, interviews, obituaries, etc.; the awesome collection and staff of the Lincoln Center Library of the Performing Arts in New York City; the American Film Institute in Washington, D.C. Such noted cinema writers/historians as DeWitt Bodeen, Richard Bojarski, Doug McClelland, and James Robert Parish all shared materials, ideas, and encouragement with me. Eddie Brandt, whose "Saturday Matinee" still shop in North Hollywood is perhaps the finest in the country, patiently allowed me to study his vast stock of portraits, stills, candids, and poster reproductions. I was fortunate too in owning or having access to books and magazine features by some of the most respected movie critics/historians of the day, whose names and works are cited elsewhere in this book.

I was determined, however, that the real adventure in writing this book would be contacting as many celebrated veterans of the series as possible and talking with them to secure their first-hand memories.

It was, indeed, a formidable task. Many of the stars, directors, writers, et al., have died. Two surviving prominent producers were terribly ill and/or sadly senile; one died while this book was in production. Robert Florey, *Frankenstein*'s original adaptor and director of the infamous 2-reel *Frankenstein* test with Lugosi, also died. One actor refused to cooperate, claiming he was saving all his stories for his own book; when his book project fell through, he confessed to me, "I can't remember a thing!" There were a couple of aging ingenues who refused to consent to interviews. And there are several once-famous movie personalities in Hollywood who, for whatever strange reasons, are keeping a stamped envelope self-addressed by Gregory William Mank, who has given up hope of hearing from them about their work in the series.

Nevertheless, the story of Universal's Frankenstein saga was told—by some exceptional people whose kindness I'll always treasure. There was Charles Barton, director of *Abbott and Costello Meet Frankenstein*, who took time from a move from Santa Monica beach to Toluca Lake, and treatment for a back problem, to reminisce warmly about the comedy team he loved, and the "monsters" he greatly admired. Sara Jane Karloff Brodsack, Karloff's only child, graciously spoke to me regarding her father's true feelings about his "dear old Monster." My friend Lillian Lugosi Donlevy told me with utmost candor why her husband Bela refused *Frankenstein*, why he played the part of the Monster 12 years later in *Frankenstein Meets the Wolf Man*—and what he thought of Boris Karloff. Josephine Hutchinson, the still-lovely actress who trembled so chicly in *Son of Frankenstein*, charmingly confided to me how "phony" it felt to act in a Frankenstein movie. Elsa Lanchester, the *Bride of Frankenstein* herself, regaled me with marvelously told tales about playing the Monster's Mate, and even coached me on how to perform that infamous hiss which she so unforgettably sounded in that classic fantasy. David Manners, Horror's greatest romantic hero, sensitively remembered Colin Clive, in whose arms he had died in 1930's *Journey's End*, while Curt Siodmak, the prolific horror/science fiction writer who scripted *Frankenstein Meets the Wolf Man* and concocted the story for *House of Frankenstein*, recalled his days at Universal with great candor and wit. Finally, the beautiful Elena Verdugo, the tragic Ilonka of *House of Frankenstein*, actually took time out from a London vacation to answer my questions about that "monster rally" of 37 years ago.

I am also grateful to such survivors as Evelyn Ankers, Ralph Bellamy, John Carradine, Mae Clarke, and Hans J. Salter, all of whom have recalled their work in the Frankenstein series in other interviews and/or their own writings. And, of course, I must thank such late-lamented artists as Lionel Atwill, Lon Chaney Jr., Colin Clive, Robert Florey, Dwight Frye, Sir Cedric Hardwicke, Boris Karloff, Erle C. Kenton, Carl Laemmle, Jr., Rowland V. Lee, Bela Lugosi, Ilona Massey, Roy William Neill, Jack P. Pierce, Basil Rathbone, Glenn Strange, Edward Van Sloan, and James Whale, who reminisced about Frankenstein adventures during their lifetimes, and whose relevant observations are quoted in this book.

There should be one note of caution: please realize that the opinions expressed by the various people interviewed for this book, regarding the professional and personal habits of their co-workers and famous acquaintances, are *their* opinions, as stated to me. They do not necessarily reflect the opinion of the author.

I must also express gratitude to Ronald Bowers (Editor of *Films in Review*), Frederick S. Clarke (Editor of *Cinefantastique*), the County Recorder of the Los Angeles Hall of Records, Michael G. Fitzgerald, Hammer Pictures, Independent-International Pictures, The Larry Edmunds Bookshop of Hollywood, Kenneth G. Lawrence, the Office of the State Registrar of Vital Statistics of California, Robert Scherl, Charles Smith (of the *Film Favorites* Still Service), 20th Century Fox Studios, and Universal Studios.

One final word of thanks: to my wonderful wife Barbara and my two beautiful children, Jessica and Christopher, who tolerated my strange moods and hours while this book was prepared.

Introduction

A Saturday night, September 1957. I was clad in my pajamas, sitting on the living room floor, staring boldly at the television set, and six years old. My parents, vigilantly seated on the couch behind me, had finally honored my heartrending pleas, and had allowed me to stay up until the ungodly hour of 11:15 P.M.—to see *Frankenstein.*

The local news ended. "Shock Theatre" began. The film flickered onto the screen, Edward Van Sloan made his entrance, looked right at me, and spoke:

> How do you do? Mr. Carl Laemmle feels it would be a little unkind to present this picture without just a word of friendly warning. We are about to unfold the story of Frankenstein, a man of science, who sought to create a man after his own image—without reckoning upon God. It is one of the strangest tales ever told. It deals with the two great mysteries of creation—Life, and Death.
>
> I think it will thrill you. It may shock you. It might even . . . *horrify* you! So if any of you feel that you do not care to subject your nerves to such a strain, now is your chance to . . . well, we've warned you!

It was at this point that I turned off the set, ran up the hallway and dived into the safety of my bed.

A few weeks later, my courage rallied, and I sat up with my father to see *Frankenstein Meets the Wolf Man.* I still remember my Dad, a very perceptive and very unpretentious judge of movies, wincing at Bela Lugosi's performance as the Monster. Then, shortly afterwards, I watched (with a shivering babysitter) *Son of Frankenstein.* Karloff's Monster and Lugosi's Ygor enchanted me, and my "love affair" with the Frankenstein saga really began on that night.

Today, few film scholars would debate the fact that Universal Studio's Frankenstein films, beginning with the 1931 milestone *Frankenstein* and ending with the 1948 farce *Abbott and Costello Meet Frankenstein,* constitute the most beloved horror film series ever produced. Cinema history has long acknowledged Karloff's interpretation of the Monster as one of *the* great film performances, and the pictures themselves have become a part of American movie folklore. Scores of films based on Mary Shelley's hapless Monster have been produced internationally, but only the Universal series has won a true following—and one that segues from generation to generation.

Historically, Universal's Frankenstein series ran distinctly parallel to the history of the Horror genre itself. The December 1931 release of *Frankenstein* (following the success of *Dracula* ten months previous) fully inaugurated Horror as a sensational genre, inspiring the creation of many of the cinema's vintage chillers. *Bride of Frankenstein,* released in May of 1935, was an audacious climax to the "Golden Age" of Hollywood Horror, while *Son of Frankenstein,* premiering in January of 1939, reawakened Horror film production after a 2½ year coma. The following serious entries—1942's *The Ghost of Frankenstein,* 1943's *Frankenstein Meets the Wolf Man,* 1944's *House of Frankenstein,* and 1945's *House of Dracula*—mirrored (for all their merits) the decline of the genre, while 1948's *Abbott and Costello Meet Frankenstein* allowed the Monster, Dracula, and the Wolf Man to make a gracefully comic exit as the more contemporary horrors of the atomic age made their entrance.

Accompanying my affection for these films was a fascination with the lives of the men and women who brought those movies to life, and with the stories of the films' productions. The deeper I probed, the more fascinated I became. The history of Universal's Frankenstein series was much more than the garden variety film book material of credits, synopses, and copied newspaper reviews. It was a dramatic story of studio politics, talent, egomania, fickle public taste, freak accidents, private and public scandal, sadism, gallantry, heartbreak, fatal illness, and even a possible murder. Against the backdrop of one studio's lucrative Horror series, many personal dramas had been played.

This book attempts to tell the complete story of Universal's Monster saga. There are detailed credits (with as many uncredited actors and crew members as my research could uncover); with a full synopsis for each of the eight films (including the now-famous dialogue lines, and notes on the plots' often-glaring inconsistencies); and a production history, chronicling each film's production adventures and misadventures, its popular and critical impact, and its place in historical film perspective. What dominates, however, is the personalities of the artists who gave the Frankenstein series its special magic.

There are the men who played the Monster: Boris Karloff, gentle, aesthetic, full of love and loyalty for the "dear old Monster" who changed this mysterious English exile into a beloved international star; Lon Chaney, Jr., a confused mixture of boisterous extrovert and violent inebriate, surviving his performance as the Monster in *The Ghost of Frankenstein* with loud complaints and a hip flask; Bela Lugosi, proud, arrogant, yet essentially warm and shy, cavalierly refusing the Monster role in *Frankenstein,* yet playing it at age 60 in *Frankenstein Meets the Wolf Man* in order to care for his family and continue acting; and there was Glenn Strange, a Texas cowboy, who did his best in the last three Frankenstein movies, yet never realized that the Monster needed more than just his natural muscles and wrinkles.

There are others too: James Whale, a true genius director and a tragically bitter homosexual, who gave *Frankenstein* and *Bride of Frankenstein* sparks of his own dramatic, eccentric personality; Colin Clive, the original Dr. Frankenstein, a tormented alcoholic, fated for an early death that the writers had kindly spared Frankenstein in the first two films; Jack P. Pierce, the brilliant makeup wizard, who brought to his job all the pride and diligence of a doting Creator; Carl Laemmle, Jr., a shy, deeply sensitive, creative man who received Universal City as a 21st birthday present from studio founder Carl Laemmle, Sr. and who never emotionally recovered from the overthrow of his power seven years later; Dwight Frye, a dapper Broadway comedy star and leading man, whose dream of stardom in the talking pictures became a nightmare after his portrayal of the hunchbacked dwarf Fritz in *Frankenstein* grotesquely typecast him; and many others.

The "Denouement" chapter covers the fates of various actors, directors, and others after the Frankenstein series ended in 1948. There is a chapter entitled "Further Frankensteins," briefly summarizing some of the more recent attempts to conjure Mrs. Shelley's Monster for the screen. And lastly, there is a Biographical Appendix, providing profiles of the lives and careers of many of the talents who made Universal's Frankenstein saga so very special.

I hope this book will express my admiration and affection for these beloved horror films, and their creators. At any rate, I hope it atones for that early act of cowardice in 1957, when Mr. Van Sloan's coy warning inspired me to forsake *Frankenstein* for the safety of my pillow and bedcovers.

Gregory William Mank
Delta, Pennsylvania
December, 1980

Frankenstein
poster.

Frankenstein (1931)

Producer, Carl Laemmle, Jr.; *Director,* James Whale; *Associate Producer,* E. M. Asher; *Screenplay,* Garrett Fort, Francis Edwards Faragoh, John Russell and Robert Florey, based upon the composition by John L. Balderston, adapted from the play by Peggy Webling, from the novel by Mary Wollstonecraft Shelley; *Cinematographer,* Arthur Edeson; *Scenario Editor,* Richard Schayer; *Special Electrical Effects,* Kenneth Strickfaden; *Technical Assistant,* Dr. Cecil Reynolds; *Makeup,* Jack P. Pierce; *Art Director,* Charles D. Hall, *Set Designer,* Herman Rosse; *Recording Supervisor,* C. Roy Hunter; *Supervising Film Editor,* Maurice Pivar; *Film Editor,* Clarence Kolster; *Musical Theme,* David Broekman.

Filmed at Universal City, California, August–October, 1931; premiere, Mayfair Theatre, New York City, December 4, 1931. Running time: 67 minutes.

FRANKENSTEIN—
SYNOPSIS

Night in the old mountain cemetery above the village of Goldstadt. A death bell sounds as mourners watch a coffin being lowered slowly into a fresh grave. Across the graveyard, past the statue of the Grim Reaper and the figure of the crucified Christ, two men furtively watch the rites. One has the eyes of a zealous dreamer; the other, the glazed stare of a mad beast.

Henry Frankenstein and the hunchbacked dwarf Fritz stay hidden as a gravedigger shovels the obligatory six feet of earth over the casket. When he follows the sounds of the weeping mourners down the hill, the two men scurry out under the rising moon, attack the grave and exhume the coffin.

"He's just resting," says Frankenstein, gently patting the casket—"waiting for a *new* life to come!"

Pulling their grisly booty on a little cart, the grave scavengers race along a mountain trail and come to a solitary gibbet, where a corpse dangles in the moonlight. With knife in mouth, Fritz slavers his way across the top beam and cuts the rope. Frankenstein lunges to catch the body, then looks up crestfallen. The neck is broken, rendering the brain useless. They must find another brain. . . .

At Goldstadt Medical College, the venerable Dr. Waldman is lecturing to a night class of anatomy students. Two jars sit on his desk—the first marked Cerebrum–Normal Brain, the other Dysfunctio Cerebri–Abnormal Brain. Waldman points out the second brain's scarcity of convolutions and the degeneration of the middle frontal lobe—characteristics that correspond amazingly with the traits of the brain's former owner, whose life was one of violence and murder. Leaving both jars on the desk for the students' further inspection, Waldman dismisses the class and the room is soon left in blackness. A window opens. In hobbles Fritz, timidly making his way with his little walking stick, bumping into a skeleton before grasping the jar marked Normal Brain. Suddenly, however, there sounds a gong, and the startled Fritz drops the jar to the floor—where it smashes. Biting his nails, the terrified cripple grabs the other jar.

The action shifts to a great house in the village. Elizabeth, Henry Frankenstein's blonde fiancée, has sent for Victor Moritz, her ardent admirer and formerly Henry's best friend. On the day of their engagement, Henry told Elizabeth that he was on the verge of a discovery so incredible that he doubted his own sanity, and now she has received her first word from him in four months—in the form of a morbid letter: "You must have faith in me, Elizabeth. Wait. My work must come first, even before you. At night the winds howl in the mountains—there is no one here. Prying eyes can't peer into my secret. . . ."

Victor admits to having encountered Henry about three weeks before, while walking in the woods. When he asked his friend if he might visit his laboratory, Henry glared at him and queerly insisted that *no one* could go there.

The Players

Dr. Henry Frankenstein	Colin Clive
Elizabeth	Mae Clarke
Victor Moritz	John Boles
The Monster	?*
Dr. Waldman	Edward Van Sloan
Baron Frankenstein	Frederick Kerr
Fritz	Dwight Frye
The Burgomaster	Lionel Belmore
Little Maria	Marilyn Harris
Ludwig	Michael Mark
Bridesmaids	Arletta Duncan
	Pauline Moore
Extra at Lecture/Wounded Villager on Hill	Francis Ford

* Revealed in the closing credits to be Boris Karloff. This billing gimmick (used in the film's opening credits) is a strange echo from the very first dramatic version of Mary Shelley's story, *Presumption or the Fate of Frankenstein,* presented in London in 1823. The program of the play listed the actor, Mr. T. P. Cooke, but billed the character of the Monster only ——! ". . . this nameless mode of naming the unnameable is rather good . . . ," wrote Mary Shelley after attending a performance.

Victor promises to call on Dr. Waldman, who had been Henry's professor at the University. Elizabeth, not content to pace the house, insists on joining him.

In Waldman's study, the keen old professor sits behind a desk lined with test tubes; over his shoulder a lineup of 10 skulls grins at Elizabeth and Victor. Waldman explains that the young Frankenstein, a brilliant but erratic pupil, had embarked on research in the fields of chemical galvanism and electro-biology far in advance of

Frye and Clive in the mountain cemetery.

Dwight Frye.

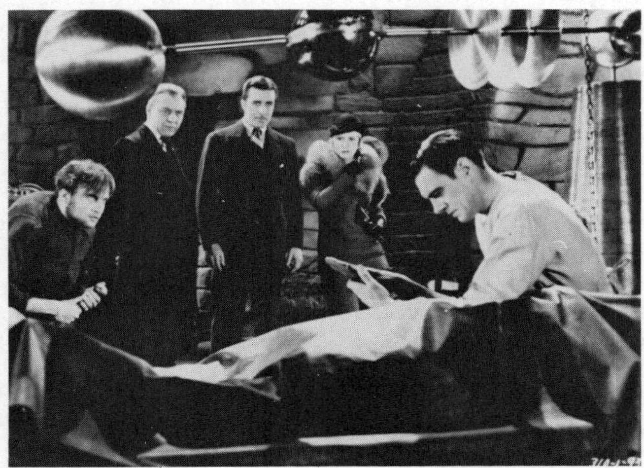

Dwight Frye, Edward Van Sloan, John Boles, Mae Clarke, and Colin Clive.

the theories endorsed by the University. "In fact," says Waldman, "they had reached a most advanced stage. They were becoming dangerous."

Too, there had been a controversy over the bodies used in the lecture room for dissection. Henry Frankenstein had deemed these cadavers inferior and demanded that the University supply him with other bodies. The researcher was blatantly unconcerned about where or how they were obtained.

Victor smiles defensively. After all, what are the lives of several rabbits and dogs?

"You do not quite get what I mean," says Waldman. "Herr Frankenstein was interested only in human life—first to destroy it, then recreate it. There you have his mad dream!"

Elizabeth begs Dr. Waldman to join them on an unannounced visit to Henry's laboratory. Waldman reluctantly agrees.

On a peak high in the mountains, an old watchtower looms over the crags, and a wicked storm shrieks and slashes through the countryside. Atop the tower, the deformed Fritz scampers about, making some electrical connections on the strange machinery that is perched on the tower roof, and then slides down a rope to the laboratory. "The storm will be magnificent!" exults Frankenstein. "All the electrical secrets of heaven. . . . Think of it! The brain of a dead man waiting to live again in a body I made with my own hands . . . *with my own hands* . . . ."

Suddenly comes a pounding on the door. Frankenstein orders Fritz to send the callers away, and Fritz scuttles off down the steps with his walking stick and lantern. He orders Elizabeth, Victor and Waldman to leave, and then returns to the tower—pausing to adjust his sock. Still, the callers per-

Edward Van Sloan, Colin Clive, John Boles, and Dwight Frye.

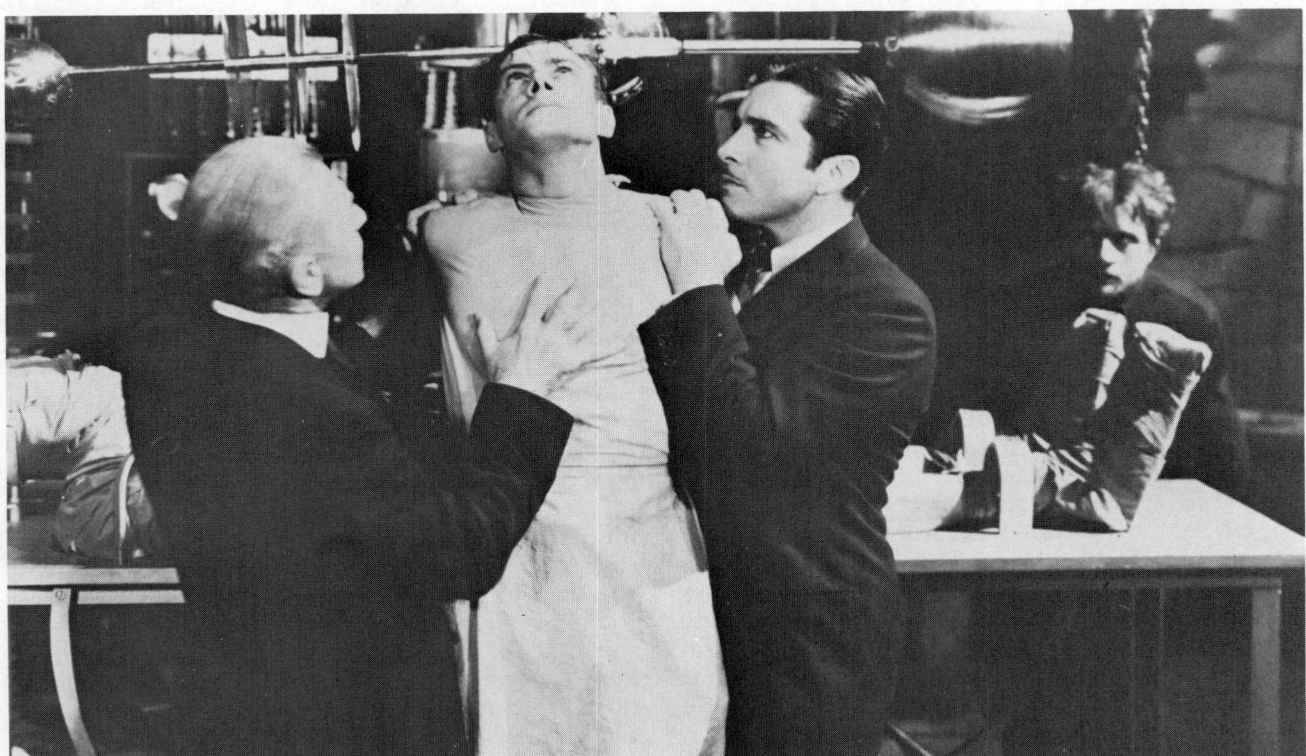

sist, and finally Frankenstein appears high above them, peering down from a barred window. "Who is it?" he demands, his voice filled with a madness that makes Elizabeth all the more determined to enter. "You must leave me alone now!" However, the entreaties of Elizabeth continue, and Frankenstein admits the group.

"Henry, you're inhuman!" says Victor, seeing the wild look in his friend's eyes. "You're *crazy*!"

"Crazy, am I?" says Henry slowly. "We'll see whether I'm crazy or not. Come on up. . . ."

In the laboratory, the young scientist reminds the professor of his famed lectures that claimed the ultraviolet ray to be the highest color in the spectrum. Not true, says Henry. Here, with his machinery, Frankenstein has gone beyond that. "I have discovered the great ray that first brought life into the world!" He feverishly details how he experimented at first only with dead animals, and then a human heart which he kept beating for three weeks. "But now I am going to turn *that* ray on *that* body and endow it with *life*!"

"And you really believe that you can bring life to the dead?" asks Waldman.

"That body is not dead," answers Frankenstein. "It has never lived. I created it! I made it with my own hands, from the bodies I took from graves, from the gallows, anywhere!" Frankenstein races to his creation, and turns to his audience.

"Quite a good scene, isn't it? One man *crazy*—three very sane spectators!"

A wild bolt of lightning streaks overhead. In feverish glee, Frankenstein and Fritz uncover the body, and in a spectacle of flashing electrical machinery, booming thunder and blinding lightning, the table carrying the creation ascends to the watchtower roof. Victor, Elizabeth and Waldman wince at the obscene flashes and deafening crashes. Fritz's face contorts in glee, and Frankenstein stares manically. The table slowly descends from the rooftop.

A hand moves.

"It's moving," gasps Frankenstein. "It's alive. . . . It's alive. . . . IT'S ALIVE. . . !"

In the welcome light of morning, Victor and Elizabeth pay a call on old Baron Frankenstein, who is convinced that his son's "experiments" conceal involvement with another woman. As Victor and Elizabeth try to convince him otherwise, Burgomaster Vogel arrives with a pompous flourish, presents flowers to Elizabeth, and asks the Baron when the wedding will be. The Baron snorts that there will be no wedding at all unless Henry comes to his senses, insults the Burgomaster, and sends him off in a huff. Disregarding what Elizabeth and Victor have told him, the Baron determines to find the other woman in his son's life who is causing all this trouble.

In the watchtower, the triumphant Frankenstein enjoys a cigar and smiles at the pacing Waldman, who insists that the newly "born" creature will prove dangerous.

"Dangerous," grins Frankenstein. ". . . Where should we be if nobody tried to find out what lies beyond? Have you never wanted to look beyond the clouds and the stars or to know what causes the trees to bud? And what changes the darkness into light? . . . if you talk like that, people call you crazy. Well, if I could discover just one of these things—what eternity is, for example—I wouldn't care if they did think I was crazy!"

Waldman is unmoved. He surprises Frankenstein by informing him that the brain stolen from his laboratory belonged to a criminal—news apparently concealed by Fritz. "You have created a Monster," intones Waldman, "and it will destroy you!"

From outside the room comes the sound of awkward, timid footsteps. The door swings open, and Frankenstein's Monster steps backward into the room. Slowly, shyly, the gaunt face turns and the insane eyes peer through the semidarkness at the men. "Come in," says Frankenstein to his Adam. "Sit down." The Monster obeys. "It understands!" rejoices Frankenstein, who now opens the skylight. The rays of the sun fall on the face of the creature who, until now, has been kept in total shadow. Fascinated, the Monster peers at the light and stands, stretching his scarred hands toward the beautiful discovery as if to embrace it. Frankenstein closes the skylight and again orders his creation to sit down. The Monster does so, his hands queerly pleading, begging for the love of his creator.

"It's wonderful," exults Frankenstein, just as Fritz, waving a torch, bursts into the room and sadistically taunts the Monster with the fire. Whimpering violently, the creature backs away, waving his hands as if to make the sight of the leering dwarf vanish—and then hurls himself at Fritz. Waldman hits him with a club, and both doctors wrestle the "fiend" to the floor, tie him up, and chain him in the tower dungeon.

The screams of the Monster echo from the dungeon. Fritz, waving a whip, runs into the cell and merrily lashes the helpless prisoner. Frankenstein, on the verge of nervous collapse, arrives and takes away the whip, begging Fritz to leave the Monster alone. However, the little hunchback's sadism is unquenched, and as Frankenstein leaves, the dwarf grabs a torch and continues torturing the prisoner, until . . .

A howl of horror rises from the dungeon. Frankenstein and Waldman rush down the stairs, throw open the door and see Fritz's twisted body hanging from a chain. The unleashed Monster glares

Colin Clive and Boris Karloff.

at the men who imprisoned him, growls, and attacks. He hysterically throws himself against the dungeon door as it is slammed in his face, roaring and shrieking in fury. Frankenstein, at Waldman's order, fills a hypodermic needle with "half grain solution." And as the Monster rushes out of the dungeon, attacking the doctors like a diabolic whirlwind, Waldman manages to plunge the needle into his victim. The Monster stares at the approaching blackness, waves his hands and collapses.

Now the old Baron, Victor and Elizabeth arrive to find Henry in a state of nervous prostration. "Oh my poor Fritz!" wails Henry. The Baron announces he is taking Henry home; Waldman promises to destroy the Monster painlessly and to preserve the records, and Elizabeth caresses her fiancé, promising him that he'll soon feel better in less morbid surroundings.

As Frankenstein recuperates in the village, Waldman prepares to destroy the Monster—by dissection. The professor is unaware, as he bends over the Monster to begin the fatal operation, that the sly creature is really awake and waiting to grasp his would-be assassin by the throat.

Minutes later, the Monster wanders down the tower steps, shrinks from the dungeon door, and strays into the black countryside.

The village is soon celebrating the nuptials of young Frankenstein and the lovely Elizabeth. As the villagers dance in the streets, the Monster is roaming the mountains. By a lake, he meets a little girl.

"Who are you?" she says. "I am Maria. Will you play with me?" The Monster looks at the little child with happy wonder. Maria takes him by the hand and walks him to the shore of the lake. "Would you like one of my flowers?"

The Monster takes the flower gingerly, looks wonderingly at it—and laughs.

"I can make a boat," says Maria as the playmates kneel by the water. She tosses her flower into the lake. "See how mine float?"

Delighted, the Monster throws his flowers, laughing joyfully as they float on the shining water. Soon his flowers are gone. In bewildered glee the Monster looks at little Maria and, in his mind, she becomes a beautiful flower. . . .

At Frankenstein Manor, the old Baron merrily toasts his son's marriage as Elizabeth, in her wedding gown, calls for Henry. She takes him to her chamber and sends away her curious bridesmaids. She has a morbid sense that something horrible is coming between them. "Oh, I'd die if I had to lose you now, Henry!"

"Why, I'll always be with you," comforts Henry. A frantic knocking at the door mocks his words.

Frankenstein leaves the room, locking Elizabeth inside. Victor informs him that Dr. Waldman's body has been discovered in the tower, and that the Monster has been seen in the hills, terrorizing the countryside. Suddenly, from upstairs, the cry of the Monster sounds. "He's in the house!" shouts Frankenstein, and he and Victor race up the stairs. Then they hear the Monster again—now in the cellars, craftily leading the men on a wild chase through the huge manor.

Elizabeth, meanwhile, sits in her boudoir. She has no idea that a giant figure is creeping up behind her. Impulsively, the nervous bride rises, walks to the door, turns—and screams.

The house is in an uproar. Guests, bridesmaids and servants run toward the sound of the heartrending shrieks. Henry appears from the cellars to unlock the door and find his bride sprawled on the bed, her blonde tresses undone, her voice hysterical with horror.

Meanwhile, in the village, Ludwig, the father of Little Maria, is marching through the streets, carrying the pathetic little bundle that was once his daughter and causing the happy cries of the villagers to turn to shrieks of bloodthirsty vengeance.

That night a light burns in every window of the village. The men ignite their torches, the gen-

Karloff as the Monster.

Mae Clarke and Karloff.

darmes prime their yelping bloodhounds, and the enraged parade marches through the village streets as women and children watch and weep. In the hills, the mob divides. The bereaved Ludwig leads his men into the woods; the Burgomaster commands the lake party, and Frankenstein himself leads men into the mountains.

"I made him with these hands," Frankenstein had told Victor as he left Elizabeth in his friend's care, "and with these hands I will destroy him."

Soon Frankenstein is separated from his men as he scales the mountain—and comes face to face with his Monster. On the edge of a towering cliff, under the black clouds of the night, the hunted creature stares at the creator who gave him life and deserted him—and then he attacks. The cries of Frankenstein echo below, and the Monster, carrying the bleeding, unconscious scientist on his back, races up a hill from the pursuing mob and bloodhounds to take sanctuary in an old windmill. The Monster climbs to the top floor and is leering from a window at his persecutors when Frankenstein awakes and tries to escape. After dodging the Monster at the grist wheel, Frankenstein runs out onto the mill balcony, where "created" pummels "creator," finally hurling the scientist off the balcony.

A vane of the windmill catches Frankenstein, then drops him—seriously injured, but alive—to the waiting mob. As the Monster kneels on the windmill balcony, remorsefully watching as the men carry away his god, there comes the cry, "Burn the mill!" Flames quickly streak up the old walls, and the Monster, screaming in hysteria, runs inside the mill, away from the savage faces and shouts of the people below. A great beam falls on the howling Monster and pins him to the floor.

As the Monster screams in terror and pain, the villagers outside scream in vengeful joy. All keep a sadistic vigil around the burning windmill, cheering the presumed cremation of a hapless creature now infamously known as Frankenstein's Monster.

Ludwig carries the corpse of his little Maria: Michael Mark, Marilyn Harris, and players.

The climax at the windmill: Clive and Karloff.

FRANKENSTEIN— PRODUCTION HISTORY

I have found it! What terrified me will terrify others; I need only describe the spectre which haunted my midnight pillow.[1]

Mary Shelley, from her introduction to *Frankenstein.*

In the summer of 1931, Universal City was three decades away from joining such sites as the Chinese Theatre, Disneyland and El Rancho La Brea Tar Pits as one of Southern California's most popular tourist attractions. It was a pastoral little movie studio, cradled in the foothills of the San Fernando Valley. Sheep grazed in the looming mountains, geese sailed on the sparkling Falls Lake, horses ran through the meadows and woods, and roosters crowed on the little chicken farm that supplemented the studio's income. The picturesque back lot sprawled into the hills like a Christmas garden, dotted with such sites as the quaint European village of *All Quiet on the Western Front;* the dusty Wild West town; the Paris cathedral of *The Hunchback of Notre Dame;* the Monte Carlo Casino of *Foolish Wives.* Indeed, aside from the sound stages that huddled under the towering hills like giant, gray mausoleums, Universal resembled not so much a studio as a Borgo Pass village in Transylvania or a Bavarian hamlet.

It appeared a splendid locale to create a Monster. And, in the predawn blackness of a 1931 summer day, the most infamous Monster of all was amok—driving his sputtering Ford through the gates of Universal and loping toward the lights of the makeup department.

It's a Universal Picture

Universal City slogan, early 1930s

Universal City, or "Little Europa" as it was nicknamed by cinema colony wags, was the kingdom of the Laemmles. Carl Laemmle, immigrant from the village of Laupheim, Bavaria, had tired of his clothing business in Oshkosh, Wisconsin; on June 8, 1912, his Universal Film Manufacturing Company was born in New York. Two years later, the enterprising Laemmle paid $165,000 for 230 acres in California's San Fernando Valley (including the historic site where Mexico's General Andres Pico and U.S. Army Colonel John C. Frémont signed the 1847 treaty by which the United States gained California), and on March 15, 1915, the

A 1932 Universal Studio soiree with James Flavin, James Whale, Bela Lugosi, "Uncle Carl" Laemmle, and Tom Mix.

gates of Universal City officially opened. Fifteen thousand stars, starlets, dignitaries, reporters, extras and curiosity seekers thronged through the portals, studio cowboys galloped through the streets firing their guns, a buckaroo blew up a dam, the band played "The Star-Spangled Banner," and actress Laura Oakley presented Laemmle with the gold key to the city, which he accepted with the none-too inspiring words: "I hope I didn't make a mistake in coming out here."

Over the years, the five-foot-three ever-smiling "Uncle Carl" (so dubbed because the Universal payroll during his reign supported no less than 70 Laemmle relatives, cronies and hangers-on), kept the studio alive with shoot-'em-up Westerns and cutesie comedies, though there were several glorious contributions to the cinema's heritage, including Erich von Stroheim's *Foolish Wives* (1922) and the Lon Chaney classics *The Hunchback of Notre Dame* (1923) and *The Phantom of the Opera* (1925). In 1931, the 64-year-old producer was proud of his erratic empire—and of his son, the shy, hypersensitive Carl junior, who on April 28, 1929, had received the post of Vice President in Charge of Production of Universal City as a 21st birthday present.

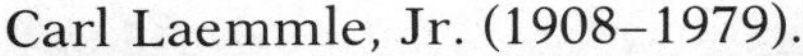

Carl Laemmle, Jr. (1908–1979).

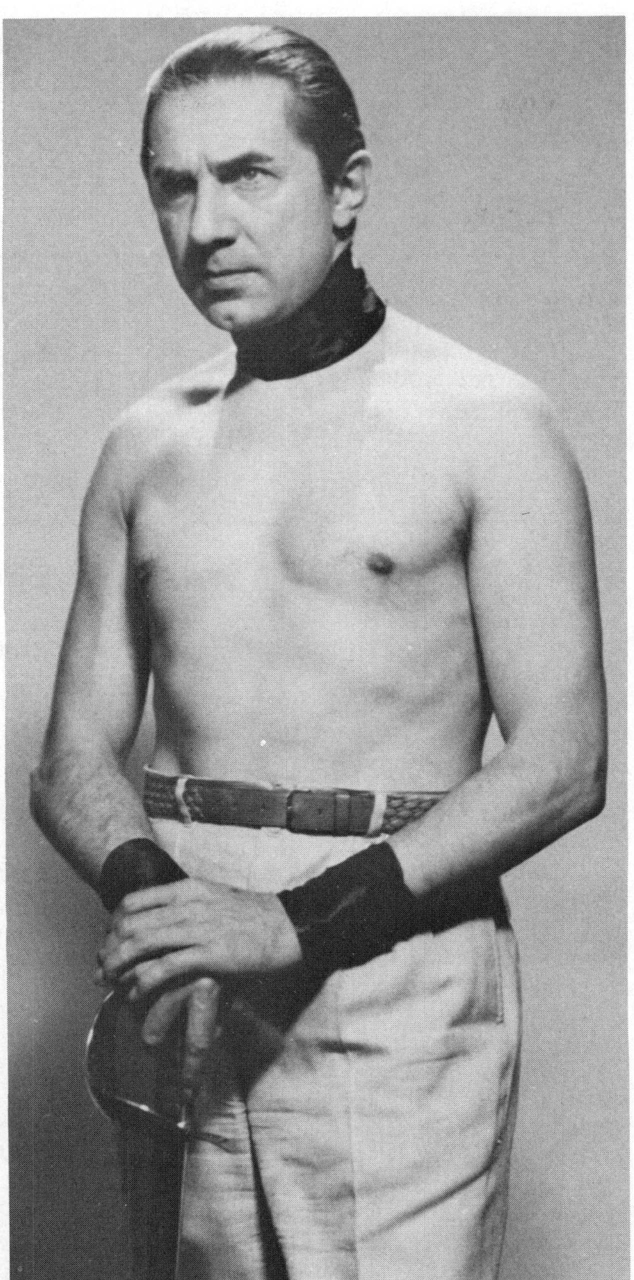

Bela Lugosi (1882–1956).

Although in the spring of 1931, the Depression was threatening a financial Armageddon for Universal, the Laemmles were glowing. "Junior's" first project, *All Quiet on the Western Front,* had proven an international triumph, winning the Academy Award for Best Picture of 1930. Junior also was enjoying great success with a film that had been released on Valentine's Day with the publicity teaser, "The story of the strangest Passion the world has ever known!" The title: *Dracula.*

Women wrote me letters. Ah, what letters women wrote me! Young girls. Women from 17 to 30. Letters of horrible hunger. Asking me if I cared only for maiden's blood . . . They hoped that I was Dracula. They hoped that my love was the love of Dracula. They gloated over the thing they dared not understand. . . .[2]

Bela Lugosi

In 1931, towering, classically handsome, 48-year-old Bela Lugosi was receiving passionate letters by the sackful. His portrayal of Bram Stoker's immortal Count in Universal's screen version of *Dracula* was a grand climax to a 30-year career. His work encompassed such roles as Romeo, Armand Duval, and Jesus Christ on Hungary's classical stage, German silent films such as *The Last of the Mohicans* (as the Indian Chingachgook), New York stardom in such plays as 1922's *The Red Poppy* (as Fernando, sexy Spanish apache dancer), 1925's *Arabesque* (as a Valentino-like sheik), and 1926's *The Devil in the Cheese* (as a dashing Greek bandit). On the night of October 5, 1927, Lugosi opened at New York's Fulton Theatre in *Dracula,* winning overnight stardom; he later toured the country as the suave bloodsucker and inspired such swoons from the flushed-cheeked ladies of the gallery that he was shocked when Universal almost passed him over in casting the film version (originally set for Lon Chaney, Sr., who died of cancer in August 1930). "Who was tested?" smirked Lugosi later. "The cousins and brother-in-laws (sic) of the Laemmles—all their pets and the pets of *their* pets! This goes on for a long time and then old man Laemmle says, 'There's nobody in the family that can play it, so why don't you hire an *actor*?' "[3] (Even when "old man" Laemmle decided to use an actor, he considered Ian Keith, William Courtenay and Paul Muni before finally signing Lugosi.)

As Lugosi reaped the pleasures of his newly won stardom, filling his Hollywood Athletic Club apartment with macho Mediterranean furniture and incessantly puffing on Havana's most expensive cigars, Universal hoped to add the Hungarian to the studio's none-too-formidable fold of contract players: Lew Ayres, Mae Clarke, Ricardo Cortez, Andy Devine, Slim Summerville, et al.

Advance publicity poster for *Frankenstein.*

Lugosi opted instead for a one-picture deal, perhaps wisely, for it indeed appeared that Universal City was about to collapse. The studio had suffered a $2½ million loss in 1930 and, in March 1931, even as the lush receipts from *Dracula* poured into the lot, the still-smiling Laemmles (still collecting their top salaries) had given pink slips to 350 employees and shut down the studio for six weeks. While many in Hollywood wondered if the studio would or could reopen, Junior directed that a new horror project be prepared for Lugosi, whom he hoped to mold into "the new Chaney." The task was assigned to a young French director-writer named Robert Florey—whose enthusiasm for the horror project was destined to turn into a bitterness he would harbor for the rest of his life.

Congenial, 30-year-old Robert Florey had every reason to hope for major cinema success. A lifelong lover of films, he had come to Hollywood in 1921 as a correspondent for the French *Cinemagazine,* and stayed to serve as foreign publicity director for Mary Pickford and Douglas Fairbanks. He became Valentino's advance manager (and good friend) on a 1923 European personal appearance tour, and later worked as an assistant

I first discussed the *Frankenstein* idea with Richard Schayer upon my return from Europe in 1931. He was not certain that the Mary Wollstonecraft Godwin Shelley work was adaptable. . . .[4]

Robert Florey

to such directors as Henry King, Josef von Sternberg, and King Vidor (for whom he also served as technical advisor on MGM's 1926 *La Boheme*). At Paramount's New York base in Astoria, Florey directed such films as *The Hole in the Wall* (the 1929 talkie debut of Edward G. Robinson and Claudette Colbert), and *The Cocoanuts* (in which Florey and co-director Joseph Santley faced the challenge of rounding up the four Marx Brothers from their bookies, the local speakeasy, the chorus girls' dressing room, or wherever to reprise the Broadway hit as their feature debut). Departing Paramount, Florey was back in Hollywood, seeking stimulating projects and delighted to confer with Universal story editor Richard Schayer over lunch at Hollywood Boulevard's Musso and Frank Restaurant regarding a horror follow-up to *Dracula*.

They discussed a variety of ideas: the Grand Guignol plays of Florey's native Paris; H.G. Wells' *The Invisible Man;* Poe's *Murders in the Rue Morgue*. However, the horror classic which most enticed both men was Mary Shelley's *Frankenstein*.

We will each write a ghost story.

George Gordon, Lord Byron, 1816

Scholars now believe it was the stormy night of Tuesday, June 18, 1816, that 18-year-old Mary Wollstonecraft Shelley conceived the story of Frankenstein. The wild, rainy night in Geneva was poetically proper, as was the company. Present were Villa Diodati's host, Lord Byron, the devilishly handsome, clubfooted poet, himself reviled in the Victorian world as a free-thinking, wanton monster; Dr. John Polidori, Byron's physician (whom the patient cruelly called "Polly-Dolly"), and a whimpering would-be poet who kept vowing to commit suicide and finally did in 1821 by swallowing prussic acid; Claire Clairmont, Mary's half sister, who was then pregnant with Byron's child Allegra; and there was Mary's lover, poet Percy Bysshe Shelley. They had fallen in love on the gravestone of Mary's mother, writer Mary Wollstonecraft, who had died giving her birth. Shelley finally abandoned his wife Harriet (who later drowned herself) and two children for his soulful mistress. On May 3, 1816, accompanied by Claire Clairmont and their love-child William, the couple fled England and began the "Grand Tour" of Europe.*

Mary Wollstonecraft Shelley.

It had been Byron's idea for each member of the little band to concoct a ghost story. Lying awake in her bedroom at Villa Diodati, listening to the storm outside, Mary closed her eyes and saw in a vision (not a nightmare) the Monster Maker—and his Monster:

> . . . I saw—with shut eyes, but acute mental vision—the pale student of unhallowed arts kneeling beside the thing he had put together. I saw the hideous phantasm of a man stretched out, and then, on the working of some powerful machine, show signs of life, and stir with an uneasy, half vital motion. Frightful must it be; for

*There is an academic theory that, in her travels, Mary visited Castle Frankenstein, a 13th-century fortress in what is now Hesse, West Germany, atop a hill along the Rhine River. It was there, legend insists, that Baron Georg von Frankenstein slew a poison-spewing dragon in 1531, and it was there that the alchemist Johann Konrad Dippel (whose notoriety *might* have contributed to Mary's conception of Victor Frankenstein) began his life. The castle is a hotel today—popular with tourists who want to know where the Monster lived!

The ruins of the actual Castle Frankenstein, above the village of Nieder-Beerbach, West Germany.

> supremely frightful would be the effect of any human endeavour to mock the stupendous mechanism of the Creator of the world. His success would terrify the artist; he would rush away from his odious handiwork, horror-stricken . . .[5]

Mary completed *Frankenstein* on April 17, 1817. Finding a publisher for this tale of blasphemy and horror was no easy task. It was the none-too-reputable firm of Lackington and Hughes that finally published *Frankenstein* (anonymously) on March 11, 1818. There was controversy indeed, and the *Quarterly Review* lambasted the book as "a tissue of horrible and disgusting absurdity."

Still, a classic had been born—a classic which would be the sole major literary achievement of Mary Shelley. Yet, when she died on February 1, 1851, treasuring the linen-wrapped heart of Shelley (who had wed her in 1818 and drowned in 1822), the long-respectable widow had the comfort of having created an immortal literary character.

Frankenstein quickly began a long, popular dramatic history. The first play version was *Presumption, or the Fate of Frankenstein,* which premiered at London's Lyceum Theatre (also known as "the English Opera House") on July 28, 1823. James Wallack played Frankenstein, while T.P. Cooke scored a great success as the Monster, eventually playing the part for 365 performances. Mary Shelley herself attended, and wrote of the play to a friend, ". . . I was much amused, and it appeared to excite a breathless eagerness in the audience . . ."[6] It also attracted righteous protestors, who picketed the theater for presenting so impious a work. Yet versions of *Frankenstein* began playing internationally (the famous Grand Guignol Theatre of Paris presented a production in 1826), and hundreds of dramatic variations, ranging from stark melodrama to silly burlesque, followed during the century.

The new art form of moving pictures had been quick to dramatize the Mary Shelley masterwork. The year 1910 saw the release of Thomas Edison's film No. 6604, *Frankenstein,* with Charles Ogle as a deformed, clawed, hairy Monster. "The formation of the hideous creature from the blazing chemicals of the huge cauldron of Frankenstein's laboratory is perhaps the most weird and fascinating scene ever shown in a moving picture!"[7] promised Edison's publicists. In the 10-minute film, the Monster plagued Frankenstein on his

Charles Ogle created his own makeup when he played the Monster in Edison's 1910 *Frankenstein.*

creator's wedding night, then vanished in a mirror as his maker's pure love for his bride vanquished his sin of impiety.

In 1915, a new version followed—Ocean Film Corporation's five-reel *Life Without Soul*, directed by Colonel Joseph W. Smiley. English thespian Percy Darrell Standing played the Monster sympathetically, but nobody cared—the film flopped. The Raver Film Corporation bought it from Ocean, and Mr. Raver decided to add some scientific footage. With new scenes of blood running through veins, cells conjugating, and, for some reason, "the reproduction of life in the fish world,"[8] *Life Without Soul* was released again. It bombed again.

There was, too, at least one European film version. In 1920, the Albertini Studios of Italy released *Mostro di Frankenstein* directed by Eugenio Testa and featuring Umberto Guarracino as the Monster.

Back on the stage, a new dramatic version of *Frankenstein* by Peggy Webling premiered at London's Preston Theatre in 1927. On February 10, 1930, there was a popular revival of Miss Webling's *Frankenstein* at the Little Theatre in London, with Henry Hallat as Frankenstein and Hamilton Deane (who had originally adapted the play of *Dracula* in 1924 and had portrayed Van Helsing) acting the Monster. Again, this drama* sympathetically treated the Monster, who learned of life from a kind, crippled girl whom he accidentally drowns. After its run at the Little Theatre, *Frankenstein* toured the provinces in repertory with *Dracula*, and Hamilton Deane enjoyed himself hugely as he nightly alternated between the Monster and the Count.

Robert Florey thought *Frankenstein* could become a great movie chiller; Richard Schayer, while admiring the story, was not confident that it was ideal movie material. As the lunch at Musso and Frank's ended, Schayer told Florey that, if he wanted the job of adapting and directing *Frankenstein* for the screen, Florey himself would have to sell the idea to Junior Laemmle. In his 1948 memoir, *Hollywood: D'hier et D'aujourd'hui,* Florey wrote of his eventful audience with Universal's Crown Prince:

> The crimes committed by the Monster were relatively easy to imagine, and during an unusual interview, while Carl Laemmle, Jr. surrendered his fingers to a manicurist, his hair to a barber, his thoughts to his secretaries, and his voice to a dictaphone, I explained the general plan of the film to him. He told me to type up the story right away and send it to the head of the scenario department.[9]

*It was this version in which the Christian names of Victor Frankenstein and his friend, Henry Clerval, were interchanged—a switch which would be perpetuated in Universal's 1931 film.

In his five-page synopsis, Florey fashioned the role of Frankenstein as a vehicle for Bela Lugosi. He also managed to reduce Mary Shelley's sly, eloquent, insidious Monster to a grunting, rampaging monstrosity. It was just what Universal wanted. With Junior Laemmle's blessing, *Frankenstein* began its slow, twisted and historical road to production.

> . . . Schayer agreed with my conception of the film and told me to go ahead with an extended and detailed adaptation—adding that the front office would insist on Lugosi playing the part of the Monster . . .[10]
>
> Robert Florey

Almost from the beginning, Robert Florey was fated for trouble with Universal.

On April 8, 1931, Universal officially purchased the rights to the play version of *Frankenstein* by Peggy Webling. (The novel, of course, was in the public domain.) The fee: $20,000, plus 1 percent of the world gross.* The strange facet of this agreement was that part of the sum went to writer John Lloyd Balderston, who had "anglicized" Hamilton Deane's *Dracula* for its New York premiere, and was fated to contribute to such classic horror films as *The Mummy, Bride of Frankenstein* and *Mad Love.* The contract engaged Balderston to provide Universal with a screen adaptation of Miss Webling's play. This must have perplexed Florey, who, after all, was supposed to be the official adaptor of *Frankenstein.*

This strange development was probably why Florey then became cautious with Universal. Receiving the green light from Schayer to proceed with a full screenplay, Florey refused to do so until Universal presented him with a contract which promised him that he would both write and direct *Frankenstein.* The studio slyly complied by devising a contract which promised Florey he would indeed write and direct—and young Florey signed it, overlooking the fact that nowhere did the document specify that the film was to be *Frankenstein.* It was an oversight he would deeply regret.

At any rate, Florey, enjoying the bliss of ignorance, began writing a complete screenplay with his friend Garrett Fort (who had worked on the shooting script of *Dracula*) assisting and writing

*These original terms later inspired a 1952 legal battle: *Universal* v. *Balderston and the estate of Peggy Webling* (who had died in 1947). The plaintiffs argued that they were entitled to 1 percent of the world gross not only on *Frankenstein,* but also on the seven subsequent films of the series. In May 1953, an out-of-court settlement was reached; while no amount was ever disclosed, Balderston claimed the payment was "highly satisfactory" and shared the settlement (estimated to be more than $100,000) with the late Miss Webling's grandnephew in England.

the dialogue. Florey is responsible for the crude touch of a criminal brain being placed in the Monster; a happier contribution was the climax in the old windmill, an inspiration Florey received after looking out his apartment window and seeing the windmill trademark of the Van de Kamp bakery.

Meanwhile, Bela Lugosi learned that Junior Laemmle wanted him to play the Monster—and exploded. Florey eagerly joined him as an ally. Why, they demanded, should a handsome star with an excellent voice be wasted in a part which, as Lugosi put it, any "half-wit extra" could play? Yet, for all the objections from Florey and Lugosi, Junior Laemmle held his ground. To the young producer, Bela Lugosi was a horror star only.

As the script neared completion, the very cooperative Florey arranged with Junior to shoot a two-reel test for *Frankenstein* to give the producer a better idea of the final product. Come the end of April 1931, Universal reopened its gates. Bela Lugosi, brooding about his casting, nevertheless pasted advance publicity about *Frankenstein* in his voluminous scrapbooks. And Robert Florey, his excitement mounting, looked forward to his test for *Frankenstein*.

How can I describe my emotions at this catastrophe, or how delineate the wretch whom with such infinite pains and care I had endeavoured to form? His limbs were in proportion, and I had selected his features as beautiful. Beautiful? Great God! His yellow skin scarcely covered the work of muscles and arteries beneath; his hair was of lustrous black, and flowing; his teeth of a pearly whiteness; but these luxuriances only formed a more horrid contrast with his watery eyes, that seemed almost as the same colour as the dun-white sockets in which they were set, his shrivelled complexion, and straight black lips.[11]

Mary Shelley's description of
the Monster in *Frankenstein*

As Robert Florey completed preparations to shoot the *Frankenstein* tests in the spring of 1931, problems abounded—especially in the makeup department.

Chief wizard of cosmetics at Universal City was Jack P. Pierce, a 42-year-old Greek immigrant and former semi-pro Chicago shortstop who arrived in Hollywood in 1910 and had worked as a nickelodeon projectionist, a theater manager for Harry Culver (founder of Culver City, home of MGM), bit player, assistant cameraman and producer. Pierce also had dabbled as a makeup artist at various studios; Universal wooed him to a permanent post after he so strikingly made a monkey out of Jacques Lerner in Fox's *The Monkey Talks* in 1926. Garbed in a white smock, his black hair slicked back and his military mustache impeccably trimmed, Pierce resembled a picaresque cross between an austere surgeon and the Demon Barber of Fleet Street as he perenially tended to such cosmetic indelicacies as the slippery toupee of Paul Lukas and the double chin(s) of Deanna Durbin. After years of sealing the wrinkles of aging glamour girls and the dewlaps of sagging matinee idols, Pierce welcomed the challenge of making a Monster. "I worked for four months on *Frankenstein,*" remembered Pierce years later, "making hundreds of sketches and models."[12]

Already, there was no love lost between Jack Pierce and Bela Lugosi. They had clashed during the filming of *Dracula,* when Pierce wanted to experiment with a special makeup for the king of vampires. Lugosi, prizing his handsome Slavic features, would have none of it. Even after the star did agree to alter his hairline and use the blue-green greasepaint (which photographed pallid gray), he insulted the makeup chief by insisting that Pierce *not* make him up. Lugosi would make up himself. Now, with Mary Shelley's description of the Monster so repulsively vague, Lugosi had to agree to Pierce's experiments—and things were very tense in the makeup studio.

"Something has got to be done for Bela Lugosi," reported the June 7, 1931, edition of the Los Angeles *Record.* A farcical situation had developed as the hapless Florey doggedly tried to rehearse and film his test. Whenever Lugosi would venture from the makeup department *en route* to the soundstage to rehearse his scene, the California sun would melt the makeup (described by the *Record* as ". . . two or three different colors, stripes, streaks, and striations") into streams of running goo—making Lugosi, in the *Record's* words, ". . . a clown instead of a menace." This happened time and again, delaying the test and, to Lugosi's greatest consternation, usually ruining the cigar he was smoking at the time.

Lugosi, meanwhile, developed ideas of his own. As Boris Karloff would remember of the Hungarian's *Frankenstein* test days, "I was once told that he insisted on doing his make-up himself—and did this awful, hairy creature, not at all like our Monster."[13] Neither Pierce nor Junior Laemmle cared for Lugosi's awful, hairy creature. Lugosi bristled, and the controversy raged on about the Monster's ultimate appearance. As Pierce would angrily carp: "Lugosi thought his ideas were better than everybody's!"[14]

Pierce continued his sketches and studies, but time was running out. Finally, Junior Laemmle and the makeup man decided on a Monster *a la* the Golem, the clay-skinned, broad-wigged giant of Jewish folklore so impressively played by Paul Wegener in 1920's *Der Golem.* At last, on a still-

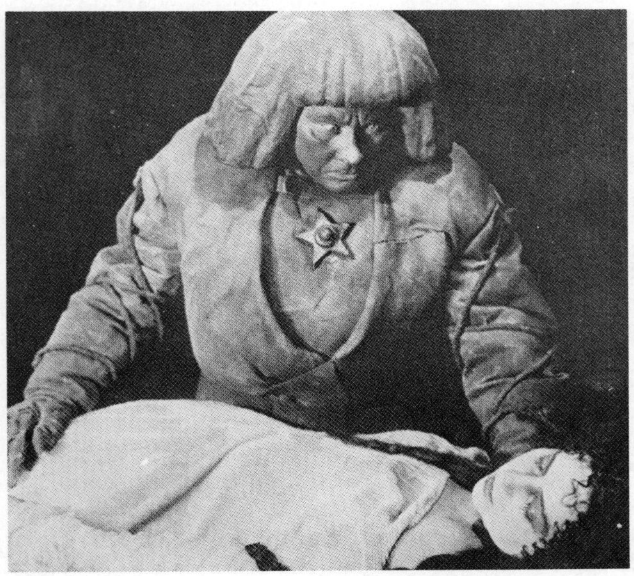

Paul Wegener and Lyda Salmanova in 1920's *Der Golem*. Lugosi's final makeup for his *Frankenstein* test was reportedly modeled after this clay monster.

standing set from *Dracula*, Florey directed his two-reel test, presenting the creation sequence (without the stunning electrical effects). The director explained his concepts to cameraman Paul Ivano, the Golemesque Lugosi (who had little to do but open his eyes and "come alive" in the last 200 to 300 feet of the test), and Dutch character player Edward Van Sloan, who had played the venerable vampire fighter Dr. Van Helsing opposite Lugosi in the Broadway, road company and movie versions of *Dracula*. As Lugosi galumphed his way onto the stage, Van Sloan was hardly impressed. Shortly before his death in 1964, Van Sloan recalled that Lugosi's ". . . head was about four times normal size, with a broad wig on it," that "he had a polished, clay-like skin," and that the total effect of his Monster was ". . . more like something out of *Babes in Toyland*!"[15]

It was a very unpleasant day. As Florey recalled:

> As I was working with the other actors, during a time when the Monster had not yet "come to life," Lugosi kept exclaiming, "Enough is enough;" that he was not going to be a grunting, babbling idiot for anybody, and that any tall extra could be the Monster. "I was a star in my country, and will not be a scarecrow over here!" he said repeatedly.[16]

The two-reel test was completed. A few days later, Florey, Lugosi and Ivano assembled in Junior Laemmle's screening room to show the producer what studio publicity had already promised ". . . surpasses in THRILLS even *DRACULA* . . . !" The lights dimmed, the test unreeled, and soon the screen filled with the face of Lugosi, his eyes gleaming into Ivano's camera.

Junior Laemmle burst out laughing.

The test reel ended. The lights came on. Junior, promising a conference, hurriedly excused himself as the director, cameraman and star stood mutely in the screening room. Suddenly the silence was broken. "Ivano!" roared Lugosi, "My close-up was *magnificent*!"[17] With that, Lugosi awarded Ivano with a bouquet of dollar cigars and strutted from the room. Ivano, not a smoker, gave the cigars to Florey, who really didn't feel like a smoke at the moment.*

Directed by James Whale (The Genius who made *Journey's End* and *Waterloo Bridge*)

Marquee publicity for *Frankenstein*

News of the *Frankenstein* test reel debacle was soon popular gossip about the Universal lot, and there whisked into Junior Laemmle's office a visitor—James Whale.

Young (38), lean, tall and swaggeringly sardonic, Whale was the studio's most prized director; Florey scornfully referred to him as the "Ace of Universal." Whale's dramatic career began in a World War I prison camp in Holzminden, Germany, where the second lieutenant acted in plays presented by his fellow prisoners. Returning to England after the armistice, Whale abandoned his job as a cartoonist for the London *Bystander* and joined the world of the theater. He played in revivals of *The Cherry Orchard* and *The Sea Gull*, worked as a stage manager, scenic designer, and director, and scored as the lunatic who helps his father (Charles Laughton) imprison a young

*In the December 1969 issue of *Film Fan Monthly*, a former agent of Lugosi, who earned notoriety by selling copies of the actor's personal effects after his death, placed this advertisement:

"BELA LUGOSI buffs: For sale: Screen test that Bela Lugosi made for the original *Frankenstein*. 35 mm sound, running time 21 minutes; same scene is shown twice with change in lighting, etc. Between scenes camera was left running and Carl Laemmle, James Whale, Colin Clive, and Lugosi can be seen and heard discussing the test and wardrobe Lugosi was wearing. Film can be examined and screened BEFORE purchase is made. Price: $4,000.00 . . ."

This offer was obviously a fraud; it was, of course, Florey (not Whale) who directed Lugosi's test, and Clive was still in England at the time. This author knows of one individual who made an appointment to see this test reel; he was stood up.

In all probability, there is no surviving copy of the famous test reel. Considering its inferior reputation, the test was probably destroyed by the studio at the first opportunity.

James Whale (1893–1957).

beauty in the chiller *A Man with Red Hair* (1928).

Then, on January 21, 1929, *Journey's End,* R.C. Sherriff's saga of the spiritual ravages of war, opened in the West End. Directed by Whale with magnificent bravura, it became the town's hottest ticket. Whale's success with the Broadway and Chicago companies won him passage to Hollywood to prepare the film version of *Journey's End* for Tiffany Studios. For experience, Whale served as "dialogue director" of Paramount's *The Love Doctor* (1929) and Howard Hughes' 1930 classic *Hell's Angels.* In the latter film, Whale was challenged to wring a performance out of platinum blonde Jean Harlow, terrified in her first starring role. Once the "Blonde Bombshell" began weeping on the set and begged Whale to *tell* her how to be seductive. Whale's reply: "My dear girl, I can tell you how to be an actress but I cannot tell you how to be a woman."[18]

Junior Laemmle had seen *Journey's End* in New York, and its impact was instrumental in his determination to film *All Quiet on the Western Front*—so much so that some wags at Universal called the picture "Junior's End." On *The New York Times* "Ten Best" list of 1930, *All Quiet* . . . placed No. 2, while *Journey's End* placed No. 3. Whale placed No. 8 on the *Film Daily's* "Ten Best" directors poll of 1929–30. Vividly remembering Whale's mobile camera, striking close-ups and dramatic pictorial style, Junior offered the laureated young director a Universal contract, promising a top salary (approximately $1,000 weekly) and instant seniority over such fellow "megaphoners" as William Wyler, Hobart Henley, John M. Stahl, Tod Browning, Edward Laemmle—and Robert Florey.

On the June morning of 1931 when Whale visited Junior's office, the director had just completed *Waterloo Bridge,* which promised to be one of the studio's major artistic and financial successes of the season. As Junior talked with the aloof, elegant artist, he did not recognize in "Jimmy" a man whose egomania, homosexuality and drinking would eventually result in his exile from the studios, or a man fated for a sordid death that remains one of Hollywood's infamous, unsolved mysteries. Laemmle saw, quite rightly, only a man blessed with a talent that could conceivably catapult Universal into being a worthy rival to Paramount, United Artists and Metro-Goldwyn-Mayer. Whale could have anything at Universal—and he wanted *Frankenstein*:

> I chose *Frankenstein* out of about 30 available stories because it was the strongest meat and gave me a chance to dabble in the macabre. I thought it would be an amusing thing to try and make what everybody knows to be a physical impossibility into the almost believable for 60 minutes. A director must be pretty bad if he can't get a thrill out of a war, murder, robbery. *Frankenstein* was a sensational story and had a chance to become a sensational picture. It offered fine pictorial possibilities, had 2 grand characterizations, and dealt with a subject which might go anywhere—and that is part of the fun of making pictures.[19]

Junior Laemmle had a choice: loyally allow Florey to flounder until he perfected his treatment, or indulge his pet director. It was an easy choice for him. Whale got *Frankenstein.*

Anybody can moan and grunt.[20]

Bela Lugosi

James Whale celebrated, Robert Florey smoldered. The outraged Frenchman, determined to win back his picture, raced for his contract. Indeed, it stated he was to write and direct, but it was not explicitly stated that the film would be *Frankenstein.* Universal's legal department shrewdly had placed Florey over a barrel.

Still, Florey did not surrender immediately. He hoped an appeal to Bela Lugosi to join him in storming Junior's office might help; after all, Lugosi was a star with influence. However, Lugosi, while sympathetic to Florey, was never thrilled by Florey's script or by the idea of playing a mute idiot, and was totally repulsed by Jack Pierce's ladles of makeup. Indeed, he had serious second thoughts about doing *Frankenstein* at all.

During this time, Bela was attracted to a pretty, 19-year-old Hungarian girl named Lillian Arch. She was destined to become the actor's fourth wife, from 1933 to 1953 ("I lasted the longest"), as well as the third spouse and widow of veteran star Brian Donlevy (1966–1972). Having long since sold the "love nest" she shared in Palm Desert with "absolute doll" Donlevy and now living in Glendale, this charming, delightfully candid lady explained to me Bela's attitude toward *Frankenstein*:

> Bela wanted out! He said, "I'll get a doctor's excuse" because it was a six-hour makeup and all that sort of stuff. Bela, you see, was the *actor*. And he couldn't see himself moaning and grunting—and that's all the Monster did in the original one. Bela thought, "You don't need an *actor* for that part! Anybody can moan and grunt! I need a challenging part—a part where I can *act*!"
>
> He had a stupid agent—this I must add! I think it was a woman. And if she had an ounce of brains, she would have said, "Look Bela. I don't care what you think. You are right now the top in horror. You did *Dracula*. Now here's the Monster. Don't refuse it." If only he had a smart agent—but he had a stupid woman.[21]

Hence, Bela asked producer Laemmle to release him from *Frankenstein*. Junior did so quite cheerfully, as Jack Pierce recalled, since Lugosi ". . . had too many ideas of his own that didn't coincide with those of the producer, Carl Laemmle."[22] Junior was happy, Bela was happy, and Florey was still unhappy, so, to soothe egos and skirt lawsuits, Laemmle presented the defeated Florey with Poe's *Murders in the Rue Morgue*, assuring him that this was indeed the film he would write and direct. Lugosi was set for the film's starring role of Dr. Mirakle, a part all believed would be a worthy challenge for his dramatic powers, and Laemmle even issued a press release stating that Universal would star Lugosi in a remake of *The Hunchback of Notre Dame* (a project never mentioned again). Thus did Robert Florey* and Bela Lugosi lose their opportunity to create the screen's most famous horror picture—which, indeed probably would not have become the screen's most famous horror film if both men had remained on the job.

Today, a small coterie of film historians insists that Florey would have delivered a *Frankenstein* superior to the product created by Whale. Judging by Florey's other work in the genre—*Murders in the Rue Morgue,* Columbia's *The Face Behind the Mask* (1941), Warners' *The Beast With Five Fingers* (1947)—it is a rather weak argument. As Boris Karloff would later reflect:

> I don't think the main screenwriter, Bob Florey, really intended there to be much pathos inside the character. But Whale and I thought that there should be; we didn't want the kind of rampaging monstrosity that Universal seemed to think we should go in for. We had to have some pathos, otherwise our audiences just wouldn't think about the film after they'd left the theatre, and Whale very much wanted them to do that. He wanted to make some impact on them. And so did I.[23]

I wasn't going to play a monster.
I was from the the-a- tuh![24]

John Carradine

Whale's revamping of *Frankenstein* began. Having read Florey's script, he perused Balderston's adaptation (which included such episodes as the Monster beholding sunlight for the first time and accidentally drowning a young girl). The director screened such German fantasies as *The Cabinet of Dr. Caligari* (1920, with Conrad Veidt as the corpse-like somnambulist Cesare), *Der Golem* (1920, which also contained a fateful meeting between the giant monster and a little girl), and Fritz Lang's *Metropolis* (1926, with its awesome electrical laboratory), as well as MGM's *The Magician* (1926, with its tower laboratory and evil dwarf assistant). He discussed these ingredients with contract writers Garrett Fort (who had worked on the script of *Dracula* and had written the dialogue for Florey's treatment) and Francis Edwards Faragoh. As a new script evolved, containing Whale's

* Not surprisingly, a great bitterness festered between Florey and Whale after *Frankenstein*. Whale opened the sore further by spitefully removing Florey's name (as a writer) on the film's opening credits. This time Universal sided with Florey, but it was too late to amend the domestic prints, and Florey's name appeared only on the foreign prints of *Frankenstein*.

Branded with the failure of the *Frankenstein* test, Florey, in later years insisted that Lugosi's makeup was very similar to Karloff's; that Pierce did not work four months on designing the makeup; that Florey himself created the idea of the neck bolts; and that Universal destroyed his test to create a "myth" for Karloff and Pierce. Considering that this makes liars out of Pierce, Karloff, Whale, Laemmle junior, and Van Sloan, it's a none-too-convincing claim.

favorite material from Florey's script, Balderston's adaptation, the silent films and his script conferences, the director turned his thoughts to casting. One fact soon became painfully obvious: playing a mute monster pieced together from the parts of fouled corpses was not the stuff that most actors' dreams are made of.

Lon Chaney was dead. Bela Lugosi was officially off the picture, the July 18, 1931, edition of *Hollywood Filmograph* reporting his departure from a role cavalierly described as ". . . a dumb character . . . a monster." With no other established horror man in Hollywood, Whale started scouting.

Hollywood legend relates that, in 1931, one of the film colony's most bizarre sights was a tall, emaciated Poe-esque young man, attired in flowing cape, slouch hat and cardboard spats, who paraded under the palm trees of Hollywood Boulevard roaring the great soliloquies and sonnets of Shakespeare. The flamboyant character called himself John Peter Richmond; he later became the celebrated Shakespearean stage star and cinema character player John Carradine.

At this time, the 25-year-old Carradine supported himself by sketching, sculpting, classical work with Los Angeles little theaters, dish washing, and in dire emergencies, the "bastard art" of movies. It was such an emergency that took him to Universal in the summer of 1931, where he *almost* tested for the part of the Monster. In 1974, a sadly arthritic, but mentally keen Carradine told Vincent Price of the indignity on an ABC special, "The Horror Hall of Fame:"

> . . . I've never played a monster . . . I was offered one and turned it down—I turned down *Frankenstein*, and Boris took it. . . .
>
> They sent me to the makeup department, and the makeup man started mixing up a bowl of plaster, and I, being a sculptor, knew just what he was up to—a life mask!
>
> I said, "Wait a minute—what is this?"
> He said, "You play a Monster."
> I said, "Oh! Do I have any dialogue?"
> "No. You just grunt."
> "This is not for me!" I said, and walked out . . . I never regretted it. . . .*

With a self-spoofing eye roll, Carradine later emphasized that he believed (as did Lugosi) that the Monster was an unworthy role for a theatrical artist. Several other actors, their names never documented, also came and went, neither impressive nor impressed. It would require the insight of a strange, mysterious, 43-year old English character player, sipping tea on a fateful noon in the Universal commissary, to realize "That Monster is one of the most sympathetic characters ever created in the world of English letters."[25]

*Ironically, Carradine was Universal's first choice 33 years later for the part of Herman Munster on the CBS series *The Munsters.* He was unavailable (". . . unfortunately for my wallet . . .") and Fred Gwynne took the part. Carradine would guest on the show as Mr. Gateman, owner of the mortuary where Herman worked, and appeared as the Munster's butler in Universal's 1966 feature *Munster Go Home.*

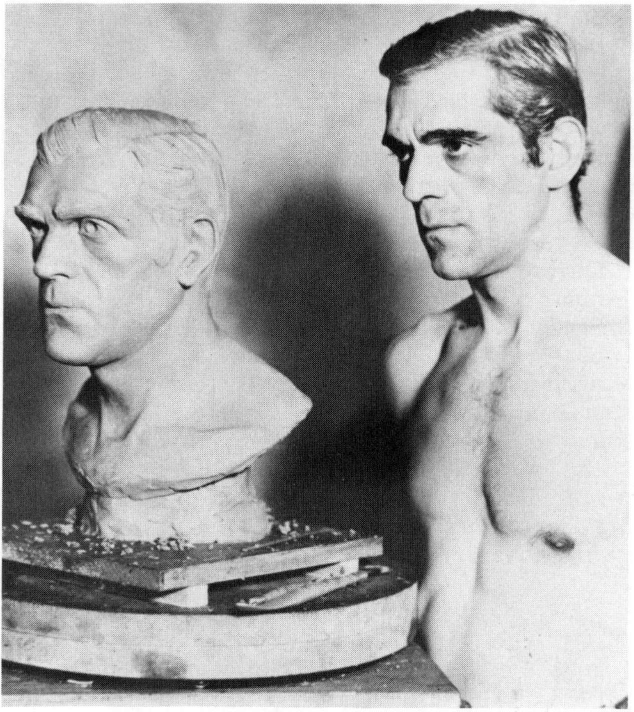

Boris Karloff.

> James Whale, the director . . . was lunching at a nearby table. Suddenly he caught my eye and beckoned me over. I leapt—he was the most important director on the lot. He asked me to sit down. I did, holding my breath, and then he said: "Your face has startling possibilities . . ." I cast my eyes down modestly, and then he said, "I'd like you to test for the Monster in *Frankenstein.*" It was shattering—for the first time in my life I had been gainfully employed long enough to buy myself some new clothes and spruce up a bit—actually, I rather fancied meself! Now, to hide all this new-found beauty under monster-makeup? I said I'd be delighted.[26]
>
> Boris Karloff

As Whale looked across the table into the hopeful calf eyes of Karloff's gaunt, haunting face, the director could recognize that he was speaking to a man for whom life had presented a full repertoire of melodramas.

Indeed, since beginning life as William Henry

Pratt in Dulwich, England, on November 23, 1887, Karloff* had survived his exile by an unloving family, the agony of near-starvation, the wrath of rent-seeking landladies, the Saskatchewan tornado of 1912, the indignities of western America's most flea-bitten stock companies, and the heartache of at least three broken marriages. Arriving in Canada in 1909, a black sheep due to his love of theater in a family of British diplomats, he had labored as a farmer and a lumberjack before making his 1910 stock debut with the Jean Russell Players of Kamloops, British Columbia, in Molnar's *The Devil*. Karloff won the job by lying about his experience. "When the curtain went up I was getting thirty dollars a week," remembered the actor. "When it descended, I was down to fifteen dollars!"[27] Still, Karloff pursued his beloved craft of acting in various gypsy-like stock troupes. As he later recalled, with his famous lisp:

> Frequently we would skip the entire second or third act simply because we were tired and wanted to go home. Besides, it served the audience right. They had no business being there in the first place, wasting their time on such terrible theatre![28]

The stage finally dumped Karloff in Hollywood. He soon found his "type" when, as a French Canadian trapper in *The Deadlier Sex* (1920), he tried to rape Blanche Sweet. However, his fortune proved elusive, and only then, in 1931, after 80-odd movie roles (including the Caligariesque hypnotist of 1926's *The Bells*), some California stage work, and a spell as a truck driver, was the skinny, bowlegged Karloff enjoying some notice. In Columbia's *The Criminal Code,* he won praise as the murderous jailbird Galloway, a role he had created in the West Coast stage company; in RKO's *Young Donovan's Kid,* he twitched as dope peddler Cokey Joe, out to hook little Jackie Cooper; and in the classic newspaper melodrama *Five Star Final,* just completed at Warners, he was an obscene joy as fake preacher/real pervert T. Vernon Isopod, leering at the fishnet hosiery of Ona Munson and inspiring Edward G. Robinson to snarl, "You're the most blasphemous thing I've ever seen—it's a miracle you've not been struck dead!" Then playing a gangster in *Graft* at Universal, Karloff was working so steadily that his fourth (possibly fifth) wife Dorothy had forsaken her school librarian job. The couple hoped even to desert the A-frame "shack" (Dorothy's word) they shared atop Laurel Canyon, where they had gaily entertained on those Prohibition evenings by brewing green beer in the bathtub.

"Monster indeed!" smiled Karloff at Whale's offer. Both director and actor were excited after their commissary chat, and Whale said later:

> Boris Karloff's face has always fascinated me, and I made drawings of his head, added sharp bony ridges where I imagined the skull might have been joined. His physique was weaker than I could wish, but that queer, penetrating personality of his, I felt, was more important than his shape, which could easily be altered.[29]

Karloff, meanwhile, ran out and bought a copy of *Frankenstein,* re-reading Shelley's masterwork. However, as both men knew, Karloff's winning the part depended on the success of the test reel. Junior Laemmle must not laugh this time. So, at first opportunity, Karloff called on Jack Pierce, whose talent and friendship he would prize all his life:

> Jack was nothing short of a genius, besides being a lovely man. He was also in the inside of the studio, knew what the score was, and was in a position to stall the test. So, at the end of the day's work on *Graft,* I would stay, and he would stay and nightly he worked on the makeup until we felt it was ready. People in production were constantly calling and saying, "Aren't you ready yet?" . . .[30]

For three hours a night for three weeks, Pierce and Karloff met nightly in the makeup bungalow to "create" the Monster. Yet, in all fairness, before the efforts of Pierce, Whale and Karloff are discussed further, it should be noted that another individual would later claim credit for the ultimate success of *Frankenstein* and the stardom of Boris Karloff. His name: Bela Lugosi.

Bela created his own Monster.[31]

Lillian Lugosi Donlevy

For a truly talented man, Bela Lugosi possessed a strange weakness for stretching the truth. In later years, he reminisced that he so passionately made love to Estelle Winwood in the play "The Red Poppy" that he fractured three of her ribs (Miss Winwood remembers no such thing); that he so impressed MGM with his performance in *Mark of the Vampire* (1935) that the studio awarded him top billing over Lionel Barrymore (Bela was billed third); and, even in the humiliation of his 1955 self-incarceration as a drug addict, that he had waged a "25-year battle" with dope when he actually had been addicted for a decade. Never-

* His *raison d'etre* for the name Boris Karloff: "As an actor, I had to change the Pratt for shall we say obvious reasons, and there was a Karloff somewhere on my mother's side. William and Karloff didn't go too well together, so I simply plucked the Boris out of a book somewhere."

theless, it can no longer be proven that Lugosi was glamorizing reality when he told the press this story about *Frankenstein* in 1935:

> I made up for the role and had tests taken, which were pronounced O.K. Then I read the script, and didn't like it. So I asked to be withdrawn from the picture. Carl Laemmle said he'd permit it, if I'd furnish an actor to play the part. I scouted the agencies—and came upon Boris Karloff. I recommended him. He took tests. And that's how he happened to become a famous star of horror pictures—my rival, in fact.[32]

Can this be true? Karloff never spoke of such a thing. "Well, why would he?" laughs Lillian Lugosi Donlevy. "*He* would never say that!" She loyally supports her ex-husband's "100 percent true" account:

> . . . Bela turned down the Monster role, after doing all the original take-offs. And he made the greatest mistake of his career—he brought Boris Karloff to Universal City. Bela said, "Here's the man who can play it"—and that put Karloff, an *extra*, on the map. It's a damn shame, for otherwise there would be no Boris Karloff today—absolutely none.
>
> Bela created his own Monster.[33]

Junior Laemmle, James Whale, Jack Pierce, and others, never related Lugosi's version of the casting; while Karloff never did publicly, could he have confessed privately that it was so? Sara Jane Karloff Brodsack, Boris' lovely brunette daughter (born, poetically enough, on November 23, 1938, her father's 51st birthday, as he was in full Monster regalia at Universal on the set of *Son of Frankenstein*), should know. A housewife with two sons, living in Yucaipa, California, she graciously told me the only version of the *Frankenstein* casting she knew:

> My father was in the cafeteria at the studio, and the man who was casting the picture, James Whale, came in and selected him. He asked him if he would like to test for the role, and then I understand he and Jack Pierce worked many long hours perfecting the makeup before the test was made.

I acquainted Mrs. Brodsack with the Lugosi account. Her calm reply: "I don't think that's true."[34]

Most people agree. In fact, while both Arthur Lennig, author of the Lugosi biography *The Count*, and Robert Cremer, author of the family-authorized biography *Lugosi: The Man Behind the Cape*, take potshots at Karloff in their respective works, neither records Lugosi's oft-told *Frankenstein* story.

Whatever story one chooses to believe, one fact is clear: Lugosi's departure from *Frankenstein* not only cost him a classic credit—it unleashed upon him a formidable and eclipsing rival. The Englishman (who thought of Bela as "a kind and lovable man"),[35] at the expense of the Hungarian (who thought of Boris as "a cold fish"),[36] was able to create the masterpiece performance of the horror genre.

Bela Lugosi created his own Monster.

A Good Cast Is Worth Repeating

Universal Closing Credit line, early 1930s

As Pierce and Karloff continued their nocturnal experiments, Whale carefully selected his other major players:

Dr. Henry Frankenstein: Mary Shelley's blasphemer was a dream part for the right actor. The Laemmles originally wanted the wrong actor—Leslie Howard, who would prove a delight as *The Scarlet Pimpernel* (1935) but was hardly ideal for the part of a renegade scientist soiling his fingers

Colin Clive (1900–1937).

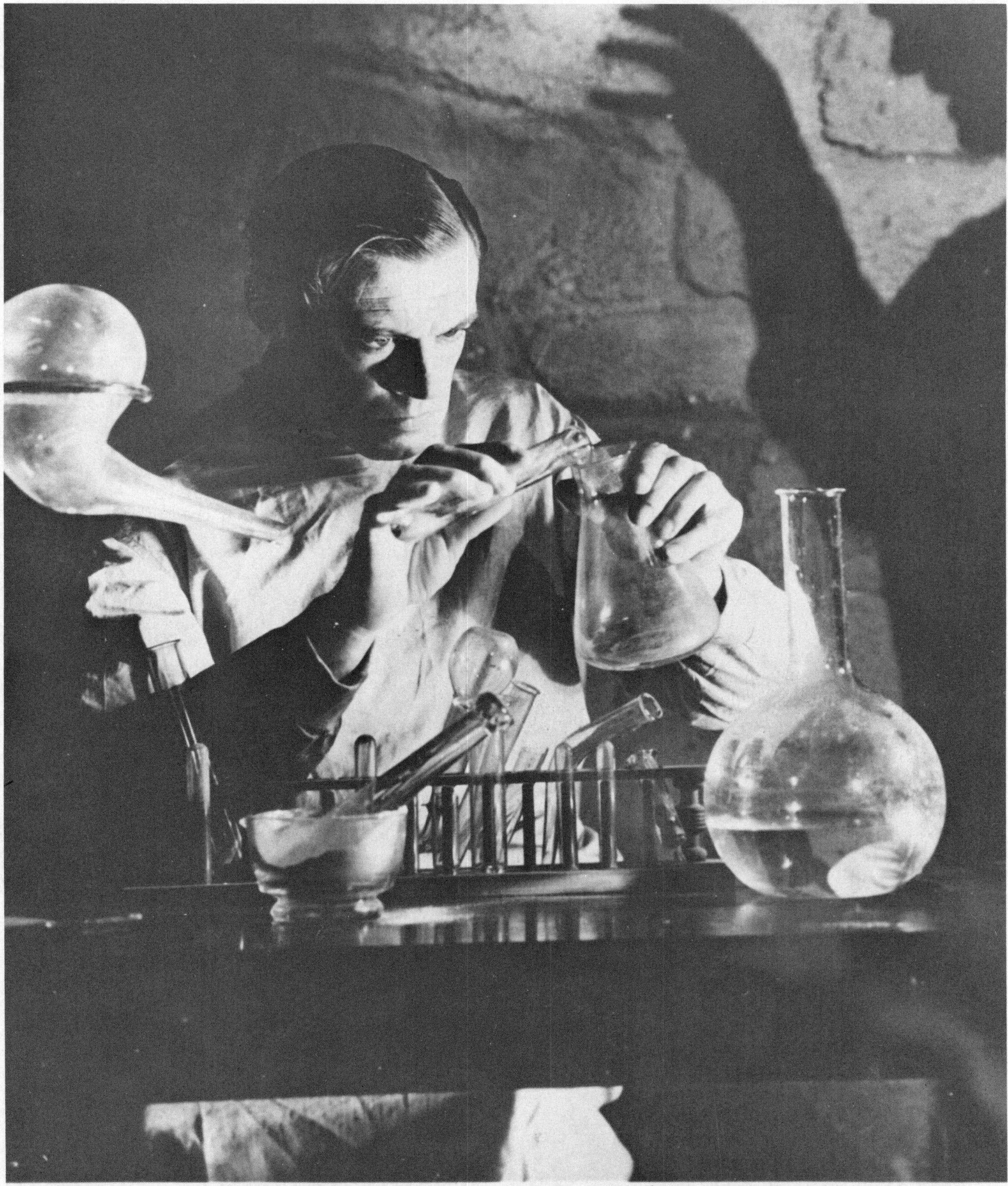

Clive as Frankenstein.

in graves and mausoleums.

Whale vetoed Leslie Howard. He remembered how cinemagoers wept at the anguish of the cadaverous, alcoholic, demon-ridden Captain Stanhope in *Journey's End*. It was a heartbreaking performance by cadaverous, alcoholic, demon-ridden Colin Clive—Whale's 31-year-old "discovery," intimate friend and only choice for the role of Frankenstein.

Most actors privileged to work with Clive remember him two ways—as a brilliant actor and as a tormented man. As David Manners, Clive's co-star of *Journey's End* and later the romantic lead of such classic shockers as *Dracula, The Mummy* and *The Black Cat,* told me:

> To me, his face was a tragic mask. I know he was a tortured man. There seemed to be a split in his personality: one side that was soft, kind, and gentle; the other, a man who took to alcohol to hide from the world his true nature. . . .
>
> Today he would find help. Every one of us wanted to help then, but when he was on the bottle, which was most of the time, he put on the mask of a person who repelled help and jeered at his own softness. . . .
>
> He was a fantastically sensitive actor—and as with many great actors, this sensitivity bred addiction to drugs or alcohol in order to cope with the very insensitive world around them.[37]

Perhaps the ideal role for Clive would have been *Dr. Jekyll and Mr. Hyde.*

By the time he starred in *Journey's End,* Clive, like Karloff, carried the aura of a man whose life had been filled with tragedy. A descendant of "Clive of India" and the son of a medal-laden British colonel, he had seen his own military dreams destroyed when a riding accident at the Royal Military Academy fractured his knee. Clive shocked his family by drifting into the theatre, training at the Royal Academy of Dramatic Art, acting in repertory and touring companies, sparkling in the chorus line of West End musicals. Fellow thespians gossiped of his drinking, bisexuality and curious marriage to French actress-playwright-mimic Jeanne de Casalis, a lesbian. Whale had thought him a natural for the spiritually ravaged Stanhope, and his superb performance on the London stage and in the cinema version made him an internationally praised star.

Whale dispatched a letter about *Frankenstein* to Clive at his 400-year-old country cottage in County Kent. As the director later explained of his choice:

> I chose Colin Clive for *Frankenstein* because he had exactly the right kind of tenacity to go through with anything, together with the kind of romantic quality which makes strong men leave civilization to shoot big game. There is also a level-headedness about Clive which keeps him in full control of himself even in his craziest moments in the picture.[38]

Clive happily accepted the offer. He later spoke of his major attraction to the story:

> I think *Frankenstein* has an intense dramatic quality that continues throughout the play and culminates when I, in the title role, am killed by the Monster that I have created. This is a rather unusual ending for a talking picture, as the producers generally prefer that the play end happily with the hero and heroine clasped in each other's arms.[39]

Little did Clive realize when he said this that a happy Hollywood ending, very similar to what he scoffingly described, would be tacked on at the last minute! Nevertheless, Universal was delighted when Clive signed for *Frankenstein.* His wonderful acting was an inspiration to the entire company, and as his "Elizabeth," Mae Clarke, would recall, "I had such deep admiration for Colin and his talent. I melted at every word he uttered."[40]

Elizabeth, Henry's Fiancee: Though Universal publicity colored her as a flowering, 21-year-old find, Mae Clarke, formerly Violet Mary Klotz of Philadelphia, was really 24 and quite experienced. In 1924, she was rolling up her tights and pursing her lips to kick in the chorus of Broadway's *Sitting Pretty* and, unbeknownst to her, inspiring Anita Loos to create the immortal dumb blonde Lorelei Lee of her play *Gentlemen Prefer Blondes.* As Miss Loos divulged in 1974:

> . . . Lorelei was born full-blown in 1924. I patterned her on a cute little blonde H.L. Mencken was escorting at the time. Her name was Mae Clarke . . . Mae Clarke certainly added something to my experience. Mencken was a beau of mine . . . It amused me to see how such a brilliant man could be amused by Mae, a cutie pie blonde.[41]

The cutie pie prospered; Broadway shows such as 1926's *The Noose* and 1927's *Manhattan Mary* won her a Hollywood bid, where she was enjoying a great year in 1931. She had played Molly, the whore who took that suicide leap in Howard Hughes' *The Front Page,* and won a footnote in Americana at Warner Bros., where James Cagney ground half a grapefruit into her face in the gangster saga *The Public Enemy.* That classic celluloid chauvinism made her nose bleed, and after director William Wellman cried "Cut!" Mae cut loose

John Boles and Mae Clarke with picture of Colin Clive, in a scene from *Frankenstein*.

at Cagney: "Oh, you son of a bitch, look what you did to me!"[42]* Universal noted the scene's impact and gave Mae a star contract. Her splendid performance as Myra, the pathetic streetwalker of Whale's *Waterloo Bridge* had established her as queen of the Universal lot, where, truthfully, there was little formidable competition for her crown at the time.† As Whale, whom Miss Clarke considered a genius, explained, "I asked for Mae Clarke for Elizabeth, because of her intelligence, fervor, and sincere belief that *Frankenstein* would claim the public's interest."[43] Years later, Miss Clarke commented, "As it developed, the part of Elizabeth was not a good follow-up to Myra rolewise, but this was more than compensated for in a continuing association with prestige pictures."[44]

Victor Moritz, Henry's trusted friend: For the thankless part of Victor, reliable hunk on hand to dry the tears (and, as originally scripted, presumably wed) Elizabeth after Henry's demise, Whale chose to use the studio's John Boles, solid, handsome leading man then alternating between roles as singing baritones in such fare as 1930's *Captain of the Guards* and *King of Jazz,* and romantic melodramas such as 1931's *Seed.* A U.S. spy in Germany, Bulgaria and Turkey during World War I, the pleasant 35-year-old, Texas-born actor was a fine solid foil to the eclectic Clive, and accepted the part as an offbeat variation on his usual assignments.

Dr. Waldman, Frankenstein's tutor: "Is that all you've learned about acting?"[45] Edward Van Sloan, 49, demanded of himself after watching his movie debut in *Dracula.* The hook-nosed, mellow-voiced veteran of some 150 plays, including the Broadway comedies *Polly Preferred* (1923) and *Morals* (1925), had played Van Helsing in the original Broadway *Dracula* in 1927; after touring in the part, he soon moved his wife and son to Hollywood. A survivor of the Florey screen test, Van Sloan was fated to win a special niche in the horror genre via three characterizations: all-wise Van Helsing of *Dracula* (and the 1936 sequel *Dracula's Daughter*), all-wise Dr. Waldman of *Frankenstein,* and all-wise Professor Muller of *The Mummy.* While these roles were the highlights of a film career largely devoted to competently played bit

Dwight Frye (1899–1943).

* The two became good friends, and acted together again in Warners' 1933 *Lady Killer* (in which he dragged her across a room by her hair and kicked her down a hallway), and Grand National's 1936 *Great Guy.* Mae was a guest of honor at Cagney's 1974 American Film Institute Life Achievement Award dinner and presented the delighted star with a grapefruit tree.

† Her only real competition for the part of Elizabeth was Bette Davis, soon axed by Universal after Junior Laemmle decreed, "She's got as much sex appeal as Slim Summerville."

Dwight Frye as Fritz in *Frankenstein.*

parts, Van Sloan regarded them cavalierly in his final years, hoping (futilely) that he would be best remembered for his stage comedies.

Fritz, Frankenstein's Dwarf assistant: "Rats! Rats! Rats!" squealed the giggling, pop-eyed, "fly-eater" Renfield of *Dracula.* It was a classic performance by Dwight Frye—listed in a late 1920's poll as one of Broadway's 10 finest actors, praised for his dynamic work in such New York hits as *Six Characters in Search of an Author, Puppets,* and *The Devil in the Cheese* (in which he co-starred with Fredric March and Bela Lugosi), and gifted as a concert pianist. Abandoning his Broadway base and the theatrical tearoom he owned and operated at 44 W. 69th Street, the 32-year-old actor was making his new home in Hollywood, with actress wife Laurette Bullivant and baby son Dwight junior, in his quest for fame in the talking cinema. Though heralded in New York City as a leading man and comedy specialist, the diminutive Frye was fast becoming (to his shock) one of the screen's most macabre creeps; in addition to *Dracula,* he had played Wilmer Cook, the psycho "gunsel" of Warners' *The Maltese Falcon* (a part later twitched in the classic 1941 remake by Elisha Cook, Jr.), and a butler who really *did* do it in Fox's Charlie Chan mystery *The Black Camel* (with Lugosi as a red herring). As such, Frye was Whale's first pick for Fritz, the sadistic hunchbacked dwarf whose inept brain-snatching and torturing of the Monster launch the creature on his rampage.

Whale carefully completed the casting of the smaller roles. As jolly old Baron Frankenstein, he cast 73-year-old Englishman Frederick Kerr (". . . an asset to any picture . . . I wanted him because he is conventionally well-bred enough not to interfere with the personal liberty of any son over 18 years old").[46] For Little Maria, the moppet who plays the fatal flower game with the Monster, Whale chose Marilyn Harris, a strange-looking little girl whose unusual "cuteness" added a very special touch to that classic vignette. Plump Englishman Lionel Belmore joined the cast as the Burgomaster, and bald Russian Michael Mark signed for the part of Ludwig, bereaved father of Little Maria. And John Ford's brother Francis, once Universal's greatest serial hero, humbly reported for two bit parts: an extra at the Goldstadt Medical College lecture and the wounded villager in the climactic chase.

All that remained was the official casting of the Monster.

Early in August 1931, The *Aquitania* docked in New York harbor, delivering Colin Clive for his train trip to Hollywood. A Universal emissary was on the docks to meet him, presenting Clive the script for *Frankenstein* and tidings from Whale. The letter enthused about the film, gave insights into Frankenstein's character,* and supplied news of the casting—noting that the film would feature ". . . Bela Lugosi or Boris Karloff as the Monster."[48]

Indeed, the Universal front office, apprehensive about the duration of the nightly rendezvous of

*To quote from Whale's letter:

"It is a grand part and I think will fit you as well as Stanhope . . .

"I see Frankenstein as an intensely sane person, at times rather fanatical and in one or two scenes a little hysterical . . . Frankenstein's nerves are all to pieces. He is a very strong, extremely dominant personality, sometimes quite strange and queer, sometimes very soft, sympathetic, and decidedly romantic. He hates causing anxiety to Elizabeth and his father, but his passionate zeal and his invention forced him to do so. . . . In the first scene in his laboratory he becomes very conscious of the theatrical drama and goes a little insane about it . . .

"There are none of Dracula's maniacal cackles. I want the picture to be a very modern, materialistic treatment of this medieval story—something of 'Doctor Caligari,' something of Edgar Allan Poe, and of course a good deal of us . . . I know you are absolutely right for it . . ."[49]

The letter also suggested that Clive talk to as many Americans as possible en route to Hollywood so to pick up a "looseness" in his English accent; noted that the script would probably undergo some revision; and informed the actor he could look forward to about three days of rehearsals and tests before shooting would officially begin.

> If the Monster looks like something I dreamt after something I ate, don't blame me—blame science![47]
>
> Jack P. Pierce

Pierce and Karloff, was seriously considering recalling the arrogant but established Lugosi for the Monster. *Murders in the Rue Morgue* was not yet ready, and with the *Frankenstein* sets completed (by Herman Rosse, who had won an Academy Award for Universal's 1930 *King of Jazz* and who designed the sets for *Dracula*), the cast ready, the crew assembled, and Arthur Edeson (cameraman of *All Quiet on the Western Front*) engaged as cinematographer, another delay could not be tolerated—even if it meant Lugosi lurching about like "something out of 'Babes in Toyland.'"

Bela's callback proved unnecessary. The face of Karloff as the Frankenstein Monster became the most frightening visage of Hollywood history. As England's *Film Weekly* reported:

The final result.

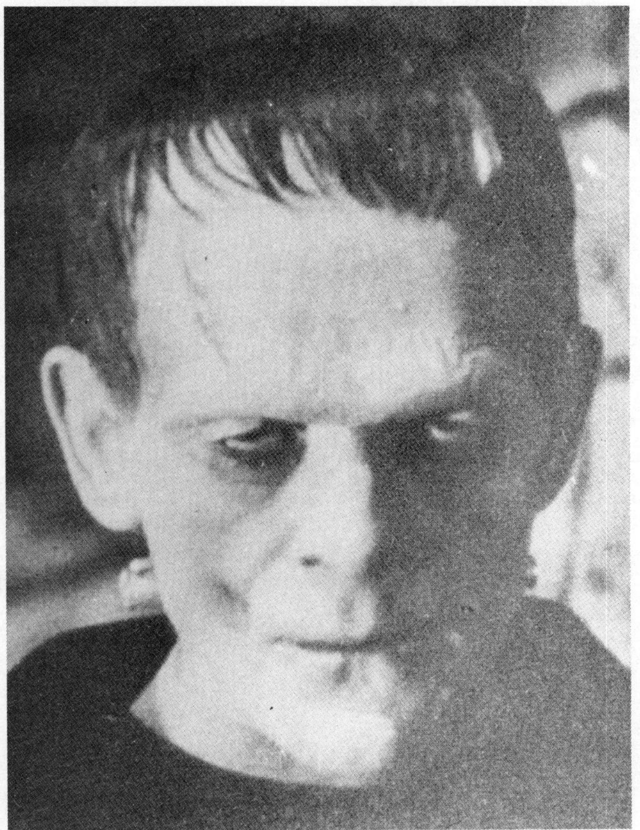

> Boris Karloff's makeup as the synthetic man pieced together from corpses is the most brilliantly horrible ever achieved on the screen . . . It is almost impossible to look at his apparently scarred, stitched, and skewered skin . . . without believing that his body has really been sewn, spliced, and glued together. The effect is completed by his emaciated face, sunken eyes, the 'barking' which is his only form of expression, and the uncanny movement of his joints . . .[50]

While the very laconic, publicity-shunning Pierce managed for years to elude interviewers asking for the story of the makeup, he finally told *The New York Times* during the production of *Son of Frankenstein* how his Monster was created:

> . . . I made him the way textbooks said he should look. I didn't depend on imagination. In 1931, before I did a bit of designing, I spent three months of research in anatomy, surgery, medicine, criminal history, criminology, ancient and modern burial customs, and electrodynamics.
>
> My anatomical studies taught me that there are six ways a surgeon can cut the skull in order to take out or put in a brain. I figured that Frankenstein, who was a scientist but no practicing surgeon, would take the simplest surgical way. He would cut the top of the skull off straight across like a potlid, hinge it, pop the brain in and then clamp it on tight. That is the reason I decided to make the Monster's head square and flat like a shoe box and dig that big scar across his forehead with the metal clamps holding it together.
>
> Those two metal studs sticking out at the sides of the Monster's neck have puzzled folks no end, so I'd better explain them. They are inlets for electricity—plugs such as we use for lamps or flatirons. Remember, the Monster is an electrical gadget. Lightning is his life force. . . .
>
> Here's another thing. I read that the Egyptians used to bind some criminals hand and foot and bury them alive. When their blood turned to water after death, it flowed into their extremities, stretched their arms to gorilla length and swelled their hands, feet, and faces to abnormal proportions. I thought this might make a nice touch for the Monster, since he was supposed to be made from the corpses of executed felons. . . . I made his arms look longer by shortening the sleeves of his coat, stiffened his legs with two pairs of pants over steel struts . . . I cover Karloff's face with blue-green greasepaint, which photographs gray. I blacken his fingernails with shoe polish. . . .[51]

Karloff himself made one significant contribution to the makeup. "Finally, when we were in the last stages . . . my eyes seemed too normal and alive and natural for a thing that had only just been put together and born, so to speak."[52] So Pierce put mortician's wax on the lids, veiling the

Jack Pierce studies Karloff's face in the makeup studio.

eyes. With cheesecloth, he simulated "pores" in the skin; with cotton strips soaked in collodion, he produced "veins;" and with a black "beauty mark," he accented Karloff's cadaverous face, (a touch Karloff further accentuated by removing a dental bridge).

Finally, in total makeup and costume,* Karloff stood more than seven feet tall and took on an incredible 48 pounds, including an unseen five-pound spine (". . . the rod which conveys the current up to the Monster's brain,"[53] explained Pierce) and the giant asphalt-spreader's boots weighing 13 pounds each. In this guise, Karloff finally reported for the critical test.

Junior Laemmle was amazed. Awed by the makeup, the producer also noted what Pierce had so wisely allowed: Karloff's gaunt, sensitive face was free for the play of emotion. Laemmle approved Karloff's casting for a natural reason rather than a cosmetic one: "Karloff's eyes mirrored the suffering we needed."[54]

Shortly afterwards, Bela Lugosi read of Karloff's casting in the trade papers. Obtaining Karloff's telephone number, he gave the Englishman a call.

"The part's nothing," said the star to the player, "but perhaps it will make you a little money."[55]

*A slightly different makeup, for which Pierce claimed Whale was responsible, was also photographed. Though quickly discarded, it was used extensively to promote the film.

. . . This was a pathetic creature who, like us all, had neither wish nor say in his creation and certainly did not wish upon itself the hideous image which automatically terrified humans whom it tried to befriend. The most heartrending aspect of the creature's life, for us, was his ultimate desertion by his creator. It was as though man, in his blundering, searching attempts to improve himself, was to find himself deserted by his God.[56]

Boris Karloff

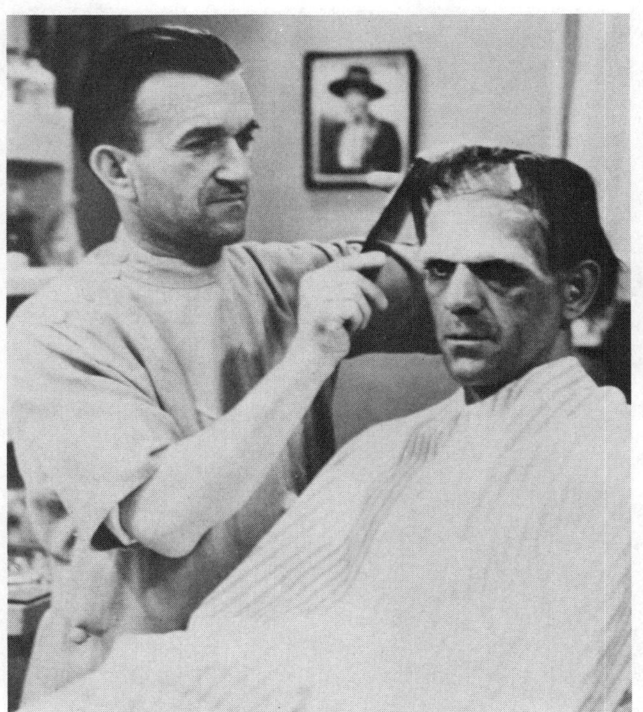

Pierce applies the Monster's wig.

From the beginning, Karloff's approach to his "dear old Monster" was one of love and compassion. To discover and convey such sympathy was an outstanding insight—considering that rarely has an actor suffered so hideously in bringing life to a character.

"It took from four to six hours a day to make me up," said Karloff. "I felt like an Egyptian mummy as Jack ladled the layers of makeup on me."[57] The company call for *Frankenstein* was 9 o'clock every morning, so Karloff piloted his old Ford onto the Universal lot at 4 A.M. to begin his makeup. The studio was like an eerie ghost town at that black hour, and often the only sound was a coyote howling in the mountains.

Come 9 A.M., Karloff, barring any makeup problems, was on the set in his 48-pound getup. The summer sun was already merciless by that hour:

> To fill out the Monster costume I had to wear a doubly-quilted suit beneath it. We shot *Frankenstein* in mid-summer. After an hour's work I'd be sopping wet. I'd have to change into a spare undersuit, often still damp from the previous round. So I felt, most of the time, as if I were wearing a clammy shroud. No doubt it added to the realism![58]

As the August heat soared, Karloff's makeup proved a torture. The mortician's wax eyelids he believed to be so necessary would melt and crumble on the sweltering set, falling into his eyes and causing terrible pain. Pierce stood by the actor's side constantly, emergency makeup box in tow, ready to fix a bolt if it loosened or adjust the wig if it slipped or share a joke when humor was a necessity.

Come lunchtime each day, Whale dismissed the company, but Karloff could not join them. "He didn't have lunch with us in the studio commissary," remembered Mae Clarke, "because it was easier for him, due to the makeup, to eat alone in his dressing room bungalow . . ."[59] Once inside this sanctuary, Karloff stripped. To keep wearing his soppy underwear in the terrible heat might have caused pneumonia. Outside, stars and starlets strolled by on their way to the commissary, mercifully unaware that inside the bungalow lurked a naked Monster. After his solitary lunch, Karloff, in fresh underclothes, a spare quilted suit and the torturous costume and boots, ventured back to the soundstage.

Worse would come. One morning, very early in the production, Karloff took a little walk to escape

Karloff and Jack Pierce, as reflected in the makeup studio mirror.

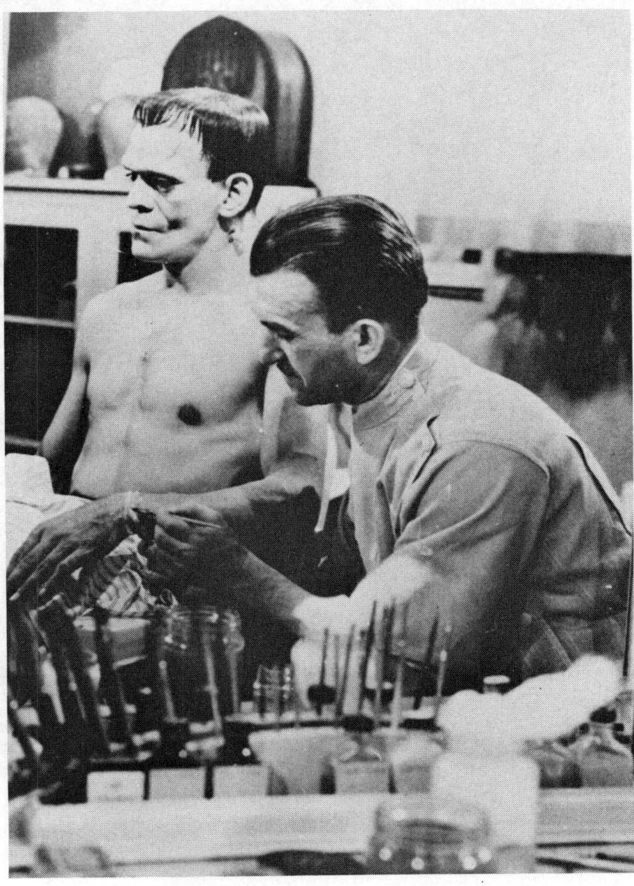

Karloff as the Monster.

the soundstage heat. As the laconic Pierce himself later validated, a pretty young studio secretary came sashaying around a corner. Karloff looked down and smiled. The secretary looked up and fainted. Word of her prostration reached "Uncle Carl." Hugely fond of issuing personal mandates (even the lot's "Keep Off the Grass" signs bore his signature), the Universal patriarch expressed concern about Karloff: "Some of our nice little secretaries are pregnant, and they might be frightened if they saw him!"[60] Hence, Universal habitués beheld the sight of Karloff, a blue veil covering his head, strolling hand in hand with Pierce as the sympathetic makeup man guided the player to and from the set. The actor was forbidden to leave the soundstage except for his bungalow lunch, and two guards (probably Laemmle relatives) took up posts at the stage door to safeguard against visitors and, presumably, an escape attempt by Boris. News of this intrigue became a popular topic around Hollywood, *Variety* cynically calling it the "kind of secrecy that makes publicity."[61]

As Uncle Carl magnanimously safeguarded against miscarriages, Karloff suffered on. Neither Junior Laemmle nor Whale considered that, as they left the studio each evening, some of Karloff's worst agony lie ahead—the removal of the makeup. For one and a half to two hours each night, burning oils, severe acids ("plus a great deal of bad language!"[62] added Karloff) stripped the makeup from the actor's face. By the time he returned to his Ford, toting his still damp morning underwear, Karloff had survived a 15-to 16-hour day—a direct violation of the Academy of Motion Picture Arts and Sciences edict that an actor work no longer than 12 hours any day (unless the subsequent rest period was appropriately expanded).

Karloff's professionalism is still legendary in Hollywood, and he was never less than bravely charming and witty throughout the shooting. But he was no fool. He had a strong sense of injustice and refused to allow Universal to exploit him. Hence, Karloff soon appealed to the Academy for relief from the studio's sadistic schedule. The Academy ruled quickly in his favor—a decision that, according to *Film Weekly*, ". . . flung the Universal lot into mourning."[63]

So, near the end of shooting, some mild concessions were made. Karloff began arriving at 5:30 A.M., and Pierce, an ally in his protest, managed to streamline the makeup application into three and a half hours. The work day also ended slightly earlier to facilitate makeup removal. However, perhaps out of sportsmanship to the studio, perhaps

Karloff, a veil covering his Monster makeup, takes a walk on the back lot with Jack Pierce, during a break from *Frankenstein*.

Jack Pierce (center) and assistant "touch up" Karloff's makeup during a tea break on the set of *Frankenstein*.

due to his own sense of the absurd, Karloff good-naturedly continued his trips to and from the *Frankenstein* soundstage sporting his tacky blue veil.

From the picture's very inception we approached it as a serious work with a serious view. I think this gave it dignity and helped make it a classic.[64]

Mae Clarke

Had visitors crept past the soundstage guards and penetrated the interiors of *Frankenstein's* closed set, they would have discovered the between-scenes atmosphere to be anything but monstrous. For all of Karloff's makeup tortures, good spirits prevailed. Star Colin Clive, "on the wagon" for most of the filming, was having a grand time in Hollywood. When later asked by *The New York Times* if he had enjoyed his movie colony sojourn, Clive replied:

Oh crikey! I should say that I did. It was marvelous . . . As a visitor to your country, and particularly an English visitor, I especially welcomed this readiness on the part of everyone to make friends . . . I had no trouble in getting golf and tennis games.[65]

English protocol ruled the set, and as Mae Clarke recalled, "There were tea breaks every mid-afternoon."[66] The grandest sight of these sabbaticals was Karloff, relaxed in a beach lounge chair, enjoying a cigarette with his tea, and making wry jokes as a fan wafted air toward his sweat-shrouded body. Whale tapped the taste and intelligence of his fine cast as he directed the classic scenes of *Frankenstein:*

The Creation Sequence: It is quite obvious that both *The Magician* (with its tower laboratory) and *Metropolis* (with its electrical creation episode) had great impact on Whale's conception of the Monster's "birth"—a sequence which he believed must be flawless:

James Whale and Colin Clive as seen from the rafters of the *Frankenstein* sound stage.

> I consider the creation of the Monster to be the high spot of the film, because if the audience did not believe the thing had been really made, they would not be bothered with what it was supposed to do afterward. . . . By this time the audience must at least believe something is going to happen; it might be disaster, but at least they will settle down to see the show. Frankenstein puts the spectators in their positions, he gives final orders to Fritz, he turns the levers and sends the diabolic machine soaring upward to the roof, into the storm. He is now in a state of feverish excitement. . . . The lightning flashes. The Monster begins to move. Frankenstein merely has to believe what he sees, which is all we ask the audience to do.[67]

The awesome electrical paraphernalia which sparked, buzzed and crackled so magnificently was the creation of Kenneth Strickfaden, who assembled and operated it with two assistants. The tower laboratory set had caused such fascination among Universal employees that Junior and Whale invited visitors to witness the creation sequence, and as Mae Clarke recalled, "Everybody for miles around came to watch when they pulled the switch!"[68] The special effects, spectacular for 1931, proved unforgettable for a generation of filmgoers. Karloff never forgot them either:

> The scene where the Monster was created, amid booming thunder and flashing lightning, made me as uneasy as anyone. For while I lay half-naked and strapped to Dr. Frankenstein's table, I could see directly above me the special effects men brandishing the white-hot, scissors-like carbons that made the lightning. I hoped that no one up there had butterfingers![69]

The Flower Game: No scene in the film aroused so much controversy as the Monster's pastoral play by the lake with Little Maria, whose celebrated failure to float is perhaps the most famous episode of the *Frankenstein* series. "Here was this beautiful direction by Whale," said Mae Clarke. "He told little Marilyn Harris, 'Here is Mr. Karloff in a funny costume who's just being friendly. You just look up at him and say, 'I am Maria.'"[70] Yet, when the players rehearsed the episode on the sunny shore of a Hollywood lake, Whale and Karloff came to an extreme difference of opinion:

Colin Clive and Dwight Frye.

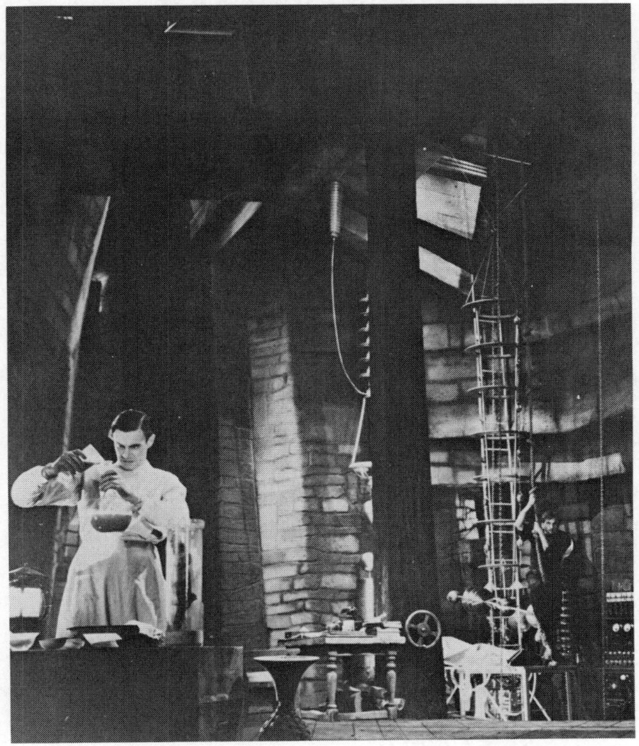

The Monster, holding a flower, smiles at his new friend, little Maria . . .

> Well, that was the only time I didn't like Jimmy Whale's direction. . . . My conception of the scene was that he would look up at the little girl in bewilderment, and, in his mind, she would become a flower. Without moving he would pick her up gently and put her in the water exactly as he had done to the flower—and, to his horror, she would sink. Well, Jimmy made me pick her up and do THAT [motioning violently] over my head which became a brutal and deliberate act. . . . The whole pathos of the scene, to my mind, should have been—and I'm sure that's the way it was written—completely innocent and unaware.[71]

The other players and crew members sided with Karloff. Indeed, they all felt that the little girl need not be killed or hurt at all—why not treat the Monster to a peaceful, happy idyll? "This was the nearest the Monster came to having a soul, without having one,"[72] Miss Clarke incisively recalled. But Whale, a director who always demanded obedience, responded, "The Death has to take place." As Karloff said:

> He fumbled for his words as he tried to convey why to us, because in a strange way we were all very hostile about it. He couldn't just bully us into acceptance. Then he said, 'You see, it's all part of the *ritual.*'[73]

Karloff had no choice but to accept Whale's ritualistic, innocent-child-killed-by-soulless-monster approach. Hence, Karloff threw Marilyn into the air and she splashed into the lake, screamed, "No, you're hurting me! Daddy!" and obligatorily sank. Still Karloff remained offended by the sadism. "I insisted on that part being removed,"[74] said the actor decades later of a scene whose fate would finally be decided by an aghast trade paper preview audience.*

Incidentally, none of this sensitivity infected little Marilyn's fanatical stage mother, who was lakeside for the shooting. After Karloff had tossed the moppet into the lake, Mrs. Harris, almost hysterically excited, squealed, "Throw her in again!"[75]

The Boudoir Scene: From a little girl, to an impatient virgin, Whale had the Monster spread his wrath, and one of *Frankenstein's* most famous moments comes when the black-clad Monster sneaks into the chamber of the bridal-gowned Elizabeth to scare her into hysterics. In rehearsals, the hysterics became almost genuine. As Miss Clarke elaborates:

> Between Karloff's perfect performance and my throwing myself so thoroughly into my role, I feared I would drop dead. I asked Boris if he knew any tricks which would help me. "Remember," he said, "when I am coming at you to keep your eye on my up-camera little finger. I'll keep wiggling it. Then you'll know it's only Boris underneath all this makeup." Fortunately for me, Boris didn't forget to wiggle his finger![76]

The Mountain Chase: "The pagan sport of a mountain manhunt" was how Whale conceived the bravura climax of *Frankenstein,* as the villagers pursued the Monster to his fiery "death" in the windmill. Whale masterfully blended actual exteriors of the torch-bearing villagers marching vigilantly in the night through the studio's little European village (previously seen in *All Quiet on the Western Front*), sailing on a back lot lake, and racing over hilly studio terrain with a soundstage set of craggy mountains, all accented by the yelping of the pursuing bloodhounds.

This sequence also proved to be the most grueling for Karloff—due to Whale's egomania. The director, resenting all the attention Karloff was enjoying on the lot and in the press, felt "upstaged" by the player and now exorcised his wrath.

*Strangely, at least one renegade print of *Frankenstein* containing the complete flowers sequence has surfaced over the decades, but only in theater revivals, never on television. Universal, meanwhile, still insists that studio policy has never tolerated the showing of edited sequences to the public, and refuses to restore the footage, or to confirm if the complete sequence is in the vaults.

The Monster and Maria (Marilyn Harris) play with flowers by the lake . . .

. . . and the game ends in death—and a deleted scene.

Boris Karloff and Mae Clarke.

Whale ordered Karloff to race up the hill to the windmill carrying the six-foot, 154-pound Clive over his shoulder literally *dozens* of times. Karloff, who used no stuntman on the picture, stoically endured the abuse, and never related it publicly—though he would remember the treatment vividly years later when suffering painful back problems.

Whale's set sadism even spread to his friend Clive. Seeking "realism," Whale demanded that Clive and Karloff tussle so long and so hard in the climax that Clive finally dislocated an arm.

"Frankenstein Finished" said the October 11, 1931, *New York Times.* The studio began dismantling the sets (though the laboratory was revamped to accommodate Lugosi and his ape of *Murders in the Rue Morgue*). Whale turned his energy to pre-production of his next film, *Impatient Maiden,* with Mae Clarke set for the title role. Colin Clive treated himself to a vacation in Hollywood enjoying rounds of tennis and golf and American coffee. Jack Pierce put away Dwight Frye's hump and Karloff's padding and boots, and returned to his usual glamorizing chores. And Karloff, having lost 20 pounds, bearing two little scars on his neck from the electrodes, and having earned a reported $500 for his portrayal of the Monster, began hunting jobs again. He had watched some of the daily "rushes" of *Frankenstein;* like so many great actors who have played great parts, he believed he had fallen very short of playing the Monster as well as he deserved to be played. One evening, after viewing the rushes, the disheartened Karloff turned to Edward Van Sloan, and commented mournfully that he thought *Frankenstein* would: "ruin my career."

"Not so, Boris, not so," smiled Van Sloan. "You're *made*!"[77]

Carl Laemmle and son hosted a special preview of *Frankenstein* for the trade press at Universal City in early November 1931. The reaction was one of numb shock. After the lights came on, the Laemmles sheepishly confessed to the reviewers

The pursuit of the Monster: Michael Mark (far left), Lionel Belmore (center), and Colin Clive lead the mob through Universal's back-lot European village.

YOU'LL BE AMAZED!

Universal Publicity Slogan for *Frankenstein*

that, in the words of *Motion Picture Herald*, "they did not know what to do about it."[78] The abashed Laemmle senior ultimately refused to release the picture until cuts were made to soften the blasphemy and horror.

Changes ensued.* The lake episode with Maria ("I won't forgive Junior Laemmle or James Whale for permitting the Monster to drown a little girl before my very eyes"[79] wailed the *Motion Picture Herald* reviewer) was cut with the Monster reaching for the girl. Added was the prologue, with Edward Van Sloan's coy warning to the audience, as well as a new ending, in which jolly Frederick Kerr toasted his son's recovery and marriage as Henry was tended in a long shot by Elizabeth. Colin Clive was heartsick at the news of the happy denouement, but Whale rather liked it. "The semi-happy ending," said Whale, "was added to remind the audience that after all it is only a tale that is told, and could easily be twisted any way by the director."[80] With severe apprehension, Universal shipped a negative of *Frankenstein* to New York, where, on a chilly Friday evening, December 4, 1931, audiences lined up in the rain outside Times Square's Mayfair Theatre to see what all reports promised to be a notorious shocker.

The result, of course, was show business history.

*Clive's climactic hysteria as the Monster comes to life (*Boles:* "Henry—in the name of God!" *Clive:* "Oh, in the name of God—now I know what it feels like to *be* God!") was later edited out only after the film's early engagements, leaving a jump cut covered on the sound track by a peal of thunder.

It's been reported that Clive referred to the Monster as "Adam" in the original release of *Frankenstein*, and that these references were later cut. However, there is no evidence of the name "Adam" in the cutting continuity script prepared by the studio at the time of the film's original release.

Frankenstein became the greatest hit engagement of the Mayfair's history, tallying a walloping first-week gross of $53,000. The 1734 seats proved too few, and the box office soon scheduled extra performances, selling advance tickets until 2 A.M. *Variety*, soon to salute the film as "the biggest money picture in the country," gave a "rave" review:

> Looks like a *Dracula* plus, touching a new peak in horror plays and handled in production with supreme craftsmanship. . . .
>
> Maximum of stimulating shock is there, but the thing is handled with subtle change of pace and shift of tempo that keeps attention absorbed to a high voltage climax, tricked out with spectacle and dramatic crescendo, after holding the smash shivver on a hair trigger for more than an hour. . . .
>
> Playing is perfectly paced. Colin Clive . . . plays it with force, but innocent of ranting. Boris Karloff enacts the Monster . . . with its indescribably terrifying face of demoniacal calm, a fascinating acting bit of mesmerism. . . .
>
> Photography is splendid and the lighting the last word in ingenuity. . . . It took nerve for U to do this one. . . .[81]

The New York Times, the East Coast's most influential paper, also praised *Frankenstein:*

> . . . a stirring, grand guignol type of picture, one that aroused so much excitement at the Mayfair yesterday that many in the audience laughed to cover their true feelings. . . .
>
> No matter what one may say about the melodramatic ideas here, there is no denying that it is far and away the most effective thing of its kind. Beside it, *Dracula* is tame. . . .[82]

Relieved and thrilled by the early reports from New York, the Laemmles and Whale took off for seaside Santa Barbara, where *Frankenstein* had its West Coast premiere on Sunday evening, December 6, 1931. Universal had sent formal premiere invitations to Colin Clive and Mae Clarke, but both declined. Clive was on holiday at his country retreat in England, where, on the very day of the Santa Barbara premiere, he tried to ride his horse over a high gate, fell, and fractured a hip. Miss Clarke, because of her simultaneous contracts with Universal and Columbia, was too exhausted to make the trip. Karloff, meanwhile, was ignored.

The West Coast premiere was not without incident. There were a number of walk-outs and, if reports are to be believed, a hysterical mother and daughter ran screaming up the aisle, through the lobby, and into the street. Afterwards, at about 2 A.M., the telephone rang in Whale's room at the Santa Barbara Biltmore. "Whale?" demanded the voice, "I just want you to know that, on account of your silly picture, I can't get to sleep. So I'll be damned if you're going to sleep either!"[83]

"Women come out trembling, men exhausted," reported *Motion Picture Herald*, which surprised Universal by giving the top laurels to Karloff:

> If Universal's production of *Frankenstein* does nothing else, it establishes Boris Karloff as the one important candidate who has arisen for the mantle of the late Lon Chaney . . . Because of his restraint, his intelligent simplicity of gesture, carriage, voice, and makeup, Karloff has truly created a Frankenstein Monster. Had he yielded to the temptation to melodramatize as the opportunity afforded, the character would have been far less formidable, horrible, terrible, and a lot of other 'ibles' . . . whether you like the picture or not, you won't deny his efficacy.

Karloff finally caught up with the movie during Yuletide of 1931, when he and Dorothy visited one of her school girl friends in San Francisco. Upon their arrival, they discovered *Frankenstein* to be playing in Oakland, just across the bay:

This early makeup experiment—with touches suggested by Whale—crept into some of the promotional materials for *Frankenstein.*

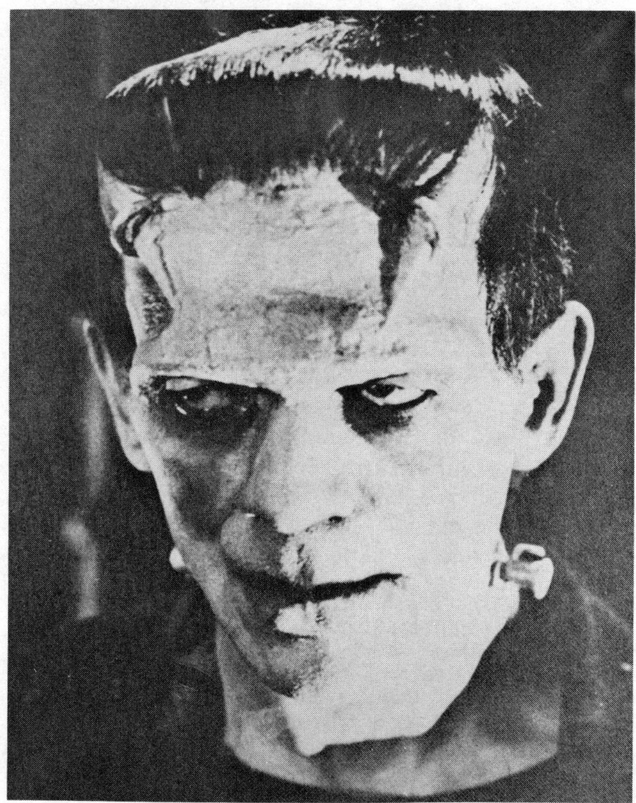

. . . What could be more natural than to invite our friend to a performance? I had, of course, seen rushes of the picture, but never a connected version, and as the film progressed I was amazed at the hold it was taking upon the audience. At the same time I couldn't help wondering how my own performance would weather all the build-up.

I was soon to know.

Suddenly out of the eerie darkness and gloom, there swept on the screen, about eight sizes larger than life itself, the chilling, horrendous figure of me as the Monster!

And, just as suddenly, there crashed out over the general stillness the stage whisper of my wife's friend. Covering her eyes, gripping my wife by the shoulder, she screamed:

"Dot, how can you live with that *creature*?"[84]

Frankenstein stirred controversy indeed. There were many who righteously sided with *Film Weekly's* attack: "It has no theme and points no moral, but is simply a shocker beside which the Grand Guignol was a kindergarten . . . it is the kind of film which could only induce nightmares."[85] The Kansas State Board of Censors banned the film, until some *four minutes* of cuts were made; in Providence, Rhode Island, some newspapers refused to run the advertisements, claiming they were "too excessive;" and in England, the film could not be shown until the censor excised the scene in which Fritz's body was discovered hanging in the dungeon, and the Monster's boudoir adventure with Elizabeth. Parent and Civic Groups who actively protested the film felt it to be totally unfit for children ("The children thought otherwise,"[86] smiled Karloff). Whale, delighted by the uproar, coolly replied, "I never intended this picture for children—but would like to make a children's version!"[87]

Yet, all these protests merely gave the film more notoriety, and *Frankenstein* (with the poster subtitle "The Man who Made a Monster") was a sensation. With a variety of publicity stunts, including ambulances parked outside theaters and nurses in attendance in movie house lobbies,* *Frankenstein* grossed more than $1,000,000 (over double the take of *Dracula*) in its first domestic goround† becoming one of Hollywood's top-grossing pictures of the 1931–32 season and one of the greatest moneymakers in Universal's history. An artistic success as well, it placed No. 7 on *The New York Times* very discriminating "Ten Best" list for 1931, played at the first Venice Film Festival in 1932, and was acclaimed as a personal triumph for Junior Laemmle, Whale, Clive, and, of course, Karloff, who, to his amazement, learned from his agent one morning that Universal would present him with a star contract.

I thought, maybe for once, I'll know where my breakfast is coming from, after more than 20 years of acting![88]

The first Frankenstein, produced by Carl Laemmle and directed by James Whale, was a brilliant creative work . . . The photography and direction remain classic . . . Karloff's performance remains a deeply moving experience.[89]

Drake Douglas, *Horror!*

Frankenstein changed Hollywood, cinema history and the lives of its creators, and in its wake came a parade of now-vintage shockers. Fredric March became the only "monster" to date to win

* Though much has been made of the fact that Universal released tinted versions of *Frankenstein* in green ("the color of fear"), this was done on only a few prints and soon discontinued, as it proved a nice touch for the Monster, but made everyone else look bilious.

† The most recent tally claims *Frankenstein* has grossed $13,000,000. It continues to earn money via television rentals, and has been marketed by MCA Video Cassette Inc.

an Academy Award, via Paramount's 1932 *Dr. Jekyll and Mr. Hyde;* MGM's Irving Thalberg, ordering Tod Browning to "out-horrify *Frankenstein,*" produced the notorious *Freaks;* screaming Fay Wray cracked Lionel Atwill's wax face in Warners' 1933 *Mystery of the Wax Museum* and, sporting a blonde wig, lured RKO's *King Kong* (1933) to his Manhattan demise. Horror was a cinema sensation—and Universal was its top peddler.

As Universal reigned supreme in the genre, so did Boris Karloff rule as Hollywood's king bogey man. His star rose at the studio as he created a gallery of superbly chilling performances, all in 1932: the hulking Morgan of Whale's *The Old Dark House;* the shrivelled Im-Ho-Tep of *The Mummy;* and (on loan-out to MGM), the infamous Yellow Peril of *The Mask of Fu Manchu.* He proved his international popularity by visiting England to star in *The Ghoul* (1933), then proved his versatility by playing in two major 1934 releases: John Ford's RKO *The Lost Patrol* (as the religious lunatic Sanders) and Fox's *House of Rothschild* (as the Jew-hating Baron Ledrantz). By the time he returned to Universal to star as the wolfish Satanic High Priest Hjalmar Poelzig in Edgar Ulmer's exquisitely morbid *The Black Cat* (Karloff's first screen union with second-billed Bela Lugosi), the star rated billing by one, all-capital word: KARLOFF.

Yet, for all the other excellent horror films and performances of this richly creative period, *Frankenstein,* and Karloff's Monster remain the most celebrated film and performance of all. Even today, in the pea-soup wake of *The Exorcist, Frankenstein* is still the most famous horror film ever made, while the Monster remains the genre's most hallowed character. Why was *Frankenstein* so fantastic a success—and why has its popularity endured so powerfully over the past half-century?

First of all, sociologically speaking, *Frankenstein* premiered in the depths of the United States' Depression. In a tragic era of "Brother, Can You Spare a Dime?", many American moviegoers could relate to the plight of Frankenstein's Monster. They too, it seemed, had been spawned then abandoned by the American Dream—or God Himself. Others found in the melodrama a welcome escape from the mundane world of breadlines in this time of America's economic disaster.

Yet there is a lasting quality in *Frankenstein.* Certainly, the film no longer horrifies, but has aged gracefully over the half-century like a beloved, Grimm Brothers fairy tale, which, a la Mary Shelley's classic, inspires a profound sympathy for the Monster.

Whatever tactics James Whale employed to win *Frankenstein* must be forgiven him today (especially in the light of Robert Florey's *Murders in the Rue Morgue,* which proved a failure upon its February 1932 release). It is the genius of Whale that gives *Frankenstein* the charm, style and aura of folk poetry which serve the classic so well today. Whale's pictorial elan creates an innocent, pastoral backdrop for his morality tale, providing the audience with rich memories: the rain-slashed mountain tower, the immaculate, electricity-charged laboratory, the lovely lake idyll, the village wedding feast (in which the happy dancing peasants become a howling, bloodthirsty mob), and the mountain manhunt that climaxes at the old, forsaken windmill. With such "modern" cinema touches as the close-up and the panning of scenes through walls, Whale exhibits a marvelous sense of cinema pace; even in the romantic interlude between Boles and Miss Clarke (by no means Whale's favorite part), the director opens on a portrait of Clive, switches to a closeup of Boles, and then to a closeup of Miss Clarke to establish cleanly and quickly the romantic triangle. Slices of Whale's bizarre humor (also apparent in his 1933 classic *The Invisible Man,* and even more so in *Bride of Frankenstein*) appear: Clive tosses a shovelful of graveyard dirt over his shoulder and into the skullface of a cemetery angel of death; Frye stops scuttling up the tower steps to adjust his sock; old Frederick Kerr snorts and blusters to amusing effect. Whale's perversely clever introduction of the Monster is itself a classic, as the director almost sadistically prolongs the suspense. First we hear awkward footsteps; then the Monster steps from out of the darkness into the light of the doorway (backward!); and then slowly turns, staring into the camera for those three famous closeups. And, of course, Whale knew how to inspire actors, as proven by the film's fine gallery of performances. If only for *Frankenstein,* Whale deserves fame as a cinema pioneer. That he is not widely acclaimed even after such credits as *The Invisible Man, Bride of Frankenstein,* and 1936's *Show Boat* is a tragedy, and one which must stem at least partially from the strange nature of his later life.

Colin Clive is a superb, apocalyptic Dr. Henry Frankenstein; his magnificent hysteria as he cackles "IT'S ALIVE!" on seeing the moving hand of the Monster is one of the truly magic moments of the horror genre. With his skeletal face and fiery eyes, fraught, twitching personality, and voice like a crazed pipe organ, the willowy actor brings the Monster Maker to blasphemous life. Yet, there is a poise, passion and intelligence in his portrayal which gives Frankenstein a strange charisma, and Clive's beautiful delivery of Frankenstein's famous soliloquy—" . . . Have you never wanted to look beyond the clouds and the stars or to know what causes the trees to bud . . . ?"—almost wins sympathy for his dream to "be God." A floridly intense actor, Clive was fated to tap his

Colin Clive and Boris Karloff.

own highly strung personality in Hollywood to create a gallery of nerve-frayed grotesques (knife-craving Orlac of 1935's *Mad Love*, Jean Arthur's sadistic spouse of *History is Made at Night*, et al.). Frankenstein remains his most famous performance, one he would happily reprise in the sequel *Bride of Frankenstein*.

Frankenstein retains extra spice today via both Edward Van Sloan's schmaltzy Dr. Waldman and Dwight Frye's slavering Fritz—a grand little goblin who, following his Renfield of *Dracula*, splashed a patina of grotesquerie on Frye's cinema image from which he could never escape. As Elizabeth, Mae Clarke appears attractive and intelligent enough to appeal to a man like Frankenstein, while John Boles is solid and stolid as Victor, whose part in the film lost much impact with the happy ending. Frederick Kerr is delightfully wheezy as the old Baron, while Lionel Belmore (as the pompous Burgomaster) and Michael Mark (as Little Maria's father, Ludwig) played so vividly that they made lasting impressions on the Universal casting department, and were hired for bits in several of the ensuing films of the series.

Best and most infamous of all is Karloff's Monster. It is a masterpiece performance, tinged with a queer and haunting beauty; as Karloff stands and raises his scarred hands to the rays of sunlight, the Monster is poignantly timeless. The nightmare of Frankenstein's blasphemy, with his insane eyes, wild tortured movements and screams of horror, the Monster is also a creature of pathetic appeal, with his pleading hands, little cries of wonder and heartbreaking bewilderment at the world that so savagely rejects him. Strangely enough, as Karloff proudly remembered, it was children who most keenly felt the Monster's pathos:

> Over the years, thousands of children wrote, expressing compassion for the great, weird creature who was so abused by its sadistic keeper that it could only respond to violence with violence. These children saw beyond the makeup and really understood.[90]

One can imagine, in watching Karloff's performance, that a Creator far greater than Frankenstein has taken pity on the Monster and given him a soul—a soul tragically hidden under the stitched and scarred booty of graveyards.

Frankenstein abandoned his Monster, but Boris Karloff never did. "My dear old Monster," said the star time and again. "I owe everything to him. He's my best friend."[91] Karloff's daughter Sara Jane echoes his sentiments:

> He was *extremely* grateful for the part of the Monster. It was what gave him his first real break, what kept him employed, and "typecast" him, which in turn kept him employed. My father never could understand why actors hated to be "typecast," because it meant he could find work constantly—and what made an actor happier than working all the time?
>
> My father was a superb actor—but the world is filled with *hungry* superb actors. Frankenstein enabled my father to be a *well-fed* superb actor.[92]

Indeed, perhaps *Frankenstein's* greatest bequest to cinema history was the overnight stardom of this most beloved of horror actors. For "dear Boris" (as he quickly became known around Hollywood), the infamy was immediate and amusing. On Halloween night of 1932, a gaggle of little ghosts and goblins, carrying jack-o'-lanterns and Trick-Or-Treat bags, giggled their way to the lights of the Karloff cottage by Toluca Lake. When Boris himself answered the door, the tricksters invited the world's most infamous bogey man to join their rounds.

"As I wasn't appropriately costumed," winked Karloff, "I had to decline."[93]

THE MONSTER WANTS A WIFE!

OR DEATH TO THE
SCIENTIST WHO
CREATED HIM!

THE
MONSTER
TALKS

The Frankenstein Monster
challenges his maker!...

To agree meant another
monstrosity roaming the
world!... To refuse meant
the end of life and love!

CARL LAEMMLE PRESENTS
KARLOFF
IN
THE Bride of
FRANKENSTEIN

A UNIVERSAL PICTURE WITH
COLIN CLIVE
VALERIE HOBSON
ELSA LANCHESTER
UNA O'CONNOR • ERNEST
THESIGER • E. E. CLIVE

SCREEN PLAY BY WILLIAM
HURLBUT AND JOHN
BALDERSTON • PRODUCED
BY CARL LAEMMLE, JR.

DIRECTED BY JAMES WHALE

Bride of Frankenstein poster.

Bride of Frankenstein (1935)

Producer, Carl Laemmle, Jr.; *Director,* James Whale; *Screenplay,* William Hurlbut (from an adaptation by Hurlbut and John L. Balderston, suggested by the original story by Mary Wollstonecraft Shelley); *Photography,* John Mescall; *Special Effects,* John P. Fulton; *Special Electrical Properties,* Kenneth Strickfaden; *Music,* Franz Waxman; *Musical Director,* Mischa Bakaleinikoff; *Art Director,* Charles D. Hall; *Editor,* Ted Kent; *Makeup,* Jack P. Pierce; *Sound Recorder,* Gilbert Kurland; *Assistant Directors,* Harry Menke and Joseph McDonough.

Filmed under the shooting title of *The Return of Frankenstein* at Universal City, California, January–March, 1935; opened at the Roxy Theater, New York City, May 10, 1935. Running Time: 75 minutes.

BRIDE OF FRANKENSTEIN— SYNOPSIS

"How beautifully dramatic! The crudest savage exhibition of Nature at her worst without, and we three—we elegant three—within . . ."

An awesomely stormy night near Lake Geneva, 1816. High in a mountain tower, in a drawing room complete with wolfhounds and a roaring fire, Lord Byron pivots on his club foot away from the great window, waves his cheroot, and smiles wickedly at his companions—the poet Percy Shelley and the gentle Mary, Shelley's 18-year-old lover.

"I should like to think that an irate Jehovah was pointing those arrows of lightning directly at my head—the unbowed head of George Gordon, Lord Byron—England's greatest sinner." He invites Mary to join him at the window to watch the storm.

"You know how lightning alarms me," says little Mary, looking up from her embroidery.

"Astonishing creature," grins Byron. ". . . Frightened of thunder, fearful of the dark—and yet you have written a tale that sent my blood into ic-y crrreeps!"

"My purpose," says Mary of her novel *Frankenstein,* which has yet to find a bold publisher, "was to write a moral lesson—the punishment that befell a mortal man who dared to emulate God."

"Whatever your purpose may have been, my dear," says Byron, "I take relish in savoring each separate horror. I roll them over on my tongue . . ." Trilling his r's, Byron remembers the chills of Mary's *Frankenstein* . . . the scavenging of the graveyard . . . the blasphemous miracle of the Monster in the mountain laboratory . . . the little child drowned. "And it was these fragile white fingers," says Byron, beholding Mary, "that penned the nightmare!"

"I do think it a shame, Mary, to end your story quite so suddenly," says Shelley.

However, the story, according to Mary, is not over at all. There is more to the saga, which Mary has placed in a future world of wanton science, and on such a perfect night for mystery and horror, she consents to tell it. "The air itself is filled with monsters. . . ."

"I'm all ears!" exclaims Byron. "While heaven blasts the night without, open up your pits of hell!"

Mary Shelley continue. her story. . . .

The old windmill is now a skeleton of blazing timbers. They collapse, and a wild bloodthirsty cheer sounds from the rabid mob that surrounds the crematory of the Monster. Minnie, the hatchet-faced old maid of the Frankenstein estate, cackles her delight at the devastation. A sudden burst of flame from the ruins gives her added thrills: ". . . his insides caught at last!" she chortles. "Insides is always the last to be consumed!" The pompous Burgomaster, however, soon dispatches the crowd . . . "We want no rioting! No riots!" . . . and decrees a funeral procession shall carry the body of Henry Frankenstein to the manor house in the village. Then he wishes the dwindling crowd a good night and pleasant dreams.

Two forlorn figures remain by the smoking

The Players

The Monster	KARLOFF
Dr. Henry Frankenstein	Colin Clive
Elizabeth	Valerie Hobson
Dr. Septimus Pretorius	Ernest Thesiger
Mary Wollstonecraft Shelley	Elsa Lanchester
Lord Byron	Gavin Gordon
Percy Bysshe Shelley	Douglas Walton
Minnie	Una O'Connor
The Burgomaster	E. E. Clive
Albert, Chief Servidor	Lucien Prival
The Hermit	O. P. Heggie
Karl	Dwight Frye
Hans	Reginald Barlow
Hans' Wife	Mary Gordon
Shepherdess	Anne Darling
Ludwig	Ted Billings
Uncle Glutz	Gunnis Davis
Auntie Glutz	Tempe Pigott
Rudy	Neil Fitzgerald
A Hunter	John Carradine
A Neighbor	Walter Brennan
Communion Girl	Helen Parrish
A Neighbor	Rollo Lloyd
The Coroner	Edwin Mordant
Priest	Lucio Villegas
A Mother	Brenda Fowler
A Hunter	Robert A'dair
Marta	Sarah Schwartz
A Neighbor	Mary Stewart
A Hunter	John Curtis
Little King	Arthur S. Byron
Little Queen	Joan Woodbury
Little Bishop	Norman Ainsley
Little Devil	Peter Shaw
Little Ballerina	Kansas DeForrest
Little Mermaid	Josephine McKim
Little Baby	Billy Barty
A Hunter	Frank Terry
Villagers	Frank Benson, Ed Piel, Sr. Anders Van Haden, John George, Grace Cunard, Maurice Black, Peter Shaw
Doubles for Thesiger	Monty Montague, Peter Shaw
Double for Barlow	George DeNormand*
The Monster's Mate	?†

*Before his death in 1975, veteran stuntman DeNormand claimed he had doubled Karloff in *Bride of Frankenstein*. Academy records, however, claim that DeNormand actually doubled Barlow in the latter's fall into the millpond.

†Elsa Lanchester.

Valerie Hobson, Colin Clive, and Ernest Thesiger.

ruins. " . . . Nothing can bring our little Maria back to us," wails the mother of the drowned child who had played by the lake with the Monster. "If I can see his blackened bones," says Hans,* the hate-consumed father, "I can sleep at night!" He begins poking about in the ashes. Suddenly, the charred floor breaks away, and Hans falls deep into the mill cellar, splashing into a well pond. As he sputters in the water and grasps for a rescuing hold, a giant figure, singed and hideous, ventures across the pond from the shadows.

"Give me your hand, Hans!" exclaims the distraught woman as a large hand rises from the ashes and beckons for help. She pulls—and is soon face to face with Frankenstein's Monster! She screams, and the Monster smacks her, her figure falling through the ruins and tumbling over the destroyed water wheel to join the corpse of her husband, floating in the pond.

Minnie, attracted by the cries, has returned alone to the unholy site. Suddenly she looks up and sees the face of the Monster staring curiously at her. Hooting with screams, she races down the mountain, and the Monster stalks off in the moonlight.

The funeral procession bears the "corpse" of Henry Frankenstein to the great house, where Elizabeth mourns over the prostrate figure of her bridegroom. She sadly remembers that she was told to beware her wedding night.† This tragedy was foretold. However, Henry's arm moves, elic-

*In the original *Frankenstein*, this character was called "Ludwig."

†In the original script, the wedding night proved even more miserable, as the shock of Henry's presumed death proved a fatal shock to the old Baron. Hence, Henry Frankenstein becomes Baron Frankenstein as he recovers.

iting a scream from Minnie, and Elizabeth weeps with joy. He is alive.

Tended by his loving fiancée, Henry soon begins to recover from his horrific adventure. Late one night, as the bells chime in the village, Elizabeth comes to his bed with a bowl of soup and listens to her lover's rantings. "I have been cursed for delving into the mysteries of Life—perhaps Death *is* sacred—and I've profaned it," says Henry. Then, his erratic mood changes. Could it be, he wonders, that God intended him to discover the secret of Life? It could be a part of the Divine Plan!

Elizabeth passionately refutes this. "It is the *Devil* that prompts you!" she says, fearing that Death, and not Life will be the end of it all. She shivers as she tells Henry of the nights she stood by his side as he tossed in a mad delirium, shrieking insanely of his desire to create life from the graves and charnel houses, and, how, as he raved, a grotesque specter seemed to enter the room, stalking her crying fiancé, like Death, threatening to take him from her.

As she breaks down into hysterics, there is an ominous pounding at the door. Minnie answers it to see the skeletal figure of Dr. Septimus Pretorius, who demands that Minnie announce to her master that he has a caller "on a secret matter of grave importance. . . ." Minnie informs Henry that he has a guest ("on a secret grave matter"), and Dr. Pretorius enters the room—inspiring a chill in Elizabeth comparable to the one induced by the apparition.

Elizabeth leaves the two men alone, and Pretorius informs Henry that Goldstadt University has "booted" him from the faculty, blaming Pretorius for the crimes spawned by Henry's creation. The lectures of Pretorius had inflamed Henry's mind to create life, and now the old wizard demands that he and Henry work together as equals instead of as master and student. For Pretorius, too, has created artificial life—and if the fascinated Henry will join him, he'll be only too happy to reveal his creations to him.

Soon the twosome climb to Pretorius' garret, where the lunatic pours two glasses of gin ("It is my only weakness") and offers a macabre toast: "To a new world of Gods and Monsters!" Then, from a locked chest, Pretorius shows the shocked Frankenstein a series of glass bottles, each containing a Lilliputian being. There is a little Queen ("Charming, don't you think?"), a little King (who, if unwatched, escapes his bottle to pursue the Queen), a little Archbishop (usually asleep), a Devil (Pretorius notes a resemblance to himself—"or do I flatter myself?"), a ballerina (who won't dance to anything except Mendelssohn's "Spring Song"—"and it gets so monotonous"), a mermaid ("an experiment with seaweed").

Anne Darling (atop rock) and Karloff.

Henry protests. He labels Pretorius' people not science, but black magic. "You think I'm mad!" responds Pretorius. "Perhaps I am!" Still, as Pretorius reminds Frankenstein, he succeeded in growing his beings from the source of life, like cultures, just as Nature does. "Leave the charnel house," tempts the satanic Pretorius, "and follow the lead of Nature—or of God, if you like your Bible stories. '. . . male and female created He them. . . .' Alone, you have created a *man*. Now, together, we will create his *mate*."

"Do you mean . . ." grimaces the aghast Frankenstein.

"Yes," leers Pretorius. "A *woman* . . . ."

In the forest, the Monster roams. Eating a wild carrot, he nears a little pond and waterfall where a flock of sheep runs in terror as the creature sprawls by the water to take a drink. The Monster sees his reflection in the water, and, offended by his ugliness, he splashes madly at the water as if to destroy the grotesque image.

A more pleasing sight is the young shepherdess atop the cascade. The Monster, hoping to win a friend, stands and beckons to her, waving his hands. She screams and falls into the pond. Keening in sympathy, the Monster saves the unconscious girl and carries her to the turf, where she awakens and screams again. Her cries attract some hunters, who naturally mistake the Monster's attentions to the shepherdess and fire at him, hitting his arm.

The entire village soon learns that the Monster is in the woods, and a mob parades through the streets, led by bloodhounds. Waving guns, clubs and scythes, and screaming for blood, they soon find the Monster, holding his bleeding arm and running from the shrieking pursuers. The creature takes refuge atop a knoll, and as the villagers draw near, he rolls a boulder down upon them. However, the Monster, in all his strength, is no match for the mob. They tie him to a tall pole, hurling sticks and curses at the Monster before dropping him into a cart and returning triumphantly to the village.

"I'd hate to find him under my bed at night! He's a nightmare in the daylight, he is!" cackles Minnie as the Monster is chained in a giant chair, conveniently just his size, in the town dungeon. But he soon escapes, racing amok through the village, leaving a trail of dead and injured villagers as he again takes sanctuary in the wilderness. At night, as he wanders forlorn in the forest, he nears a little cottage and hears the strains of music. An old bearded man is playing "Ave Maria" on his violin, and the Monster shyly spies through the window. When the hermit hears a sound and goes to the door, the Monster retreats into the shadows, but after the hermit returns to his violin, the Monster throws open the cottage door with a roar. "Who's there?" asks the gentle Hermit. ". . . You must please excuse me, but I am blind. . . . Come in, my poor friend." The Monster happily whimpers to the Hermit, his giant hands pleading for love, just as they had pleaded for Henry Frankenstein's love what seemed so very long ago.

The Hermit soon realizes that the Monster is hurt and he gives him refuge in the cottage. As the Monster gratefully sounds his inarticulate cries, the Hermit wonders if perhaps the stranger is afflicted too. He is blind, and the stranger cannot speak.

The Hermit gives the Monster food, and has him lie down to rest. "We shall be friends," he promises. Over the Monster's wounded body, the Hermit kneels and prays to the crucifix on the wall, thanking his God Who has taken pity on his loneliness, and Who " . . . now out of the silence of the night hast brought two of Thy lonely children together—and sent me a friend, to be a light to mine eyes and a comfort in time of trouble, Amen."

The grateful Hermit breaks down and weeps. And a tear runs down the Monster's cheek too. . . .

The ensuing days are joyous. The Monster learns to speak some basic words—"Good," "Bad," "Bread," "Wine," "Smoke," "Wood," "Fire," and "Friend." On this day, the Hermit and the Monster have their lesson at the table, where the Monster devours bread, becomes a bit drunk on the wine and hiccups, and puffs on a cigar. "Alone, bad. Friend, good! Friend, *good!*" rejoices the Monster, and he hands the Hermit the violin. Moving rhythmically, cigar in hand, he enjoys the Hermit's playing of a merry tune.

There arrive two hunters at the cottage, who have lost their way. At the sight of the Monster, the two men panic. "This is the fiend that's been murdering half the countryside!" warns the first hunter, while the second informs the Hermit that his "friend" is a Monster, made by Frankenstein out of dead bodies. Thus, the Monster learns of his origin, and the reason that he is despised by mankind.

The first hunter attacks. The Monster strikes him, and in the battle, the cottage catches on fire. The two hunters pull the dazed Hermit from the blaze, while the Monster, crying "Friend," breaks through the flaming walls, runs past a religious shrine, frightens some schoolgirls, and races miserably into the mountains.

Come the night, a new mob of villagers seeks the Monster with lanterns and weapons. Their prey is now in the old mountain graveyard, where, violently bitter over his soulless being, he topples a giant statue of a bishop. As the hunters draw near, he lifts the slab of a tomb and climbs into the catacombs below. Not far from where the Monster hides, Dr. Pretorius and his two gallowsbird assistants are plundering a grave of one Madeleine Ernestine—aged 19 years, 3 months. "Pretty little thing in her way, wasn't she?" quips Karl, Pretorius' trusted ghoul, as they lift the casket lid and gaze at the remains. "I hope her bones are firm!" grins Pretorius, who stays in the tomb as evil Karl and Rudy take their leave. "If there's much more like this, what you say, pal, we give ourselves up and let 'em hang us?" says Karl outside the grave. "This is no life for murderers!"

Remaining behind, Pretorius enjoys some gin and toasts the skull of Miss Ernestine, now atop a neat pile of bones on the coffin lid. "I give you, the Monster!" laughs the drunken Pretorius to the bones. Even as he speaks, the Monster emerges from the shadows. "Oh! I thought I was alone,"

The Monster hears "Ave Maria"—O.P. Heggie and Karloff.

The Monster, Boris Karloff.

murmurs Pretorius, who offers the Monster a cigar ("They are my only weakness"). Up until now unsuccessful in persuading Henry Frankenstein to help him create a mate for the Monster, he thinks he now sees a very forceful way to persuade him.

"Do you know who Henry Frankenstein is—and who you are?" asks Pretorius.

"Yes," answers the Monster. "I know. Made me from dead. I love dead—hate living."

"You're wise in your generation," answers Pertorius, who soon has an ally in his quest to create a mate.

"Woman," smiles the Monster. "Friend." And, then with a strange tenderness, "Wife."

Elizabeth is now Baroness Frankenstein, and she and her husband are preparing to leave the village on the midnight express to Vienna when Pretorious arrives. " . . . I knew it!" cries Frankenstein. Elizabeth informs the smirking Pretorius that his visit is most unwelcome and leaves to oversee the baggage loading as Pretorius again demands that Frankenstein commit further blasphemy. When the nerve-frayed Frankenstein again twitches his refusal, Pretorius opens the manor door to reveal—the Monster!

"Sit down!" booms the Monster's cavernous voice, echoing Frankenstein's early order to him. Frankenstein meekly obeys, but still vehemently refuses to cooperate in the diabolical plan. Pretorius sends the Monster out, and shortly afterwards, the heartrending screams of Elizabeth sound from her bedroom. The Monster has kidnapped her!

In the pandemonium, Minnie screams, and Frankenstein demands search parties. Pretorius breaks a vase, warning that the only way to get Elizabeth back safely is to do nothing. Nothing, he intones, laying his skeletal hand on the shocked Henry, "except what *he* demands."

The old watchtower is soon ablaze with new electrical machinery, as Frankenstein and Pretorius prepare to give life to a new artificial being. A synthetic brain has been created by Pretorius, graves have been rifled, charnel houses pillaged; and, when a stolen heart stops beating, Karl, unbeknownst to Frankenstein, slays a young girl in the village to obtain a replacement.* Finally, another electrical storm strikes the mountains, and Frankenstein, his cadaverous face alight with mad fervor, sends the table with the would-be mate up to the rooftop and to the heavens, where large kites soar in the stormy skies to attract the lighting's life-giving rays to the new creation's mummified body.

Even as life begins, there is death. The Monster, arriving atop the tower, is repulsed by Karl and a torch. The enraged Monster wrestles the torch from his hand and hurls the screaming murderer off the tower roof to the rocks hundreds of feet below.

*In early script conferences, Balderston, Hurlbut, and Whale had discussed the idea of Elizabeth's heart being given to the Female Monster.

Valerie Hobson and Karloff.

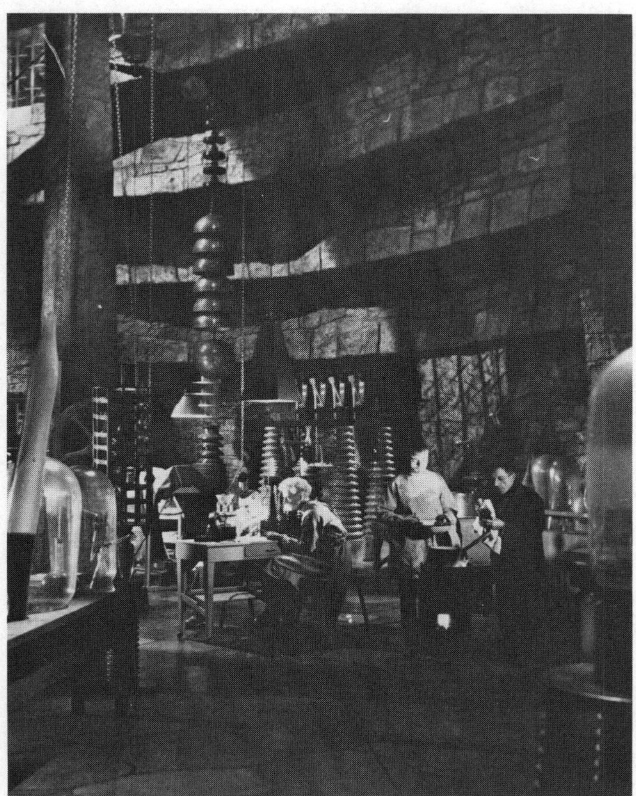

The laboratory: Colin Clive, Ernest Thesiger, Dwight Frye, and Ted Billings.

The table descends. The mummy groans softly. The two wizards remove the strip of bandages from the eyes—which are open!

"She's alive! ALIVE!" rejoices Frankenstein.

The female Monster stands in the laboratory, shorn of her bandages. Her Nefertiti-style hair, streaked with two dashes of white; her doll-face, with a livid scar on the neck; her towering body, covered with a long white gown; all appeal strongly to Pretorius, who exclaims, "The Bride of Frankenstein!"

The Monster enters. He gazes lovingly at his Mate and approaches her.

"Friend?" he timidly asks.

The female Monster turns, looks up at him—and screams.

Frankenstein and Pretorius encourage her to pay heed to her suitor. The Monster again approaches her, gingerly takes her hand and strokes it, peering hopefully into her face.

Again, she screeches in rejection.

"She hate me—like others!" mourns the Monster, who now rampages through the laboratory and grabs an ominous lever. "Look out!" cries Pretorius " . . . You'll blow us all to atoms!"

It is now that Elizabeth, having escaped from the cave where the Monster had imprisoned her, arrives at the tower and races to Henry. Fearing that the Monster will pull the lever at any moment, he urges her to go back. "But I can't leave them," he shrieks, refusing to desert his creations a second time, "I can't!"

"Yes," says the Monster, his voice breaking with emotion. "Go! You live! Go!" And then, to Pretorius: "You—stay. We belong dead!"

As Henry and Elizabeth run down the tower steps, the Monster takes a final look at his Bride. The female Monster viciously stares back, opens her mouth and savagely hisses like a mad swan. The Monster, a tear falling down his face, pulls the lever.

As Henry and Elizabeth embrace and watch, the old watchtower explodes, falling into ashes, the flashes and explosions joining the wrath of the stormy heavens—where a jealous and triumphant God keeps His watch.

BRIDE OF FRANKENSTEIN—PRODUCTION HISTORY

. . . I demand a creature of another sex, but as hideous as myself. . . . It is true, we shall be monsters, cut off from all the world; but on that account we shall be more attached to one another. . . . Oh! my creator, make me happy . . . do not deny me my request![94]

The Monster pleads with his Maker, Volume II, Chapter IX of Mary Shelley's 1818 edition of *Frankenstein*

Elsa Lanchester and Karloff.

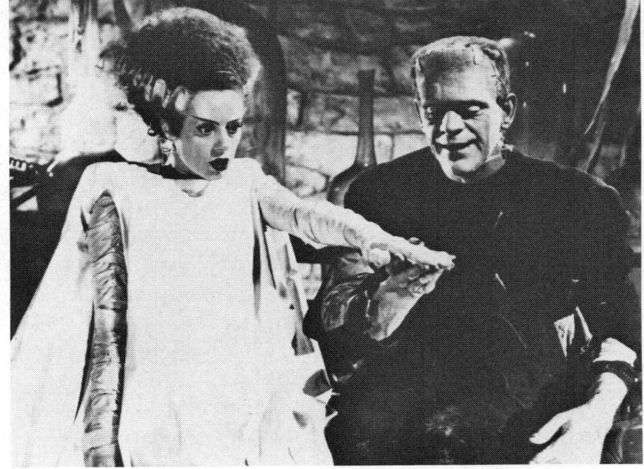

The climax of 1931's *Frankenstein,* with the hapless Monster howling piteously in the blazing windmill, did more than inspire a strange pity in audiences. It caused true mourning at Universal, where the lot lamented the premature cremation of so popular an attraction. Indeed, by 1934, the men who had prospered so in *Frankenstein*'s wake increasingly regarded the mob's roasting of the Monster as a savage and socially irresponsible act.

"God bless the old boy!" rejoiced Boris Karloff of the creature who had catapulted him to such wonderful celebrity. Thanks to his "dear old Monster," Karloff now lived in a lovely Mexican farmhouse at 2320 Bowmont Drive, high in the honeysuckled wilds of Coldwater Canyon. Katharine Hepburn had deserted the hacienda, vowing it had a "ghost." Now it was "dear Boris," looking like an amok scarecrow in his favorite private apparel of skimpy swim trunks and top hat, who haunted the pastoral aerie. Far above the eyes of Hollywood, Karloff pursued his hobbies: tenderly caring for the flowers, vegetables and fruit trees, playing ball with his Bedlington terriers and Scotties, floating in his pool reading Joseph Conrad novels and English poetry, pampering the chickens and turkeys, cavorting with such offbeat pets as a squawking parrot, a giant tortoise and his celebrated 400-pound pig Violet, and burying under the roses the cremated remains of old stock company cronies whose last wish was to rest in their now-famous friend's Eden. (Parts of the Karloff estate have been sold to a real estate developer, and these ashes now repose under slab-based, overpriced houses.) Ever the "happy rabbit" of the Hollywood Cricket Club, and a founder of the Screen Actors Guild, Karloff was still charmingly punch-drunk about his "overnight" stardom. Close friends like C. Aubrey Smith, James Gleason and Robert Armstrong, who often visited "the little farm" to enjoy his barbeque, tennis court and conversation, found Boris Karloff to be, in his daughter Sara's words, "an awfully nice man. He had a wonderful sense of humor, and a very quick wit—he was a typical English gentleman."[95]

James Whale was also relishing his Hollywood fame. "That they should pay such fabulous salaries is beyond ordinary reasoning!" crowed Whale, who in 1935 became one of the cinema's highest paid directors with his $105,000-a-year salary at Universal. "Who's worth it? But why not take it? And the architecture! And the furnishings! . . ."[96] Since *Frankenstein,* Whale had enjoyed success in a variety of genres: the romance *Impatient Maiden* (1932), the charming farce *By Candlelight* (1933), and, of course, the nightmare tales *The Old Dark House* and *The Invisible Man.* Still, his unorthodox private life was causing concern. To the delight of Hollywood's more devout gossips, the elegant, wispy homosexual would win movie colony notoriety for all-male parties around the pool of his Gothic villa at 788 South Amalfi Drive, above the cliffs of the Pacific Palisades. Be that as it may, Whale was the "Ace" of Universal, and he could have anything he wanted at the studio, as long as Junior Laemmle was in power.

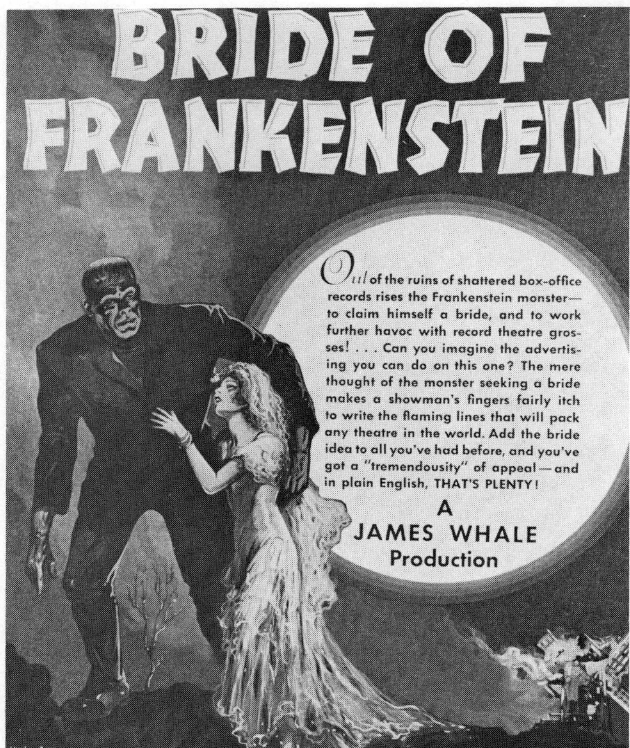

Advance publicity for *Bride of Frankenstein.*

As the Laemmles, senior and junior, joined the star and director of *Frankenstein* in mourning the Monster, a happy thought soon surfaced. In the realm of the cinema, there were no laws against grave-robbing, and moviemakers enjoyed divine power over life and death. And, as Karloff remembered of the Laemmle divinity:

> The producers realized they'd made a dreadful mistake. They let the Monster die in the burning mill. In one brief script conference, however, they brought him back alive. Actually, it seems he had only fallen through the flaming floor into the millpond beneath, and could now go on for reels and reels![97]

The resurrection of "dead" monsters would become the pet miracle of Universal City. Just as the Phoenix arose from the ashes, Karloff's Monster would arise from the millpond for *Bride of Frankenstein*—the finest and most outrageous fantasy of Hollywood's Golden Age of Terror.

Note the Calvary-like effect in this lobby card.

THE MONSTER DID NOT DIE!
He lives—and wants love!

Universal Publicity, 1935

The miracle of reviving the Monster was long in coming. As early as the summer of 1933, Universal had unfurled plans for *The Return of Frankenstein;* the star was to be Karloff and the director was to be Kurt Neumann, a young German protégé of the Laemmles. Universal's fiscal 1933 loss of $1,062,216 derailed the project, and no more was heard of it until December 1933. By that time, the almighty Whale had usurped the project from Neumann, and was reportedly preparing it with scenarist Philip MacDonald. In early 1934, while Lugosi was sneering at Karloff (on camera and off) in their first screen union, *The Black Cat,* (a stylized mixture of devil worship, necrophilia, and bastardized Poe), the publicity department announced that *The Return of Frankenstein* would soon enter official production and might co-star Boris and Bela. However, Whale now immersed himself in R.C. Sherriff's production of *One More River,* and the *Frankenstein* sequel was again postponed. It appeared that the project might lie in the same studio crypt that entombed such died-aborning Universal horror films as *Bluebeard* and *A Trip to Mars.*

Come the Christmas season of 1934, things had changed. Whale, who had basked in the praise for *One More River* after its August premiere at Radio City Music Hall, now felt comfortable about returning to the horror genre. Fiscal 1934, thanks to

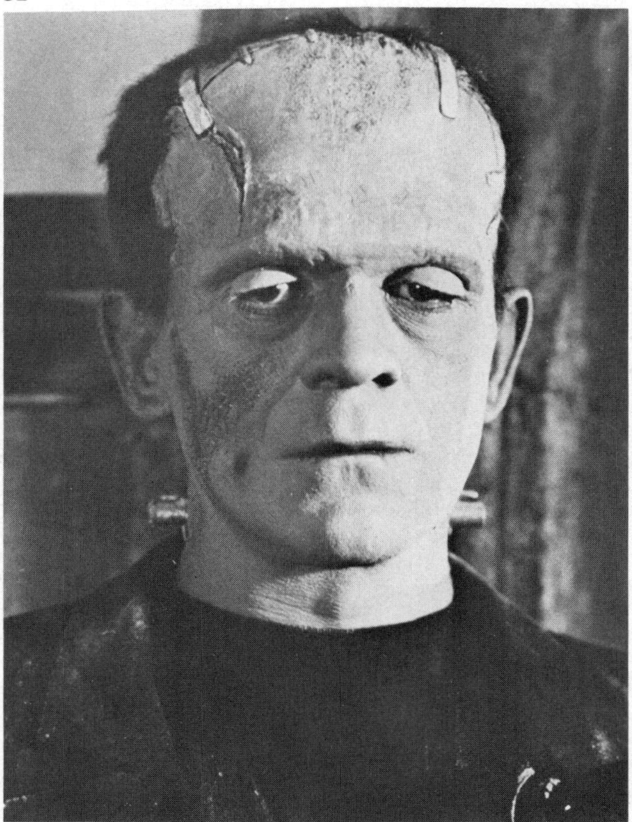

Boris Karloff's makeup in *Bride of Frankenstein*, showing the ravages of the mill fire.

Whale's *The Invisible Man* and *One More River* and the Karloff and Bela Lugosi *The Black Cat*, had bequeathed the studio a $238,292 profit, while Universal's Claudette Colbert soap opera, *Imitation of Life*, was doing outstanding business across the country. Whale believed the time was perfect to create the Swiftian extravaganza he envisioned to perpetuate the Monster's misadventures.

With Junior Laemmle enthusiastically and personally producing, Whale detailed his conception to writers John L. Balderston and William Hurlbut. All thought it proper now to consult Mary Shelley's original masterwork, and the writers became intrigued by several of the book's episodes: the Monster's doomed attempt to save a drowning girl; his meeting with a blind man in the woods; his learning to speak; and his demand for a mate.

As Balderston adapted the story and Hurlbut worked on the actual screenplay, casting began. Karloff, naturally set for the Monster, was now Universal's most popular and powerful star. In June of 1933, after his great successes in *The Old Dark House* and *The Mummy*, he had wisely walked out on Universal when the studio weaseled out of the salary hikes promised in his contract. In July 1933, repentant Universal lured him back with a luxurious contract which boosted his salary (now approximately $2,000 weekly), provided freelance clauses, and promised top-billing by surname only. MGM had GARBO. Universal had KARLOFF.

The creation had surpassed his creator; Colin Clive, borrowed from Warner Brothers to reprise Henry Frankenstein, had to accept second billing. Clive had followed *Frankenstein* with such films as RKO's 1933 *Christopher Strong* (as Katharine Hepburn's married lover), Monogram's 1934 *Jane Eyre* (as Rochester), and Universal's *One More River* (as Diana Wynyard's sadistic spouse who ravages her with a riding crop), and with such Broadway plays as 1933's *The Lake* (again with Hepburn). Yet, despite his success, Clive's face was more terribly tragic than ever as the "Hyde" side of his nature was now waxing tragically in Hollywood. "In the '30s, I think everybody out here knew Clive was brilliant," veteran screenwriter/film historian DeWitt Bodeen recently wrote me, "but also an alcoholic, and often unreliable."[98] Liquor and James Whale remained the fragile Clive's two closest friends in California, and he sometimes sought escape from his torment at the all-stag, poolside soirees which Whale hosted. Clive welcomed the *Frankenstein* sequel. He still believed that Henry Frankenstein should die to atone for his impiety, and enjoyed the shooting script's plan to destroy the blasphemer in the climactic laboratory explosion (". . . the thunders of a jealous and triumphant Jehovah roll for positively the Final *FADE OUT* . . .").

Four o'clock tea break on *Bride of Frankenstein:* Boris Karloff and Colin Clive.

The third veteran of *Frankenstein* whom Whale engaged for the sequel, was Dwight Frye, who was also a personal friend of the director's (he had played a bit as a reporter in *The Invisible Man*). Frye was now haplessly typecast as a giggling psycho. On the set of Majestic's *The Vampire Bat,* in which he played a bat-petting village idiot named Herman, Frye lamented:

> If God is good I will be able to play comedy in which I was featured on Broadway for eight seasons and in which no producer of motion pictures will give me a chance! And please, God, may it be before I go screwy, playing idiots, half-wits, and lunatics on the talking screen![99]

To showcase Frye's talents at lunacy and comedy, Whale combined two separate roles of the original script: Karl, "a bit of a village idiot," quoth the script, and Fritz, the "first ghoul" who assists Pretorius, into simply Karl, who became both a village idiot and a ghoul and one of Frye's most memorable performances.

Mae Clarke had departed her "throne" at Universal in 1932. Her career had suffered a sad reversal, compounded by the exhaustion of being "owned" by Universal and Columbia simultaneously, as well as by a 1933 car accident (while on a date with actor Phillips Holmes) which broke her jaw. Hence Universal's new "Elizabeth" was 17-year-old contractee Valerie Hobson.*

There were two players from Whale's *The Invisible Man:* Irish Una O'Connor (whose ever-swooning Mrs. Hall had won special praise from H.G. Wells) as Minnie, the Frankensteins' hysterical maid ("her aged emotions are fed and gluttoned on violence, obscenity and death" noted the script), and Britisher E.E. Clive (whose walrus-moustachioed cop P.C. Jaffers had marvelled " 'E's all eaten away!" as raving Claude Rains unraveled himself) as the blustery Burgomaster (". . . very pompous, very officious—something of the schoolmaster giving commands to children").

For the saintly role of the Hermit (". . . a small venerable bearded old man not less than 75"), Australian O.P. Heggie was signed. And, for the grandly grotesque role of Dr. Septimus Pretorius (". . . this man's entrance into a room is something to make a witch's skin creep" claimed the script), Whale originally sought Claude Rains.

*Miss Hobson's later stardom in such acclaimed English films as *Great Expectations* (1946) and *Kind Hearts and Coronets* (1949) has been eclipsed by the dignity she displayed as the loyal wife of John Profumo, the ex-British Secretary of State for War whose love affair with call girl Christine Keeler (who had a Soviet Embassy lover simultaneously) created an international scandal and brought on the downfall of Harold MacMillan's Tory Party government in 1964.

Colin Clive and Valerie Hobson enjoy a repast on the set of *Bride of Frankenstein.*

When he was unavailable, Whale sent for his dear chum Ernest Thesiger, the shrill, 56-year-old thespian and crochet king who had so memorably minced as the prissy Horace Femm ("Do you like gin? It is my only weakness") in *The Old Dark House.*

Playing bits in the film were two actors on the eye of fame. John Carradine, who would win celebrity as the snarling Sergeant Rankin of John Ford's 1936 *The Prisoner of Shark Island,* played one of the hunters who destroyed the Monster's peaceful idyll with the hermit ("It was only a day's work,"[100] recalls Carradine). And Walter Brennan, who would receive the Academy's first Best Supporting Actor Award for 1936's *Come and Get It,* was glimpsed as "a neighbor."

However, the role that most excited everybody's imagination at Universal was the Monster's Mate. As Pretorius leered in the film: ". . . A woman . . . That shall be *really* interesting!"

Who will be the Bride of Frankenstein? Who will *dare*?

Universal Publicity, 1935

In a publicity ploy reminiscent of David O. Selznick's heralded 1939 quest for the perfect Scarlett O'Hara, Universal began "leaking" the names of possible choices for the Monster's Mate. Would it be Arletta Duncan, a shapely brunette who was glimpsed as one of Mae Clarke's bridesmaids in

Frankenstein and was dispatched to Karloff's farm for a picnic and publicity shots? Would it be Phyllis Brooks, a willowy blonde destined to become a cult favorite, recently praised by William Saroyan as ". . . the strange beautiful super-real girl of motion picture art itself . . . ?"[101] Would it be Brigitte Helm, who had played the saintly Maria and her sinuously evil, robotrix twin in Lang's *Metropolis*?

If the vanity of any of these ladies bristled at being considered for the part of a Female Monster, it would not have helped to learn that they were all merely victims of the studio's quest for bogus publicity. For, despite the publicized screen tests (which the studio considered worth their cost in publicity), James Whale knew from the film's inception exactly whom he wished to cast not only as the Monster's Mate, but also as Mary Shelley of the Prologue as well. He recalled his days as the stage manager of a 1926 London revue called *Riverside Nights,* in which a slender, elfin girl with wild red hair, a black top hat, a white ballerina tutu and bare legs, sang risque Cockney ballads—and became a rage. The love child of Socialist vegetarians, this actress would bolt out the stage door after each performance in search of a taxi, as she was concurrently performing across town in another revue entitled *Midnight Frolics.* She changed her costume nightly in the back of the cab. One night a policeman stopped her taxi for speeding in Green Park—and discovered a naked lady in the back seat.

Elsa Lanchester (1902–   ).

This elfish bohemian was also a founder of The Cave of Harmony, London's legendary theatrical nightclub; had been a protégée of H.G. Wells; had played the sly Anne of Cleves in England's international movie hit *The Private Life of Henry VIII* (1933); and was now in Hollywood, living at The Garden of Allah with her husband, Charles Laughton.

I do have an odd face, and James was absolutely dead set that my face was the face for the Bride of Frankenstein![102]

Elsa Lanchester in interview with author, June 1979.

"What she has that others lack is grace. . . . It absolutely shatters me to watch her, for it's something I can't do,"[103] said Charles Laughton of his wife of 33 years, Elsa Lanchester. An actress for more than 60 years, Miss Lanchester lives today in the Hollywood Hills in a pre-World War I house, with a tower and lovely gardens. It is the house where Laughton died in 1962, and it is where the still red-haired, still elfin, but now-round Miss

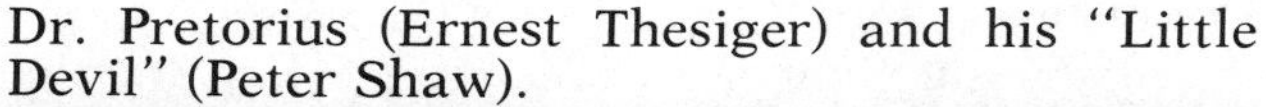

Dr. Pretorius (Ernest Thesiger) and his "Little Devil" (Peter Shaw).

An aerial view of Universal's back-lot European village.

Lanchester reminisced for me about *Bride of Frankenstein:*

> James Whale was a very strange personality. He was tall and thin and had a face like a rather nice-looking monkey. (Not a bad-looking monkey!) He was a bitter man—very bitter. I think it was because he had been in love with a lady painter, named Zinkheisen, whom he'd bring with him to the Cave of Harmony. They didn't marry, and I think he believed that was to blame for his not having a "normal" life.
>
> We met him for supper at the Brown Derby the first night we arrived in Hollywood; Charles would appear shortly afterwards in James' *The Old Dark House.* James said that night, "You'll like it here, Charles—I'm pouring the money from my hair!" James had an Italianate, Gothic house near the ocean, and he always had the portrait of that lady painter in his dining room.
>
> He *was* brilliant—such an imaginative mind—but so bitter. And, of course later, he just retired completely from life, save for a few friends—young men and such.

Miss Lanchester had just played in *David Copperfield* and *Naughty Marietta* at MGM, where she was on contract. "It was a little nothing of a contract," she says, "just to keep me busy, since Charles was here." As such, Universal found it easy to borrow her services, and she soon met with Whale, learning his reason for having the same actress play both Mary Shelley and the Monster's Mate:

> James' feeling was that very pretty, sweet people, both men and women, had very wicked insides . . . evil thoughts. These thoughts could be of dragons, they could be of monsters, they could be of Frankenstein's laboratory. So, James wanted the same actress for both parts to show that the Bride of Frankenstein did, after all, come out of sweet Mary Shelley's soul.

Billed only as Mary Shelley, Miss Lanchester sportingly allowed a "?" to identify the Monster's Mate in both the opening and closing credits.

Meanwhile, Universal's publicity department had much to revel in as *The Return of Frankenstein* began shooting. Charles D. Hall was supervising the quite wonderful sets. Outstanding among these were the 70-foot tower laboratory (in which Kenneth Strickfaden was once again erecting spectacular electrical machinery), the awesome crypt (already glimpsed in *Dracula*), and the village dungeon (curiously accoutred with a giant chair just the Monster's size). John P. Fulton was preparing some splendid special effects. The most noteworthy of these placed Pretorius' homunculi repertory of King Henry VIII (a Whale "in" joke: Elsa's husband, Charles Laughton, had just won the Academy Award for *The Private Life of Henry VIII*), his queen, a mermaid, a ballerina, an Archbishop, and Satan himself,* in glass bottle prison (by means of the "magic" of rear-screen projection and, of course, giant bottles).

In January of 1935, with John Mescall (who had photographed *The Black Cat*) as cinematographer, Whale began filming *The Return of Frankenstein.* And, to prepare the public for the sequel, Universal cut from *Frankenstein* (still in circulation) the happy denouement, which would remain forsaken in the studio vaults until the sale of *Frankenstein* to television in 1957.

The watery opening scene of the sequel, *Bride of Frankenstein,* was filmed with me wearing a rubber suit under my costume to ward off chill. But air got into the suit. When I was launched into the pond, my legs flew up in the air, and I floated there like some sort of obscene water lily while I, and everyone else, hooted with laughter. They finally fished me out with a boat-hook and deflated me.[104]

Boris Karloff

The "obscene water lily" failed to mention that, shortly after the hooting stopped, he fell into the pond and dislocated a hip. While Junior Laemmle and Whale despaired about a possible production

*Cut from the release print was another homunculus—a baby, played by veteran midget performer Billy Barty. The original script, hoping for an inside joke, noted: "In the jar is a baby—already as big as the Queen and looking as if it might develop into a Boris Karloff. It is pulling a flower to pieces." Remarked Pretorius: "I think this baby will grow into something worth watching."

The Monster (Karloff) crucified.

shutdown, Karloff visited the studio doctor, had the hip strapped and bandaged—and returned to work!

Once again the 47-year-old star's schedule was a terror in itself:

4:30 A.M. The butler awakened Karloff at the hacienda. The actor took a cold shower and an infra-red ray treatment for his injured hip.

5:10 A.M. A toast and black coffee breakfast.

5:20 A.M. Karloff began the 15-mile drive through the still-dark hills of Coldwater Canyon to Universal City.

6:00 A.M. A cosmetician massaged, soothed and oiled the star's face to prepare for the makeup application.

7:00 A.M. Jack P. Pierce began applying the face and body makeup. There were new touches, such as a livid face scar on the right cheek, exposed metal skull clips where the hair was singed, and a charred stubble of hair which grew in as the story progressed. Resultantly, the makeup, which took three-and-one-half hours to apply by the final week of *Frankenstein,* required five hours for the sequel.

12:30 P.M. Karloff, after a brief rest, donned the body padding, costume, and giant shoes with the help of Pierce and his assistants. The costume and makeup weighed 48 pounds in the original film. Now they weighed 62 pounds.

1:30 P.M. Lunchtime. Tea and a sandwich.

2:00 P.M. Karloff began acting on the set.

4:00 P.M. The tea break. Sometimes, Karloff managed to strip off his costume and padding for this treat, and the company enjoyed the sight of the Monster sipping his tea in robe and silk ascot.

7:00 P.M. Whale ended shooting for the day. Karloff, two makeup men, began removing the makeup with oils and acetic acids.

8:00 P.M. A cold shower, a light supper, and of course, tea, after which the actor drove home to Bowmont Drive.

8:30 P.M. A massage for the exhausted body, and another infra-red ray treatment for the painful hip.

9:30 P.M. Karloff climbed into bed—with his script to study the next day's shooting.

As Karloff's Monster was trussed to a pole, waved about the soundstage forest, and pelted with sticks by the jeering villagers, it seemed strange sport for a tea-and-cricket-loving Englishman. Yet Karloff, be he racing through the cobbled streets of the Tyrolean village or overturning a giant statue, never complained, and found much to enjoy in the engagement:

Karloff relaxes in his special "Monster chair."

> I remember, during the early days of the picture, that there were ten small girls working in one of the sequences. These children were most friendly. They gathered round me, lifting my enormous shoes, pinching my padded legs and trying to find out just what the Monster really was.
>
> Youngsters are thrilled but not frightened by my fantastic get-up. It seems to be the adults who are scared![105]

With Karloff now a major star (as well as one of the 13 founders of the very controversial, very aggressive Screen Actors Guild), Universal did make some concessions to the actor during the shooting. The studio built him a special "Monster chair," (preserved for the later films of the series) in which he could rest between scenes. They gave the star one or two Saturdays off, which he spent at the cricket club. And, needless to say, there was no longer a blue veil to be worn to and from the soundstage.

His great charm and humor won Karloff, again, the admiration of the entire company—except as before, from James Whale. The very conscientious star had implored the very headstrong director to scrap the Monster's dialogue:

> The speech. . . . stupid! My argument was that if the Monster had any impact or charm, it was because he was inarticulate . . . this great, lumbering, inarticulate creature. . . .[106]

Whale cavalierly ignored Karloff's concern. Elsa Lanchester believes the reason was as much one of arrogance as conception:

> That was a thing in which James Whale was rather nasty. He was very derogatory about Boris Karloff; he'd say, "Oh, he was a *truck driver.*" Maybe in the early days, he had to do some hard work, but Boris Karloff was a well-educated, very gentle, nice man.

Egomania was the villain here. Whale still bristled that it was Karloff who had won the lion's share of attention for *Frankenstein.* Some days on the set of the sequel, Whale even seemed to be competing with Karloff for the attention of the ever-vigilant publicity photographers. The director struck comic poses with the iron Monster stand-in (built due to the impracticality of making up a live double), posed elegantly with cheroot in hand, and feyly dabbed "muck" on Karloff's costume. It was all a sad conceit of the

Karloff, at peace in his "Monster chair," gets a light from Colin Clive.

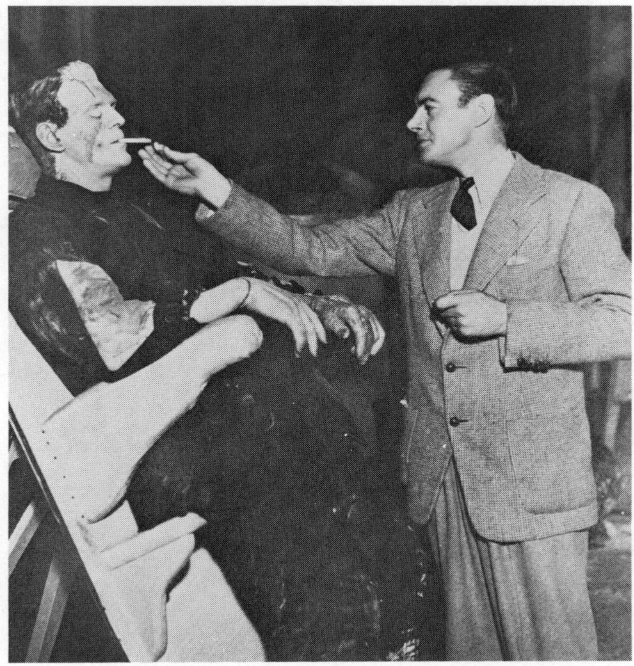

nouveau riche Whale, who had conveniently forgotten that his own father had been an iron laborer—and who was then mercifully unaware that the last lover in his life would be a gas station attendant.

The Monster's script dialogue (a far cry from the rich, literate monologues of the novel's creature) did threaten to make the Monster sound like Tarzan of the Apes. But Karloff, despite his objections, managed to pull it off. He created a cavernous voice for his Monster, one in accord with the original conception, one that wavered from the quavering "Friend?" as he timidly approaches the Bride, to the booming "We belong dead!" as he detonates the tower laboratory. So impressed, in fact, was the front office that one of the film's key advertising slogans became, "The Monster Talks!"

Meanwhile, there was another accident. Colin Clive suffered a bad fall on the set (it was rumored he was thoroughly "tight" at the time) and ripped the ligaments in his knees. Whale had to direct his friend to play much of his part seated, while Clive used crutches for his closeups.

Elsa Lanchester enjoyed the *Frankenstein* sequel. She loved playing Mary Shelley, and wearing that beautiful dress:

> The dress that I wore cost a fortune. For weeks and weeks, they had 17 Mexican ladies creating it completely by hand. It had the finest possible net, and a train at the back which you don't get to see (I don't think I stood up in the scene). It was embroidered with pearl sequins in the figures of stars and moons and butterflies. It was a beautiful work, all done by hand—and it hardly shows in the film.

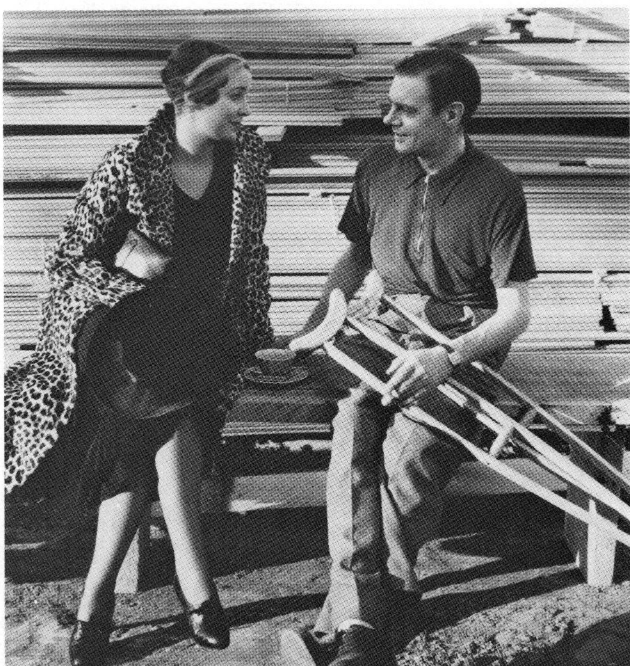

Valerie Hobson consoles Colin Clive after his fall on the set.

"Jimmy" Whale, clowning with the Monster's dummy stand-in.

---

§ELSA LANCHESTER
wishes to express her gratitude to that charming director . . . .
JAMES WHALE
and to
UNIVERSAL STUDIOS
for their courteous cooperation of one of the most interesting and distinctive roles of her theatrical experience.
Playing the Monster's Mate in The Bride of Frankenstein with Karloff was a Great Pleasure . . .
E. L.

Advertisement placed in *The Hollywood Reporter* by Elsa Lanchester, 1935.

Less appealing were the bandages of the mummified Bride, which she sported as she was brought to life by old London friends Clive and Thesiger:

> Charles and I had stayed in the country with Colin Clive and his wife, Jeanne de Casalis, once or twice. . . . Theirs wasn't a very happy marriage. She was very precious, very affected. . . .

Elsa Lanchester as Mary Shelley in *Bride of Frankenstein.*

> He was very nice, an English gentleman. . . .
>
> Ernest Thesiger was a delightful laugh for anybody who saw him or talked to him—a weird, strange character! Very acid-tongued—not a nasty person at all, just *acid*!
>
> I was tied up in those bandages, so I had to be carried to and fro, once or twice, to a wicker lounge. There my feet would be untied, and I could relax for tea.

Whale and Thesiger together formulated the idea for the appearance of the Female Monster, which they conceived as "a creature born of a thunderstorm, a wild jungle animal in captivity, with a suggestion of pride and dignity." Finally, there came the early morning that Miss Lanchester reported to Jack Pierce's makeup studio to become the Monster's Mate:

> Jack Pierce did really feel that he *made* these people—like he was a *God* who created human beings. In the morning he'd be dressed in white, as if he were in a hospital to perform an operation. He'd say "Good morning," perhaps—but you shouldn't say it first. You didn't bounce in and say "Hello"—oh no!
>
> As for the Bride makeup . . . he took *ages* to make a scar that hardly shows under my chin. For a whole hour he would draw two lines of glue, put a red line down the middle, then start making up the white edges of the scar—*meticulously* done. Well, frankly, I'm sure he could have bought such a scar for ten cents in a joke shop! But he started fresh every morning, drawing in that scar which is rarely even seen.
>
> After the scar came the eyebrows, and the hair. It's my own hair. I had it lifted up from my face, all the way around; then they placed a cage on my head and combed my own hair over this cage. Then they put the gray-streak hair-pieces in afterwards.

Pierce required three to four hours to make up Miss Lanchester. "He took so long to make Karloff up and so long to make me up, we'd only have an hour or two together," recalls the actress remembering the Academy/Screen Actors Guild dictate regarding the 12-hour day. Towering seven feet tall in her long white gown, Miss Lanchester was a truly horrendous apparition. Yet it was a clever inspiration of the actress which really brought the Bride to grotesque life:

Elsa Lanchester primps on the set of *Bride of Frankenstein.*

Charles and I used to go to Regent's Park in London to feed the swans. Swans get very, very angry. If you throw them food, that's all right, but if you walk too near them, and they've got their young around them, they *hiss*. It's like a noise through the nose, as if you're going to blow your nose and there's nothing in it. Try it!

With the patience she must have given to her dance students in England during World War I, Miss Lanchester directed me in hissing. All the while she was performing wild hisses herself. "I'm going to be sick!" she finally laughed.

So I practiced these hisses, and I did a very large hiss from my throat . . . I did get a very sore throat, what with the long shots, medium shots, retakes, and so forth. With the hisses and the screams, I lost my voice. It hurt very much, and I had codeine. Charles finished the same day on *Les Miserables* at Fox. We got on the train the next day, after we were sure we were free from retakes, departed for New York and London—and *slept*!

It was a "super horror" movie and demanded hauntingly eerie, weird, and different music.[107]

Franz Waxman

In the Hollywood of the 1930s, German screenwriter/actress Salka Viertel was the favorite hostess of "Europe's exiled intellectual elite." At her salon at the foot of Santa Monica Canyon, one could behold such sights as Garbo, Chaplin and Dietrich chatting as they enjoyed the chocolate cake. It was at Ms. Viertel's that James Whale met Franz Waxman, a German refugee whose score for Fritz Lang's *Liliom* (1933), with its impressionistic echo effects and electronic instruments, had been internationally acclaimed. Whale told Waxman, who had just arrived in California, of the new picture.

"Nothing will be resolved in this picture, except the end destruction scene," said Whale. "Will you write an unresolved score for it?"[108]

Intrigued, Waxman accepted Whale's invitation to watch the shooting of the *Frankenstein* sequel—and created one of the first Hollywood scores to use a symphony orchestra to impressionistic effect. A milestone in film music, Waxman's score produced leitmotifs for the major characters (including a four-note broken chord theme for the Monster that varied between the terrifying and the bewildered), and beautifully scored the various episodes: the mournful (and premature) dirge as the funeral procession bears Frankenstein home from the mill; a satirical yet stirring march as the simple-minded townspeople parade off to capture the Monster; the lovely scoring of "Ave Maria" as the Monster meets the Hermit; the whimsically sinister theme as the Monster and Pretorius share their supper in the crypt; and climactically, the magnificent score for the Creation of the Female Monster,* in which a thumping tympanum suggests the beating of the Bride's heart and a cacophany of wedding bells heralds her unveiling. This marvelous music and its crescendo, praised by cinema music historian Page Cook as "one of filmusic's most exciting moments,"[109] has itself become a classic, and is featured on the RCA album *Sunset Boulevard: The Classic Film Scores of Franz Waxman*, performed by Charles Gerhardt and the National Philharmonic Orchestra.

Whale, who himself suggested a "big dissonant chord" to close the film, was delighted with Waxman's work—as was Universal. In the wake of the success of *Bride of Frankenstein*,† Waxman (who was to win Oscars for his scoring of Paramount's 1950 *Sunset Boulevard* and 1951 *A Place in the Sun*) was hired as the music director of Universal Studios, writing more than a dozen scores and conducting and supervising the music of over 50 Universal pictures before departing for MGM during Universal's 1936 debacle.

. . . We are all three infidels, scoffers at all marriage ties, believing only in living fully and freely in whatever direction the heart dictates. Such an audience needs something stronger than a pretty little love story. You say look at me; I say look at Shelley—who would suspect that pink and white innocence, gentle as a dove, was thrown out of Oxford University as a menace to morality, had run away from his lawful spouse with innocent me but 17, that he was deprived of his rights as a father by the Lord Chancellor of England, and reviled by society as a monster himself. I am already ostracized as a free thinker, so why shouldn't I write of monsters?

A monologue of Elsa Lanchester's Mary Shelley, cut from the release print of *Bride of Frankenstein*.

Production of the sequel "wrapped" in March of 1935. Karloff, having sweated away more than 20 pounds, took refuge at his farm and the cricket club, leaving behind at Universal a storm of tense

*Portions of this Creation Sequence music bear an incredible similarity to "Bali Ha'i," of *South Pacific*, the Rodgers and Hammerstein musical which opened on Broadway in 1949.

†Waxman's score for the *Bride* . . . was later re-arranged by Charles Previn, and used in the Universal *Flash Gordon*, *Buck Rogers*, and *Radio Patrol*, serials, as well as some studio potboilers of the era.

Dwight Frye and Gunnis Davis in an episode cut from the release print.

egos, Junior Laemmle was worried about the humor of the picture and upset that Whale had not played up more horror, as Junior had requested, then ordered, then begged him to do. John Balderston, meanwhile, bitterly resented the few horror flourishes Whale had given to the satire Balderston had written, and disowned the film! And Colin Clive was heartbroken because Whale had opted again to film a happy ending, in which the actor had to caress Valerie Hobson rather than enjoy the dramatic satisfaction of being blasted to atoms. (At the time the climax was filmed, Whale still planned to kill both Frankenstein and Elizabeth in the tower, and a figure resembling Clive can be glimpsed very briefly amidst the explosions.)

Hence, with pride, excitement and considerable anxiety, the nervous Laemmles presented a series of previews during the first week of April of the feature they had commercially retitled *Bride of Frankenstein*. Critical reaction was laudatory:

> *The Hollywood Reporter:* . . . one of the finest productions that has come off the Universal lot for many a day. Mounted extravagantly, gorgeously photographed, excellently cast . . . Karloff is superb as the Monster . . . Elsa Lanchester, in a dual role . . . is excellent . . . Una O'Connor walks away with the feminine honors with as neat a bit of acting as has come to our eyes and ears for some time . . . Exhibitors can guarantee a fine production of a creep yarn, beautifully acted and directed. . . .[110]

Nevertheless, both producer and director agreed that the 92-minute feature could benefit by cuts. Seventeen minutes worth were made! On the cutting room floor fell some bravura dialogue from the opening sequence, excisions that distress Miss Lanchester ("I especially enjoyed doing the Mary Shelley bit . . ."). Far more upset was Dwight Frye. Out of the film came a little subplot in which Frye's Karl took evil advantage of the Monster's rampage in the village to murder his Uncle and Auntie Glutz and to steal their money ("Very convenient to have a Monster around!" he gloated). Excised, too, was one of Frye's scenes with Pretorius, in which he glimpsed the wizard's miniature people, as well as a sequence with E. E. Clive's insufferable Burgomaster, who, moments after dismissing the villagers as "superstitious infidels" and the Monster as "some wild beast from the mountains," was yanked out of his office window by the "wild beast" and pummeled in the street. To bridge the gap left by these and other cuts, Whale recalled Karloff for a single vignette in which the Monster happens upon gypsies in the forest at night, scares them away, and burns his hand while trying to snare their meal from the fire. Because this scene was filmed at the last minute, it was the one sequence totally without music.

Karloff and E. E. Clive in another sequence doomed to the cutting room floor.

Finally, on Thursday evening, May 9, 1935, the Roxy Theatre in New York City was the scene of a special preview of *Bride of Frankenstein.* By the time the doors opened at 10:30 the next morning, for the film's "official" opening, there was a line outside the 5,886-seat movie house. It was a big time for Horror on Broadway: MGM's *Mark of the Vampire* was in its second week at the Mayfair, while Universal's *Werewolf of London* had just opened the day before at the Rialto. *Bride of Frankenstein,* however, instantly reigned as the critical and popular favorite:

> *The New York Times:* . . . Boris Karloff comes again to terrify the children, frighten the women, and play a jiggling tune upon masculine spines as the snarling, lumbering, pitiful Thing. . . .
>
> . . . Mr. Karloff is so splendid in the role that all one can say is "he is the Monster." Mr. Clive, Valerie Hobson, Elsa Lanchester, O.P. Heggie, Ernest Thesiger, E.E. Clive, and Una O'Connor fit snugly into the human background before which Karloff moves. James Whale . . . has done another excellent job; the settings, photography, and the makeup . . . contribute their important elements to a first-rate horror film.[111]

> *Variety:* And now Frankenstein's Monster has a bride and Universal has another moneymaker . . . an imaginative and outstanding film . . . .
>
> . . . Karloff (the Boris is shelved) is, of course, at top form as the Monster . . . manages to invest the character with some subtleties of emotion that are surprisingly real and touching. . . .
>
> Runner-up position from an acting standpoint goes to Ernest Thesiger as Dr. Pretorius, a diabolic characterization if ever there was one . . .
>
> . . . John Mescall at the camera managed to create a great number of unusual angle and process shots which help the film tremendously. It is this excellent camera work coupled with an eerie but lingering musical score by Franz Waxman . . . that gives a great deal of the film its real horror . . . And, of course, all due credit to James Whale for welding the component parts into a homogenous whole. . . .[112]

"On Broadway *Bride of Frankenstein* . . . is grabbing the business, so far outdistancing everything else . . . there is no comparison"[113] reported *Variety.* Meanwhile, *Bride of Frankenstein* opened at the Pantages Theatre on Hollywood Boulevard, playing an incredible 11-shows-per-day schedule in the 2,812-seat movie house. Business was outstanding, and *Bride* . . . soon smashed the attendance record set at the Pantages by *Imitation of Life.* In some of the key movie houses where the picture played across the country, Elsa Lanchester's Mary Shelley dress was displayed in the lobby.

Bride of Frankenstein did run into one problem. In England an apoplectic censor decided that the scene in which the Monster tenderly gazes at the corpse of the young girl in the crypt reeked of necrophilia! The scene was cut in Britain, where the film, lauded by *Kinematograph Weekly* as a "spectacular thriller, a macabre morality play,"[114] performed top business.

A box office bonanza for Universal, *Bride of Frankenstein* became the only film in the series and the only one of Universal's golden age horrors, to rate an Academy nomination—in the category of "Best Sound" for Gilbert Kurland. He lost to Douglas Shearer (Norma's brother) for MGM's *Naughty Marietta.* It also inspired a 252-page novelization by Michael Egremont, published in England in 1936.

A few terror classics followed *Bride of Frankenstein* before the genre's "Golden Age" ended in 1936: *The Raven,* Universal's 1935 rendezvous of Karloff, Lugosi, and Edgar Allan Poe; MGM's *Mad Love* (1935), with a slavering Peter Lorre making his U.S. debut and Karl Freund directing in the grand Germanic tradition; Warner Brothers' *The Walking Dead* (1936), starring Karloff as a scientifically resurrected vessel of divine retribution. Yet *Bride of Frankenstein* dominated them all. And, with the release of this striking fantasy, Hollywood's "Golden Age of Horror" fully blossomed.

Bride of Frankenstein remains the biggest-budgeted, best-dressed, highest-polished, finest-finished horror film in history; a first-class Hollywood product made with all the artistry and technology a top studio normally lavished upon only its most commercial ventures. It was Whale's best work—and his last in the genre; he felt he could not top it.[115]

Denis Gifford, *A Pictorial History of Horror Movies*

Bride of Frankenstein reigns, widely if controversially, as the most laureled of the Classic Horror Films. Some are offended by its "sick" humor and "camp" style; yet it is certainly James Whale's masterpiece, a three-ring Swiftian circus of sardonic wit, theatrical flourishes of terror, and bitter morality. Whale did more than conjure up the Romantic theory which Mary Shelley had evoked: that there can be no sympathy in our prearranged universe for a being created by man and not God. With elegant audacity, Whale went Mrs. Shelley one better and made Karloff's Monster a bizarre Christ symbol, who laughs and weeps and pleads with those great, scarred hands with an almost heartbreaking humanity. As such, *Bride of Frankenstein* powerfully portrays the classic irony of

Creator and Monster at their leisure.

"hero," pathetically splashing at his unholy reflection in the forest pool (an exquisite piece of mime by Karloff), and portraying a wider range of human qualities than any other character in the film. Charisma has deserted Henry Frankenstein. No longer the attractive, zealous dreamer of the original film, the Monster Maker (as played by the dissipating Clive) is a living wound, a shrill neurotic, too painfully tormented by the creation and abandonment of his Monster to be truly sympathetic. As Clive glares at the heavens while the Bride receives his electrical miracle of Life, his cadaverous face is haunting and grotesque, leering with the agony of an addict hooked on blasphemy. Whale shrewdly allowed the very young Valerie Hobson to play Elizabeth as little more than a pious poseuse, while he directed Una O'Connor to pull out all stops as the shrieking Minnie (". . . I'm glad to see the Monster roasted to death before my very eyes—it's too good for him!"), a harpy ever at the forefront of the bloodthirsty villagers. Indeed, after the Monster, the two most appealing characters are the Hermit (stirringly played by O.P. Heggie), a holy man who has removed himself from the "civilized" world, and, in another wicked irony, the evil and Godless Dr. Pretorius, whom Ernest Thesiger brings to macabre life with an irresistibly demonic charm. And, in the climactic twist, Elsa Lanchester's Monster's Mate, herself doomed to the world's hatred and rejection, the Frankenstein legend—the persecution of a man-made, soulless creature by God-made, soul-possessing beings.*

Against a strange pastoral backdrop—the quaint Tyrolean village that houses the vicious villagers, the awesome mountain graveyard with its looming religious statues, the dead, bleak forest with its waterfall and little lambs and communion girls—Whale creates his tragic fairy tale, ingeniously weaving it from the Monster's viewpoint. The nightmarish Monster, sewn together from the booty of scavenged graveyards, becomes our

". . . not a modern instrument, but one which might have been imagined by a scientist of the period" is how the script described this primitive telephone, which served as a prop for Dwight Frye and Valerie Hobson.

* Originally, the shooting script offered this episode: "Long shot . . . an imposing monument . . . night . . . set against the sky—a huge Christus. The Monster comes upon it suddenly. In the dim light, he sees it as a human figure, tortured as he was in the wood. He dashes himself against the figure, grappling with it. The figure is overturned. He tries to rescue this figure from the cross . . ." Since this vignette allying the Monster with Jesus Christ appeared doomed to be cut from the release print, Whale directed Karloff to topple the statue of the bishop, not far from where the statue of the crucified Christ stood on the studio's graveyard set.

Karloff attacks Frye atop the tower; Ted Billings watches.

screams in the hapless face of her charnel house bridegroom, proudly allying herself with his persecutors.

Bride of Frankenstein, with its mad strokes of black comedy and bizarre religious touches, was audacious indeed for 1935. Only Whale would have dared present the Monster crying as a saintly old hermit prays, "Ave Maria" plays stirringly in the background, and a crucifix glows above—just as only Karloff had the grace to play it. Yet the film never becomes pretentious. Whale fashioned *Bride of Frankenstein* as a *show,* a well-paced, picturesque Monster epic. Coy humor garnishes the tale (e.g., an owl cavalierly watches as the Monster drowns Hans in the mill water); and, while Whale's satirical sense at times verges on burlesque (especially when the Monster hiccups on the wine and almost dances with cigar in hand as the Hermit fiddles a happy tune), the director's taste and Karloff's artistry prevail. The production values are excellent, and the creation of the Bride is still a spectacle. The original script had accented here, "We must feel that a MIRACLE is about to be performed," and a miracle is what Whale presents: the kites tempting the lightning in the stormy night sky, the electrical machines flashing and roaring, the fireballs of voltage cascading over the mountain laboratory roof as the Bride comes to life. John Mescall's lush camerawork is flawless, the sets of Charles D. Hall splendidly stylized, the Special Effects of John P. Fulton (especially Pretorius' Lilliputian homunculi) expertly executed, and the score by Franz Waxman a classic in itself. And, of course, all of the members of the exceptional supporting cast—Dwight Frye as Karl, lamenting "This is no life for murderers!"; E. E. Clive, snorting "Monster indeed!" as the pompous Burgomaster; Gavin Gordon, waving his cheroot and trilling his "r's" with flamboyant abandon as Lord Byron—acquit themselves with honor.

In a gallery of superb performances, special praise must go to Ernest Thesiger, whose arch, effeminate Pretorius has all the guile and unholy persuasion of Eden's serpent. Even more memorable is Elsa Lanchester, whose sly, precious Mary

Shelley and vainglorious, hissing swan of a Monster's Mate are both fascinating conceptions.

The top laurels, of course, must go to Karloff. "His Monster was a marvelous creation," says Miss Lanchester. "That *gentleness*!" It is in *Bride of Frankenstein* that Karloff's Monster runs most magnificently amok. As he hangs crucified on the pole in the forest, nobly beautiful as the villagers screech in vicious joy, Frankenstein's Monster enjoys his most profound cinema vignette.

Today, *Bride of Frankenstein* has taken its honorary place as one of the most revered, celebrated films of the thirties and of the entire horror genre. Elsa Lanchester finds adulation in her mail box constantly:

> I have so many fan letters now—more than I used to receive. Little children who have seen *Bride of Frankenstein* recognize me in grocery stores! I've changed, of course, after all these years, but I still have a lot of hair, and it blows around, and I'm still recognizable. Whatever James Whale saw in my face, it didn't leave me.

The Bride's climactic hiss.

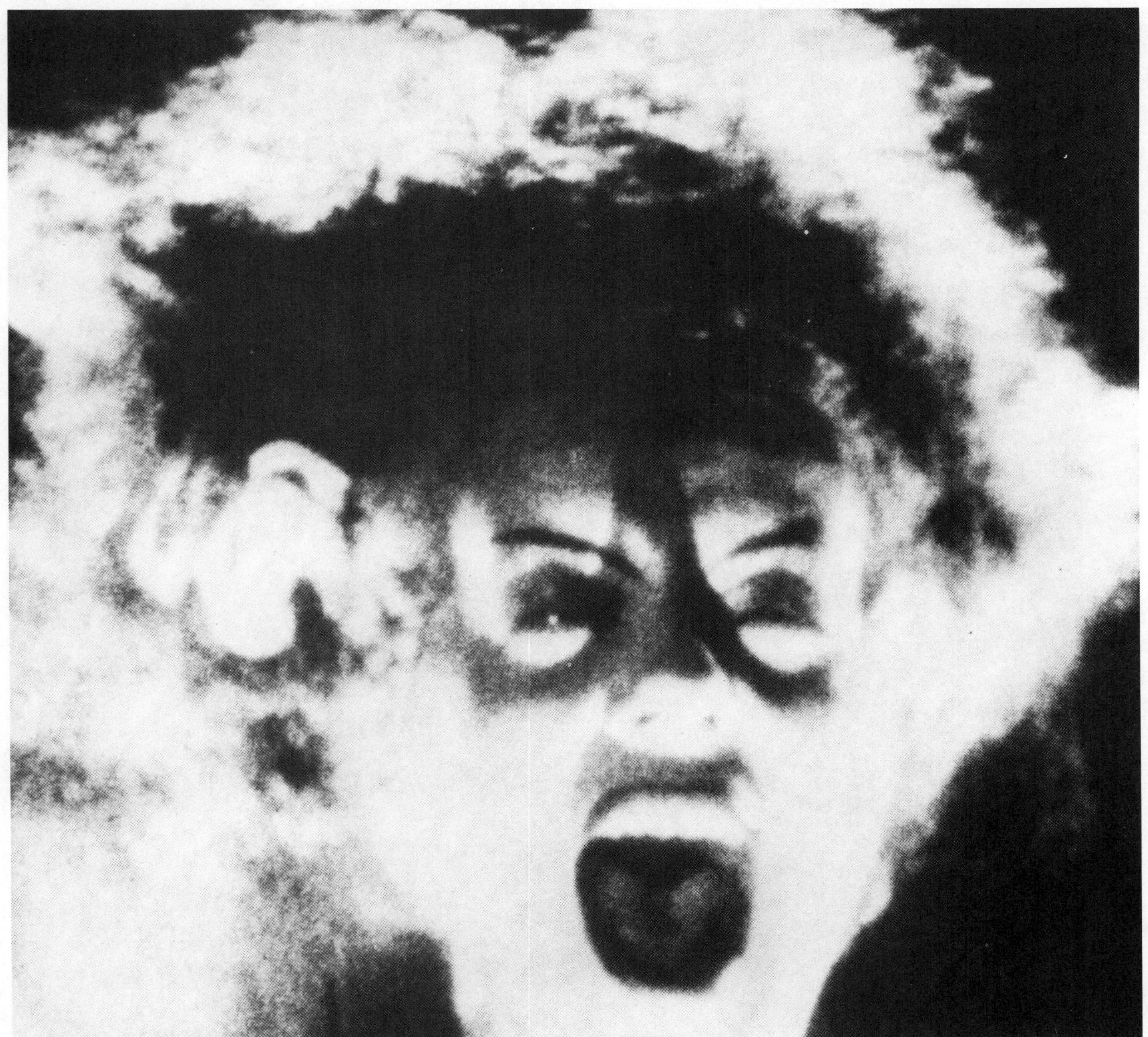

Son of Frankenstein poster.

Son of Frankenstein (1939)

Producer/Director, Rowland V. Lee; *Screenplay,* Willis Cooper; *Photography,* George Robinson; *Special Effects,* John P. Fulton; *Editor,* Ted Kent; *Art Director,* Jack Otterson (*Associate,* Richard H. Riedel); *Set Decoration,* Russell A. Gausman; *Music,* Frank Skinner (*Director,* Lionel Newman; *Arranger,* Hans J. Salter); *Costumes,* Vera West; *Makeup,* Jack P. Pierce; *Assistant Director,* Fred Frank; *Sound Director,* Bernard B. Brown.

Filmed at Universal City, California, October–December, 1938; Premiere, Pantages Theatre, Hollywood, California, January 13, 1939. Running Time: 96 minutes.

SON OF FRANKENSTEIN— SYNOPSIS

A train roars over the creaking trestles, through the mountains. A violent storm lashes the countryside, the gnarled, dead trees looming through the mist like mournful ghosts.

"What strange looking country," remarks an attractive redhaired passenger named Elsa. Her little son, Peter, is resting in another compartment; her husband, Dr. Wolf von Frankenstein, the eldest son of Dr. Henry Frankenstein, sits beside her.

"Out there in the darkness, a new life lies before us!" smiles the handsome Wolf, who had been a professor at an American college before receiving his inheritance. He and Elsa excitedly laugh about the medieval castle they are to inhabit. Perhaps there's a moat . . . a drawbridge . . . a dark old tower . . . a haunted room. . . .

"Yes, there's sure to be a haunted room," says Wolf. The castle itself is supposed to be haunted—haunted by the blasphemous deeds of Henry Frankenstein, who died there repentant. Wolf's mother had told him stories when he was a child in England, stories of the bungling assistant who stole a criminal brain for the artificial being of his father's creation. "How my father was made to suffer for that mistake!" laments Wolf, recalling how Henry Frankenstein's name had become synonomous with horror and monsters. "Why, nine out of ten people call that misshapen creature of my father's experiments . . ."

"Frankenstein," announces the conductor.

Outside, in the terrible storm, the villagers stand mutely under umbrellas, advancing for a close look at the son of Frankenstein. The Burgomaster and the gentlemen of the Council are there too. "We come to meet you," speaks the Burgomaster. "Not to *greet* you." The Burgomaster presents Wolf with two boxes—a large one that contains papers relevant to the estate, the small one containing the key that will open it.

Naturally theatrical, Wolf begins a speech to the townspeople. He insists that his father was the unwilling cause of tragedy in their village; he is sorry that he himself does not remember his father because he's been told of what a good man he was. At this the villagers issue a low, threatening groan, and begin departing. Wolf calls after them to insist that he, his wife and their son want so much to be their friends—but to no avail. The villagers have gone.

A car bears the Frankenstein family up the mountain to Castle Frankenstein.* For a moment the headlights illuminate a deformed bearded figure, with a strangely bulging neck, cowering in the castle shadows . . . but he is not noticed, and there is soon a happy reunion as the family butler, Benson, and the family housekeeper, Amelia, greet Wolf, Elsa and Peter. Elsa goes upstairs to freshen up and prepare Peter for bed; Wolf goes with Benson to the library.

A large, full-length portrait of Henry Frankenstein dominates the Gothic study, where a welcoming fire burns. Wolf envies his father's genius as he stands in the very room where his infamous sire conceived his theory of the source of life.

*Castle Frankenstein in this movie has inexplicably moved from its earlier village location to a site a mile distant from the community. Of course, considering the implied wealth of the Frankensteins, it is conceivable that the family owned domiciles in both the village and the mountains!

The Players

Baron Wolf von Frankenstein	Basil Rathbone
The Monster	Boris Karloff
Ygor	Bela Lugosi
with	
Inspector Krogh	Lionel Atwill
Elsa von Frankenstein	Josephine Hutchinson
Peter von Frankenstein	Donnie Dunagan
Amelia	Emma Dunn
Thomas Benson	Edgar Norton
Fritz	Perry Ivins
The Burgomaster	Lawrence Grant
Emil Lang	Lionel Belmore
Ewald Neumuller	Michael Mark
Frau Neumuller	Caroline Cook
Councillors	Gustav von Seyffertitz
	Lorimer Johnson
	Tom Ricketts
Dr. Berger	Edward Cassidy
Guard at gates	Ward Bond
Villager	Dwight Frye*
Double for Karloff (in pit fall)	Bud Wolfe†

* Footage deleted.
†While Wolfe took the fall into the sulphur pit, the accompanying scream was sounded by Karloff. In fact, this scream is actually a re-recording of the howl Karloff sounds in the film when discovering the dead Ygor.

"Here he planned a miracle," marvels Wolf, "and saw it come to pass—a miracle that the good people of Frankenstein called a Monster."

Under his father's portrait, Wolf reads Henry Frankenstein's last words to him. There, with the estate papers, are all of Frankenstein's records, charts and secret formulas. The letter requests that, if Wolf regards the work with distaste, he destroy them. "But," continues the letter, "if you, like me, burn with the irresistible desire to penetrate the unknown, carry on. Even though the path is cruel and torturous, carry on. . . . You have inherited the fortune of the Frankensteins. I trust you will not inherit their fate."

As Wolf stares proudly at his father's portrait, he does not see the bearded stranger, peering in through the window.

There is a cavernous thundering echoing through the castle. Benson opens the door and there enters a stiff, puppet-like man, with monocle and uniform and cape. He is Inspector Krogh, chief of police. The Inspector clicks his heels, smacks his strangely stiff right arm into a salute, and states that he comes to promise Wolf protection ". . . from a virulent and fatal poison."

"Oh," smirks Wolf. ". . . Am I to be poisoned then?"

"You're poisoned already," replies Krogh, "by your *name.*"

Wolf is in no mood for such remarks. As the Inspector warms himself by the fire, Wolf begins a passionate defense of his father, opining that the stories of the Monster have been so exaggerated over the years as to be totally ludicrous. After all, did Krogh know of one actual crime this "poor creature" had committed? In fact, Wolf demands, did he ever even see him?

"The most vivid recollection of my life," answers Krogh, removing his monocle, wedging it into his gloved right "hand" as he polishes it. "I was but a child at the time—about the age of your own son, Herr Baron. The Monster had escaped and was ravaging the countryside—killing, maiming, terrorizing. One night he burst into our house. My father took a gun and fired at him, but the savage brute sent him crashing to a corner. Then he grabbed me by the arm. . . ."

Krogh smacks his wooden arm against the wall. "One doesn't easily forget, Herr Baron, an arm torn out by the roots."

It was Krogh's lifelong ambition to be a soldier. But for his wooden appendage, he, who commands seven gendarmes in the little mountain village of Frankenstein, might have been a general.

Wolf, speechless, offers Krogh a brandy. Krogh accepts, apologizing for possibly arousing Wolf's sympathy; he notes that explaining his affliction makes it less of a "curiosity." As the two men drink, Krogh tells Wolf about six prominent village men who have died recently. Krogh has not been able to solve the murders; neither has a special agent from Scotland Yard, nor the French police. All of the victims died of a concussion at the base of the brain, and an autopsy on each one revealed that the heart was ruptured—burst, in fact—reviving stories of a murdering ghost that the villagers call Frankenstein. The townsfolk, learning Wolf is a doctor/scientist, and seeing the strange electrical machinery which preceded his arrival, fear a possible future Monster—hence Krogh's warning.

Inspector Krogh informs Wolf that *when*—not *if*—he needs help, he should ring the alarm bell in the old castle tower and Krogh will rush to his defense. Elsa arrives as Krogh prepares to leave, asks him to come for dinner some evening, and joins her husband in the library to watch the storm.

The lightning thrills Wolf, since nothing in Nature is terrifying, he says, when it is understood. That lightning, he tells Elsa, is the very substance that his father drew from heaven to give life to a being he had created with his own hands. "Why should we fear anything?"

Neither Wolf nor Elsa know that, as they watch the storm, the bearded, broken-necked stranger is peering through a door upstairs, grinning wickedly at their sleeping son.

The next morning is gloriously sunny. As they breakfast, Elsa questions Wolf about that "queer-looking structure across the ravine." The structure is Henry Frankenstein's laboratory,* destroyed in the Armageddon-like explosion that supposedly killed the Monster. After breakfast, Wolf, rifle in tow, sets out to explore it.

Inside the ruins, he is fascinated. Stalagtites and stalagmites of destroyed laboratory machinery loom in the cavernous laboratory . . . an awesome lake of bubbling sulphur boils and fumes through the open roof. . . .

And a boulder narrowly misses crushing Wolf.

Whirling about, Wolf aims his gun at the would-be assassin, and orders him to come down from atop the ruins. Down a long chain slides the bearded, broken-necked scoundrel who had spent much of the previous night spying on Wolf and his family.

"... My name ... is Ygor," rasps the villain in a gruff, coarse voice. "... You see that?" he asks, pointing to the broken bone that bulges within his neck. "They hanged me once, Frankenstein. They broke my neck. They said I was dead. And they cut me down. . . ."

"Why did they hang you?" questions Wolf.

"Because I stole bodies . . . er . . . they *said*. They threw me in here, long ago. They wouldn't bury me in holy place, like churchyard. . . . So," rejoices Ygor with an evil cackle, "Ygor is dead!"

"Nobody can mend Ygor's neck. It's all right," says the madman, merrily rapping on the petrified skin covering the broken bone.

Since Wolf is a doctor, Ygor invites him to accompany him on a secret journey. The bearded rogue pulls a large slab away from the walls of the ruins, and leads Wolf through a dark catacomb. There Wolf discovers the coffins of his grandfather and his father, the latter with a scrawled legend: "Maker of Monsters."

There is more to see. Deeper inside the catacomb, lying on a large table, is the Frankenstein Monster, dressed in a sheepskin jersey.

"He's alive!" shouts Wolf as the Monster's hand moves at his touch.

"He's my friend," grins Ygor slyly. "He . . . he does things for me." The vagrant tells Wolf of the accident that long ago rendered the Monster comatose. While the creature was outside, "hunting," a great storm brewed, and as the Monster passed under a tree, lightning struck. Ygor glows as he tells Wolf that the Monster *cannot* be destroyed because Wolf's father made him to live forever. Now that the Monster is sick, Ygor demands that Wolf make him well.

"Your father made him, and Heinrich Frankenstein was *your* father too!" says Ygor.

Wolf asks if Ygor is implying that the Monster is his brother.

Ygor nods. "But his mother was light–e–ning!"

Fascinated, Wolf surrenders to his scientific zeal and agrees. Before leaving the laboratory, Wolf takes a torch, and changes the blasphemy on his father's coffin to read: "Maker of Men."

Soon, Wolf has moved the Monster up from the tomb and onto a large platform above the sulphur lake. Assisted by Ygor and Benson, the scientist soon makes fascinating discoveries about the Monster: the abnormal pituitary that accounts for his great size . . . the bullets that are lodged in his still-beating heart . . . the super-human blood cells that appear to battle each other, as if they had a conscious life of their own.

Meanwhile, the gentlemen of the council summon Ygor to appear before them and tell them what Wolf von Frankenstein is doing. Ygor affects the innocence of a schoolboy; he can't understand a scientist's business; he's only a blacksmith. One

* In a famous inconsistency of the series, the "abandoned old watchtower" in Goldstadt here becomes a building that is situated near the Frankenstein estate.

Basil Rathbone as Wolf von Frankenstein, with Karloff's Monster in the background.

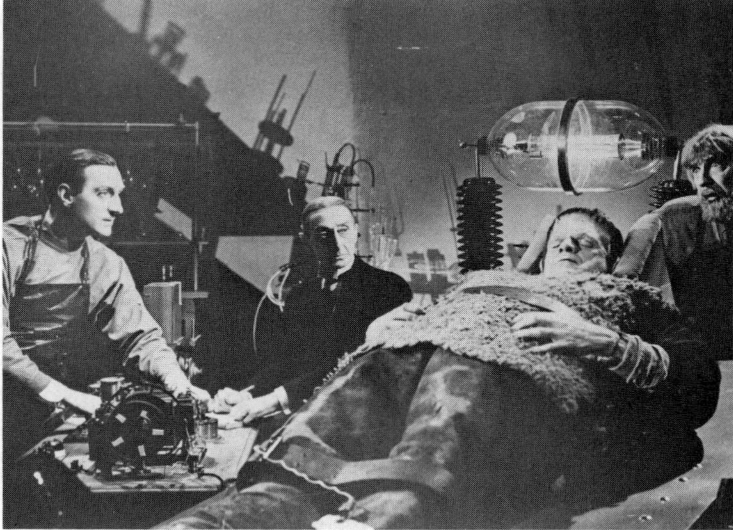

Rathbone, Edgar Norton, Karloff, and Lugosi.

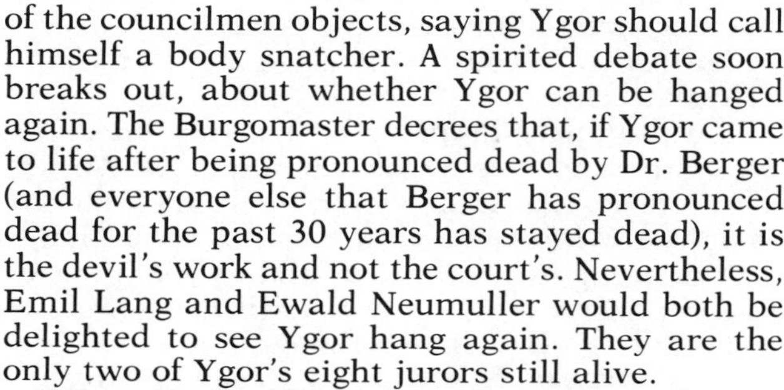

of the councilmen objects, saying Ygor should call himself a body snatcher. A spirited debate soon breaks out, about whether Ygor can be hanged again. The Burgomaster decrees that, if Ygor came to life after being pronounced dead by Dr. Berger (and everyone else that Berger has pronounced dead for the past 30 years has stayed dead), it is the devil's work and not the court's. Nevertheless, Emil Lang and Ewald Neumuller would both be delighted to see Ygor hang again. They are the only two of Ygor's eight jurors still alive.

"They die *dead,*" laughs Ygor of his six former judges. "I die *live*!" The abashed Burgomaster dismisses Ygor, and the madman leaves, but not before spitting on Neumuller. ". . . Sorry. I cough. You see, bone get stuck in my throat!"

Back in the laboratory, the day arrives when Wolf will try to revive the Monster. Hoping to vindicate his father's name by turning the living Monster over to scientific research, Wolf orders Benson to turn on the generator, and the electrical machinery blazes and whirrs. Ygor, fearful for his friend's safety, rushes to the Monster's side and grabs his wrist, suffering an electrical shock. The Monster awakes, growls at Benson, and then lapses back into a coma.

Wolf returns to the castle to discover Inspector Krogh enjoying tea with Elsa. Over their teacups, the two men spar with each other, Krogh suavely questioning Wolf about his experiments in the laboratory, Wolf just as suavely evading them. Wolf reveals to Elsa that the old laboratory, according to family history, was built by the Romans above a natural sulphur bath, which over the centuries has intensified to more than 800 degrees farenheit. Even the staunchest Roman, ventures Krogh, could not wade in that lake today without being parboiled to the bone, and Wolf is suggesting that the Inspector try it as Peter enters. The lad lectures Krogh for shaking hands with his left hand and for wearing a glove in the house.

". . . You see," says the embarrassed Krogh, "I only have one real arm. This one isn't mine."

"Well, whose is it?" asks Peter.

Wolf manages to ease the situation, telling Peter that Krogh lost his real right arm in the war, and that he is something more than a general—he's an inspector. Peter begins relating his adventures hunting elephants and tigers, and claims that his nap wasn't long—a giant came into his room and woke him up. It was a nice giant, too. So nice that Peter has given him his story book. "Are there lots of giants around here?" asks Peter.

"Only one that I ever heard of," replies Krogh, suspiciously glancing at Wolf.

Wolf rushes Peter upstairs, and asks him about the elephants and tigers . . . and the giant. Peter admits that the first two were just pretend, but that the giant was real. And, when Peter imitates the Monster's walk, Wolf races madly to the laboratory ruins.

Calling for Ygor and running about the laboratory, Wolf has his back to the giant figure that is slowly advancing behind him. A heavy arm on the scientist's shoulder turns him around, and he finds himself staring into the curious face of the Monster. Fascinated by Wolf's expressive face, the Monster toyingly changes the man's expressions, stretching Wolf's face into a warped smile. The ailing Monster than wanders away, and sees in a laboratory mirror the same hideous face that had stared at him from the little pool many years before. Upset by his grotesqueness, the Monster drags the handsome Wolf over to the mirror, so to confirm his image, and groans at the confirmation. As the sad Monster whirls away, Ygor arrives and turns the mirror to the wall.

In horror, Wolf watches as the Monster lovingly obeys Ygor's simple direction to go. "He just do what I tell him—always!" With a vicious leer, Ygor refuses Wolf's demand that he experiment further to make the Monster well. "He's well enough for me," snarls the madman, *"and you no touch him again!"* As Wolf stares in fascination, Ygor, laughing in evil glee, rubs the creature's massive chest, the Monster looking down at the cripple with love.

That night, Neumuller drives his carriage past the old castle tower, where Ygor's face appears in a high window. Neumuller spits at him. As the councilman rides away, the Monster joins Ygor at the window, and nods at the orders he is given.

Along a gloomy mountain trail, Neumuller passes under a shadowy tree. The Monster swings from a branch with one hand and grasps Neumuller's neck with the other. The Monster then places the body on the road and leads the horses over it, mutilating the corpse of the man who had treated his friend Ygor so cruelly.

Meanwhile, at Castle Frankenstein, Benson is missing. Fritz, a servitor actually spying on the household for Krogh, says that Benson was last seen going up to the nursery for the baby's supper tray.

Wolf again rushes to the laboratory and finds Ygor nursing the Monster through a nightmare. Ygor claims that Benson came to the laboratory to see the Monster walk and then ran into the woods. Wolf asks Ygor if he's sure he didn't kill him. "Why?" laughs Ygor. "I *scare* him to death. I don't have to *kill* him to death!"

Later that evening, Ygor again roosts in the castle tower, playing his shepherd's horn, as the Monster stalks into the village. Councilman Lang, sitting up late in his shop, senses something behind him, and turns to see . . .

The villagers, in an uproar, storm the castle gates, where Krogh has stationed guards. Krogh pays an accusatory call on Wolf, and Wolf pays an accusatory call on Ygor. Abandoning his dream to repair the Monster's warped brain and vindicate his father, Wolf is about to crush the sleeping Monster's skull with a rock.

"No touch him, Frankenstein!" shouts Ygor, who now gleefully admits his guilt. "Eight men say Ygor hang. Now eight men deaaaad! *All dead!*" Wolf orders Ygor off the estate, but Ygor refuses to leave. "He's *mine!*" rasps Ygor of the Monster. "He no belong to you! You go away, not *me!*" At this, the Monster rises and grabs Wolf with a roar of hatred. Ygor intervenes.

When Wolf returns to the castle, Inspector Krogh has arrived. He leaves his hat on—for he is there on official business—to arrest Wolf in order to keep the villagers peaceful. Wolf, too proud to admit to Krogh his actions, suggests that the "Monster" could be old Ygor, but Krogh laughs. Ygor has a perfect alibi for all the murders, having been

The Monster and Ygor.

Rathbone, Karloff, and Lugosi.

Lionel Atwill as Inspector Krogh.

in the castle tower, playing his horn. Nevertheless, Wolf, with Krogh's permission, visits the laboratory to order Ygor off the estate. Ygor attacks with a hammer, and Wolf shoots him.

In the library, Wolf informs Krogh that he has killed Ygor. Krogh confronts Wolf with the news that Benson is dead; the inspector discovered his body in a secret passageway off the nursery. He also shows the shocked Wolf Benson's watch, which was in the possession of Peter, given to him by the Monster. "There's a Monster afoot and you know it!" snaps Krogh. "He's in your control! By heaven, I think you're a worse fiend than your father. Where is it, Monster? . . . I'll stay by your side until you confess. And if you don't, I'll feed you to the villagers like the Romans fed Christians to the lions!"

In the laboratory, the Monster finds Ygor sprawled on the floor. Worried, he bends over his friend, moaning in sympathy. He takes the hand of his friend, pats it, sees blood and sounds a scream that echoes ominously throughout the laboratory.

As Wolf and Krogh match wits in the study, via rounds of darts (which Krogh carries by sticking them into his prosthesis), the Monster tenderly carries Ygor to the catacombs. Then, in a violent fury, he goes mad, smashing the machinery in the laboratory, hurling apparatuses into the sulphur pit and discovering Peter's Fairy Tale book. The Monster grins, crumbling the book in his giant hands as he decides how to revenge himself on Wolf von Frankenstein.

Through the passageway, the Monster appears in Peter's room. As Amelia faints, the Monster kidnaps Peter and leads the trusting boy through the passage and to the laboratory. Amelia regains consciousness, screams of the atrocity to Elsa, who herself goes running and screaming to the laboratory. Alerted by these cries, Wolf and Krogh run to the "Monster's home."

The Monster and Peter arrive. Peter turns after reaching the platform, and offers to help the Monster up. The Monster raises Peter and is about to throw him into the sulphur, but he cannot do it. Little Peter has treated him as a friend.

Wolf, Krogh and Elsa burst into the ruins. The Monster wedges Peter under his foot, and as Krogh fires his pistol, the Monster recognizes the Inspector and again tears off his wooden arm! Waving the arm like a club, the Monster roars at his enemies as Wolf, climbing atop the ruins, grabs a chain and swings down and kicks the Monster off the platform. With a terrible scream, the Monster falls into the 800-degree lake of boiling sulphur, sinking beneath the surface as Wolf and Elsa embrace Peter.

Shortly afterward on a sunny morning, Wolf von Frankenstein stands with his family at the railroad station, again confronting the villagers. He bequeaths to them the castle and estates of Frankenstein, with which they may do as they

The Monster (Karloff) waves the artificial arm of Krogh (Atwill), while Peter (Donnie Dunagan) cries for help.

will. "And may happiness—and peace of mind—be restored to you all. Goodbye!" The villagers cheer as the exiles board the train and say a final farewell to the gentlemen of the council. As the train pulls out of the station, the new wooden arm of Inspector Krogh is snapped to a salute.

SON OF FRANKENSTEIN— PRODUCTION HISTORY

I have been cursed for delving into the mysteries of Life. . . .

Colin Clive as
Dr. Henry Frankenstein in
Bride of Frankenstein.

On a June night in 1937, a line of people snaked down Venice Boulevard, outside the old Edwards Brothers Colonial Mortuary in Los Angeles.

"Who's dead?" asked a passerby, noting the strange queue.

A young blonde, with a movie magazine in one hand and her high heels in the other, spun around to reply.

"Frankenstein!" gasped the blonde with an excited smile.

Inside the mortuary, the painted, skeletal cadaver of Colin Clive lay propped in a large funeral bed which the public could pass in gawking tribute. Consumption had killed the tormented, alcoholic Clive, 37, on the morning of June 25. The wonderful actor's neurotic nature and drinking had taken a terrible toll. Some months before his death, while playing Jean Arthur's diabolically jealous husband in *History is Made at Night,* Clive had become hysterical during a dramatic scene, sobbing bitterly as the company watched in shocked silence.

For three days Clive's body was showcased in the Colonial Mortuary. So sad was his private life that, after cremation, his ashes were unclaimed for more than a week at Hollywood's Rosedale Crematory, unwanted by any loved ones. An Edwards Brothers undertaker finally picked them up. Their final disposition is a mystery.

Clive's corpse was tragically symbolic of the horror genre in the late Thirties—embalmed by the producers and sentenced to an ignoble limbo. And, Universal's financial troubles had continued, despite warnings from associates.

The creativity, imagination and flair of *Bride of Frankenstein* represented the finest qualities of the Junior Laemmle reign at Universal—a reign that was doomed. Even the profits from *Bride* . . . could not save the studio from yet another financial disaster. Fiscal 1935 had closed with a loss of $677,185, one hundred and twenty-five studio workers had been laid off, and stockholders were exasperated.

The Laemmles panicked. On November 1, 1935, "Uncle Carl" closed a deal for emergency funds to survive the financial tempest. It came with a cutthroat option from J. Cheever Cowdin's Standard Capital Corporation and magnate Charles R. Rogers, a shrewd money man with movie ambitions. Rogers and company agreed to lend the Laemmles $750,000, provided they receive the option to buy Universal within 90 days at a cost of $5.5 million. Desperately, the producers agreed.

The new year of 1936 began wonderfully for Universal; the week ending January 22 proved the most successful in the studio's history as audiences flocked to the Irene Dunne/Robert Taylor sudser *Magnificent Obsession* and the new Karloff and Bela Lugosi chiller *The Invisible Ray.* So optimistic was the glowing Laemmle senior that he had refused to grant the Cowdin-Rogers forces a two-month extension. He did, however, grant a one-month extension, and days later sportingly extended the option until March 13, trusting that the intended usurpers could never gather the money in time.

They did.

Cannot sell expensive features. Change policy.

Telegram from exhibitor/producer
Sol Lesser to Carl Laemmle, Sr., the 1930s

Junior will not change policy.

Laemmle Senior's reply

Speak to Junior; convince him to change policy.

Lesser's reply

Do not persist. You will give Junior a breakdown.

Laemmle Senior's reply

Junior will break down Universal if policy is not changed.

Lesser's final reply[116]

On March 14, 1936, the Laemmles experienced their own ultimate horror as the Standard Capital Corporation gobbled up the empire that Uncle Carl had founded 24 years before. By April 3, 1936, it was official; the old Universal was dead, the "New Universal" was born as 90 percent of the stock became the property of Standard Capital. Laemmle senior took down the old "It Can Be Done" sign from above his desk and resigned. Robert Cochrane, his co-founder, became president; J. Cheever Cowdin became Chairman of the Board; and Charles Rogers himself took the nerve-frayed, heartbroken Junior's post as Vice President in Charge of Production. Happily, the old regime managed to surrender with a wonderful success: the 1936 musical version of *Show Boat,* starring Irene Dunne, produced by Junior and directed by James Whale was a stirring swan song for the Laemmles.

Uncle Carl lived for three more years, playing his beloved card game of fargo and lavishly tending to his many charities. On the morning of September 24, 1939, Universal's 72-year-old founder suffered three heart attacks and died at his palatial domain at 1275 Benedict Drive in Beverly Hills. His $5 million plus estate generously remembered his family, servants and charities. Forty years to the day after Laemmle senior's demise—September 24, 1979—Junior Laemmle, crippled, addled and largely forgotten, died of a stroke at age 71. A "has-been" at 28, Universal's broken Crown Prince died four decades later in his old mansion at 1641 Tower Grove Drive above Beverly Hills, where he had vegetated for most of his post-Universal days.

He never produced another picture.

Step out with the *New* Universal!

Publicity slogan of the
Rogers regime, 1937.

As the old Universal globe with its revolving airplane metamorphosed into a swirling planet with glittery stars and that famous razzmatazz theme music, "the New Universal" proved itself a power to be feared. Its first act was to oust more than 70 Laemmle relatives, friends and hangers-on from the payroll. (Many of these beneficiaries reported to the lot only on payday, and at least two weekly paychecks were being made out to parties who were dead!) Front office policy, so sympathetic and respectful in Junior's day, now became dictatorial. Rogers approved all projects, and directors were to shoot in strict accordance with his pre-arranged schedule. The creative choice that directors had enjoyed with Junior was now passé, as extinct as the "Keep off the Grass" signs that had featured Uncle Carl's signature and the little chicken run bulldozed by the new regime.

With the change in studio policy came a change in studio output. After reaping the profits of Junior's *Show Boat,* the new management garnered a $1 million gross per film with the Carole Lombard/William Powell screwball comedy *My Man Godfrey,* and the musical *Three Smart Girls,* in which a plump, pubescent soprano named Deanna Durbin won major stardom and became the trilling talisman of the new Universal. The accent was now on wholesome musicals and comedies and cheap "B"-actioners; horror, a genre that Rogers perceived as a socially deleterious fascination of the eccentric Laemmle reign, was out. *Dracula's Daughter,* released in May of 1936, closed Universal's first wave of talking cinema horror as Rogers axed similar projects and cancelled the new Karloff/Lugosi vehicle *The Electric Man,** which was all set for shooting.

It was England that drove the final nail into Horror's coffin. On January 1, 1937, the British Censor *banned* horror films from England. Presumably the march of Hitler was enough to keep the British nervous. Hollywood, ever fearful of alienating the lucrative English market, embalmed the genre. For the talents who had made their names in horror films, the true test of their box office clout had arrived.

I lived then in the horror medium . . . waiting for telephones that did not ring, to ring. . . .[117]

Bela Lugosi

As the horror genre withered, so did a pall descend on the careers and lives of some of its most gifted veterans.

James Whale, calling *Show Boat* his "pride and joy," sailed in June 1936, to England, where he was to direct Marlene Dietrich and Robert Donat in *Knight Without Armour* for United Artists, and Charles Laughton in *Goodbye Mr. Chips* for MGM. Both jobs strangely fell through.† So did his next proposed project for Universal, *Time Out of Mind,* based on the Rachel Fields best seller.‡ His five-year contract with Universal expired in 1936, and he signed a new non-exclusive pact with the lot, beginning work on *The Road Back* (the long-promised sequel to *All Quiet on the Western Front*). The "Ace" of the old Universal soon discovered that the New Universal had severely cut the power he

*Also titled *The Man in the Cab,* it later became Universal's 1941 *Man Made Monster,* with Karloff's electrical freak role passing to Lon Chaney, Jr. and Lionel Atwill inheriting the Lugosi-slated part of the mad scientist.

†*Knight Without Armour,* Alexander Korda's depiction of the Russian revolution, was directed by Jacques Feyder and released in 1937. MGM eventually produced *Goodbye Mr. Chips* in 1939, with Sam Wood directing. Robert Donat, who replaced Laughton in the title role, won the Best Actor Oscar for his performance.

‡Whale discussed forming an independent production company with exiled Junior Laemmle to produce this project, but nothing came of the scheme. Universal finally produced it in 1947, and Robert Siodmak directed.

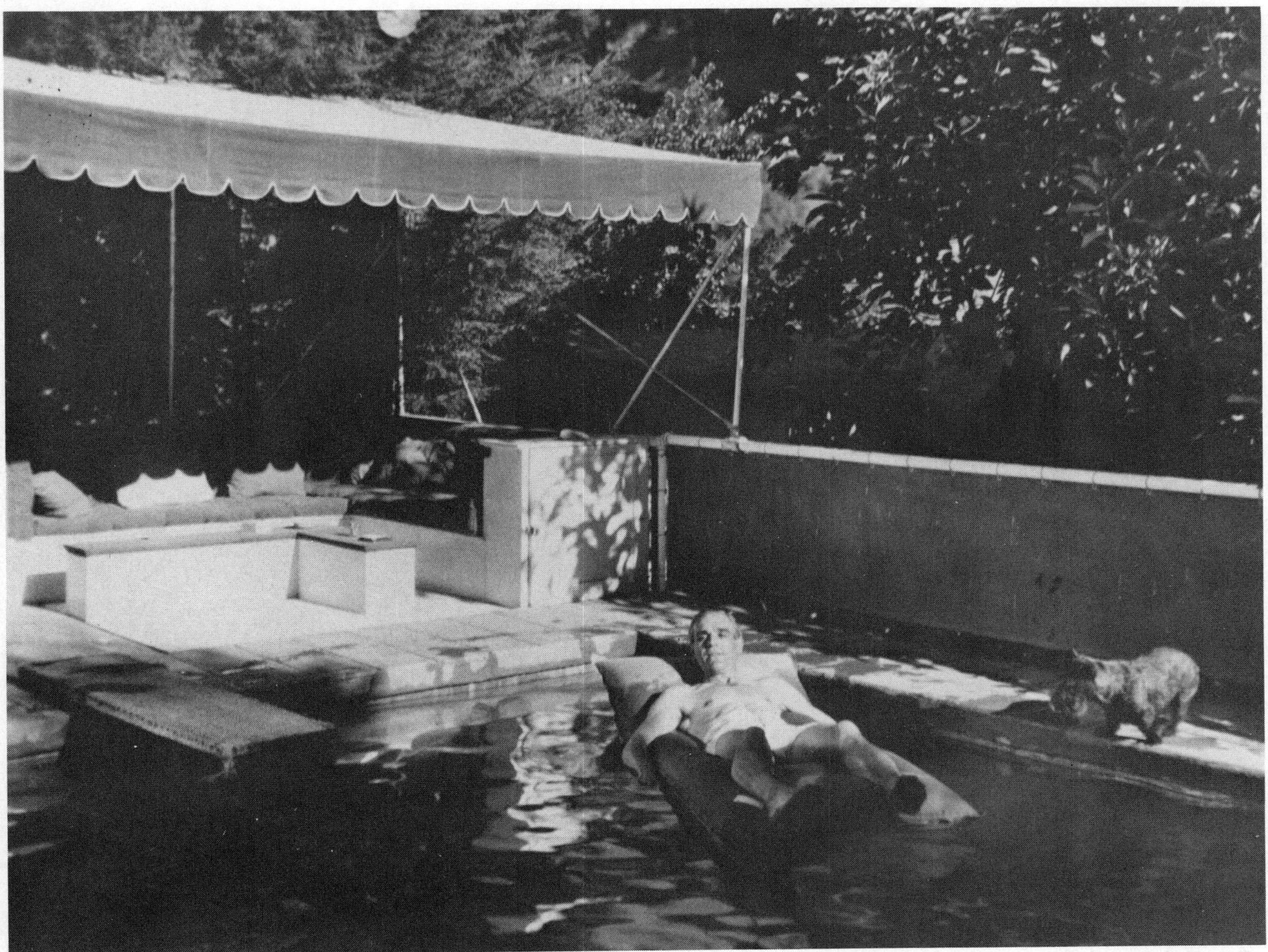

Karloff enjoying his Coldwater Canyon estate.

had enjoyed in the Laemmle regime. Nor did Charles Rogers have any tolerance for Whale's eccentricities. When, on *The Road Back,* Whale arrived each day costumed as a German WW I officer and dressed his crew as "Huns," Rogers made no disguise of his disgust. And, when previews of *The Road Back* revealed an overly dramatic feature, Rogers angrily withdrew it, put the film back into production, and assigned contractee Ted Sloman to "tone down" some sequences and direct a new ending.

The Road Back did at least prove to be one of the top moneymakers of Hollywood's 1936–37 season. The same could hardly be said for *The Great Garrick,* a richly festooned costume comedy starring Brian Aherne and Olivia de Havilland, which Whale directed at Warner Bros. So foul an egg did this strange froth lay at theaters that an outraged Jack Warner reputedly banned Whale from ever again setting foot on the Warner lot!

Whale did enjoy a few more successes, such as MGM's *Port of Seven Seas* (1938) and United Artists' *The Man in the Iron Mask* (1939), but it was clear that his grand days were behind him. Whale would say goodbye to Universal with *Green Hell* (1940), an absurd Inca temple melodrama with an incongruously chic Joan Bennett sashaying through headhunter-infested jungles. The following year, Columbia engaged Whale to direct *They Dare Not Love,* an anti-Nazi opus. Whale stalked off the set after an argument, and Charles Vidor finished the picture. By this time, the stories of Whale's arrogance, drinking and sodomy were such that he had little choice but to retire to his Pacific Palisades mansion, where he painted, partied and looked after his vast real estate holdings and investments.

Karloff, meanwhile, discovered that he was seeing more of Dorothy, the little farm and Violet the pig, but he survived nicely. He signed a five-

Universal gathers its most impressive attractions as of November 1938. From left to right: Edgar Bergen and Charlie McCarthy, Rathbone, Lugosi, Deanna Durbin, Karloff, Jackie Cooper, Bing Crosby (actually on loan from Paramount for *East Side of Heaven*), W.C. Fields (then at work sparring with Bergen's McCarthy on *You Can't Cheat an Honest Man*), and, in front, the Little Tough Guys.

picture star contract with Warners, commencing with his haunting performance in *The Walking Dead* (1936). He also benignly starred in Universal's 1937 "B" *Night Key,* began the *Mr. Wong* series at Monogram, guest-starred on such radio shows as Edgar Bergen and Charlie McCarthy's *Chase and Sanborn Hour* and *Lights Out,* and even performed Poe's "The Tell-Tale Heart" in vaudeville. Dwight Frye also retained solvency, playing on the West Coast stage in *Night Must Fall* as Danny (the psycho who murders an old lady and carries her head in a hatbox), playing in movie potboilers like *The Shadow* (1937) as a "twist-backed horse handler" who leers and lunges at Rita Hayworth, and doing bits for Whale in *The Road Back* and *Sinners in Paradise.*

Bela Lugosi, however, discovered himself to be in the same limbo that imprisoned the horror genre. Few people were happier when horror films faded than Lugosi, who trusted that his versatility would now be able to come to the fore. Instead, offers declined, and after a week's work in the Republic serial *S.O.S. Coastguard* (1937), the star entered a 15-month stretch of unemployment. When Bela Lugosi, Jr., was born in January 1938, the Motion Picture Relief Fund humiliated the proud father by "leaking" the news that it had paid for the delivery. "Whatever Became of . . .?" columns in trade papers publicized Lugosi's plight as the abashed actor took refuge in the library of the colonial mansion he had built at 2227 Outpost Drive in the Hollywood Hills, escaping the trauma via his beloved sociology books.

Finally, even this refuge was denied Lugosi; late in 1938, the mortgage company took away his house. As Bela moved Lillian, Bela Junior and the Great Danes to a rented home in San Fernando Valley, he could have taken solace in the fact that no Universal film of the 1937–38 season had been listed among the period's top grossers. Indeed, except for *My Man Godfrey* and the Deanna Durbin hits, Rogers' reign at Universal had proven a dreadfully dull failure, both artistically and commercially. Fiscal 1936 had ended for Universal with a loss of $1,835,419; fiscal 1937 closed with a loss of $1,084,998; and the first 26 weeks of 1938 would report a loss of $588,285. For all his big business acumen and front office pontifications, Rogers was reaping more depressing financial reports than idealistic Junior Laemmle ever did.

Finally, in February 1938, Robert Cochrane resigned as president, and Nate Blumberg took over. Then, on May 19, 1938, Charles Rogers himself resigned, and Cliff Work, formerly of RKO, assumed the post of Vice-President in Charge of Production. There was a new New Universal.

While Blumberg and Work conferred about studio product, Los Angeles' Regina Theatre, in a last-ditch attempt to seduce live bodies into the nearly bankrupt movie house, rented cheap prints of *Dracula, Frankenstein* and *Son of Kong.* On Friday, August 5, 1938, the triple-feature horror show opened—and soon became the talk of Hollywood. Lines formed outside the Regina until well past midnight, and Universal, hearing of the sell-out business, rushed out *Dracula* and *Frankenstein* on a double bill.

One wonders what Junior Laemmle and Charles Rogers thought of the new, outrageously lurid trailers which Universal prepared to attract audiences to the double bill. For *Dracula,* the coming attractions proclaimed, "In all the annals of living horror one name stands out as the epitome of evil—Dracula . . . the very mention of the name brings to mind things so evil, so fantastic, so *degrading,* you wonder if it isn't all a dream, a nightmare!" A film of Dwight Frye leering "Rats! Rats! Rats!" followed. In the Frankenstein trailer, an eerie voice reeking of suggestive sensuality accused the Monster of trying "to prey upon the innocence of children," accompanied by a carefully excised clip that showed the Monster and Little Maria walking hand in hand!

Whatever the effect of the trailers, the box office response was incredible. The double feature drew record business from Waterbury, Connecticut, to Salt Lake City, Utah, and even outgrossed the film's original receipts in many cities. Delirious over the profits and not so sensitive about the unsavoriness of cinema horror, Universal patted La Durbin on her girdled derriere and vowed to unleash a new wave of cinema terror, beginning with a new adventure of the Frankenstein Monster.

> Terror strikes! A horrible creature . . . made from the flesh & bones of dead men . . . waiting to pounce upon the unwary to satisfy his lust to kill!
>
> Teaser line from *Son of Frankenstein* publicity

When Universal began production of the third saga of Frankenstein on Monday, October 17, 1938, the studio had no conception of *Son of Frankenstein* as the epic classic it has become. The front office simply hoped for a quick-profit moneymaker, allotting $250,000 to its modest budget—$25,000 less than was allowed the original film more than seven years before.

Rowland V. Lee had other ideas. The director of such films as *Zoo in Budapest* (1933), *The Count of Monte Cristo* (1934), and *The Three Musketeers* (1935), was now one of Universal's major power figures, enjoying studio *carte blanche* almost to the degree that the now-humbled Whale had enjoyed during the Laemmle days. Recognizing the epic potential of *Son of Frankenstein,* the aggressive Lee managed to railroad the studio into doubling the budget. He also recruited Willis Cooper, creator of radio's *Lights Out,* to write the screenplay,* assigned Frank Skinner to create a full musical score, engaged Jack Otterson to design the sets, and planned to shoot the film in full color.†

Best of all, he assembled a superb cast.

Originally, Universal planned to borrow Peter Lorre from 20th Century-Fox to play Wolf von Frankenstein, the original blasphemer's first son. Lee opted instead for the high-priced favorite Basil Rathbone. Since climaxing his long classical stage career as Romeo to Katharine Cornell's Juliet in 1934, the lean, incisively elegant Rathbone had become the cinema's villain supreme, whipping Freddie Bartholomew in *David Copperfield,* sneering at Garbo in *Anna Karenina,* and engaging in glorious swordplay with Errol Flynn in *Captain Blood* and *The Adventures of Robin Hood.* Oscar-nominated for his fiery Tybalt of Metro's 1936 *Romeo and Juliet,* as he would be honored again for his sly King Louis of Paramount's 1938 *If I*

*Cooper's first draft, written after he screened *Bride of Frankenstein,* was something of a mess. In it, Wolf von Frankenstein drove to his father's old estate and discovered the remains of the Bride, Pretorius and the homunculi. The Monster, fully intact, returned to life via a lightning bolt, retained his powers of speech, demanded a friend, kidnapped Frankenstein's son, and planned to remove the child's brain and transplant it into a corpse to obtain this friend. The climax found the army attacking the Monster, hurling him into a bottomless pit and tossing hand grenades in it after him to insure his demise!

†Though much of the scenery was designed especially for color photography (as was the Monster's new sheepskin costume), the plans for color production were reportedly abandoned after executives noted the poor effect of Karloff's makeup in color tests.

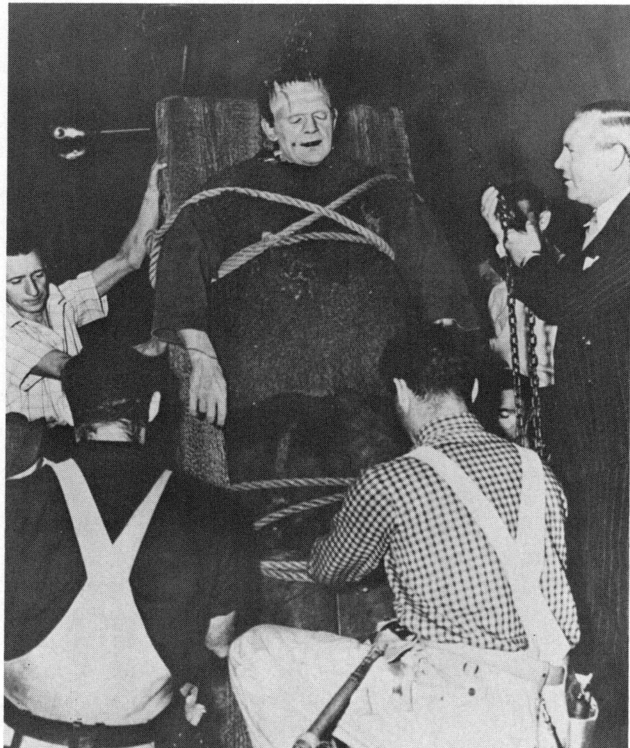

Rowland V. Lee supervises the hoisting of Karloff's Monster during the shooting of *Son of Frankenstein.*

*Were King,** the 46-year-old Rathbone was true Hollywood aristocracy, his wife Ouida being the cinema colony's most elegant hostess and his showplace house at 5254 Los Feliz Boulevard the site of some of Hollywood's most exquisite soirees. Offstage a genuinely warm, kind, gentle man with a delightful sense of humor and a great love of dogs and children, Rathbone cavalierly considered *Son of Frankenstein* a "penny dreadful"[118] movie, but nevertheless brought all his stylish professionalism to the project and claimed top billing.

Karloff was once again Boris Karloff, and second billed in *Son of Frankenstein.* The actor was not at all happy after reading Cooper's final script despite the fact that the Monster was again inarticulate. "He was going downhill. We had exhausted his possibilities. He was becoming a clown,"[119] lamented Karloff of his Monster, who spent much of the time simply sprawled upon a huge table. Nor was Karloff pleased when the Monster received a new costume—a sheepskin jersey, presumably a gift from his friend of the piece, the mad shepherd Ygor. The jersey, which Karloff described as "furs and muck," was miserably heavy, and made the Monster look like a circus sideshow attraction. Karloff frequently would shed it between scenes, quite a sight in his exposed muscle padding and suspenders. Though displeased with the script, Karloff still loved his Monster, and sought ways to display the creature's pathos and humanity.

Third billed was Lugosi as Ygor, the broken-necked blacksmith/shepherd. Hollywood studios have never been acclaimed for their charity, and *Son . . .* is a good example. In negotiating the contracts for the leading players, Universal assured Rathbone and Karloff of lucrative deals, but, aware of Lugosi's financial plight, brutally tried to take advantage of it. As Lillian Lugosi Donlevy told me regarding the studio's financial arrangements with her then-husband:

> . . . they cut Bela's salary from $1,000 per week to $500. Then they planned to shoot all his scenes in the picture in one week! When Rowland V. Lee heard about this, he said, and I

The Monster's "New Look."

* He lost both times to Walter Brennan, nominated for *Come and Get It* and *Kentucky.*

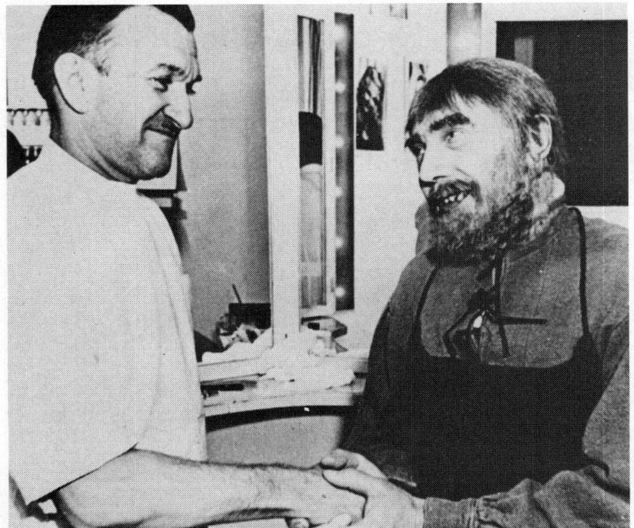
Bela Lugosi thanks Jack Pierce for turning him into "Ygor."

quote, "Those God-damned sons of bitches! I'll show them. I'm going to keep Bela on this picture from the first day of shooting right up to the last!" And he did.[120]

Universal's front office was outraged, but Lee defiantly kept his word. As the director built up Lugosi's role, adding dialogue and entire sequences, the actor had a wonderful time as Ygor, surprising Jack Pierce by delighting in the grisly makeup of mangy beard and hair, snaggle teeth and bulging neck. He also disguised his cultured Hungarian accent with that unforgettable, raspy voice, enjoyed himself hugely. "Bela loved it," says Lillian of her husband's role of Ygor. "He loved any challenging part."

For 4 hours daily, Lugosi sat at the mercy of Pierce, whom he had treated so cavalierly during the days of *Dracula* and the tests for *Frankenstein.* First, the makeup man applied the rubber broken-neck piece, which was secured to the left side of the actor's neck by an elastic strap which ran under Lugosi's right arm. Then Pierce glued yak hair on Lugosi's face, and stretched a wig over the star's head; Pierce then clipped and curled and combed to create the desired mangy effect. Then Pierce pasted on a yak moustache, and shoved in a set of snaggle teeth. A *New York Times* reporter, who visited Pierce's studio during the shooting, noted that the makeup man couldn't resist a smug smile as he detailed how former adversary Lugosi had learned ". . . the futility of attempting to escape one's destiny in the hands of the makeup man."[121]

With Rathbone, Karloff and Lugosi signed for above-the-title billing, Universal added a bonus to the featured players: Lionel Atwill. After a sterling stage career in which he romanced such ladies as Nazimova, Katharine Cornell and Helen Hayes, the bombastic Atwill had embraced a movie career of scavenging morgues, leering at heroines and inspiring hisses. As Atwill told an interviewer after settling in Hollywood:

> See—one side of my face is gentle and kind, incapable of anything but love of my fellow man. The other side, the other profile, is cruel and predatory and evil, incapable of anything but the lusts and dark passions. It all depends on which side of my face is turned toward you—or the camera. It all depends on which side faces the moon at the ebb of the tide.[122]

Atwill was a wicked delight in such films as *Mystery of the Wax Museum* (offering Fay Wray immortality as a wax-coated Marie Antoinette), *Murders in the Zoo* (tossing Kathleen Burke into a crocodile pool), *The Song of Songs* (lecherously treating Marlene Dietrich to a horrifying wedding night), *Captain Blood* (lashing Errol Flynn), etc., etc. Perhaps Atwill's greatest performance was as the Spanish officer Pasqual in von Sternberg's ex-

Lionel Atwill, Josephine Hutchinson, and Basil Rathbone take a stroll on the sound stage of *Son of Frankenstein.* (From the collection of Josephine Hutchinson)

Michael Mark, Bela Lugosi, Lawrence Grant, Lionel Atwill et al. Note the steaming kettle, far left.

otic *The Devil is a Woman*, in which his masochistic glee as Dietrich figuratively wipes her spiked heels on him is one of the most striking episodes of perversity in the cinema. A strange man who enjoyed attending sensational murder trials and who was chauffeured about in a Rolls Royce mysteriously pockmarked by bullet holes, "Pinky," as he was called by his cronies, was, like his friend Rathbone, a member of Hollywood's *crème de la crème*. The 53-year-old actor was then wed to Louise Cromwell MacArthur (Douglas' ex-wife), a multimillionairess, and lived in splendor on the Pacific coast. The role of Inspector Krogh, whose childhood memories of the Monster center around his wooden arm, was a treat for Atwill's flair for the bizarre, and he happily developed a repertoire of tricks to perform with the unnerving prosthesis.

The role of Elsa, Wolf's jittery wife, was presented to Josephine Hutchinson, the lovely, red-haired actress formerly of Eva Le Gallienne's famed Civic Repertory Company and then under contract to Universal. Donnie Dunagan, a child actor with the bountiful curls of Shirley Temple, was cast as little Peter; while Emma Dunn, who played the mother of Lew Ayres' Dr. Kildare in that MGM series, acted Amelia, the Frankensteins' maid. Edgar Norton, who had been "Poole," the butler of Fredric March's Dr. Jekyll seven years before, here became Benson, the Frankensteins' loyal retainer. The Universal casting department placed some very interesting faces on the town council. Gustav von Seyffertitz, who had tried to drown Mary Pickford in quicksand 20 years before in *Sparrows*, took a seat on the bench, as did two veterans of the original *Frankenstein*—Lionel Belmore (who had played Burgomaster Vogel) and Michael Mark (who had acted Ludwig, Little Maria's father). The splendid English character player Lawrence Grant (who had played the title role in MGM's 1918 *To Hell With the Kaiser*) presided as the Chief Magistrate.

Rathbone, Josephine Hutchinson, Donnie Dunagan, and Emma Dunn.

Come Halloween 1938, *Son of Frankenstein* began shooting.

It was a strange picture, you know.[123]

Josephine Hutchinson

The only surviving star of *Son of Frankenstein* is the still striking Josephine Hutchinson. Best remembered for her cinema performances in *Oil for the Lamps of China* and *The Story of Louis Pasteur,* she graciously spoke with me in her charming penthouse in a stylish old Manhattan apartment house on the East Side:

> I had beautiful clothes in it—that was fun, as was working with Basil and Pinky, both pros and charming men. Emma Dunn was a dear, and the little boy, Donnie, was nice. I wasn't around for most of the scenes with Karloff and Lugosi, as most of my scenes were with Basil and Pinky.
>
> Of course, doing a Frankenstein film is kind of a phony bit—you don't have to delve too deeply! Altogether, though, it was a pleasant engagement.[124]

Indeed, the *Son of Frankenstein* soundstage became the most popular site on the lot. For the days that Karloff and Lugosi (after long mornings in the makeup department) reported to the stage for their scenes, Universal was amazed at the flood of requests for passes to the set—mostly from young females! So voluminous was the demand that Lee, at times, placed a "No Visitors" sign on the soundstage door. Universal celebrities, of course, were always welcome, such as Edgar Bergen and Charlie McCarthy, who took a break from swapping venom with W.C. Fields on the neighboring *You Can't Cheat an Honest Man* set to trade quips with the Monster and Ygor.

Leading the laughs each day were Rathbone and Karloff, who inspired mischief in each other. The crew soon became used to such sights as Basil and Boris blowing up surgeon gloves like balloons, and reveling in practical jokes. As Karloff happily reminisced:

> In the scene where Bela slowly tells Basil, "He—does things for me," and there I am, all stretched out on this dais—well, we all just doubled up, including everyone else on the set, the entire cast, crew, and even Rowland, who said he didn't mind the extra takes for the chuckles it gave everyone.[125]

There was one sad side to the shooting: Lugosi's lingering loathing for the "half-wit extra" Karloff. Ever since they had first teamed in Universal's 1934 *The Black Cat* (in which Bela enjoyed himself hugely by skinning alive the top-billed, better-paid Boris in the wild climax), the Hungarian had resented "the cold fish" whose stardom and popularity was a constant pain to him. Now, on *Son of Frankenstein,* Bela was not only forced to work with Boris again, but to see his rival each day in the very guise that helped Karloff snatch away

Edgar Bergen (who appears to have been careless putting on his toupee) and Charlie McCarthy take time out from Universal's *You Can't Cheat an Honest Man* to trade quips with Karloff and Lugosi.

Happy Birthday Boris!

Lugosi's horror crown. To make things worse, Lugosi personally found Rathbone, widely regarded as one of Hollywood's nicest stars, as indigestible as Karloff. Explained Lillian:

> Basil Rathbone was *verrrry Brrrritish.* He was a cold fish, and Karloff was a cold fish. Bela, who actually was very warm, couldn't tolerate either one of them![126]

Ironically, Rathbone would prove to be especially friendly and encouraging to Lugosi 17 years later when, after Bela's grotesquely overpublicized drug cure, they played together in *The Black Sleep.*

There was another problem on the set. Although Lee was working with some of the cinema's best trained actors, he forced upon them a very sophomoric method. As Miss Hutchinson relates:

> I do remember that the director had a theory that dialogue learned at a moment's notice would be delivered more naturally. For actors like Basil and Pinky and myself, trained in theatre technique, this is not true. Nevertheless, Mr. Lee did some rewriting on the set. We spent a lot of time in separate corners pounding new lines into our heads, which, of course, one can do, but it adds pressure.

Still, good spirits prevailed, buoyed by English humor, and the most colorful sideshow of *Son . . .* came on November 23, 1938, as Karloff turned 51. The company treated him to a surprise birthday party. In full Monster regalia, Karloff beamed before a properly monstrous cake as Rathbone and Lugosi flanked him with happy smiles. That very morning, Karloff's wife Dorothy gave birth to his daughter Sara Jane, news greeted by the first-time father with joyful tears.

Whatever Lugosi's personal feelings about Karloff, Karloff always considered Lugosi to be "a kind and lovable man,"[127] which, indeed, he was very often. Five days after Sara Jane's birth, Lugosi brought Lillian and 11-month-old Bela junior onto the set with a present for the Karloffs' new baby. During the visit, the little Bela revealed family loyalty by bursting into tears when posed with Karloff's Monster.

Son of Frankenstein was completed during the holiday season of 1938, and both Karloff and Lugosi costumed themselves as Santa Claus at their

Lillian Lugosi and 11-month-old Bela junior visit a proud husband/father on *Son of Frankenstein* sound stage.

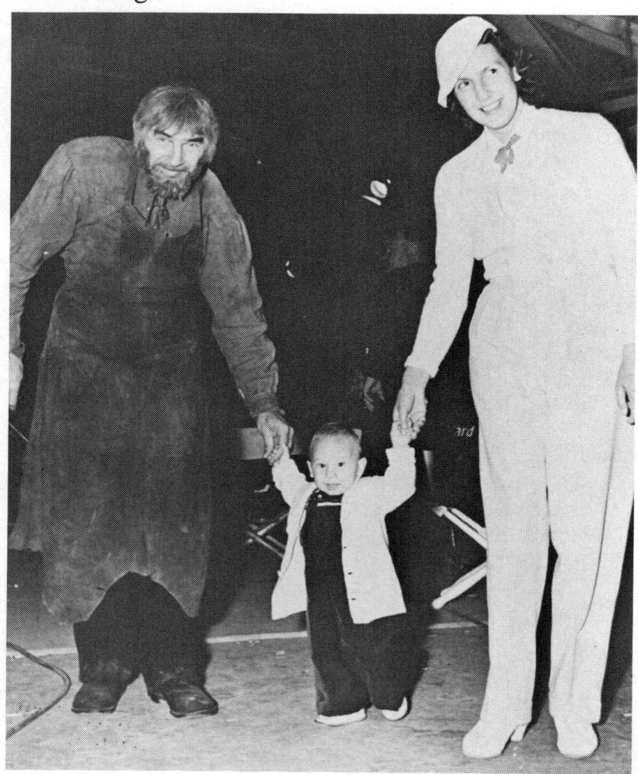

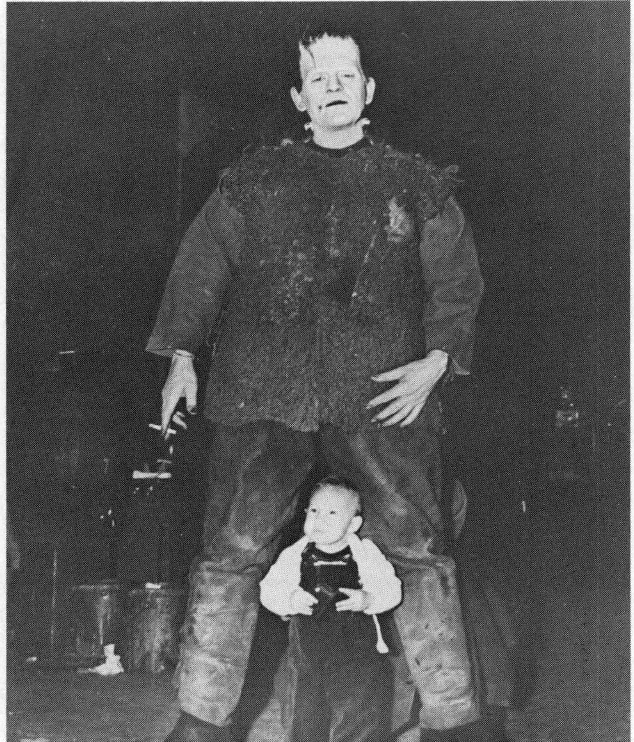

Boris Karloff and Bela Lugosi, Jr., today an L.A. lawyer, make friends.

respective homes. A major factor in post-production was the musical score, composed by Frank Skinner and orchestrated by Hans J. Salter—a German immigrant whose marvelous music saved many a horror film from mediocrity. Skinner and Salter had a frantic two weeks to create the score, and Salter remembered the battle to meet the release date deadline:

> I remember, there was one stretch, pretty close to the recording date, where we didn't leave the studio for 48 or 50 hours. He would sit at the piano and compose a sequence, and then he would hand it to me. I would orchestrate it and he would take a nap on the couch in the meantime. Then, when I was through orchestrating, I would wake him up, and he had to go back and write another sequence while I would take a nap. And this went on for 48 hours or so, so that he could make the recording date.[128]

While the score was completed, another problem arose: cuts. In its original form, the film ran longer than one hundred minutes, and proper pacing demanded excisions. If Dwight Frye was upset by the cuts in his role in *Bride . . .*, he was devastated by the cuts in *Son . . .* which eliminated his entire part as an angry villager! While Universal has never clarified the nature of the cut scenes, the fact that Ward Bond, then winning status as a popular character player, is glimpsed only as a policeman in a mob scene at the Frankenstein gates, shouting at the horn-playing Lugosi, "Ygor! Shut up! You've been playing that thing all night!" implies that at least some of the footage was devoted to the police and their handling of the mobs.

The Menace of Basil Rathbone! The Fright of Boris Karloff! The Horror of Bela Lugosi! The Hate of Lionel Atwill!

Advertisement for *Son of Frankenstein*

Hence, on Friday the 13th of January 1939, Universal proudly premiered *Son of Frankenstein* at Hollywood's Pantages Theatre. Reviews were excellent:

> *Motion Picture Herald:* Artistically, *Son of Frankenstein* is a masterpiece in the demonstration of how production settings and effects can be made assets emphasizing literary melodrama. Histrionically, the picture is outstanding because of the manner in which Basil Rathbone, Boris Karloff, Bela Lugosi and Lionel Atwill, as well as the members of the supporting cast, sink their teeth into their roles. . . .[129]

> *The Hollywood Reporter:* Universal hereby offers a brand new picture for 1939 release that will chill and thrill audiences, and speak through that universal language, Fear. It's a knockout of its type for production, acting, and effects . . .
>
> . . . Rowland V. Lee's direction creates and keeps a chillingly sombre mood, and the grim humor that's in it, he handles very well indeed . . .
>
> . . . Basil Rathbone gives still another excellent performance as von Frankenstein. Lionel Atwill is something very special in the way of inspectors, and makes the part rich. Bela Lugosi is quite horrible, and very impressive as the living dead man, Ygor. And, of course, Boris Karloff as the Monster . . . is mechanically quite perfect, and not exactly a household pet . . .[130]

On January 28, 1939, *Son of Frankenstein* opened in New York at Broadway's 2,092-seat Rivoli Theatre, where it played midnight shows, attracted packed houses and collected mostly good reviews:

> *New York Daily Mirror:* . . . a star-spangled horror epic . . . The Messrs. Lugosi and Karloff vie with each other in being horrible and it is touch-and-go all the way . . .[131]

There were also laudatory reviews—in England! The self-righteous ban on Horror had been lifted, and *Son of Frankenstein* was respectably reviewed in the influential journal *The Cinema:*

> Grand Guignol melodrama. Forceful narration frankly out to frighten, and abundantly succeeding on wealth of thrilling detail and physical horror of monster's incarnation. . . . Horrific highlights . . . all colorfully emphasized by Karloff's characterization of hideous monster who yet inspires pang of pity, and Bela Lugosi's portrait of misshapen and crazy fiend. Whenever the pair are together the incident is interesting indeed.[132]

Still, screen horror remained a controversial subject in many circles. Such august bodies as the California Congress of Parents and Teachers and the Daughters of the American Revolution were aghast, and the Women's University Club fired off this attack:

> It is hard for anyone who does not like horror pictures to understand why anybody should want to see one. This production has a fine cast, is technically extremely good, and perhaps fascinating to those who are not repelled by its hideousness. The close-up detail of facial expressions of the Monster and of those whom he terrifies make the picture sickening to look at. . . . Adol. 12–16—Very Bad. Children 8–12—Terrible.[133]

With such detractors very much the minority, *Son of Frankenstein* resurrected the horror genre. In Los Angeles, Boston and Richmond, the picture outgrossed any Universal release to that date, and the studio proudly took a full page advertisement in *The Hollywood Reporter* boasting the names of cities where hold-over dates were necessary. Showcasing both Karloff and Lugosi, the film made Boris busier than ever, and set Bela back on the road to solvency. Perhaps Bela had mellowed, or maybe he was just being privately sarcastic, but while en route to England to star in *The Human Monster* in 1939, he told *The Brooklyn Eagle* that he and Karloff, as freshly blessed fathers, ". . . often get together and talk about when our children grow up and how nice it would be if they fell in love with each other."[134]

"That's news to me," Sara Jane Karloff Brodsack told me, "and I'm sure it would be news to Mr. Lugosi's son!"[135]

Widely cherished as the last true "classic" of the Frankenstein series, *Son of Frankenstein* contains more all-around appeal than any of its siblings. Rather than the eccentric, pastoral, bizarre quality of Whale's first two sagas, the film flaunts an aura of grand epic melodrama, garnished here and there by Lee with bits of the charming, fairy tale poetry of the first entries. There is terrific atmosphere; the sunshine that reflected on the mountain lake and the little village in *Frankenstein,* is rarely in sight, replaced by a pervading gloom of misty days and lightning streaked nights, as if the Monster's legend has warped the very elements. Otterson's gargantuan "psychological sets," fashioned in the German expressionistic style of cavernous ceilings, looming shadows, monstrous beams, and that stunning wreck of a laboratory; Skinner's dynamic score; and the scenery-gnashing performances create a wonderful show—lacking much of the genius of its predecessors, but still a most worthy perpetuation of the Monster's misadventures.

An expensive, nothing spared picture . . . brilliantly mounted, lavishly set, excellently played—a fine farewell for Karloff as the Frankenstein Monster. . . .[136]

Denis Gifford, *Karloff: The Man, The Monster, The Movies*

A great blessing of *Son . . .* is the presence of Basil Rathbone as the elegantly excitable Wolf von Frankenstein. Tall, slender and handsome, Rathbone indeed appears a son to Colin Clive (whose beautiful full-length portrait hangs in the castle's study in the film). As Wolf, he not only has that Rathbone charisma, but also zeal and a most welcome comic timing (as when he charmingly offers to take the suspicious Atwill to see the boiling sulphur pit—and parboil him!). That there is a spice of "ham" in his performance, especially in his battle of wits with Atwill, is neither offensive nor surprising. The two actors were old acquaintances (Atwill had directed Rathbone in the 1930 Broadway comedy *A Kiss of Importance*), and quite naturally tried to "top" each other (as they would in *The Hound of the Baskervilles, The Sun Never Sets,* and especially *Sherlock Holmes and the Secret Weapon,* which pitted Basil's Holmes against Lionel's Moriarty). Still, Rathbone's Wolf is a three-dimensional character—proud, funny, surly, charming and heroic—and it is unfortunate that Rathbone, who in later years became apoplectic when identified with horror films, didn't personally think more highly of this film and performance.

As for Atwill, he was delighted by *Son of Frankenstein,* and rightly so—his Inspector Krogh is a masterpiece of macabre comedy. With his arch military bearing and superb delivery of dialogue (who can forget his vow to Rathbone, ". . . I'll feed you to the villagers—like the Romans fed Christians to the lions!") the actor also performs marvelous bits of gallows humor with his wooden arm—saluting with it by smacking the prosthesis with his left arm, situating his monocle between the gloved wooden "fingers" as he suavely pol-

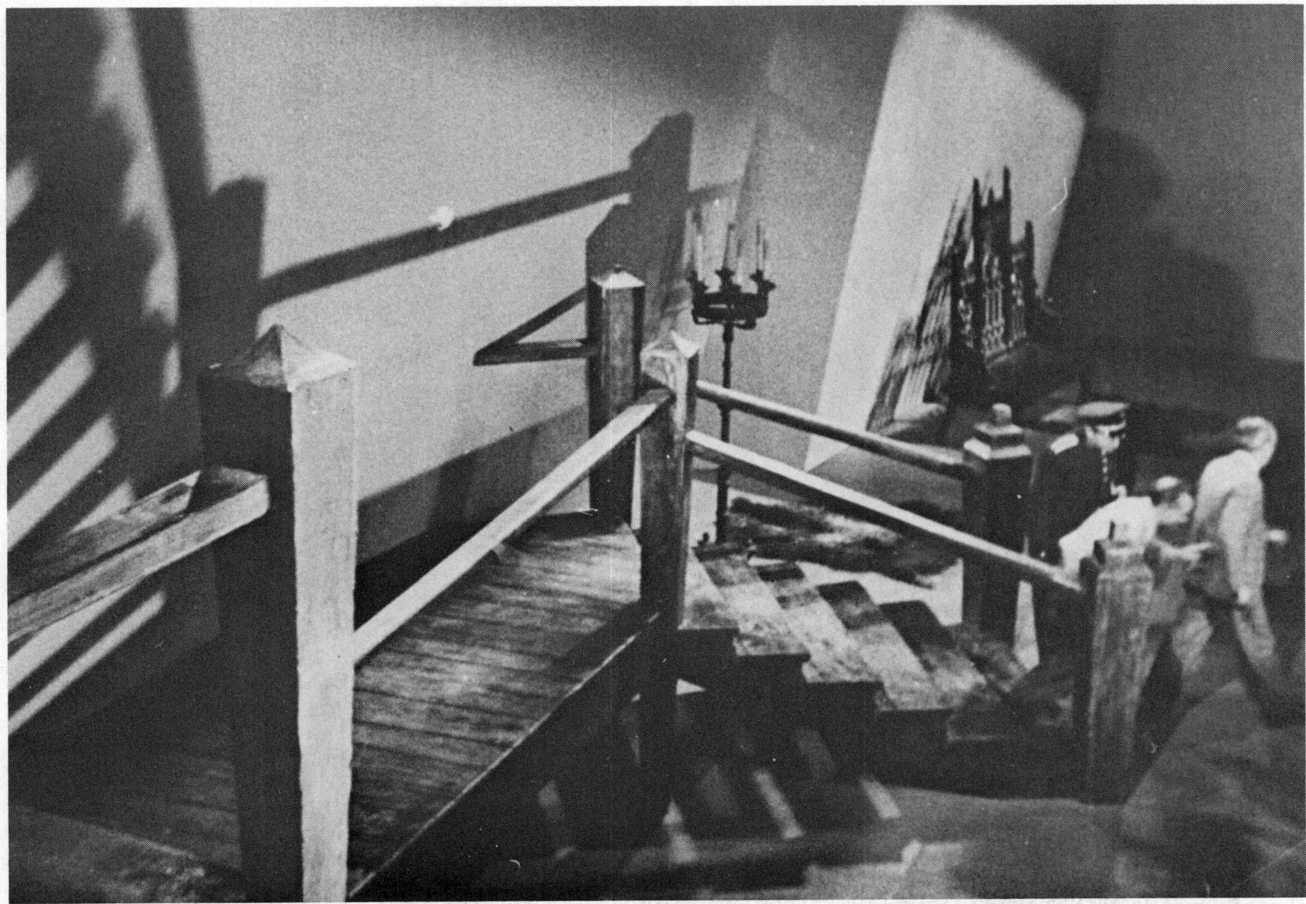

". . . the angles and masses were calculated to force an impression of a weird locale without intruding too strongly into the consciousness," said Jack Otterson of his "psychological sets" for *Son of Frankenstein.*

ishes the eyepiece, sticking darts into it between rounds of a game, etc. Winning the prize for the outstanding "featured" performance of the entire series, Atwill as Krogh is a delightfully "sick" character, one that foreshadows the black humor of the 1960s cinema (*Dr. Strangelove, The Loved One*, etc.) and one that inspired a special take-off in Mel Brooks' spoof, *Young Frankenstein.*

The supporting cast is uniformly excellent, especially Josephine Hutchinson, who elicits true sympathy for Elsa, a refined, cultured lady who suddenly finds herself living in an awesome old castle where a maid recites nonsense: "If the house is filled with dread, place the beds at head to head." The complete loss of her sleek composure when she discovers that Peter has been kidnapped, and her ensuing manic screams that would shame Fay Wray, are especially satisfying. However, the performances that attracted—and attract—the most attention are those of Lugosi and Karloff.

"God, he was cute!"[137] rejoiced Lugosi of his mirthful, broken-necked old Ygor, a performance that drove a stake for all time through the pique that all he could play were variations on Count Dracula. As Rowland V. Lee later saluted:

> We gave him his sides as Ygor and let him work on the characterization; the interpretation he gave us was unique, imaginative, and totally unexpected. . . . He played Ygor as a rogue, but one that evoked sympathy. There was warmth in his voice and a twinkle in his eye that made him almost lovable. His eyes were like prisms that caught and reflected the light in a most unusual way. . . .[138]

Rapping on the broken bone that bulged out of his neck, mischievously spitting on juror Mark ("Sorry . . . bone get stuck in my throat!"), enraging the villagers by playing his shepherd's horn in the castle tower all night as his friend the Monster terrorizes the village, or cackling as he massages the Monster's chest, Lugosi's Ygor has become

Rathbone, Lugosi, and Karloff.

Karloff's Monster takes a swing during an all-star Hollywood baseball game for charity in 1940. That's Buster Keaton behind the catcher's mask.

one of the classic performances of Horror's Golden Age. Lillian Lugosi Donlevy verbalized the sentiments of many a fantasy buff when she told me of her husband's Ygor, "I thought it was a great performance—an Academy Award performance."[139]

"There was not much left in the Monster to be developed; we had reached his limits. I saw that from here on, he would become rather an oafish prop, so to speak, in the last act or something like that, without any great stature,"[140] said Boris Karloff. Indeed, save for the beautifully played scene before the mirror, where the Monster rediscovers his reflection, Boris has precious little opportunity to show his stuff throughout most of the film. The actor contented himself by creating vivid little moments, such as his pathetic parading for Ygor as the blacksmith shows off for Wolf, his surprisingly graceful acrobatics as he swings out of a tree to pluck Mark fatally from his carriage, and his crying out from a nightmare. But after Rathbone pumps three bullets into Bela, the movie focuses on the Monster, and Boris plays a last act that is magnificent. In the film's most powerfully played vignette, the Monster discovers the slain Ygor; kneeling over the deformed body, the creature realizes his only friend is dead and unleashes a scream as bloodcurdling as it is heartrending. The ensuing climax presents Karloff at his best—ravaging what's left of the smoky laboratory in a howling frenzy, grinning wickedly as he discovers the Fairy Tales book and conceives his plan for revenge, kidnapping Frankenstein's son but being unable to destroy the innocent child, ripping off Atwill's wooden arm as he roars at his enemies before being destroyed a third and most spectacular time. The last reel of *Son . . .* finally allows Karloff's Monster to be what he truly is— the most celebrated terror character in cinema history.

Although *Son of Frankenstein* was a great success, Karloff respectfully vowed never again to play the Monster. He had spent, by Jack Pierce's calculations, nearly 900 shooting hours in the famous makeup and costume, but exhaustion wasn't the reason. "I owe him so much," Karloff later said with true sentiment, "that I owe him a little respect, a little rest."[141] While he never played the Monster in a feature, Karloff did don the makeup for a 1940 all-star charity baseball game at Los Angeles' Gilmore Stadium (tapping the ball, he scored a home run as such infielders as Buster Keaton and the Three Stooges fainted), as well as for the October 26, 1962, episode of CBS' *Route 66* entitled "Lizard's Leg and Owlet's Wing," wherein Peter Lorre donned cape and top hat and Lon Chaney, Jr., hammed as the Hunchback of Notre Dame, the Mummy, and the Wolf Man.

However, if Boris Karloff cared enough for his Monster to offer him "a little rest," Universal did not share the sentiment. *Son of Frankenstein* was the first of a parade of studio hits that gloriously closed the decade for Universal: *Three Smart Girls Grow Up,* starring the increasingly popular, increasingly girthy Deanna Durbin; *Love Affair,* pairing the profiles of Irene Dunne and Charles Boyer; *Destry Rides Again,* with Marlene Dietrich warbling "See What the Boys in the Back Room Will Have." Relishing a $1,153,321 profit for fiscal 1939, Universal Studios ventured confidently into the 1940s and was hellbent on doing so with its profitable Monster right in tow.

The Ghost of Frankenstein poster.

The Ghost of Frankenstein (1942)

Producer, George Waggner; *Director,* Erle C. Kenton; *Original Story,* Eric Taylor; *Screenplay,* W. Scott Darling; *Photography,* Milton Krasner and Woody Bredell; *Art Director,* Jack Otterson, (*Associate,* Harold H. MacArthur); *Film Editor,* Ted Kent; *Sound Director,* Bernard B. Brown, (*Technician,* Charles Carroll); *Musical Score,* Hans J. Salter; *Gowns,* Vera West; *Set Decorations,* Russell A. Gausman; *Assistant Director,* Charles B. Gould; *Makeup Artist,* Jack P. Pierce.

Filmed at Universal City, California, December 15, 1941–January 15, 1942; opened at the Rialto Theatre, New York City, April 3, 1942. Running time: 67 minutes.

THE GHOST OF FRANKENSTEIN— SYNOPSIS

"There's a curse upon this village—the curse of Frankenstein!"

Lights burn in the windows of the old town hall in the village of Frankenstein as the Burgomaster and his Council listen to the citizens vent their hatred for the name of Frankenstein. They blame the legend for the village's downfall. The countryside shuns the village. The fields are barren. The inn is empty. Children cry in their sleep; there is no bread.

"You talk as though these were the Dark Ages!" admonishes the Burgomaster. After all, he reminds them, the Monster perished in the sulphur pit of Frankenstein's tower laboratory, and Ygor was riddled with bullets from the gun of Wolf von Frankenstein himself.

The villagers do not believe Ygor is dead. Just as he survived hanging, the madman has survived bullets, they assert. "Haven't I seen him," asks one villager, "sitting beside the hardened sulphur pit, playing his weird horn, as if to lure the Monster back from death, to do his evil bidding!"

"Destroy the castle!" shouts the village agitator. "Strike the last traces of these accursed Frankensteins from our land!"

The Burgomaster, fearing for his re-election come fall and persuaded by the Council, finally agrees to allow the people to do as they please with the castle. "We'll blow it up!" screams the agitator, and the mob storms out into the night, running up the mountain to the old castle that overshadows the village. As they reach the estate, brandishing torches and dynamite, there suddenly appears a new reason for the villagers to destroy the castle—old Ygor is seen laughing sadistically atop the castle tower! Viciously delighted with this opportunity to rid themselves of him once and for all, the villagers begin planting their explosives as Ygor hurls down massive stones onto his shrieking adversaries. The first explosion, however, sends the broken-necked maniac scurrying into the castle, where the old walls crumble and crash. As Ygor pulls himself from some rubble, he looks at the massive wall of sulphur that had so strangely hardened after Wolf von Frankenstein's departure. A hand is groping through . . .

"My friend!" rejoices Ygor as he aids the sulphur-caked Frankenstein Monster from its erstwhile tomb. "The sulphur was good for you, wasn't it? It preserved you . . . Now you live forever!" As the villagers cheer each new explosion, Ygor and the Monster escape. Soon they are in a graveyard during an electrical storm. As Ygor cries after him, the Monster roams about the cemetery, reaching toward the violent heavens until he is struck by a bolt of lightning. "Your father was Frankenstein," remembers the exultant Ygor, "but your mother was the light-e-ning!" Together, the two fiends set off in the storm for a new destination.

In the beautiful village of Vasaria is a large chateau behind a high wall that bears the sign "Ludwig Frankenstein, M.D. Diseases of the Mind." Inside, three men—the promising young surgeon Dr. Kettering, the disreputable Dr. Theodor Bohmer and Dr. Frankenstein—have completed a history-making operation: a human brain has been removed from a skull, subjected to surgery and then replaced.

"With success, we *hope,*" smirks Bohmer, refer-

The Players

Dr. Ludwig Frankenstein	Sir Cedric Hardwicke
Erik Ernst	Ralph Bellamy
Dr. Theodor Bohmer	Lionel Atwill
Ygor	Bela Lugosi
Elsa Frankenstein	Evelyn Ankers
Cloestine	Janet Ann Gallow
and	
The Monster	Lon Chaney
with	
Dr. Kettering	Barton Yarborough
Hussman	Olaf Hytten
Martha	Doris Lloyd
Chief Constable	Leyland Hodgson
Magistrate of Vasaria	Holmes Herbert
Burgomaster of Frankenstein	Lawrence Grant
Hans	Brandon Hurst
Sektal	Julius Tannen
Frone	Harry Cording
First Councillor	Lionel Belmore
Second Councillor	Michael Mark
Villager No. 1	Otto Hoffman
Villager No. 2	Dwight Frye
Constables	Ernie Stanton
	George Eldredge
Double for Chaney	Eddie Parker

ring to the patient's violent dementia praecox (schizophrenia).

Dr. Ludwig Frankenstein, second son of Henry and brother of Wolf, looks the bitter Bohmer in the eye. He reminds his colleague that medical science has advanced a great deal since Bohmer performed *his* operation—a dream that proved a nightmare never even discussed in the orthodox scientific world. "But you blazed the trail," comforts Frankenstein, as Bohmer glares. As the learned scientist leaves for the library to complete his notes, Bohmer violently snaps off his rubber surgical gloves.

Young Kettering cannot seem to understand why Bohmer has allowed that one awful "mistake" to embitter his life. "Mistake?" snaps Bohmer. "Oh no, no, no, no, no. Just a slight miscalculation. . . . In those days I was the master. Frankenstein was just the pupil. But I made a slight miscalculation. . . ."

Meanwhile, as a flock of geese scatters in fear, the Monster and Ygor pass through the gates of sunny Vasaria. As Ygor looks for the Frankenstein estate, the Monster sadly watches some village boys bullying a little girl named Cloestine, kicking her ball up onto a roof. "Hello. . . . Are you a giant? . . . Can you get my ball?" These kind words from the innocent child warm the Monster, who carries Cloestine to the rooftop to retrieve her ball. A frightened mob gathers. Soon a villager climbs to the rooftop to attack the monstrous stranger, and the Monster knocks him from the roof to his death on the cobbled street. Cloestine's father is panic-stricken. The Monster is promised that no one will hurt him and he descends at a nod from Ygor who has joined the crowd. However, as he reaches the streets, the mob leaps upon him, beating the Monster and carrying him off to jail.

Shortly afterward, town prosecutor Erik Ernst, the fiancé of Frankenstein's lovely blond daughter Elsa, calls on the doctor. He asks Frankenstein to come immediately to the village to examine the prisoner. "He's huge, a monster!" Frankenstein promises to come, but before he can leave, his maid Martha announces a caller—from the village of Frankenstein.

"How does it feel to face a man you thought your brother killed, Doctor?" asks Ygor. The scoundrel informs Frankenstein that the prisoner in the town jail is indeed the Monster, and that the doctor must harbor him. "You can harness the

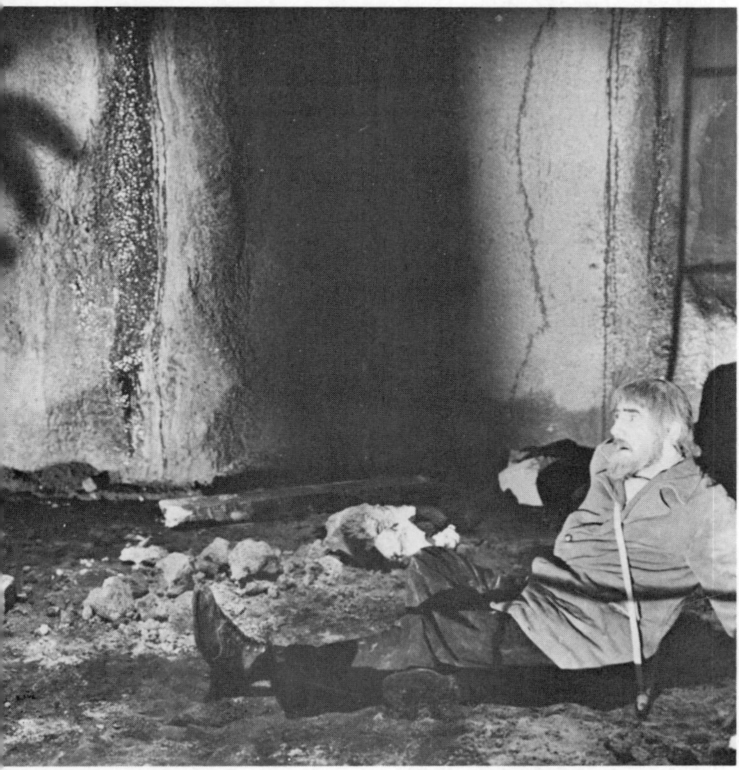

Old Ygor (Bela Lugosi) sees the Monster's shadow break forth from the hardened sulphur pit tomb.

Lon Chaney, and Bela Lugosi.

Evelyn Ankers, Lionel Atwill, and Sir Cedric Hardwicke.

light-e-ning," smiles Ygor, "give him back the strength he once had. . . ."

"Ever since the day my father put life into that thing it has been a curse!" replies Frankenstein. "The terrible consequences of his creation killed my father, drove my brother into exile. The Monster shall not ruin my life!"

Ygor has other plans. He threatens to inform the village, Elsa and Frankenstein's friends of the family's horrible past unless Frankenstein convinces the police to turn the Monster over to him. Frankenstein agrees, then orders Ygor out of his house. As Ygor leaves, he sees Elsa on the staircase—and smiles evilly at her. "He *smiled* at me," a shaken Elsa tells her father. "A cruel smile . . . It was dreadful!" Her father calms her and departs for the town.

The courtroom of Vasaria overflows with villagers who have come to gawk at the Monster, now chained and harnessed in a witness chair. The Monster pays no heed to Erik's questions, but appears to warm to little Cloestine, who fearlessly approaches the Monster and gently asks him his name. Then Frankenstein enters the courtroom. The Monster eyes him strangely, with a slight grin as if recognizing the family aura. Frankenstein, however, denies any knowledge of this fiend. "I never saw this 'man' before in my life. I know nothing about him."

Again rejected by a Frankenstein, the outraged Monster rips his chains from the floor and, as the villagers flee in horror, confronts the doctor. By force of personality, Frankenstein bravely stares the Monster into non-violence. Suddenly, Ygor's shepherd's horn is heard from a carriage outside. The Monster escapes the courtroom, climbs into the carriage, and Ygor drives madly away, the villagers in futile pursuit.

That night there is a terrific storm. Elsa, nervously pacing the castle, enters her father's study and sees on the desk a book of records compiled by her grandfather, with additional notes by her uncle, *The Secrets of Life and Death.* Morbidly fascinated, she pages through the book and shivers at the entries, such as the one dated May 20th:

> The body of my creature is complete. Every physical part carefully chosen and the whole assembled. Now, the brain. . . ."

Suddenly, in a flash of lightning, Elsa turns around and sees the Monster and Ygor peering through the windows. She screams, while, outside, Ygor points at the door, shouts "Frankenstein!," and exhorts the Monster to pound down the door. In a rampage, the Monster stalks the corridors, grabs the howling Kettering and slays him. Frankenstein and Elsa race to the scene, where the Monster snares the shrieking woman. However, before she is harmed, Frankenstein releases a sulphuric gas that renders the Monster, Ygor and Elsa unconscious. He then summons Dr. Bohmer, who, after staring in keen fascination at the Monster, helps Frankenstein in trying to save Kettering's life. They fail.

Later that night, a despondent Frankenstein confesses the family's infamy to Elsa. She had suspected something horrible from the moment she had seen Ygor, and now begs her father to forswear anything to do with these horrors. "*Please* don't let it spoil our lives!" says Elsa. Frankenstein promises.

Ludwig decides to destroy the Monster by dissection. Bohmer righteously refuses to assist him, so Frankenstein decides to do it alone. However, as he prepares to destroy the Monster, the apparition of Henry Frankenstein appears:

"My son . . . Would you destroy that which I, your father, dedicated his life to creating?"

". . . But it has brought death to everything that it's touched!" protests Ludwig.

"That is because, unknowingly, I gave it a criminal brain . . . What if it had *another* brain?"

Ludwig realizes he has found his answer. Summoning Bohmer to the laboratory, he breathlessly announces that he will give the Monster the brain of Kettering, whose death has not yet been reported to the police. The Monster thereby will cease to be evil and become a man of character and learning.

Ygor, who has come into the laboratory after hearing the electrical machinery beginning to strengthen the Monster for his operation, protests Frankenstein's plan. "You're going to make him *your* friend, and I will be alone," he argues. He proposes a different plan. "Doctor . . . Ygor's body is no good . . . You can put my brain in his body!

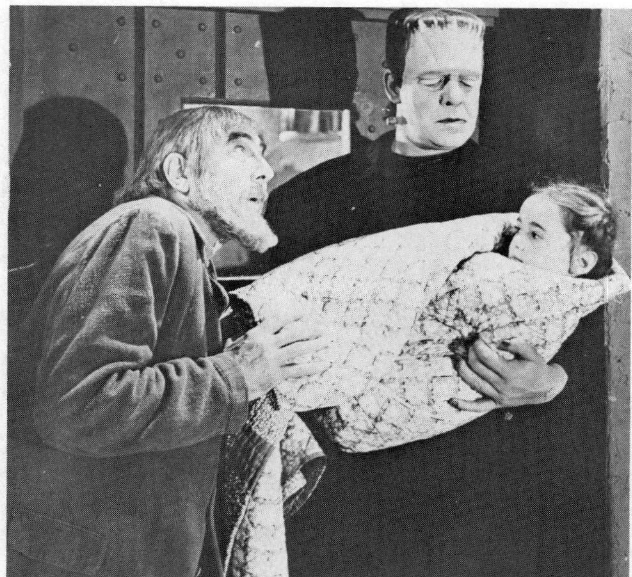

Lugosi, Chaney, and Janet Ann Gallow. "Tonight, Ygor will die for you. . . ."

You can make us one . . . We'll be together always . . . My brain . . . His body . . . together!"

"Ha! That would be a Monster indeed!" Frankenstein laughs as he denies the request.

As the Monster revives, Ygor hisses "A new brain!" at his friend, trying to make the creature understand his impending operation. "He is the first time happy in his life!" laughs Ygor of the Monster. Ygor is surprisingly merry too, despite Frankenstein's decision. He believes he has found the way to get his wish through the jealous Bohmer. Meeting Bohmer on the sly, Ygor tempts him with the thought of ruling the medical world. "You weave a pretty fairy tale, crooked neck," sneers Bohmer. Ygor, however, promises it will happen—if Bohmer sees to it that the brain of Kettering does not go into the Monster's skull. Instead, Ygor's brain must be substituted. And, if Bohmer helps him, Ygor will see to it that the frustrated man has everything he wants.

As the date of the operation nears, Erik demands that Frankenstein allow him to search the estate. Warning his future son-in-law that he may find himself unwelcome in the future, Frankenstein agrees. However, the Monster cannot be found! He has escaped the mansion and entered the village, where he kidnaps Cloestine—for it is her brain he wishes to inherit. In fleeing with Cloestine, the Monster accidentally knocks over a lamp and the house is burned to the ground. Cloestine is believed to have been killed in the fire.

"Ygor has a better idea!" cries the broken-necked villain when the Monster returns with Cloestine. "You will have the brain of your friend Ygor! . . . Tonight, Ygor will die for you." The Monster rebels. Throwing Ygor against the wall, the Monster slams back the laboratory door, inadvertently crushing Ygor behind it.

That night, Frankenstein and Bohmer begin the operation. Bohmer warns the broken Ygor that this could be the end of everything for him. "Better death, than a life like this," responds the dying cripple, "now that I have seen the promise of a life—forever." With clockwork precision, a new brain is placed into the Monster's skull. Frankenstein wonders what Kettering will think when he resumes life in the Monster's body—whether he will thank the doctors or whether he will object to reawakening in the Monster's frame.

Two weeks pass. As the Monster slowly recovers from the major operation, the villagers are becoming restless. Hussman has never believed that Cloestine perished in the fire because no bones were found. And nobody can understand why the giant maniac who escaped from the jail cannot be located. Believing Frankenstein to be protecting the Monster, surly villager Frone and his mob march with their torches to the gates of the Frankenstein sanitarium, where Erik intercepts them on horseback. He bargains with the crowd for time, enters the house, and insists to Frankenstein that the time has come for a showdown.

Frankenstein agrees. He explains to Erik how the Monster had killed Kettering, but that he lives again in the body of his murderer. Believing that he has made amends for the misdeeds of his father and his brother, and that he has restored the good name of Frankenstein, the doctor confidently leads Erik to the dungeon—and to the Monster.

He does not see the mad grin on Bohmer's face.

"You recognize me?" Frankenstein asks the Monster.

The Monster nods.

"Tell me. Who am I?"

"You are—Dr. Frank-en'shtein."

"And you are," replies Frankenstein at the gruff voice, "you are Dr. Kettering!"

"I am *not* Dr. Kettering. I—am—Ygor! . . . I have the strength of a hundred men. I cannot die! I cannot be destroyed! I—Ygor—will live forever!"

"I've created a hundred times the Monster that my father made!" gasps Frankenstein, who hurls himself at the gloating Bohmer. The Monster intervenes. He stops short of killing Ludwig Frankenstein since he realizes that the senior Frankenstein gave him life and this man has given him a brain.

Meanwhile, the restless townspeople have broken into the estate. Elsa returns little Cloestine, and Erik races up from the cellars with the news that the madmen have turned on the gas. As Bohmer turns up the toxic fumes, Frankenstein tries

Left to Right: Olaf Hytten, Ralph Bellamy, Doris Lloyd, Janet Ann Gallow, Evelyn Ankers, and players.

to stop him and is fatally beaten by the Monster.

Then suddenly . . .

"Bohmer! I can't see!" cries the Monster.

"Your dream of power is over, Bohmer," sighs the dying Frankenstein. For Bohmer had not realized that, while the Monster's blood was the same type as Kettering's, it was not the same as Ygor's. It will not feed the sensory nerves.

"Bohmer! You played me a trick!" roars the Monster. "What good is a brain without eyes?" The creature's huge arms toss the trembling Bohmer into a giant piece of electrical machinery which blasts thousands of volts into the bumbling doctor's body.

Blind and furious, the Monster crashes through the laboratory, overturning highly combustible chemicals, short-circuiting electrical equipment, causing the estate to explode into a giant inferno. Groping through the flames, his clothes ablaze, his face blistering, the Monster finally falls under a huge beam, imprisoned once again in a tomb of searing fire.

Outside, Erik and Elsa watch the horrible disaster. Erik turns his fiancée away from the catastrophe which has taken her father, and walks with her to a nearby cliff. The dawn is breaking.

THE GHOST OF FRANKENSTEIN—PRODUCTION HISTORY

The 1930s ended triumphantly for Universal with its 1939 $1 million profit, and the new decade promised even greater riches. A $2,390,772 profit for 1940 followed the success of the Deanna Durbin vehicles *Spring Parade* and *It's a Date,* the W.C. Fields comedies *The Bank Dick* and *My Little Chickadee* (with his "little brood mare," Mae West), the rowdy western *When the Daltons Rode,* and, of course, a fresh batch of horror concoctions. The 1940 shockers included *Black Friday,* a brain transplant yarn and the sixth tandem feature of Karloff and Lugosi (committing the cardinal sin of not pairing the stars in a single scene); *The Invisible Man Returns* (with a 28-year-old Vincent Price in the title role); and *The Mummy's Hand* (with arthritis-plagued western star Tom Tyler succeeding Karloff as the bandaged one). As 1941 began, Universal happily continued building up its contract roster* of stars and players.

Other studios, too, followed the horror revival spawned by *Son of Frankenstein.* Columbia produced Karloff's "Mad Doctor" series, beginning with 1939's *The Man They Could Not Hang;* MGM released 1941's *Dr. Jekyll and Mr. Hyde,* with Spencer Tracy's brilliant (albeit controversial) performance; Paramount unleashed Albert Dekker as 1940's *Dr. Cyclops,* the movies' first full-Technicolor grotesque; RKO slapped together 1940's *You'll Find Out,* a Kay Kyser hooplah in which Karloff, Lugosi, and Peter Lorre were originally set to sing (they didn't); and Monogram was churning out replicas *a la* 1941's *The Invisible Ghost,* with Lugosi.

Then, suddenly, a near-calamity threatened havoc for future horror production: terror superstar Boris Karloff defected to Broadway.

Boris Karloff as Jonathan Brewster in *Arsenic and Old Lace,* Fulton Theatre, New York City, 1941.

Look at that puss. He looks like Boris Karloff!

from *Arsenic and Old Lace*

"The happiest role of my life"[142] was how Boris Karloff remembered his maniacal Jonathan Brewster of Joseph Kesselring's classic comedie noire *Arsenic and Old Lace.* Opening January 10, 1941, at Broadway's Fulton Theatre (now named for Helen Hayes), the play hilariously dealt with two homicidal old ladies, their nephew who thinks he's Teddy Roosevelt, and his fiendish brother transformed by a drunken plastic surgeon to resemble the cinema's infamous bogey man. When Karloff's Jonathan explained his murder of one Mr. Spenalzo with a bitter "He said I looked like Boris Karloff!" the packed house never failed to roar. Though originally terrified by the prospect of his New York stage bow ("I was scared stiff about how they'd like me"),[143] Karloff, who had starred in no less than nine movies released in 1940, found himself to be an overnight Broadway sensation. He starred in the New York company for a year and a half,* then embarked on a 66-week road tour, recalling the long run as "one of the happiest periods of my life."[144]

A continent away, Hollywood producers mourned the loss of the horror king. Not so Bela Lugosi. Although he envied Karloff's Broadway hit, Lugosi contented himself with the fact that he now had the chiller market all to himself, with contracts at Universal and Monogram (where he was churning out rot like 1941's *Spooks Run Wild* with those ever-nauseating Bowery Boys). However, Universal had little respect for the aging Hungarian, and believed an entirely new leading horror man was in order.

*Collecting weekly paychecks at Universal in 1941 were such leading men as Richard Arlen, Lon Chaney, Jr., Buster Crabbe, Robert Cummings, Andy Devine, Dick Foran, Allan Jones, and Robert Stack; such leading ladies as Evelyn Ankers, Deanna Durbin, Jane Frazee, Nan Grey, Anne Gwynne, Irene Hervey, Gloria Jean, Constance Moore, Peggy Moran, Helen Parrish, Baby Sandy, and Maria Montez. Universal also held special contracts with such stars as Marlene Dietrich, The Andrews Sisters, W. C. Fields, Loretta Young, Brian Donlevy, Irene Dunne, Bela Lugosi, and Abbott and Costello.

**Arsenic and Old Lace* ran three and a half years (1,444 performances) on Broadway; Karloff's initial successor as Jonathan was Erich von Stroheim. In the 1944 screen version, Warner Bros. economically cast contractee Raymond Massey as Jonathan, who was made up to look like Karloff.

Lon Chaney, Jr. (1906–1973).

Ironically, while it was Karloff who became the new Chaney, it was a Chaney who became the new Karloff.

George . . . Tell me what you done before . . . about the rabbits . . . Please? . . . Go on, George. . . . Tell about the rabbits and how I get to tend them . . .

Lon Chaney, Jr. as Lennie in *Of Mice and Men*

In the finale of Universal's *Man of a Thousand Faces,* the 1957 biopic of Lon Chaney, Sr., the dying Chaney (played by James Cagney) beckons his only child Creighton to his deathbed, takes his famous makeup box, and adds a "Jr." to his name—hence passing the acting heritage to his son.

Nothing could have been further from the truth.* When cancer killed Chaney on August 26, 1930, it was a comfort to the dying man to know that his 24-year-old son was well on his way to becoming a master plumber. "He's happy in business and he's got a great wife" insisted the rigidly stoic Chaney when asked if his son would follow in his dramatic footsteps. Rarely allowed to attend the gala premieres, forbidden to make the rounds of the glamorous parties and left virtually nothing of his father's estimated $1.5 million estate, Creighton Tull Chaney was to make it on his own—and not by acting.

Nevertheless, Lon Chaney had not been interred at Forest Lawn quite two years before Creighton Chaney made his movie bow, dancing in the chorus of RKO's *Girl Crazy* (1932). The young man plunged happily into the movies:

> I worked under five names. I did extras under one name, stunts under another name, bits under another and leads under my own name. I'd get a call to do a fight, so I'd go on the set and I'd go quick to the assistant director and I'd say "How long's the fight going to take? And how long am I going to be here?" And he'd say about 20 minutes. "And when are you going to do it?" He'd say about an hour from now. "Okay, I'll see you." I'd run to the next set and work under a different name. And between the three or four sets I'd come off smelling like a rose.[145]

The rose soon wilted. That "great wife" (Dorothy Hinckley) divorced him, winning the small nestegg left by his father and leaving Chaney with two sons (Lon and Ronald) to raise. Job offers dwindled, and the desperate actor changed his moniker to Lon Chaney, Jr.,—not without traumatic guilt ("They starved me into it"). A player's contract with 20th Century-Fox totally wasted Chaney in humiliating bits. The only attention he won came in the summer of 1938 in Pineville, Missouri, on location for *Jesse James*—he fell off his horse in a chase sequence and was trampled by the following herd. Director Henry King blamed the accident on Chaney's nightly drinking and sent him back to Hollywood, where he was dropped by the studio a few months later. In 1939, Lon Chaney, Jr., with a new wife (model Patsy Beck), two sons and a growing drinking problem, found a finance company repossessing his car and furniture.

Then lightning struck. Chaney won the part of the moronic giant Lennie Small in the West Coast company of John Steinbeck's *Of Mice and Men.* His shattering performance (14 curtain calls on opening night) earned him the role in Lewis Milestone's 1939 film version. So movingly pathetic was Chaney's Lennie as he lovingly but fatally stroked a bird, a puppy and (ultimately) an oomphy Betty Field, that he suddenly captured stardom. After Chaney scored again as the scarred old

*Chaney junior, who sold the rights to his father's story to Universal, later lamented that the studio put five writers to work on it the day after the purchase to distort the facts.

Two of the stars of *The Ghost of Frankenstein* in an advertisement that appeared shortly before the film's release.

warrior of RKO's 1940 *One Million B.C.*, Universal offered him a contract, and he was soon sweating for his paycheck: rabid Lionel Atwill shot him full of electricity in *Man Made Monster,* savage Indians all but burned him alive in the serial *Riders of Death Valley,* and, finally, lycanthropic Bela Lugosi gnawed him to top stardom in *The Wolf Man.* In that box office bonanza ($1 million domestic gross), Chaney created the classic character of Lawrence Talbot and established himself as Universal's new great white hope of Horror.

"The studio received more mail for me during that period than any other star," Chaney later boasted, "and they immediately rushed me into a Frankenstein picture."[146]

One of the most powerful men of Universal during the war years was George Waggner, one of the few men in Hollywood with a producer/director/writer contract. Director and associate producer of *The Wolf Man,* the energetic Waggner was convinced that the time was ripe for a new chapter in the Frankenstein saga. Hence, Eric Taylor, who had contributed to Universal's *Black Friday* and the 1941 *The Black Cat,* hatched a new story, and W. Scott Darling wrote the screenplay.* Erle C. Kenton, the veteran director whose credits included Paramount's 1932 *The Island of Lost Souls,* had joined Universal, specializing in rapidly churning out "B" pictures, and was assigned the megaphone for *The Ghost of Frankenstein.*†

*The first draft story drastically differed from the final product. The original story again concerned Wolf von Frankenstein, who had moved to Vasaria to operate a sanitarium. Ygor and the Monster arrive in town, and Ygor finds an evil soulmate in Wolf's deformed assistant Theodor. When Wolf decides to give the Monster a new brain, Ygor and Theodor conspire and Ygor's brain is placed in the Monster's skull. Wolf, in trying to undo his wrong, is thrown into the electrical machinery, which blows up and kills the rest of the cast. One especially ludicrous feature of the original story was the Monster and Theodor raiding the village and wiping out the entire police force.

†The Monster, incidentally, had made a gag appearance in Universal's Olsen and Johnson comedy *Hellzapoppin* in 1941. Stuntman/bit player Dale Van Sickel donned the makeup. Olsen and Johnson also planned for the Monster to play a "cameo" in their 1944 Universal comedy *Ghost Catchers,* but he does not appear in the release print.

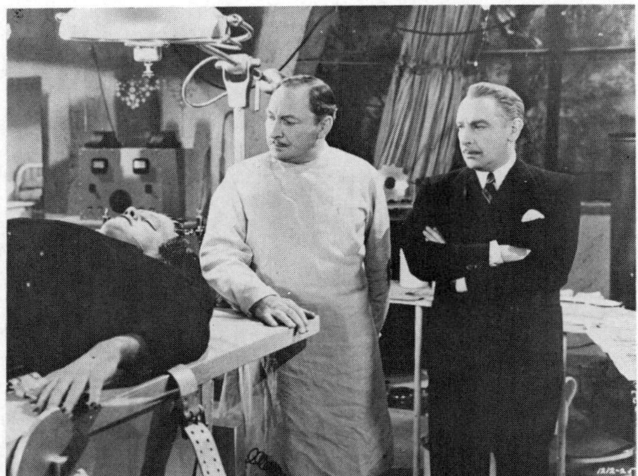

Lon Chaney, Lionel Atwill, and Sir Cedric Hardwicke.

With "Master Character Creator" Chaney promised special billing as the Monster, top billing went to Sir Cedric Hardwicke, who starred as Dr. Ludwig Frankenstein, the Monster-Maker's second son. "You are my fifth favorite actor," George Bernard Shaw once quipped to Hardwicke, "the other four being the Marx Brothers."[147] Knighted in 1934 for his Shavian stage work, the short, bald, 48-year-old thespian had become a favorite, top-priced Hollywood character star, especially adept at villainy (e.g. the wicked justice of RKO's 1939 *The Hunchback of Notre Dame,* the evil Mr. Jones of UA's 1940 *Victory,* and Death himself in MGM's 1939 *On Borrowed Time*). With toupee, mustache, blue double-breasted suit and patrician elan, Hardwicke sold his stature to a Frankenstein film with no shame—at least no more than he suffered regarding his usual presence in Hollywood. As he later reflected, "I believe that God felt sorry for actors so He created Hollywood to give them a place in the sun and a swimming pool. The price they had to pay was to surrender their talent."[148]

The role of Erik, town prosecutor and "hero" of the melodrama, was passed to Ralph Bellamy. Fatigued by his image of a girl-losing dolt in sex comedies such as *The Awful Truth* (1937), and freshly liberated from Columbia's *Ellery Queen* series, Bellamy had signed with Universal in hopes of securing some solid dramatic parts (he had just played the town constable in *The Wolf Man*). It was a peculiar career phase for Bellamy who was soon to prove himself a superb actor on Broadway.

As Dr. Bohmer, Frankenstein's wicked, bitter assistant, Waggner cast Lionel Atwill, who had earned a lewd reputation in Hollywood circles. "Women are cat creatures," quoth Atwill in a 1930s interview. "Their preference is for a soft fireside cushion, for delicate bowls of cream, for perfumed leisure, and for a master—which is where and how they belong."[149] In 1939, Louise Atwill left her "master," citing his adultery, drinking and threats of physical violence, and in her absence, "Pinky" was the host of parties which inspired no end of gossip. In the spring of 1941, shortly after the actor received word that his only son John had been killed in action with the Royal Air Force, two women, a Cuban dress designer and an unwed, pregnant 16-year-old, testified before the Los Angeles County Grand Jury in a very sordid rape trial. Their testimony touched on a 1940 Christmas holidays orgy they attended in the Pacific Palisades mansion of a Hollywood celebrity who showed the pornographic movies *The Daisy Chain* and *The Plumber and the Girl,* and then led the guests in stripping and reprising the films' carnal antics on a tigerskin rug while a pianist played Viennese waltzes. The voluptuary's name: Lionel Atwill. Deeply humiliated ("I might as well make a hole in the water somewhere and jump in!" he wailed to his lawyer),[150] Atwill, black arm band marking his son's death, took the witness stand, vehemently denied the women's stories, and convinced the jury that his get-together was only "an innocent party." The outraged prosecutors kept working on the case, convinced that Atwill was lying. Sadly, as would later be proven, he was.

The *millions* who were lured to the box office by the flesh of Frankenstein's terrifying Monster . . . will storm your theatre anew to see his fearful apparition stalk again! You will *thrill* to a NEW Weird creation of Horror! NEW Terror! A NEW spine-chilling story . . . with an *all-star* cast . . . with the screen's sensational new character creator, *Lon Chaney. . . !*

Trade advertisement for *The Ghost of Frankenstein*

Things were a bit happier for Bela Lugosi, who reveled in the chance to reprise old Ygor. Thanks to his Universal and Monogram contracts, he had recently moved Lillian and Bela junior into what became his favorite Hollywood home—a Gothic house, complete with gargoyles and a magnificent two-story latticed window, just north of Universal City on Whipple Street. It became known as Lugosi's "Dracula House," and in his final years, long after his dwindled fortunes forced him into a tiny apartment, Lugosi would occasionally turn up on the doorstep, ring the bell and announce to the owners, "I am Bela Lugosi, and I have come to see my house." (It has since been demolished.)

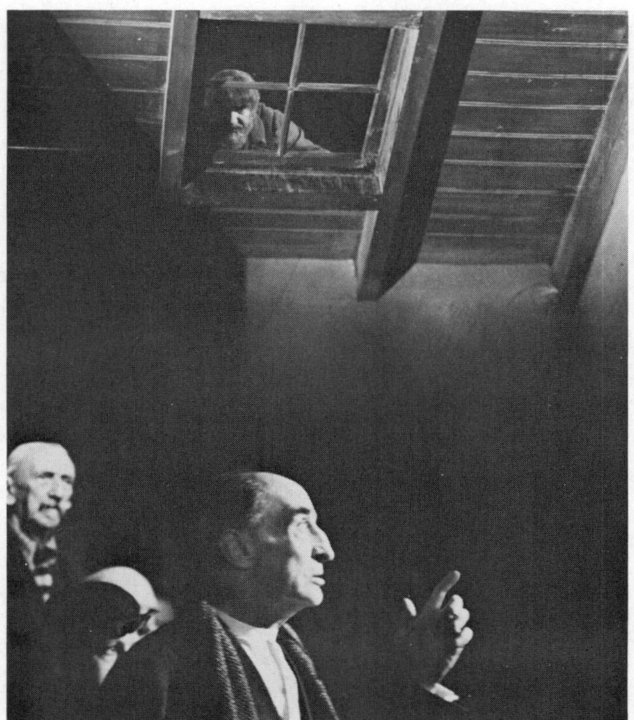

Bela Lugosi as Ygor in a scene cut from the release print of *The Ghost of Frankenstein*.

stein's maid Martha), Leyland Hodgson (as the Chief Constable), Olaf Hytten (as Cloestine's father), and Holmes Herbert (as the chief magistrate of Vasaria). Also in the film's opening, but unbilled, was Lawrence Grant who repeated his role of the Burgomaster from *Son of Frankenstein*, as well as Michael Mark and Lionel Belmore as the very jurors whom the Monster had killed in the previous film! A studio publicity release explained their presence: "Policy enters the scene through the custom of the studio of endeavoring to spot the same faces in each succeeding feature of the *Frankenstein* series."[153] Also cast in the opening sequence, where he raves, "Destroy the castle . . . We'll blow it up!," was poor, pale Dwight Frye, making his fourth appearance in the series. Frye was grateful for the day's work. Not long before, he had been reduced to playing in a stag film as a voyeur hiding in the bushes, watching a nudist colony volleyball game.

On Monday, December 15, 1941, shooting officially began on *The Ghost of Frankenstein*.

Boisterous, hard-drinking, bully-boy Lon Chaney, Jr., was a very complex man. Curt Siodmak, who wrote the screenplay for Chaney's *The Wolf Man* (as well as many exceptional horror films of the 1940s), came to know the actor—and his private tortures—very well over the many years they

The last player to receive feature billing was Universal's lovely 23-year-old starlet Evelyn Ankers. Born in Chile of British parents, she took her dramatic training in London. Signed by Universal after screaming so lusciously in the 1940 Broadway chiller *Ladies in Retirement*, Miss Ankers, fresh of *The Wolf Man*, was fated to become the studio's "Queen of the Horrors." A fine actress whose talents at the studio ran the gamut from slick comedy *(All by Myself)* to sleek villainy *(Weird Woman)*, Miss Ankers was never delighted by her reputation as the Fay Wray of the 1940s; she rapidly tired of adjusting her girdle between swoons and brushing greasepaint and yak hair off her oft-mauled body. "It was always nerve-wracking and a tremendous effort for me,"[151] remembers the lady today, having long retired to lush Maui, Hawaii, with actor husband Richard Denning (their 1942 marriage proving one of the movie colony's longest and happiest). Still, as she began playing Elsa Frankenstein, Miss Ankers sportingly told the publicity department, "I'd just as soon play in mysteries and horror films forever—as long as my scream holds out."[152]

Following a screen test with Chaney, four-year-old Janet Ann Gallow was signed to play little Cloestine. Also cast were Barton Yarborough (as the doomed Kettering), Doris Lloyd (as Franken-

Lon Chaney and Evelyn Ankers.

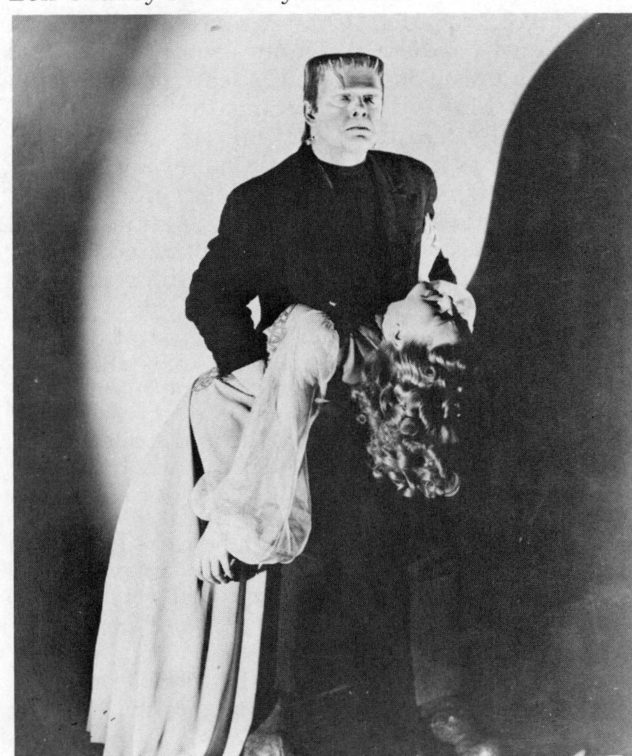

Ankers and Chaney appear to be discussing possible war strategy between scenes.

would work together. Chaney related to Siodmak stories of the sadism of Chaney senior, who would order his only son to fetch a leather strap, and then beat him with it, forcing the crying child (who usually had done nothing wrong) to count the whippings in a loud voice. Chaney could never escape the agony of such terrible memories of his illustrious father. Very graciously, Siodmak shared with me this insight into the complicated Chaney junior, from the screenwriter's autobiography:

> Alive or dead, his father dominated him to the end of his days, endangering his masculinity . . .
>
> The "macho" image which some male actors portray on the screen is often deceiving. Over six feet tall with a craggy face and a deep voice, Lon conveyed a strong virility. But I couldn't believe his love scenes and therefore never created an ardent one for him in the numerous pictures I wrote for him. Though he raised children and was married to an understanding wife, Lon was sexually confused . . . he could not adjust to a sexual preference he was unable to accept . . .[155]

Following Boris Karloff as the Monster was an awesome challenge for any actor. With Karloff's reputation at Universal almost saintly in its nature, all eyes were on Chaney, challenging him not only to match his father but also now to equal or surpass Karloff's performance and professionalism. The fact that Chaney failed is perhaps more a compliment to Karloff than an indictment of Chaney.

They cast me as the Frankenstein Monster. It took four hours to make me up. Then they led me to the set. They dug a hole in the cliff and put me in. They stuck a straw in my mouth and covered me up with cement. It took till twelve o'clock to get me sealed in. Then everybody went to lunch![154]

Lon Chaney, Jr.

Problems began in the makeup department. While Jack Pierce's favorite horror performer was Karloff ("He was a gentleman, always on time, and everything an actor should be,")[156] Chaney made a less favorable impression. Hot-tempered, impatient and a bit arrogant about his newly won

Jack Pierce prepares Chaney for the film's opening sequence.

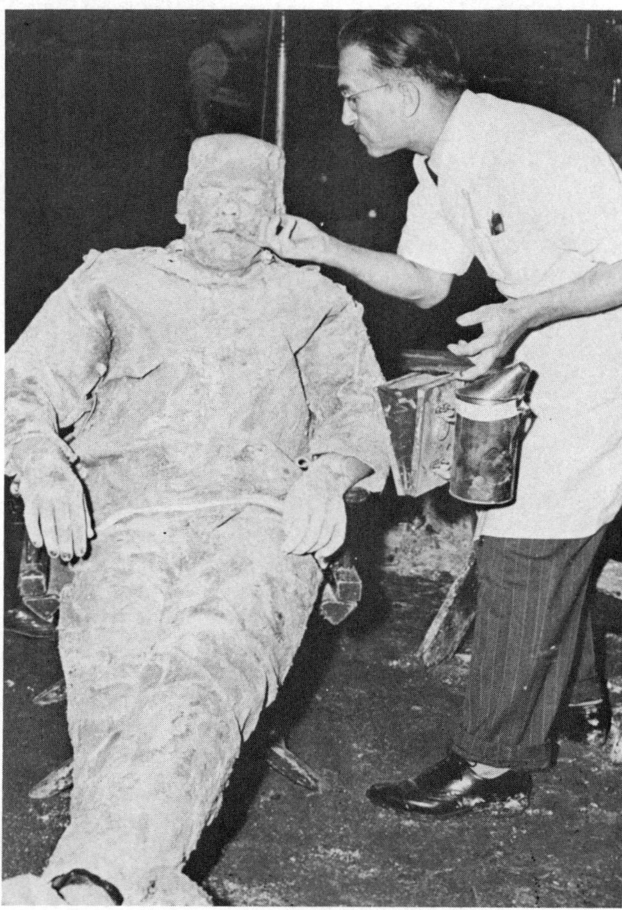

stardom, Chaney proved a trial to Pierce during some sessions. When Pierce was asked years later if he enjoyed working with Chaney, he laconically replied, "Yes and no. That's about all I can say."[157]

There was another problem: alcohol. Hard knocks had left an insatiable thirst in Chaney, and a directors' warning soon followed the actor through the Universal soundstages: "Be careful that you don't work too late with him, because in the afternoon he gets thirsty, and then he'll be difficult."[158] Hence, as *The Ghost* . . . began shooting, some studio employees caught sight of the Frankenstein Monster stepping outside the soundstage between scenes, enjoying a snort from the "flask" that Chaney faithfully toted.

Naturally, drinking and playing Monsters don't mix, and there was soon trouble. Jack Otterson, whose psychological sets for *Son of Frankenstein* were so successful, designed a bizarre maze of corridors leading to and from the laboratory of *The Ghost*. . . . So intricately constructed was the set that director Kenton had to film some scenes through a window, unable to see the actors in action. "Most of the shots through the window feature troupers like Sir Cedric Hardwicke, Lionel Atwill, Bela Lugosi and Ralph Bellamy," said Kenton. "Why should I worry about them?"[159] However, Kenton did have to worry about Chaney. Standing six-foot-nine and weighing 284 pounds in complete costume and makeup, Chaney had a difficult time maneuvering (especially after a few quaffs) and one afternoon became lost in the maze. Though never farther than 50 feet away from the camera and crew, who were shouting encouragement, Chaney took 10 minutes to find his way clear.

As if Chaney weren't having enough trouble, publicity-craving Universal soon exhumed a ghost from the past—Karloff's blue veil. "Since civilians' nerves are keyed-up as the result of blackout tests and other wartime activity," noted the studio, "Universal studio officials have reissued an order of years ago to prevent the Frankenstein Monster from appearing in public even within studio confines."[160] Chaney took the indignity with less humor than did Karloff.

The worst torment, however, was the rubber forehead piece which was snugly set against Chaney's own forehead and caused him intense aggravation. One long day, Chaney was especially upset by the discomfort and demanded that the piece be removed. It was an unfortunate case of "crying wolf." Chaney's complaints were nothing new, and Kenton and crew ignored him. Outraged, the angry actor tore the forehead piece off and ripped open a wound in his forehead, the blood running over his face. Chaney felt no pangs about taking a week off from the film following the awful accident.

Despite Chaney's incapacitation and the arrival of Christmas in the midst of production, Kenton briskly "wrapped" the shooting on Friday, January 15, 1942, just slightly beyond the 24-day shooting schedule. The filming proved great fun for cameraman Milton Krasner, who, using a one-inch wide-angle lens, photographed Chaney from ominous low angles to accentuate his size. *The Ghost* . . . also provided checks for some 300 extras, who gathered in the backlot village for the Monster and Ygor's arrival in Vasaria and waved torches in the climactic storming of the estate, as well as for ace movie double Eddie Parker, who substituted for Chaney in the fiery finale. Universal also mined footage of Colin Clive and Dwight Frye from *Frankenstein,* as well as some spectacular creation sequences and some Clive close-ups from *Bride of Frankenstein* used in flashback as Evelyn Ankers shivers over her "grandfather's" *Secrets of Life and Death.** And finally, Hans J. Salter created an exciting musical score complete with leitmotifs for the principal characters.

As with most Universal features of the era, *The Ghost of Frankenstein* was filmed with the accent of speed and potential profit. Ralph Bellamy would later remember how director Kenton, with a little hyperbole, set the tone of the production:

> . . . We finished a scene and Kenton said to Cedric Hardwicke and me, "We have to go down to the backlot for a staircase to shoot a silent shot. Why don't you sit here and relax?"

*In an especially fine piece of editing, footage of Clive and Frye uncovering the Monster in the laboratory of *Frankenstein* cuts to a pair of hands unwrapping the Monster's bandaged face—and revealing Chaney in the makeup.

Lugosi as Ygor.

So Cedric and I had a pleasant hour, two hours, and finally decided to go down to see how they were doing. There was a lot of hollering and running around, and the assistant director finally went to this little director and said "We're ready." He picked up the megaphone and almost bumped the assistant as he turned it around. He said, "Get Evelyn Ankers at the top of the stairway." He started to pace, back and forth, with the megaphone, and said, "Now Evelyn, you're all alone in this dim, dark, dank, dingy, ancient, oozing, slimey castle at four o'clock in the morning. Your mother's been carried off by the Frankenstein Monster, your father's been killed by the wolf man, the servants have fled, your lover is being chased across the moors by the dogs. I want to get the feeling from you, as you come down this stairway, that you're fed up with it all!"

Anytime Cedric and I saw each other anywhere in the world after that—and it was a lot of places—we'd say, "You fed up with it all?"[161]

As *The Ghost of Frankenstein* entered post-production, anxiety swept Universal: could the *Frankenstein* series survive without Karloff? The studio was determined to prove it would, saturating Chaney with publicity, and even issuing the trade papers a prepared review (just fill in the name of the theatre) which vowed that Hardwicke was "effectively cast," Bellamy "strong," Atwill played "with his customary finesse," Lugosi was "extremely menacing," Ankers was "both attractive and capable," and Chaney, as the Monster, ". . . defies critical analysis. Suffice it to comment that he is completely terrifying. . . ."[162] Universal previewed the picture for a press audience on February 27, 1942, set the official release date for March 13 (a Friday), 1942, and dispatched a promotional tour for the film—one that Evelyn Ankers remembers with embarrassment:

> . . . I found myself engaged in conversation with a charming, cultivated man, quiet-mannered and a little shy. We talked about Hollywood, motion pictures, and life in general, and before parting, the gentleman informed me that he had enjoyed working in the picture with me. I uttered a vague thank-you and only later learned that I had been talking to Bela Lugosi . . .[163]

The son of the "man with a thousand faces" is fast becoming known as the "man with a thousand talents."

Universal publicity for *The Ghost of Frankenstein.*

So complete had Lugosi's metamorphosis been to Ygor on the set that his own co-star had not recognized him!

Universal soon sighed in relief: the early reviews were good. Noted *The Hollywood Reporter:*

> Nothing will kill Frankenstein's Monster, which is, of course, to the monstrous delight of Universal . . . This latest is called *The Ghost of Frankenstein,* and inventively stands on an imaginative par with all of its interest-gripping, quasi-scientific predecessors . . . Erle C. Kenton's direction makes magnificent use of every element of suspense and Lon Chaney, having dropped the Jr., comes into his traditional own as the giant Monster. The cast is definitely above average . . . Hardwicke plays the third of the Frankenstein scientists and acquits himself with honor . . . Bela Lugosi is again a splendid Ygor . . . Jack P. Pierce duplicates everything he devised for the first Monster in making up Chaney in the image of Karloff. . . .[164]

Motion Picture Herald also enjoyed:

> The current installment in the continued adventures of the Frankenstein Monster maintains a standard of performance, effectiveness and quality exceeding the average for horror films by a considerable margin . . . Sir Cedric Hardwicke . . . gives the assignment his usual polished performance, while Lon Chaney as the

Monster achieves an equivalent distinction in point of terrifying uncouthness. . . .[165]

However, when *The Ghost of Frankenstein* opened April 3, 1942, at New York City's favorite horror house, the 1,750-seat Rialto, *The New York Times* critic Bosley Crowther was quick to sneer:

> Don't look now, gentle reader, but Frankenstein's Monster is loose again. . . . Gorgons, hydras and chimeras dire! Aren't there enough monsters loose in this world without that horrendous ruffian mauling and crushing actors? . . . the thought that he may yet return for further adventures with his body and Lugosi's sconce fills us with mortal terror. That is the most fearful prospect which the picture manages to convey.[166]

Various other critics were also patronizing toward *The Ghost . . .*; indeed, with America now in World War II, the Monster was upstaged by the horrible headlines hawked outside the theatres. Still, with a grab bag of exploitative gimmicks for exhibitors,* *The Ghost of Frankenstein* proved a hit—but as a *programmer,* not as a lavish fantasy venture. Clearly, Frankenstein's Monster was going downhill.

Action on the back lot. Note that an obvious dummy is "doubling" for little Janet Ann Gallow in this shot.

> . . . *The Ghost of Frankenstein* is probably the least appreciated of the entire series. Too often dismissed, because it isn't as good as the first three (and there's no denying that it isn't), and because it heralds the reduction of the series to programmer status . . . If *The Ghost* . . . is already an assembly line job, it's a good, thoroughly professional and highly entertaining one. . . .[167]
>
> William K. Everson, *Classics of the Horror Film.*

Most horrorphiles divide the Universal Frankenstein series into two unequal halves: the first three with Karloff as the Monster, and the succeeding five with his successors. As such, *The Ghost of Frankenstein* has been widely branded as the harbinger of the decline of the saga. It's unfortunate, and not really fair, for there is much in the film that is grand fun—but the assets cannot cancel out the deficits that pockmark the film's reputation.

The film's first flaw is Chaney's Monster. Perhaps wisely, Chaney chose in following Karloff to eschew the Englishman's powerfully emotional style, and to underplay the part, hence creating a nice contrast to the superhuman strength he so potently displays. This is especially effective in his rampage through Frankenstein's estate, as he pounds down the door, murders Yarborough and grabs Evelyn Ankers before succumbing to the gas. The Chaney Monster is an awesome beast, but nothing more than that; he makes no real impact on the audience other than passing thrills. While Karloff's face displayed a repertoire of emotions, Chaney is stone-faced; while Karloff roared in terror or laughed in wonder, Chaney is strangely, totally mute (until the climax when it is, of course, Lugosi's dubbed voice that sounds from his lips). Even in the specially contrived scenes with little Janet Ann Gallow, Chaney fails to sustain any real sympathy or depth, and their tandem scenes only remind one of Karloff's tender joy with Little Maria in *Frankenstein.* Truly it is unfair to gauge Chaney's performance by Kar-

*Universal did all it could to hatch money-making ideas in exhibitor's minds for promoting all studio products, and the horror films were a specialty. On *The Ghost of Frankenstein,* suggestions included hiring a local rooftop to erect a "monster," with a sheet for a body and a head cut out from a 24-foot poster of the film; a "Find the Ghost," contest, in which a theater employee would dress up like the Monster ("it is suggested you soften down the Monster's makeup so that it is not too frightful or scarey for women and children," warned the pressbook), with local radio commercials cackling, "The Ghost of Frankenstein will prowl the West End section of the city tonite and clutches in his awful hand ten one-dollar bills and twenty free passes to give to those with nerve enough to find him . . ."; offering a Defense Bond and several books of Defense Stamps for the best essay answering the question, "Will the Nazi Frankenstein Monster Follow the Famous Legend and Destroy Its Makers!"; and others.

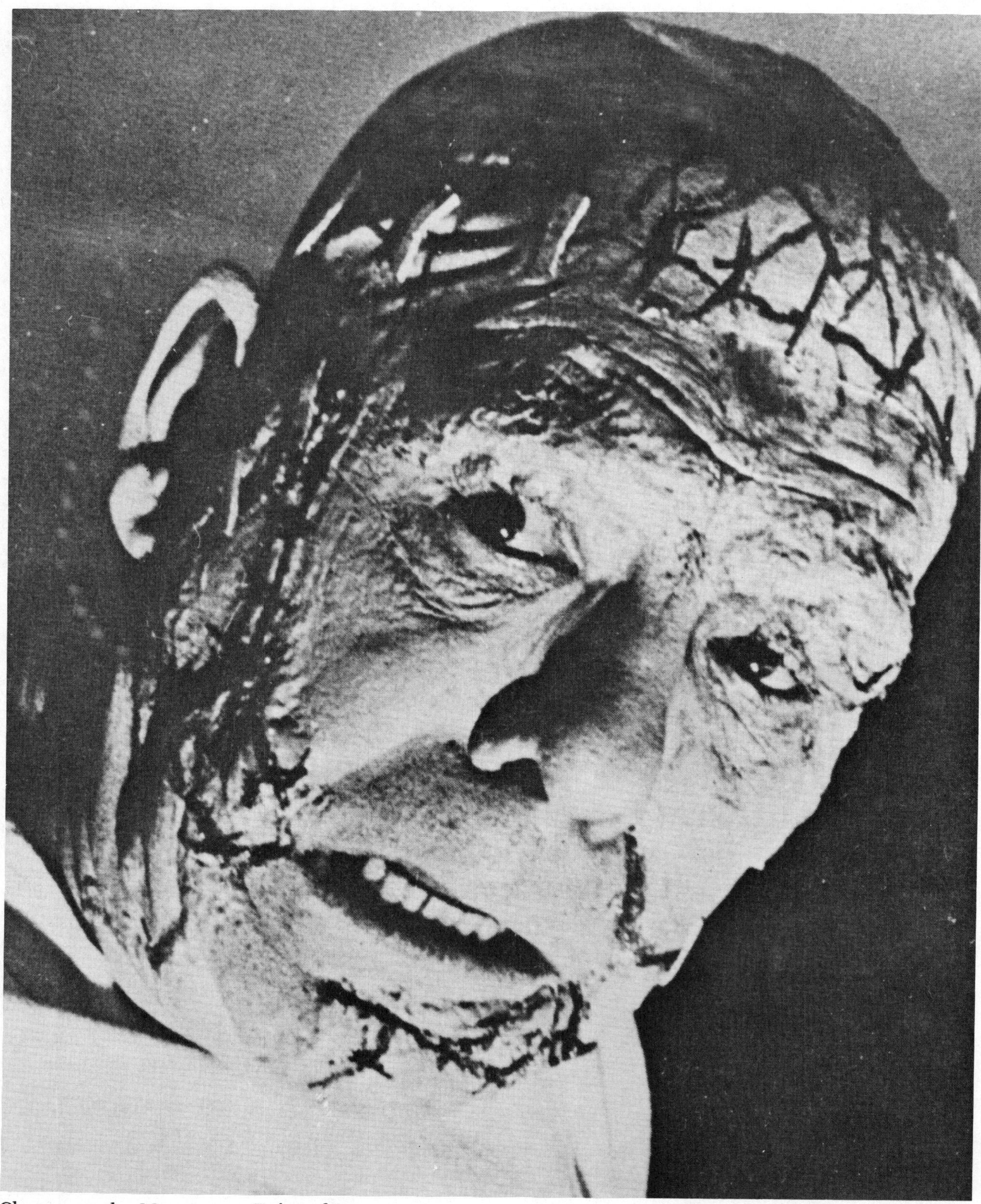

Chaney as the Monster on *Tales of Tomorrow*.

loff's guidelines, but it is also inevitable. As posterity has proven, Karloff's shadow loomed over all those actors who replaced him as the Monster, eclipsing their efforts.

The other major fault in *The Ghost . . .* is the climactic idea of the brain transplant. While the popping of Ygor's brain into the Monster's body did present a crowd-pleasing chill, it was not a fresh idea (Universal's *Black Friday* of 1940 already had covered that gimmick), and ludicrous in execution (if Ygor's mind was in the Monster's super carcass, why did the creature still speak as if its neck was broken?). Technically, the finale presented confusion regarding any sequels: would they be the adventures of the Monster, or Ygor? While Universal opted for the latter view that this brain-switching only made the Monster more evil without changing his identity, the Monster would conversely appear less evil, less crafty and progressively moronic.

Nevertheless, if one doesn't want to probe into the plot and can ignore Karloff's conception of the Monster, *The Ghost of Frankenstein* is top quality escapism, a swift-paced panorama of the slick film factory that was Universal in the war years. The film is puffed with little spectacles—the opening with its dynamiting of the castle, the grand sequence in which the Monster is struck by lightning in the stormy graveyard and the fiery climax. The old backlot village looks especially picturesque (a delightful touch is the gaggle of geese that squawk in terror as the Monster and Ygor enter Vasaria), and the Jack Otterson sets, while not "grand" like those of *Son . . .*, are claustrophobically effective. The low angle camerawork serves splendidly, and Hans J. Salter's truly exciting score proved such an asset that other studios would pirate Universal horror films he scored and run them for their contract composers as examples of what they wanted to achieve in their horror films.

However, the best feature of *The Ghost of Frankenstein* is its marvelous cast. Hardwicke's masterful aplomb sets a tone of respectability for the film; he is also excellent in his brief apparition as the title spectre. Bellamy, too, lends earnestness and sincerity to the melodramatics, while Atwill, as ever, is a wicked delight, especially grand as he beams with joy as his rival Hardwicke realizes that Ygor's brain is in the Monster's skull. No cinema villain ever smiled quite so obscenely! As for Miss Ankers, she is lovely, unleashing two soulful screams and delivering painful lines such as "Father . . . It's as if a great cloud has come over you" with graceful elan.

Top acting honors, however, go to Bela Lugosi for his old Ygor. When he leers his "cruel smile" at Miss Ankers on the staircase, he presents a truly frightening madman; when he fidgets over Yarborough's body and pulls the Monster away ("Come, no one will know who did it"), he suggests a guilty schoolboy; and when he offers his brain to the Monster ("Tonight, Ygor will die for you"), he transcends the penny dreadful plot and hoke to reveal a truly twisted and fascinating character. Lugosi's wonderful performance carries *The Ghost of Frankenstein*, and causes one to wonder just what kind of marvelous actor Bela Lugosi was on Hungary's classical stage before Hollywood largely reduced him to an oily vehicle.

While *The Ghost of Frankenstein* did not, as Universal and Chaney hoped, advance the new horror star's popularity, it did sustain it nicely. Frankenstein's Monster, however, would prove an unhappy memory for Chaney—for more reasons than his 1942 performance. In 1952 Chaney played the Monster, with bald dome and scars (due to Universal's copyright of the makeup) on television's *Tales of Tomorrow*. Prior to the live telecast, Chaney became inebriated, got confused and played the televised performance believing it was the final dress rehearsal. As the director and crew battled hysteria, Chaney cursed under his breath and gingerly picked up and put down the breakaway props which were supposed to crumble in his mighty grasp. Chaney was mortified to learn of his *faux pas*, and the abashed actor later claimed it took him several weeks to recover emotionally from this debacle.

If Frankenstein's Monster craved rest, Universal Studios refused to give it to him. As proven by the reception afforded *The Ghost of Frankenstein*, the Monster, while no longer a phenomenon, was still a revenue winner potently aiding Universal on its way to a $3 million 1942 profit. Several resurrections and indignities loomed before the studio's soulless Monster would be allowed to return to ashes.

A re-release advertisement for *Frankenstein Meets the Wolf Man*.

Frankenstein Meets the Wolf Man (1943)

Producer, George Waggner; *Director,* Roy William Neill; *Original Screenplay,* Curtis Siodmak; *Director of Photography,* George Robinson; *Art Director,* John B. Goodman (*Associate,* Martin Obzina); *Director of Sound,* Bernard B. Brown (*Technician,* William Fox); *Set Decorations,* Russell A. Gausman (*Associate,* E.R. Robinson); *Film Editor,* Edward Curtiss; *Gowns,* Vera West; *Musical Director,* Hans J. Salter; *Assistant Director,* Melville Shyer; *Special Photographic Effects,* John P. Fulton; *Makeup Artist,* Jack P. Pierce.

Filmed at Universal City, California, October 12–November 11, 1942; opened at the Rialto Theatre, New York City, March 5, 1943. Running time: 74 minutes.

FRANKENSTEIN MEETS THE WOLF MAN—SYNOPSIS

It is midnight in the old, windswept cemetery of Llanwelly Village in Wales. Moonlight shrouds the headstones as two grave robbers pry their way into the mausoleum of the Talbot family, once the countryside's most wealthy and celebrated natives. A marker at the base of a coffin directs the grave molestors to the corpse they seek:

LAWRENCE STEWART TALBOT
Who Died at the Youthful Age of 31
R.I.P.

Heeding the town rumors that young Talbot was buried with money in his pockets, they open the casket and find the cadaver covered with wolfbane. They shiver as they recall the old Balkan legend:

"Even a man who is pure at heart,
and says his prayers by night,
may become a wolf when the wolfbane blooms,
and the moon is full and bright."

Meanwhile, the rays of the full moon shine on Talbot's body—and a hand rises from the casket.

Shortly before dawn, a policeman finds a young man sprawled in a Cardiff street, many miles from Llanwelly. He appears to have a severe skull fracture,* and is taken to Queen's Hospital, where the young, brilliant scientist/surgeon Dr. Frank Mannering operates to save his life. To Mannering's amazement, the patient is sitting up in bed and speaking only hours later. He informs Dr. Mannering and blustering Inspector Owen that he is Lawrence Talbot of Llanwelly Village. The Inspector calls Llanwelly Police Station to inform them of Talbot's accident, stating, "We've got him up here in our hospital."

"I wouldn't want him in *our* hospital," replies the Sergeant. "He died four years ago!"

That night the moon is full again, and in the morning, a few streets from Queen's Hospital, a Constable is found viciously slaughtered as if by some sort of wild animal.

Meanwhile, the nurse who checks on Talbot that morning finds the windows open and a disheveled Talbot sprawled on his bed. Mannering rushes to his patient, and Talbot demands he call the police, claiming he has murdered the Constable. Talbot shows Mannering and the Inspector a wound on his breast: "See that scar? That's where I was bitten by a wolf. Only it wasn't a real wolf—it was a man—a werewolf. I killed him. Now, I turn into a wolf when the moon is full. . . . Won't you believe me? Help me!"

*In the 1941 film of *The Wolf Man,* Talbot was "killed" when his father, Sir John Talbot, dealt a mortal blow to his son's head with a silver-headed cane. According to the script of *Frankenstein Meets the Wolf Man,* Sir John Talbot "died of grief" shortly after his son's demise and was laid to rest in the same crypt that was fouled by the grave robbers.

The Players

Baroness Elsa Frankenstein	Ilona Massey
Dr. Frank Mannering	Patric Knowles
The Mayor	Lionel Atwill
The Monster	Bela Lugosi
Maleva	Maria Ouspenskaya
Inspector Owen	Dennis Hoey
Franzec	Don Barclay
Vazec	Rex Evans
Rudi	Dwight Frye
Guno	Harry Stubbs
and	
Lawrence Talbot, the Wolf Man	Lon Chaney
with	
The Festival Singer	Adia Kuznetzoff
Erno	Torben Meyer
The Constable	Charles Irwin
The Nurse	Doris Lloyd
The Grave Robbers	Tom Stevenson
	Cyril Delevanti
The Sergeant	David Clyde
Grave Digger	Jeff Corey
Rudi's Wife	Beatrice Roberts
Village Girl	Martha MacVicar*
Double for Lugosi	Eddie Parker

* Later Martha Vickers.

Dr. Mannering thinks Talbot is suffering from a delusion; the Inspector suspects he is an imposter, hiding behind a dead man's name. However, before the hospital orderlies can wrestle Talbot into a straightjacket, he roars, "You think I'm insane? . . . Well, you just look inside of that grave where Lawrence Talbot is supposed to be buried, and see if you find a body in it!"

Lon Chaney, Maria Ouspenskaya, and Rex Evans.

The Doctor and Inspector visit the crypt. There is *no* body in Talbot's casket. And that evening, Talbot escapes from Queen's Hospital—after tearing the straightjacket to shreds with his teeth.

Fleeing to Europe, Talbot seeks Maleva, the old gypsy woman and mother of Bela, the werewolf whom Talbot had killed. Finally locating her in a gypsy camp, he pleads for her help. "It's not in my power to help you," she quaveringly replies, "but I will guide you, and take care of you, as I took care of my own son. I know a man who has the power to help you." Together, Maleva and Talbot depart for Vasaria and the sanitarium of Dr. Ludwig von Frankenstein.

Early one night the wanderers finally reach Vasaria and inquire in the village inn for directions to Frankenstein's estate. The innkeeper, Vazec, points out a pile of ruins perched atop a mountain above the village: "There—that's his burial place! The fire destroyed him and all his misdeeds. He harbored a Monster, a thing created by black magic!" Shortly after Vazec evicts the "beggars" from his inn, the full moon rises. The young serving girl of the inn is found murdered, her jugular vein severed.

As Vazec carries the girl's body home, the villagers swarm behind him. "Could it be the Monster again—Frankenstein's Monster?" asks Rudi.

Chaney with Ilona Massey.

"An *animal* bit her to death!" cries another. Just then the howl of a wolf is heard from near the Frankenstein ruins, and the townspeople charge up the hill to kill the beast. Running from the mob, with its howling dogs and guns, the Wolf Man crashes through the ruins of the Frankenstein estate and tumbles into a deep cavern coated with thick, glistening ice. Unable to escape, he loses consciousness. The townspeople content themselves with arresting Maleva and marching her back to the village.

The next morning, a transformed Talbot awakes in the cavern. As he tries to escape, he perceives what appears to be a body suspended in the ice. He breaks the ice away and is soon staring at the rectangular skull, bolted neck and flaring nostrils of the living Frankenstein Monster. Freeing the Monster from his prison, they search together for the records of Dr. Frankenstein. All they find, however, is a portrait of a beautiful blond young woman, inscribed, "To my dear Father." "So she's the one who can help me," sighs Talbot.

Determined to locate the records, Talbot, calling himself Lawrence Taylor, asks Vasaria's plump, pleasant Mayor to give him Elsa Frankenstein's address, claiming he wishes to buy her ruined estate. The mayor refuses to divulge her whereabouts—Elsa has left Vasaria—but he does arrange a meeting between the two in his office. There Talbot reveals his true desire, to which Elsa replies: "I don't have any records! If I had, I would have destroyed them long ago. The house burned down, and I have never set a foot on that ground again and never shall." Before they leave, the mayor asks Elsa and Talbot to be his guests that night at Vasaria's Festival of the New Wine.

Talbot and Elsa sit together at the Festival in the town square, where the villagers joyously accompany the Festival Singer in a boisterous folk song:

> Come one and all and sing a song, Faro-La, Faro-Li!
> For Life is short but Death is long, Faro-La, Faro-Li!

The singer leads his chorus to Elsa's and Talbot's table, where his next chorus incenses Talbot:

> To them I toast, come drink with me,
> That they may ever happy be,
> And may they live eternally . . .!

Talbot explodes. "Stop it! I don't want to live eternally!" As the villagers draw back in terror, Talbot recognizes a familiar face in the crowd—Dr. Frank Mannering.

Mannering informs Talbot that he has been seeking him ever since his escape from Queen's Hospital. Newspaper accounts of horrible murders led Mannering to Vasaria, and after the mayor escorts Elsa away for a spirited dance, Mannering insists Talbot return to England with him: "Talbot, you're a murderer. You're insane at times and you know it. Why don't you let me take care of you? Perhaps we could cure you!" Talbot refuses.

Chaney, and Lugosi as the Monster.

Lionel Atwill, Ilona Massey, Patric Knowles, Maria Ouspenskaya, Dwight Frye, Harry Stubbs, and players.

"I only want to die. . . . Dr. Frankenstein left a diary. In it are his records of the Secrets of Life and Death. If I could find this diary, I could break this curse and find peace in death." Vazec has been eavesdropping on this morbid conversation, but before he can do anything, the screams of Rudi and his wife shatter the gaiety: "It's the Monster! The Monster!"

The townspeople scream in fright as the Monster stalks through the square. Talbot races to the Monster's side and helps the creature into the back of a carriage filled with wine barrels. As the village men rally and charge the carriage, Talbot whips the horses, racing through the square and toward the castle ruins as the Monster kicks wine barrels into the path of his pursuers. They escape.

Vazec is soon exhorting the villagers into a frenzied mob, calling for the arrest of Elsa, as well as Mannering. However, both the mayor and Mannering succeed in calming the townspeople, and the doctor vows, "I promise you, if you'll help me I'll rid Vasaria of this curse once and for all."

The next morning Mannering, Elsa and the released Maleva climb up to the ruins. They say they'll aid Talbot, and Elsa reveals that she *does* know where her father kept *The Secrets of Life and Death*. The fascinated Mannering reads the words of the tragic Dr. Frankenstein:

> . . . This, my creation, can never perish unless its energies are drained off artificially—by changing the poles from plus to minus. . . .

Mannering immediately begins repairing Frankenstein's electrical equipment, promising to drain the energies away from both the Monster and Talbot.

Meanwhile, in the village, Vazec is still raving about the dangers of leaving the little band in the ruins alone. "Blow up the dam above the castle, and they'd all drown like rats—all of them!" he urges. "You're drunk, Vazec," replies the mayor, who does not take the intoxicated man seriously, otherwise he says, "I'd order you arrested for con-

Massey, Knowles, Chaney, and Lugosi.

spiring to endanger the lives of this community!"

As the days pass, Mannering grows fascinated with the prospect of returning the ailing Monster to his full power. Elsa recognizes this, and pleads with him: "Listen to me, Frank. I saw my father become obsessed by his power. He died a horrible death, just as my grandfather did. It is in your hands to undo the crimes my father and grandfather committed. We must clear the name of Frankenstein!" Mannering agrees to heed her words.

That night Mannering places both Talbot and the Monster on operating tables and prepares to drain away their lives—"I hope I bring peace to both of them." However, his scientific curiosity proves too much for his resolves, and he gasps, "I can't destroy Frankenstein's Creation! I've got to see it at its full power!" The whirring and buzzing of the electrical equipment awakens Elsa, who rushes in her nightgown to the laboratory. She stares in horror as the Monster, bolstered with artificial energy, opens his eyes and grins a wicked smile of gratitude at the awestruck Mannering. "Frank! You're making him strong again!" she cries as she lunges for a switch to stop the blasphemy. Before Mannering can stop her, Elsa pulls the switch and the machinery explodes. But the Monster escapes his bonds on the operating table and stalks toward Elsa! Mannering is beaten back when he tries to save her. Meanwhile, the moon has risen . . .

As the Monster walks off with Elsa in his arms, the Wolf Man leaps upon him. Frankenstein's creation tumbles, dropping his lovely load, and as Elsa and Mannering escape, the two horrors viciously battle, the werewolf leaping and clawing at his electroded foe, the Monster tossing about his hirsute opponent. Meanwhile, above the ruins, Vazec is scuttling across the dam, planting dynamite. The old dam explodes, and cascades of water sweep down the mountain, crashing into the ruins and sweeping the still-battling monsters to their (presumably) ultimate demise.

FRANKENSTEIN MEETS THE WOLF MAN—PRODUCTION HISTORY

> Even a man who is pure in heart,
> and says his prayers by night,
> may become a wolf when the wolfbane blooms,
> and the autumn moon is bright. . . .
>
> Curt Siodmak's famous poem from
> *The Wolf Man* (1941)

In the wake of Frankenstein, Boris Karloff, via *The Old Dark House* and *The Mummy,* was a sensation; in the wake of *The Wolf Man,* Lon Chaney, via *The Ghost of Frankenstein* and *The Mummy's Tomb,* was not. A popular star whose chiller features proved to be nice draws in the exploitation houses, Chaney failed to become a *top* attraction and soon was battling with the front office. He incessantly waged war to prevent the studio from billing him simply as "Lon Chaney," a war he would lose. He hated playing the crumbling Kharis of the *Mummy* series, arguing during the shooting of *The Mummy's Tomb* that the rubber mask gave him an allergy; and, despite the fact that grotesques like Lennie and Larry Talbot had won him stardom, Chaney claimed he was fed up with horror parts. "When I got my break in pictures, in *Of Mice and Men,* I was Lennie, the imbecile," Chaney groaned to the studio publicists. "Now,

Lugosi, and Chaney as the Wolf Man.

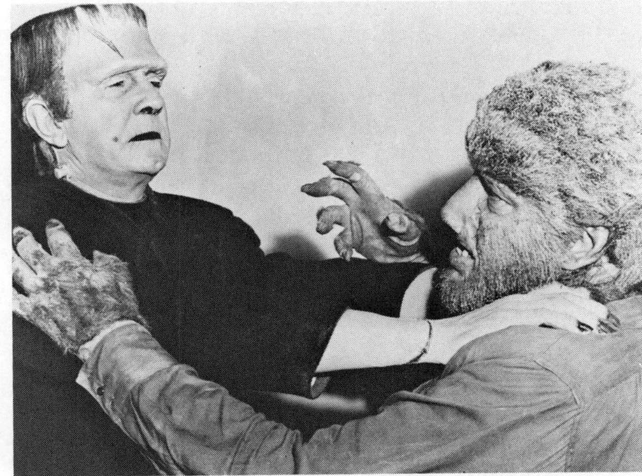

I'm typed as an ideal horror man. I scare women and children and give the men shudders."[168] In the opinion of the six-foot-two, 220-pound actor, his proper *metier* was the Charles Boyer type of role.

Universal paid no heed to Chaney's demands and remained determined to get their money's worth out of the "Master Character Creator." When none of Chaney's follow-ups to *The Wolf Man* won him the reception that his werewolf enjoyed, the studio decided a resurrection of Lawrence Talbot was in order. And soon, while lunching with George Waggner in the Universal commissary, screenwriter Curt Siodmak joked . . .

Universal was always on the verge of collapsing. And the studio was kept alive, actually, by the horror films—notably the Frankensteins. They would have been broke without those pictures![169]

Curt (aka Curtis, Kurt) Siodmak

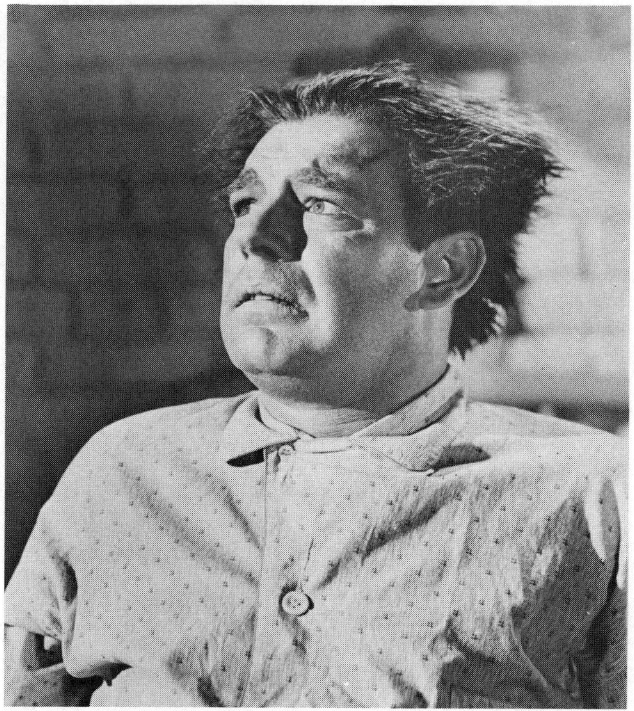

Lon Chaney, as Lawrence Talbot, beholds the moonlight . . .

By 1942, Teutonic Curt Siodmak had become the top fantasist among Hollywood screenwriters. After success with UFA in Germany (where he wrote the 1933 science fiction classic *F.P.1 Antwortet Nicht*) and Gaumont-British in England (1935's *Transatlantic Tunnel*), he brought his wife to Hollywood in 1937, where he was soon creating such scripts for Universal as *The Invisible Man Returns* (with Vincent Price, 1940), *Black Friday* (Karloff and Lugosi, 1940), *The Invisible Woman* (John Barrymore and Virginia Bruce, 1941), and climactically, *The Wolf Man*. As Siodmak himself explains his international survival as a writer:

> Story construction—that's why I got paid in every damn country. I could construct a story out of the blue sky. Most writers are dialogue writers, and they produce very worthy dialogue, but there are really very few constructionists who started from scratch. That's why I got jobs.[170]

Siodmak would never sign a contract with Universal; Universal, in turn, would never boost Siodmak's salary of $400 per week, even after the bonanza of *The Wolf Man*. "Cliff Work, the studio boss, always said I could go anywhere else in town," says Siodmak, "and get the money I wanted after working on Universal pictures. Ha!" Still Siodmak was very much in demand at the studio, and told me, with his still heavy German accent, of the evolution of *Frankenstein Meets the Wolf Man:*

> My producer at Universal was George Waggner. He was very nice, and he made lots of money for Universal. He was very German in his tastes, and his fun was to drink beer and sing songs—a typical German-American.
>
> Well, I went to his office once a week, and gave him all the honey I could think of, telling him what a great man he was. I thought, "One day he must find out that I'm kidding!" He never found out, of course. He *never* found out. Anyway, with *Frankenstein Meets the Wolf Man*, what really happened was this: I was sitting in the Universal commissary, and George Waggner came by, and we had lunch together. And I made a joke. I said, "George, why don't you make a picture, *Frankenstein Wolfs the Meat Man*—er, I mean, *Frankenstein Meets the Wolf Man*?" He didn't laugh.
>
> So, it was during the war, and I wanted to buy an automobile, and I wanted to get a new assignment so I could afford it. George would talk to me every day, and say, "Did you get the car?" And I'd say, "No! What's my new job?" And George would say, "Never mind, get the car."
>
> Well, one day I had to pay to get the car. George said, "Did you buy it?" and I said "Yes, I bought it." George said, "Okay! Your job is *Frankenstein Wolfs the Meat Man*, er, I mean *Frankenstein Meets the Wolf Man*. I give you two hours to accept!"

With car payments to make, Siodmak accepted. Soon, he had developed a clever slant for the film:

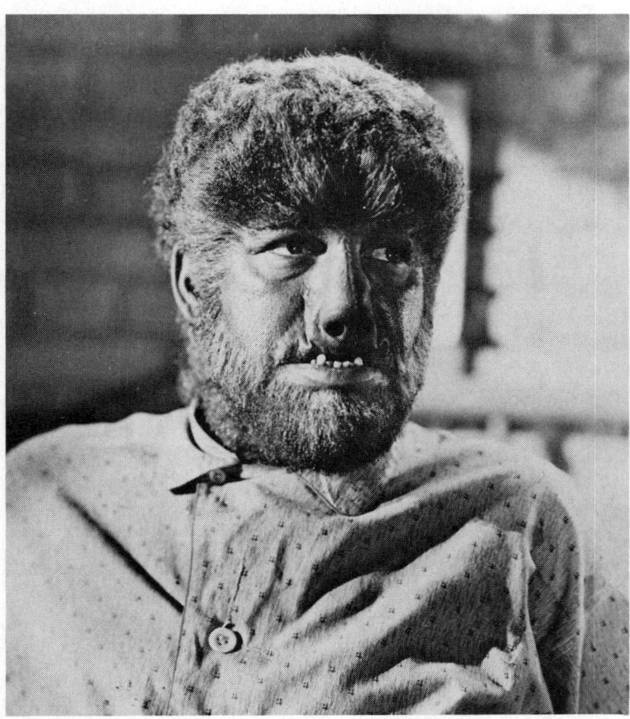

. . . and becomes the Wolf Man.

> It was a very interesting idea. The Wolf Man wants to *die,* because he does not want to commit murder. And he meets the Frankenstein Monster, and the Monster wants to *live.* So they want to find Dr. Frankenstein's secrets of Life and Death.

Still, Siodmak could not be totally serious about forming a rendezvous with Universal's two most popular nightmares:

> I wrote a funny thing in there . . . the Wolf Man was talking with the Monster, and he says, "I change into a wolf at night." And the Monster says, "Are you kidding?"
>
> George Waggner found those lines when he read the script and took them out!

Lon Chaney Jr. plays a double header as both Monsters in *The Wolf Man Meets Frankenstein,* which goes to bat at Universal this week. . . .

Variety, October 14, 1942

The original title of the final shooting script was *The Wolf Man Meets Frankenstein* and rightfully so, because Siodmak had devoted far more attention to the lycanthrope's character than to the Monster's. Producer Waggner recruited Roy William Neill, then very busy at Universal as the director of the Rathbone/Bruce *Sherlock Holmes* series, to direct the shocker, and outlined with Neill a plan: Lon Chaney would play *both* the Wolf Man and the Monster! The employment of stunt men and doubles, claimed Waggner, would create the proper illusion, and Chaney could enjoy an avalanche of publicity. However, the cost and trouble of such a procedure (as well as Chaney's erratic reputation) caused the producer to scrap the dual role idea at the last minute, and Waggner was content to cast Chaney as the Wolf Man. Surprisingly, Chaney recognized Frankenstein's creation as the top horror of Universal's repertoire, and he initially griped that he wanted the Monster role. A perusal of the Siodmak script, in which the Wolf Man dominated, changed his mind, as did his affection for the lycanthropic Talbot. As Chaney would crow of his Wolf Man, "He was my baby!"

So what of the Monster? The two most logical candidates were Boris Karloff and Bela Lugosi. Siodmak knew them both:

> I knew Karloff very well. He came to my house quite often. He lisped in life—it was funny—and he had a very dark complexion. I don't know what kind of country background he originally had. . . . He was very, very nice—very soft-spoken, and he loved to read children's stories to little boys and girls.

Besides having vowed never to play the Monster again, Karloff was unavailable, having begun his road tour in *Arsenic and Old Lace.* This left Bela Lugosi. Says Siodmak:

> Bela! I met Bela, of course, but he was a pest. He always called me and said "Curt! Can you get me zat part? Huh? I want to play zat part!" When I met him, he was very unrealistic. He could never act his way out of a paper bag! He had those Hungarian movements. He had created one character—Dracula—and the character had stuck.

Despite Lugosi's magnificent performance as Ygor in *Son of . . .* and in *The Ghost of Frankenstein,* there were important men at Universal who shared Siodmak's opinion of Lugosi's talent. One only had to see Lugosi's unfortunate casting in such Universal horror films as the caretaker in 1941's *The Black Cat,* the cameo as the gypsy of *The Wolf Man,* and a butler in *Night Monster* to trace his decline in his producers' eyes. Still, Lugosi did seem the logical choice. Since the closing of *The Ghost of Frankenstein* found the brain of Bela's evil old Ygor popped into the Monster's skull, it appeared fitting that the Hungarian undertake the part. Anyway, Lugosi owed Universal

Bela Lugosi as the (originally) blind and speaking Monster. *The Ghost of Frankenstein* carefully prepared audiences for a Hungarian-accented Monster, *Frankenstein Meets the Wolf Man* did not.

a film on his contract. However, as Bela had never tired of informing the press, it was he who had turned down the Monster role in 1931, outraged by the prospect of playing a mute "scarecrow." Would he be willing to play the part now?

At this point in his career, Bela Lugosi was willing to play almost anything. As Siodmak relates:

> Lugosi was glad to get a job again. He was really hard-up. He was already under financial pressure in those days, and there were really few jobs about for him. Karloff did much more.

Lugosi's 4th wife, Lillian, admitted to me that Siodmak's sentiments are true:

> Isn't it crazy? After turning down the original, Bela winds up doing it anyhow—*The Monster Meets the Wolf Man,* or something? He finally did it because of MONEY. He didn't do it any other way![171]

Bela humbly signed on—but with some solace. Perusing the script, he saw that the part of the Monster might be more challenging than he thought. In Siodmak's original, the Monster was blind (as he had been in the climax of *The Ghost . . .*), and spoke! Hence, the proud actor could accept the part with his original objections honored and speak the dialogue in a sinister variation on his Ygor voice.

Ironically, top-billing was awarded neither Monster. That honor was afforded Ilona Massey, blonde Hungarian soprano with a true beauty mark, who played Elsa von Frankenstein (the part acted in *The Ghost of Frankenstein* by Evelyn Ankers). It had been a sad cinema topple for the lovely Ilona, who had arrived in Hollywood in 1937 as the pampered protégée of no less than Louis B. Mayer. During one of his extravagant European talent-seeking junkets, the movie potentate had met Ilona at the Hotel Imperial of Carlsbad, where she enchanted the mogul with her bountiful blonde perfection and lovely voice (then showcased in the Vienna State Opera's production of *Aida*). Ilona's conquest was complete after a merry evening of wine and dance. While the pair danced a passionate rhumba, Ilona's gown just happened to snap at the shoulder, providing "L.B." an eyeful as the lady shrewdly blushed in charming embarrassment before rushing away to make repairs. An MGM contract was signed very shortly thereafter.

Ilona Massey and Bela Lugosi.

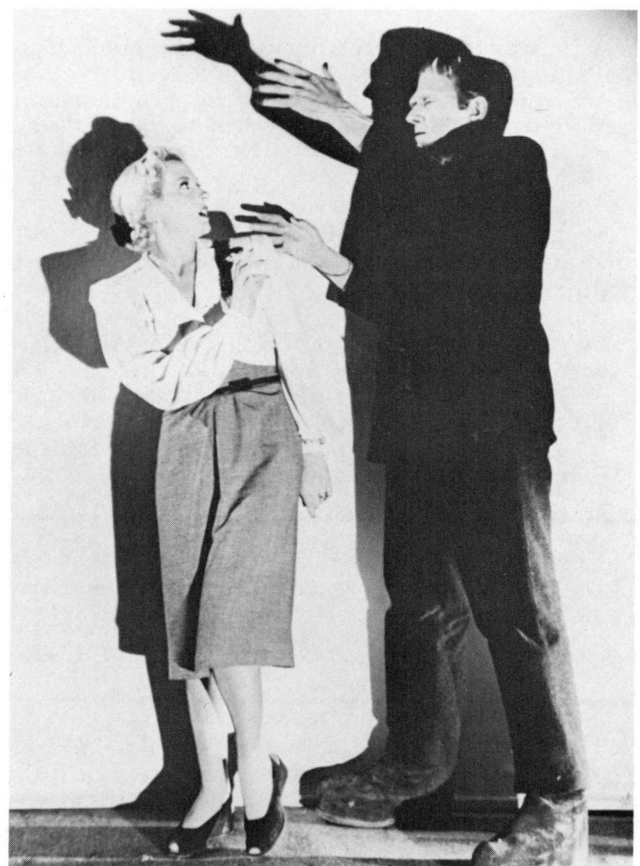

Back at Culver City, Metro spent as much as $300 a day supplying "The Singing Garbo" with English lessons and vocal training. She scored a great success in 1937's *Rosalie,* the outlandish musical classic with Nelson Eddy and Eleanor Powell. Then for two years Ilona did nothing but collect her weekly studio paycheck and serve as a front office threat to another Mayer "pet," Jeanette MacDonald. She left MGM after 1939's *Balalaika* (again with Eddy); as her star rapidly dimmed, she signed a two-picture pact with Universal. It wasn't a happy stay. She despised playing in 1942's *Invisible Agent,* in which she stooged for Jon Hall's Invisible One; she was especially aghast at John Fulton's special effect of dangling her in midair (supposedly hoisted by Hall) by stringing wires to her corset. Miss Massey was much happier with *Frankenstein Meets the Wolf Man.* "Personally, I love horror films," said the singer late in her life. "And that's why I did this one. I thought it would be wonderful to do a horror film. I really enjoyed it."[172]

Chaney and Lugosi did not even get second billing in what the publicity department was heralding as "The Battle of the Century!" Immediately following Ilona in the cast list was Patric Knowles, formerly of Warner Bros. where he played his most famous part (Will Scarlet of 1938's *The Adventures of Robin Hood)* opposite his close crony Errol Flynn. Having become an all-purpose leading man at Universal (where, incidentally, he had played Evelyn Ankers' fiancé in *The Wolf Man*), Knowles was well-cast as Dr. Frank Mannering, being a fine enough actor to sound sincere when he cries, "I can't destroy Frankenstein's creation! I've got to see it at its full power!" and handsome enough to give Ilona somebody to cling to in the final reel.

Universal appeased Chaney with special "and" billing in the credits, but Bela had to settle for billing in the opening credits* below yet another actor—Lionel Atwill. The portly "Pinky," having just provided Basil Rathbone with a marvelous toad of a Moriarty in *Sherlock Holmes and the Secret Weapon,* was cast as the jolly Mayor of Vasaria. Atwill was grateful for the role, as he had been through some humiliating courtroom adventures regarding his Yuletide orgy that provided a horror show of their own. After perjuring himself *twice* before the Los Angeles County Grand Jury, Atwill finally confessed in Fall 1942 that he did indeed host such a frolic. On October 15, 1942, three days after *Frankenstein Meets the Wolf Man* began shooting, Atwill was sentenced to five years probation for his perjury, and the shocked Hays office issued a mandate to Hollywood studios *not* to hire the profligate. While rumor circulated that Universal would fire Atwill after his sentencing, he remained on the picture. "But for the courage and magnanimity of one particular studio," said Atwill later of Universal, "I guess I should be a dead egg now."[173]

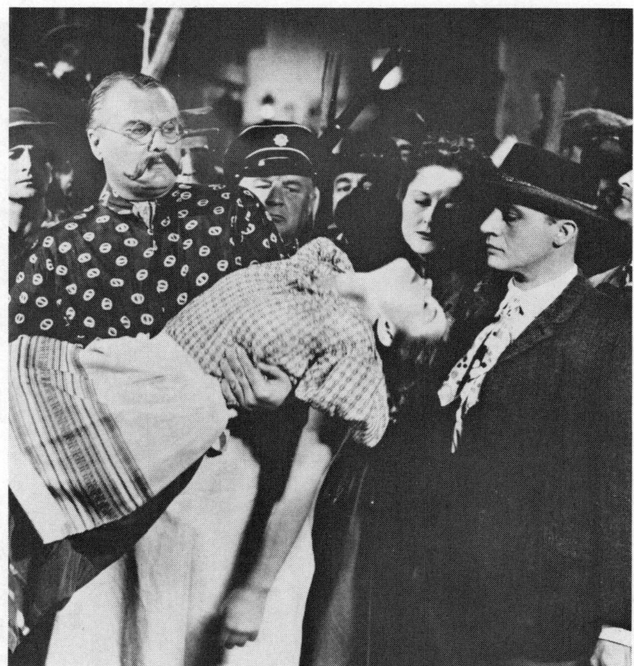

Martha Vickers plays dead in the arms of Rex Evans, as Harry Stubbs (in police hat), Beatrice Roberts, and Dwight Frye look on mournfully. Ms. Vickers died in 1971.

The supporting cast was nicely stocked. Grand, 66-year-old Maria Ouspenskaya of the Russian Art Theatre, reprised her role of Maleva, the gypsy sage of *The Wolf Man.* Dennis Hoey, then winning popularity as the thick-skulled Lestrade of the *Sherlock Holmes* series, was in his blustery element as Inspector Owen. Stout Rex Evans, memorable as Katharine Hepburn's butler of MGM's *The Philadelphia Story* (1940), enjoyed the role of Vazec, the raving innkeeper. Poor Dwight Frye made his fifth appearance in a Frankenstein film, this time as Rudi, a nervous villager. Adia Kuznetzoff, the Russian bass of gypsy roots who rolled his eyes and operatic tones in many Hollywood films, was cast as the Festival Singer, who belts out the famous "Faro La Faro Li" song. And Martha MacVicar, who later became Martha Vickers the oomphy Warner star of the late 1940s (and the third Mrs. Mickey Rooney), made her film bow as the lineless victim of the Wolf Man during his first evening in Vasaria. With his cast assembled, director Neill began shooting on October 12, 1942.

*In a billing compromise, Universal billed Atwill above Lugosi on the film credits, but billed Lugosi above Atwill on posters and lobby cards.

The Festival of the New Wine.

The TWO most terrifying creatures of all time . . . electrified with every awesome passion that thrilled millions in all of their spectacular predecessors . . .!

from the *Frankenstein Meets the Wolf Man* pressbook

While Frankenstein's Monster had never before met the Wolf Man, Bela Lugosi had certainly met Lon Chaney—and a peculiar relationship it was.

Naturally, it pained Lugosi to realize how strangely movie history had repeated itself—at his expense. Just as *Frankenstein*, for which he had been offered the Monster role, catapulted Karloff to glory in December 1931, so had *The Wolf Man*, whose title role had been sought by Lugosi, established Chaney as screen horror's great white hope in December 1941. While Lugosi certainly would have been miscast as Lawrence Talbot (too old and too Hungarian), he still brooded over the roles, money and clout that Chaney was enjoying at Universal. Chaney, meanwhile, ever-sensitive that he was "cashing in" on his father's name and reputation, appeared to resent Lugosi's flair, style and flamboyance—qualities lacking in his own performances.

Off screen, the aloof, dignified Lugosi had very little in common with the ebullient, bully-boy Chaney, aside from the fact that both men were alcoholics. Lugosi, whose professional ethics were far too high for him even to consider sipping his beloved brew of Scotch and beer during soundstage hours, consequently had strong feelings about his flask-brandishing co-star. While Lugosi had despised those 4 P.M. tea breaks that Karloff loved, he faced in Chaney a co-star who by 4 o'clock was sometimes too intoxicated to work at all. Nor did Lugosi care for Chaney's nickname for him—"Pop." Still, both men worked together relatively amicably, albeit quite distantly, and the relationship never took on the emotional, bitter aura that colored Bela's adventures with Boris Karloff.

In 1956, Reginald LeBorg, who had directed Chaney at Universal in such films as 1944's *The Mummy's Ghost* (Chaney, ever seeking a father figure, called LeBorg "Pappy"), was director for UA's *The Black Sleep*, a "B" chiller that employed Basil

Lon Chaney, his dog "Moose," and Ilona Massey enjoy a break in the shooting.

Rathbone, John Carradine, Akim Tamiroff, Chaney and Lugosi. LeBorg has remembered sensing "great antagonism"[174] on the set of this picture between the horror stars. It was not very surprising. One day on *The Black Sleep* set, the ever-boisterous Chaney crept up behind the frail Lugosi, grabbed him and lifted the Hungarian up in the air over his head. For a 73-year-old man who had recently survived a cold turkey purging of drug addiction, was a member of Alcoholics Anonymous, and was coping with heart trouble and deafness, this just wasn't fun.

Bela Lugosi was a very nice man, but by then he was getting old, and most of his stunts were done by a stunt man and not by him . . .[175]

Ilona Massey

Frankenstein Meets the Wolf Man began shooting under very pleasant conditions. Waggner ordered splendid sets for the film. Set decorator Russell Gausman gaily festooned the backlot village for the Festival of the New Wine sequence, in which 500 extras celebrated, and the old graveyard set never looked more bleak and foreboding than it did for the opening scene desecration of the Talbot mausoleum. Lon Chaney, too, was generally on his best behavior and charmed leading lady Ilona Massey:

> I think Lon Chaney is one of the nicest, sweetest people in the world. It was a great deal of fun. You know it took four hours to put on his makeup and when it was on, it was hot under the lights. It was very difficult for him to eat. He mostly had soup which he sipped through a straw and just for fun, we put hot peppers in it! We had a lot of fun. . . . I never had any difficulty with my co-stars, but Chaney was something special.[176]

John P. Fulton, Universal's special effects maestro, perfected the famed metamorphosis, and for the first time, Chaney's Talbot changed from man to wolf before the audience's eyes. (He had only reverted from wolf to man in *The Wolf Man*.) Chaney remembered the ordeal well:

> The day we did the transformations I came in at 2:00 A.M. When I hit that position they would take little nails and drive them through the skin at the end of my fingers, on both hands, so that I wouldn't move them anymore. . . .[177]

The crew then built a plaster cast of the back of Chaney's head, starched the drapes behind him, weighed the camera down with a one ton weight so it wouldn't quiver, set targets for Chaney's eyes, and shot five or ten frames of film. Then Jack Pierce would arrive, and put a new makeup on the still pinned and immobile Chaney. Then another five or ten frames would be shot, the makeup changed again. As Chaney later grunted:

". . . We did 21 changes of makeup and it took 22 hours. I won't discuss about the bathroom!"[178]

Chaney could take it; he was only 36 years old. Bela Lugosi, in the midst of filming turned 60 on October 20, 1942. Although he lived at the time in his lovely Whipple Street house just across from the Universal lot, his wife Lillian still remembers the engagement as a terrible strain:

> I, of course, drove Bela to work (he never did learn to drive; my father offered to teach him how once and Bela said, "No, I want Lillian to drive me where I want to go"). Anyway, when he played the Monster he had to be at the studio at 5:00 in the morning. That headpiece weighed five pounds; those boots together weighed over 20 pounds;* the whole schmeer took like four hours to get on. They had a special chair on the set for the Monster to sit in. . . .[179]

*Bela might have been spared the agony of those weighted boots, but for Karloff. In 1935, when Boris was at work on *Bride of Frankenstein*, the wardrobe department created new boots out of cork to create the same effect. The ever-stoical Boris, out of loyalty to his Monster's original conception, decided to keep the original shoes. Subsequently, the wardrobe department decided that, if the 13-pounders were good enough for Karloff, they were good enough for his successors.

Sadly, it was quickly obvious to all that Lugosi's casting as the Monster was a grievous mistake. First of all, Jack Pierce's beauty clay couldn't dominate Bela's patrician nose, dimpled chin and noble features; a new, smaller, specially designed forehead piece (molded by Ellis Burman Sr., who made Universal's rubber makeup pieces) didn't help. Secondly, Lugosi's health was failing, and he simply could not tolerate the mercilessly heavy costume, four-hour makeup torture each morning, and 15- to 16-hour work days. The very professional Lugosi did all he could to rise to the occasion, even getting up at 2:30 A.M. to soak in a hot tub to prepare himself for each day's challenge. Still, it was painfully clear that the actor could never play the more demanding scenes of the script, especially the climactic fight with the Wolf Man.

To make matters worse for himself, Lugosi gallantly was organizing the American Hungarian Defense Federation in Los Angeles during his stint as Frankenstein's Monster. The 10,000 Los Angeles Hungarians managed to donate $1,600 to the Red Cross, buy $65,000 in war bonds in one day, and completely equip an ambulance for overseas action, but they could do nothing to help Lugosi in his battle against the rigors of portraying the Monster.

Finally, Waggner and Neill decided that emergency action must be taken. It was too late to remove Lugosi from the role without embarrassing repercussions for the actor and the studio. So what to do?

The panacea for the sensitive production ailment arrived in the six-foot-four form of Eddie Parker, 41-year-old Hollywood stunt man and bit player, then busy at Universal. A few months earlier, the strapping Parker had won a special niche in action cinema by taking the nastier knocks in the classic John Wayne/Randolph Scott slugfest in Universal's *The Spoilers.* More relevantly, Parker had doubled for Chaney, both as the Monster in *The Ghost of Frankenstein* and as Kharis in *The Mummy's Tomb.* Waggner and Neill recruited Parker, unbilled and sworn to secrecy, to don the Monster guise (busy days for Jack Pierce!) and lurk in the soundstage shadows, prepared to step before the camera whenever Bela was overwhelmed. Ironically, Parker, with his great neck muscles, looked much more impressive in the Monster makeup than did Lugosi—so much so that Neill used *Parker* in the opening shot of the ice-bound Monster to bolster the audience's first impression of the creature! (This was fine with Bela, who hardly cherished the thought of cramming his aching body behind the wall of ice.) As Bela sat in the special "Monster chair," puffing a cigar as he watched Parker perform the more strenuous action, he was a bit embarrassed by his situation, though not much more than he was by the part itself. Once, after unleashing a fearsome growl when Massey, Knowles and Ouspenskaya approached the ruins, Lugosi abashedly turned to Neill, shook his head and smiled: "That *yell* is the worst thing about the part. You feel like a big jerk every time you do it!"[180]

With Parker in tow, production ran smoothly, and the picture's one major disaster ironically concerned not Lugosi, but Lon and Madame Ouspenskaya. Riding atop a carriage on a bumpy back-lot lane, both players were toppled and pinned beneath the cart when it overturned in a rut. Had the horse bolted, both actors, entangled in the reins, almost certainly would have suffered dismemberment or death. However, the docile nag halted in its tracks. Lon escaped unharmed, while the fragile Ouspenskaya was required to wear a cast throughout the rest of production while her multiple injuries healed. For a time, the horse had a special friend in Lon, who daily visited his stall to treat him to sugar lumps.

On Wednesday, November 11, 1942, *Frankenstein Meets the Wolf Man* completed shooting. A relieved Bela removed the makeup, boots and costume for the last time, and post-production began in the areas of musical score and editing. Hans Salter drew the assignment of scoring the film, and rarely did he perform so nobly. In an interview with Preston Neal Jones in *Cinefantastique* magazine (Summer 1978), Salter recalled:

> In those days we had no idea we were writing for "eternity." We were just trying to keep up with the frantic pace of picture after picture. Let's say it was Monday—the producer showed you his picture. You had to write a score, and orchestrate it, and be ready to rehearse and record with the orchestra the following Monday. It was like a factory, where you'd have to produce a certain amount of red socks, a certain amount of green socks. . . . They'd screen one of those pictures for us without the music, and it would be *nothing.* All those pictures we saved for them! But those executives, they never knew what they had. We never heard a word from them. They were afraid if they gave us a compliment, we'd ask for a raise.[181]

Salter created some chilling musical effects, reprising themes from the milestone score that he, Charles Previn, and Frank Skinner had created for 1941's *The Wolf Man.* A special highlight is the now-famous "Faro-La, Faro-Li" song (with lyrics by Curt Siodmak), sung at the Festival of the New Wine. Salter remembers that the ebullient Kuznetzoff "was a very pleasant fellow. He was a Russian gypsy by heritage, and when we prerecorded this song he just ate it up. He loved doing it."[182]

In the spring 1977, when Salter was honored by the University of California at Los Angeles Extension and the Los Angeles International Film Exposition in a program devoted to Fantasy, Horror, and Science Fiction, the first reel of *Frankenstein Meets the Wolf Man* was shown to exemplify the artistry of Salter.

Editing was not so fortunate.

After Salter scored *Frankenstein Meets the Wolf Man,* Waggner, Neill, Siodmak and various members of the production staff congregated in a studio screening room to see the finished product. All were enjoying Neill's superbly atmospheric direction and Chaney's better-than-usual performance—until there came a scene which originally followed Talbot's rescuing of the Monster from the ice. The two nightmares shared a fire in the ruins, and had the following conversation:

> *The Monster:* I can't see you. I'm blind, I'm sick. Once I had the strength of a hundred men. If Dr. Frankenstein were alive, he'd give it back to me . . . so I could live forever.
> *Talbot:* Do you know what happened?
> *The Monster:* I fell into the stream when the village people burned the house down. I lost consciousness. When I woke, I was frozen into the ice.
> *Talbot:* Buried alive. I know! I know!
> *The Monster:* Dr. Frankenstein created my body to be immortal. His son gave me a new brain, a clever brain. I will rule the world forever if we can find the formula that can give me back my strength. I will never die. I will never die!
> *Talbot:* But I *want* to die. If you wanted to die, what would you do?
> *The Monster:* I would look in Dr. Frankenstein's diary. He knew the secret of immortality. And he knew the secret of death![183]

By this time, the audience in the screening room was almost in hysterics. Curt Siodmak explains:

> Do you know why they took the Monster's dialogue away? Because Bela Lugosi couldn't talk! They had left the dialogue I wrote for the Monster in the picture when they shot it, but with Lugosi it sounded so Hungarian funny that they had to take it out! Seriously!
> Lugosi was good as Dracula, because it supplied him with a Hungarian part. But a *Monster* with a *Hungarian accent*?!

For the staff in the screening room, the "topper" came in a scene at the Frankenstein ruins after the Monster had crashed the Festival of the New Wine. "What made you come out?" demanded Chaney's Talbot. " . . . You spoiled our last chance! I was working on the doctor, on Elsa. I almost persuaded them to help. Then I had to run and save you from the people of Vasaria. And now I daren't come out!"

In a scene wisely cut from the release print, Chaney and Lugosi snuggle in the Frankenstein ruins.

"I was afraid," said the Monster, voice choked with Hungarian emotion, "you had left me."[184]

That did it. After the screening, Waggner, terrified that "the beast battle of the century" would reap laughs, directed editor Edward Curtiss to cut all of the Monster's dialogue. Out came the scene by the fire, and the "I was afraid . . ." vignette. In another sequence, in which Talbot discovers the portrait of Elsa von Frankenstein and is told by the Monster who she is, the Monster's dialogue was simply erased from the soundtrack—poor Lugosi stands there, his mouth flapping mutely! To make matters even worse, all references to the Monster's blindness were expunged as well. Hence, Lugosi's stretching and groping mannerisms no longer made any sense. The damage dealt to Lugosi's sincere but weak performance was devastating.

Universal's butchered release print of *Frankenstein Meets the Wolf Man* previewed in Los Angeles on February 18, 1943.

Variety was impressed:

> Here's a strong dish for the mass of customers who go for the bizarre, the weird, the creepy. . . .

The beast battle of the century . . . The SHOCK-SHOW of the Year . . . Diabolical Murder monsters . . . Lusting for a DEATH-DUEL!

Lobby card for *Frankenstein Meets the Wolf Man*

> Picture, cannily produced by George Waggner and skillfully directed by Roy William Neill, also benefits from excellent performances by Chaney, Lugosi, Patric Knowles as a doctor, Maria Ouspenskaya, a gypsy . . . Spectacular and sensational effects are properly emphasized in the script by Curtis Siodmak and in the fine camera work by George Robinson. . . .[185]

Variety's only complaint was the "spotty performance" of Miss Massey. "She is permitted to be too casual in a number of scenes which should have been dominated by more reactionary terror." However, other critics found less to praise, and *The Hollywood Reporter* gave a snide appraisal:

> Roosevelt meets Churchill at Casablanca, Yanks meet Japs at Guadalcanal—and yet these events will fade into insignificance to those seemingly inexhaustible legions of horror fans when they hear that *Frankenstein Meets the Wolf Man*. Yay, brother! . . .
>
> . . . opens in the Langwelly (sic) Village graveyard. . . . The corpse comes to life, severs the jugular vein of its would-be robber, and goes out to make his place in the world for a second lifetime. . . .
>
> In Vesaria (sic) . . . the goon squad has burned the good (?) doctor's castle . . . the Wolf Man kills another girl and takes to the castle ruins . . . Uh-huh, he finds the Monster frozen . . . and that one, like a faithful dog, shows him the old doctor's records. It's really quite a touching scene, the two ogres playing in the castle ruins. . . .
>
> Third episode rears another ugly head—SEX! . . .
>
> . . . Ilona Massey, of whom it once was reportedly said that she'd look naked even in a fur coat, enters the scene in a filmy negligee. . . .[186]

And so on. However, it remained the privilege of the *The New York Times'* Bosley Crowther to deliver the most obnoxious review, and when *Frankenstein Meets the Wolf Man* opened at New York's shriek hall, the Rialto, on March 5, 1943, he did not disappoint:

> We confess a great disappointment. For weeks we had been waiting breathlessly for *Frankenstein Meets the Wolf Man*—as pregnant a prospect as any one could wish . . . Well, we've seen it happen . . . And—would you believe it!—the Wolf Man all but greeted his arch competitor with a "Dr. Frankenstein's Monster, I presume. . . ."
>
> Too bad. Not very horrible. Universal will have to try again. Only next time we have a suggestion: why not unite with Monogram and turn out a horror to end all horrors—*Wolf Man and Monster Meet the East Side Kids*?[187]

Such critical reports were no longer surprising to Universal, which had prepared other methods of luring audiences. In the February issue of many major magazines, a Max Factor makeup advertisement featured a beautiful portrait of Ilona Massey and a "plug" for *Frankenstein Meets the Wolf Man*. The movie's pressbook offered exhibitors a variety of schemes to stir local interest (including a "Where would the Wolf Man and Frankenstein hide in your town?" contest, calling for essays and photographs). Business across the country was excellent. Of the Universal horror releases of 1943—*Captive Wild Woman* (which introduced Acquanetta as "Paula the Ape Woman"), *The Mad Ghoul* (with juvenile David Bruce in the withered title role) and *Son of Dracula* (starring Lon Chaney)—*Frankenstein Meets the Wolf Man* was *the* top horror product of the season, its receipts greatly contributing to the studio's walloping $3.8 million profit in fiscal 1943. And, to Waggner's relief, the audiences didn't appear to notice the presence of Parker or the indelicacies of the post-production editing.

There were several professional and personal repercussions in the wake of *Frankenstein Meets the Wolf Man*.

Curt Siodmak's 1943 novel, *Donovan's Brain*, made the best-seller charts and consolidated the writer's reputation as a major fantasy author. (There have been many film versions.)

Ilona Massey, free of her Universal bonds, temporarily fled Hollywood for Broadway. On April 1, 1943, she opened in a new edition of *Ziegfeld Follies*, co-starring with Milton Berle and Arthur Treacher. The lavish revue presented Ilona with stunning costumes and lovely songs, and ran for 553 performances.

Tragically, *Frankenstein Meets the Wolf Man* would prove to be the final Frankenstein saga for the peaked Dwight Frye. In order to support his wife and son, contribute to the war effort and maintain his home at 2590 N. Beachwood Drive in the fashionable Hollywood Hills, Frye had been designing bombsights on the night shift at the Douglas Aircraft plant in Los Angeles. By day, he haunted studio casting offices, maintaining an exhausting pace that finally ended on Sunday night, November 7, 1943 when the 44-year-old actor suffered a fatal heart attack. The little man, who never forgot his days of Broadway stardom and never lost his pride, would have been humiliated to learn that his death certificate listed his occupation as "tool designer."

Lugosi as the Monster.

Finally, for Bela Lugosi, *Frankenstein Meets the Wolf Man* completed his Universal pact. While his dismal performance as the Monster wasn't totally his own fault, studio executives preferred to believe it was. Left to the mercy of Monogram and other poverty-row studios, Lugosi soon took to the road in a touring company of *Dracula* and then a road tour of *Arsenic and Old Lace.* Lugosi played, of course, the Karloff role of Jonathan—with the altered line, "He said I looked like Bela Lugosi!"

Bela Lugosi, who missed his chance in 1931, finally portrayed the Monster this time around. It would be kind to say only that he was awful in the role . . .[188]

Radu Florescu, *In Search of Frankenstein.*

In the second "half" of Universal's Monster saga, *Frankenstein Meets the Wolf Man* enjoys (arguably) the most popularity. Neill's direction is sure and sound and atmospheric. Especially impressive is his colorful staging of the Festival of the New Wine episode, which gives the film a touch of the Grimms' fairy tale quality with which James Whale had garnished the first two *Frankenstein* adventures. John P. Fulton's supervision of the special effects, including the superb transformations of Chaney and the excellent miniatures of the Frankenstein ruins, is impeccable, while Hans J. Salter's beautiful score, accented by gypsy motifs, is of inestimable assistance.

The climactic, 110-second fight between the Monster and the Wolf Man remains an exciting horror film "event." Closeups of Lugosi leering and roaring are expertly intercut with footage of Eddie Parker performing the real action, and the brawl is punctuated by the flying machinery, the snarls of the combatants, and the awesome, well-staged flood. The deluge conveniently pleased special fans of each horror character by leaving the fight a draw.

The cast, generally, is excellent. Star-billed Ilona Massey has little to do. The blonde diva sashays through the horror with the vapid pose of a model displaying too-tight lingerie. Her screams, too, are anemic indeed when compared to the howls of her swooning predecessors, Josephine Hutchinson and Evelyn Ankers. Still, Miss Massey was a great beauty, and she does bring a touch of MGM class to the film. While one might miss in Patric Knowles' Dr. Mannering the hysteria of Clive, the swagger of Rathbone and the aplomb of Hardwicke, the actor's restraint here is welcome. He never competes for attention with the title ogres, and he strikes a comfortable balance between bland horror film hero and determined scientist. The "legitimacy" that both Miss Massey and Knowles bring to *Frankenstein Meets the Wolf Man* is of great value. Lionel Atwill's jolly burgomeister has the proper Tyrolean touch, and the

That's stuntman Eddie Parker, *not* Bela Lugosi, hefting Ilona Massey in this production still.

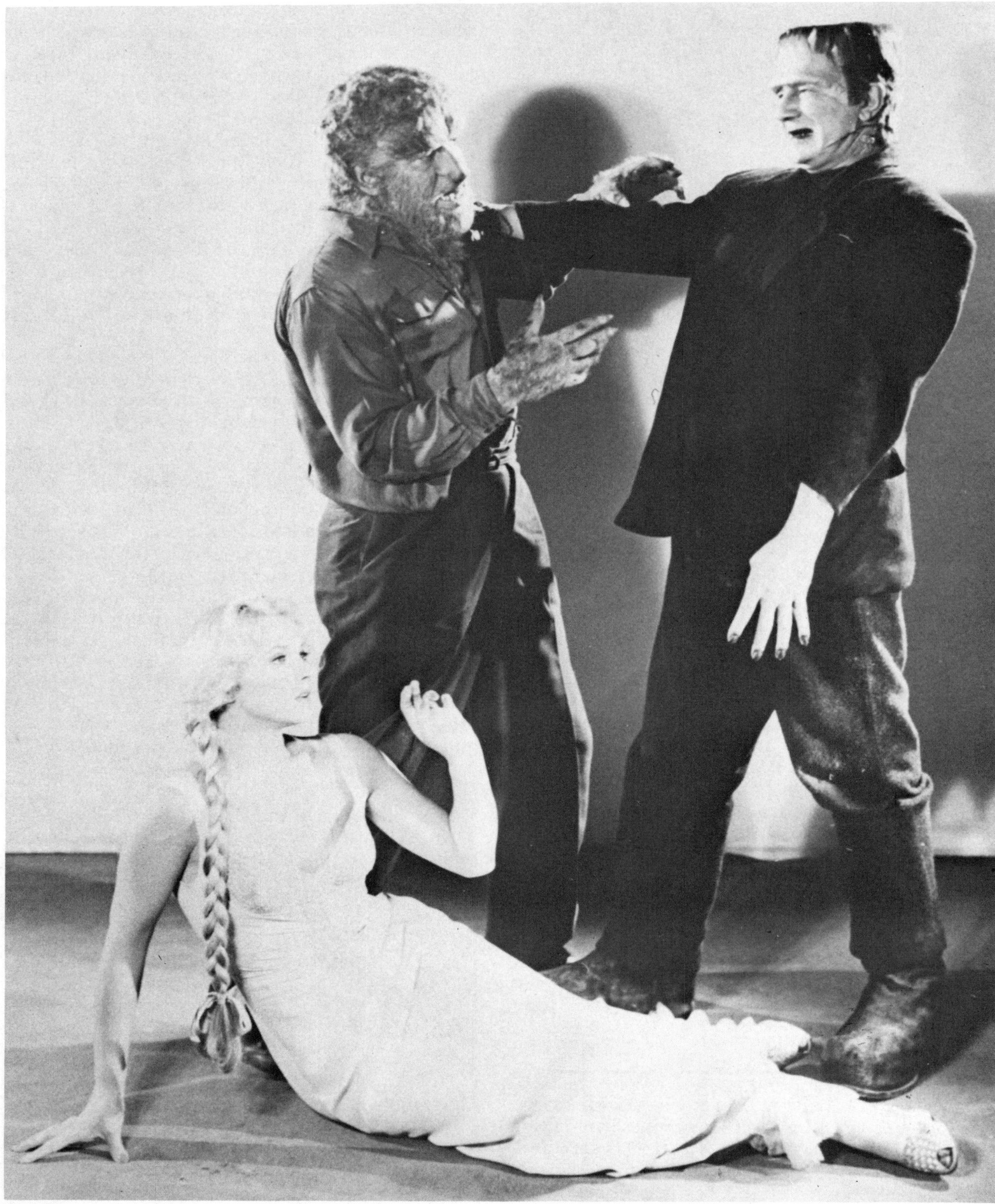

Ilona Massey, Lon Chaney, and Bela Lugosi.

actor reveals himself to be quite the dancer as he twirls the beaming Miss Massey about in a spirited folk dance at the festival. Madame Ouspenskaya's reprise of Maleva is chocked with Stanislavskian fervor, though one wishes the film were more specific about her fate—did she escape the flood, or was she washed away with the monsters? (Presumably the former, as Karloff and J. Carrol Naish do not discover an old lady suspended in the cavern's ice in the next entry, *House of Frankenstein.*) Among the minor cast members, Rex Evans is especially strong as Vazec, crazed in his manic fervor to rid the community of the creatures.

It is Lon Chaney, however, who carries *Frankenstein Meets the Wolf Man.* His performance is the best of his Universal sojourn, and he creates and sustains a pathos that conveys the tragedy, and not just the melodrama, of the lycanthropic Talbot.

Then there's Bela Lugosi. His performance of the Frankenstein Monster is undoubtedly the most maligned, panned and roasted performance of the Golden Age of Horror. Bela's unfortunately cavalier attitude toward the Monster shows only too well in his lamentable performance. *TV Guide* still synopsizes the film with the tag line, "Bela Lugosi plays the Monster, with blatant gestures." While Universal cut the Monster's dialogue because the effect was "ludicrous", it is hard to imagine a performance more ludicrous than the one in the final print. Bela had been claiming for a dozen years that he refused the original *Frankenstein* because it was a part for a "half-wit extra," so it is not so surprising that Bela's delineation presents a half-wit Monster. His performance *does* have its moments; the evil smile that flickers on his face as Knowles restores him to full power (and sight) is far more impressive than anything Chaney did in *The Ghost of Frankenstein.* As Denis Gifford notes in his book *A Pictorial History of Horror Movies,* "He (Lugosi) brought to the Monster his own curious interpretation, a hissing evil that snarled through the makeup."[189] Indeed, after watching Lugosi's performance (and learning of the behind-the-scenes mayhem), one does not feel scorn for the performance as much as pity for the actor. It's sad enough that an aging, humbled, desperate Lugosi had to accept a role he had so proudly declined a decade before. That Lugosi's appearance, acting style, and age all conspired with the lamentable editing to turn his Monster into a farce makes one fatalistically believe that Lugosi had meddled in a part he was meant to leave alone. It is both poetic and pathetic that the actor who had so vehemently opined that Frankenstein's Monster was a role unworthy of a skilled actor would so disastrously prove his own theory.

While the Monster suffered yet another indignity in his plunge to programmer revenue, Boris Karloff was playing to Standing-Room-Only houses in the national company of *Arsenic and Old Lace.* Boris never commented specifically on Bela's Monster—no doubt he avoided seeing it—but years later, he did quip about those who inherited his electrodes:

> Oh, with all that makeup on it's impossible for anyone to tell it isn't me. Every time they make another Frankenstein picture, I get all the fan mail. The other fellow gets the check![190]

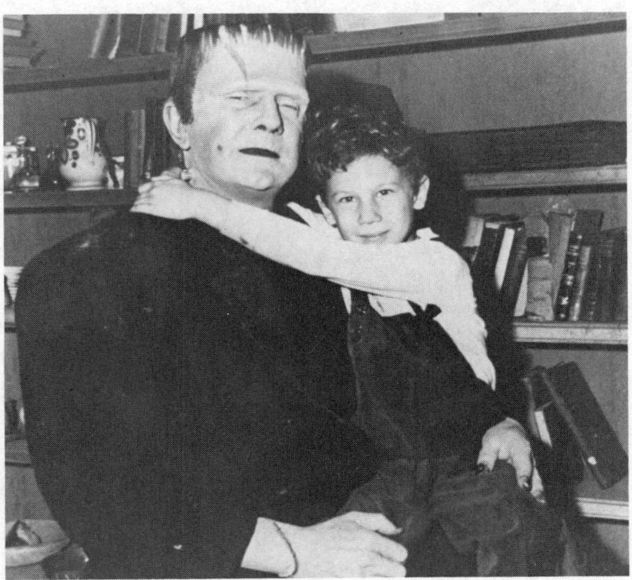

Four-year-old Bela Lugosi, Jr. gives his proud dad a hug on the set.

House of Frankenstein lobby card.

House of Frankenstein (1944)

Producer, Paul Malvern; *Executive Producer,* Joseph Gershenson; *Director,* Erle C. Kenton; *Original Story,* Curt Siodmak; *Screenplay,* Edward T. Lowe; *Director of Photography,* George Robinson; *Art Direction,* John B. Goodman and Martin Obzina; *Musical Score and Direction,* Hans J. Salter; *Director of Sound,* Bernard B. Brown; (*Technician,* William Hedgcock); *Set Decorations,* Russell A. Gausman and A. J. Gilmore; *Film Editor,* Philip Cahn; *Gowns,* Vera West; *Assistant Director,* William Tummel; *Special Photography,* John P. Fulton; *Makeup,* Jack P. Pierce.

Filmed under the shooting title of *The Devil's Brood;* Completed, Universal City, California, May 8, 1944; opened at the Rialto Theatre, New York City, December 15, 1944. Running Time: 70 minutes.

HOUSE OF FRANKENSTEIN—SYNOPSIS

An awesome storm batters the ancient walls of Neustadt Prison for the Criminally Insane. In a foul dungeon he has inhabited for 15 years, a man with wild gray hair, a long beard and a lunatic eye, sketches on the dank wall of his cell.

"Now, friend Daniel," lectures Dr. Gustav Niemann to the wide-eyed little hunchback who clings to the bars of the neighboring cell, " . . . this brain, taken from the man and transplanted into the skull of the dog, would give him the mind of a human being." Niemann shows Daniel where the infamous Dr. Frankenstein would have severed the spinal cord—though he's not certain that the famed scientist was right.

The fascinated Daniel asks Niemann if he knew Frankenstein. Niemann did not—but he claims that his brother assisted him, learned his secrets, and, before his death passed them on to the prisoner.

"Then," gleams Daniel, "you could give me a new body!"

"If I had Frankenstein's records to guide me," grins Niemann, "I could give you a *perfect* body!"

As if to punctuate Niemann's promise, a renegade bolt of lightning smashes into the prison, and the walls of the cells crumble into jagged blocks. Together, Niemann and Daniel escape into the storm.

Not far from Neustadt, the two maniacs approach a colorful carnival wagon, festooned with the words "Professor Lampini's Chamber of Horrors." The strangers help the owner extricate his coach from a rut in the rain-slashed road, and Professor Bruno Lampini invites them to enjoy the warmth of his wagon quarters.

"I have a collection of the world's most astounding horrors!" says Lampini, whose prized attraction is the skeleton of the legendary Count Dracula. Lampini says he took it ("pardon me, *borrowed* it") from the cellar of Castle Dracula in the Carpathian Mountains of Transylvania.* Lampini spread in the coffin a layer of Transylvanian soil, so that the skeleton of the vampire's earthbound spirit could lie in peace within its grave.

Niemann remembers the bloodthirsty legend of Dracula. He recalls that the withdrawal of the wooden stake from the vampire's skeleton would set him free again—to quench his unholy lust for blood. And soon, an evil idea enters his crazed brain.

"Do you ever exhibit your show in—Visaria?"†

Lampini does not. He claims Visarians have had no appetite for horrors ever since " . . . a Dr. Niemann tried to give a dog the mind of a human

* In none of Universal's *Dracula* films had the Count been destroyed in his Carpathian domain. In 1931's *Dracula,* he was killed in England's Carfax Abbey, where, in 1936, *Dracula's Daughter* (Gloria Holden) cremated his remains. In 1943's *Son of Dracula,* Lon Chaney's bloodsucker, caught in the rays of the sun, plopped into a Louisiana swamp.

† Note that the spelling of V*a*saria has changed in this film to V*i*saria.

The Players

Dr. Gustav Niemann	Boris Karloff
Larry Talbot	Lon Chaney
Count Dracula	John Carradine
Rita Hussman	Anne Gwynne
Carl Hussman	Peter Coe
Inspector Arnz	Lionel Atwill
Professor Bruno Lampini	George Zucco
Ilonka	Elena Verdugo
and	
Daniel	J. Carrol Naish
with	
Burgomaster Hussman	Sig Rumann
Fejos	William Edmunds
Toberman	Charles Miller
Muller	Philip Van Zandt
Hertz	Julius Tannen
Meier	Hans Herbert
Born	Dick Dickinson
Gerlach	George Lynn
Strauss	Michael Mark
Hoffman	Olaf Hytten
Ullman	Frank Reicher
Dr. Geissler	Brandon Hurst
The Monster	Glenn Strange
Urla	Belle Mitchell
Driver	Eddie Cobb
Prison Guard	Charles Wagenheim

being." The professor relates how this Niemann was thrown into prison as a would-be Frankenstein who had used the bodies of the newly dead to aid his experiments. Lampini also tells them that old Hussman—the man who had led the campaign to imprison Niemann—is now the Burgomaster of Reigelburg, a small place which is too far away to make a special trip.

"Nevertheless," announced Niemann, "*that* is where you are going"—and seconds later, Daniel has strangled the howling Lampini.

The following morning, the two madmen, shaved and shorn, masquerade as the proprietors of the Chamber of Horrors. Niemann, in natty cap and jacket, poses as Lampini, while Daniel stretches the carnival costume of the deceased driver over his deformed back. They ride the wagon across the countryside, "free to move on," as the vengeance-crazed Niemann purrs, "toward those for whom I have unloving memories."

There is soon a midnight horror show in Reigelburg. A crowd gathers in the foggy, chill night, including the beautiful Rita Hussman, her bridegroom Karl, Inspector Arnz and Burgomaster Hussman, Karl's grandfather. Rita gasps as the strange man in the top hat reveals the skeleton of Count Dracula, but the Burgomaster dismisses the spiel, skeleton and stake as rubbish. Still, this "Lampini" makes him uneasy. He reminds Hussman of someone—someone he can't quite recall . . .

"Perhaps you will remember later, Herr Burgomaster," replies Niemann, the curtain closing on his ghastly show.

Behind the curtain, Niemann removes the stake from the skeleton, and the cadaverous form of Count Dracula materializes. As the vampire's eyes open he sees Niemann poised with the stake poised over his heart. If Dracula moves, Niemann threatens to send his soul back to limbo, but if the vampire does as he asks, Niemann promises to serve

Boris Karloff, J. Carrol Naish, and George Zucco.

him faithfully, guarding and protecting the coffin of native soil.

"For that," responds Dracula, "I will do whatever you wish." Niemann's unholy revenge begins.

"It's like being wrapped in the arms of a gigantic ghost," Rita says of the fog as she, Karl, the Burgomaster and Inspector Arnz make their way home. Shortly after Arnz takes his leave, a coach creeps up behind them. A spidery but elegant man in top hat and cape invites the trio to enjoy the comfort of his coach, and introduces himself as Baron Latos of Transylvania. As the little group decides to visit the Hussman house for some wine, a strange, deep passion appears to be binding the "Baron" and the newly wed Rita.

At the house, the Burgomaster falls asleep; Karl visits the wine cellar; and Rita falls completely under the spell of Dracula. She stares at the large ring on his skeletal hand, a ring that bears the Dracula crest. "I see glimpses of a strange world," she says, "a world of people who are dead—and yet alive."

"It is the place from which I've just returned," replies Dracula.

"It frightens me!"

"Wear it. It will drive away your fears," says Dracula. The large ring magically becomes smaller, fitting itself to her finger, as the bond

Elena Verdugo, Boris Karloff, and J. Carrol Naish.

that links the vampire and the young woman. Rita's fear begins to ebb, replaced by a morbid passion.

"I will come for you before the dawn," promises Dracula when he takes his leave and Rita ascends to her bedroom. Meanwhile, the Burgomaster looks through his records, trying to remember where he had met the showman Lampini and realizes that the man he saw tonight was Gustav Niemann.

However, it is too late for action. The garden door opens and Dracula's demonic eyes paralyze the Burgomaster. Seconds later a large bat sucks the life from Hussman, and Dracula, with the spellbound Rita as a captive, races his coach away toward the sanctuary of his coffin.

Karl discovers his grandfather's body and the abduction of his wife. Soon Inspector Arnz is leading mounted gendarmes on a wild chase after Dracula's coach. Dracula madly whips his horses and the coach careens over the hills and through a stream and across a bridge. Niemann and Daniel, riding ahead, look back to see the pursuit. Afraid of being entangled in the chase, Niemann betrays Dracula, and Daniel tosses the vampire's precious casket of native soil out of the wagon. Terrified, Dracula loses control of his coach and it plunges down a hillside. The vampire races to his coffin on the hilltop and as he reaches the crest, the dooming rays of the dawn assail him. Unleashing a bestial scream, Dracula falls to the earth, slavering his way to the casket. Arnz, the gendarmes and Karl arrive to find only a putrid, bleached skeleton where Dracula's body had been but a moment before. Karl rushes to the unharmed Rita, who, as the Dracula ring falls from her finger, takes refuge in her husband's arms.

In the village of Frankenstein*, a spirited gypsy girl named Ilonka dances zestfully for the crowd. Niemann arrives to search for the Frankenstein records, and as he and Daniel drive the coach into town, the little hunchback watches the lovely girl dance. The Chamber of Horrors receives no welcome in Frankenstein, however. Inspector Gerlach tells Niemann that the villagers here, like those of Visaria, have seen enough horrors. "Our village has been quiet and peaceful since the dam broke and swept the Wolf Man and the Frankenstein Monster to their destruction several years ago," spits Gerlach, pointing toward the ruins that loom above the hamlet. "No one ever mentions that place, nor does anyone ever go near it." Gerlach orders the Chamber of Horrors out of town at once. However, before they can leave, Daniel sees Fejos, the gypsy leader, sadistically whipping Ilonka. In a mad desire to help the pretty dancer, he attacks Fejos, wrenches the whip from him, and maniacally lashes the gypsy before Niemann stops him. "May I take her with us?" pleads the lovesick Daniel over the unconscious form of Ilonka. " . . . Please, master, she's hurt!" Niemann, to calm Daniel, agrees.

That night, Ilonka awakes on the wagon to see the face of Daniel who offers her tea. Daniel happily talks to the stranded gypsy, offering to take her to Visaria. "You could sleep here," he says, pointing out the little space beneath the driver's bench, "and talk to me when I drive. I get so lonesome when I have no one to talk to . . . You're pretty!" Ilonka flirts with her protector, and seductively beckons him to sit beside her "where I could see you better." Daniel happily leaps atop the wagon and sees Ilonka's expression turn to one of repulsion as she sees his hunched back.

"But you will talk to me . . . sometimes . . . won't you?" begs the heartsick cripple.

"Of course I will," answers the gypsy, trying to disguise her disgust. "You've been kind to me . . . and I like you."

Niemann interrupts. He needs Daniel to accompany him to the castle ruins in a search for those famed records. The two men climb up the mountain and soon penetrate the ominous fortress. As

* Note that the village where the Monster met the Wolf Man is called Frankenstein in this movie. *Vasaria* (changed as previously noted to *Visaria*) has been given a whole new history and location that has nothing to do with either the Monster or the Wolf Man.

they search the rubble, Daniel asks Niemann if, once they find the records, the doctor will really make him like other men.

"To please your little gypsy girl? smirks Niemann. "Friend Daniel, I'll make you an Adonis!" Suddenly the floor collapses and Daniel tumbles into the bowels of the ruins. Niemann descends to his aid, and they discover a cave, where the waters of the dam have been frozen into a glacial ice cavern. Niemann lifts his lantern toward a horizontal slab of glistening ice, and sees the imprisoned form of the Wolf Man. "Master!" cries Daniel, who leads Niemann to another bizarre sight—that of a square-skulled giant trapped behind a thick wall of ice. "The undying Monster!" exclaims Niemann. "The triumphant climax of Frankenstein's genius!" Hoping these fiends might know where the records are, Niemann and Daniel build a huge bonfire to thaw the mammoth ice layers. As the ice melts, the claws of the Wolf Man jut through the ice, and on this moonless night, the beast reverts to human form. Soon, as Daniel cowers, a tall, husky man ventures from the cave.

"Who are you?" demands Lawrence Talbot (for, of course, it is he). "Why have you freed me from the ice that imprisoned the beast that lived within me?" Niemann comforts Talbot. He promises that if Talbot can find the Frankenstein records, he will build a new brain for the lycanthrope that will lift the curse from him forever. Talbot finds the records, the comatose Monster is extracted from the ice, and the caravan departs for Visaria.

To Daniel's dismay, Niemann orders him to remain in the wagon to help him treat the Monster's ice-damaged tissues. Ilonka awakes to find Talbot driving.

"My names's Ilonka. What's yours?"

"Lawrence."

"Lawrence? Do they call you Larry?"

"They *used* to."

The strange entourage soon reaches Niemann's long abandoned castle in Visaria, where a reign of terror begins. The scientist and Daniel kidnap two old enemies of Niemann: Ullmann, his ex-assistant, who had testified against him, and Strauss, who had told the court that he had seen Niemann scavenge a body from a grave. Niemann informs his quivering captives of the fates that await them: Ullmann's brain is to be placed in the skull of the Monster, while Strauss will receive the brain of the Wolf Man.

That night in the laboratory, the brains of Ullmann and Strauss are removed from their bodies. Niemann, however, is fascinated by the prospect of restoring the Monster to full power, and becomes obsessed with new, mad plans. Daniel recognizes the doctor's mania, and reminds him of his promise to reward him with a perfect body.

Glenn Strange as the Monster, Karloff, and Naish.

Having sadly watched Ilonka fall in love with the handsome Talbot, Daniel now begs the doctor to give him Talbot's body—"He's big, he's strong." But Niemann has other plans for Talbot's body. Rather than save the lycanthrope as promised, he has decided that the Wolf Man's body is the ideal home for the Monster's warped brain. Daniel implores the doctor to keep his promise to him, but Niemann refuses. "You think I'd wreck the work of a lifetime because you're in love with a . . . a gypsy girl?" The madman stalks away, and Ilonka enters, looking for "Larry."

The gypsy soon realizes that Daniel is jealous and teases him. But Daniel is concerned for her and recites a poem:

"Even a man who is pure in heart, and says his prayers by night. . . ."

Ilonka shivers. She knows the poem well. And she battles hysteria as Daniel begs her to stay away from Talbot. "When the moon is full again he'll turn . . . and he'll kill . . . he'll *kill*!"

Ilonka, heartbroken, screams at Daniel that he's making his horrible story up out of jealousy. "You're mean, and you're *ugly*!" cries the girl, glaring at Daniel's pathetic deformity. "I hate you. I HATE YOU!"

She runs out of the castle. Weeping, Daniel scuttles over to the comatose Monster, wailing, "She hates me because I'm an ugly hunchback! If it wasn't for you, *I'd* have Talbot's body!" Grabbing a laboratory table strap, the frustrated Daniel madly lashes the unconscious Monster.

Soon there appears in the heavens a full moon—and Talbot changes into the beast, ripping open the neck of a villager. The next morning, Ilonka visits him in the garden and recites the werewolf legend. They embrace, but both are aware that

Strange, Karloff, and Chaney.

only death can bring them peace of mind. Talbot laments that a werewolf doesn't just die by any natural means—"He must be killed . . . Killed by a silver bullet." "Fired by the hand," continues Ilonka, "of one who loves him enough to understand."

Ilonka spends the rest of the day fashioning a silver bullet.

Niemann remains fascinated with revitalizing the Monster, and Talbot confronts him. He, like Daniel, reminds the doctor of a broken promise; although he had found the Frankenstein records for Niemann, the scientist has made no effort to help him. "Last night I suffered the tortures of the damned!" roars Talbot. "I killed a man! Tonight the moon will be full again . . . operate on me or I swear I'll . . .!" Losing control, Talbot grasps Niemann by the neck.

"You'll destroy your only hope of release?" Niemann cooly asks.

That night, the moon is indeed full. As Niemann shoots 100,000 megavolts of electricity into the Monster's body, reviving the creature, Talbot awaits the dreaded rays of the moon. Soon a werewolf savagely crashes through glass doors and onto the estate grounds, where the loving Ilonka, brandishing a pistol, pursues him into the forest. From the trees comes a scream of terror followed by a shot. The Wolf Man lunges from the woods and falls, changing back into Lawrence Talbot. There is a look of peace on the corpse's face, a look that comforts the dying Ilonka, who manages to pull herself to "Larry's" body to die with her head on his chest.

Daniel finds Ilonka's body. Tenderly, he carries her into the castle. " . . . The only thing I ever loved," mourns the hunchback, whose grief soon turns to frenzy as he leaps and grabs the treacherous Niemann by the throat.

Suddenly there is the sound of straps breaking. The Frankenstein Monster, protective of the man who has restored his life, breaks his laboratory table bonds, pulls Daniel off Niemann, and carries the wiggling cripple across the room. Lifting the hunchback above his head, the Monster throws Daniel through the great window. Landing on the sloped castle roof, Daniel futilely grasps for a hold, but slides down the roof to fall, screaming, to his death.

A band of torch-bearing villagers witness this. The vigilantes had gathered to seek the werewolf, and the flashes of high-voltage electricity attracted them to Niemann's castle. Storming the laboratory, they find the Monster, carrying the seriously wounded Niemann under his arm. They pursue him with their torches, and the Monster lopes down the castle steps and into a bog. "Quicksands! Quicksands!" rasps Niemann in warning, but the Monster nevertheless wades into the mire, sinking under the slime and dragging the gasping Niemann to his doom.

HOUSE OF FRANKENSTEIN—PRODUCTION HISTORY

Among the writers at Universal, there was a game we played regarding the Monster. If you got the assignment of writing a Frankenstein picture, you always killed the Monster in such a way that nobody could survive it. You'd reduce him to cinders or ashes, so the next guy who had to write a Frankenstein film couldn't revive him. But then, there was always another picture, and somebody had to find a way of putting the Monster together again.

Curt Siodmak.

Glenn Strange, Boris Karloff and "villagers."

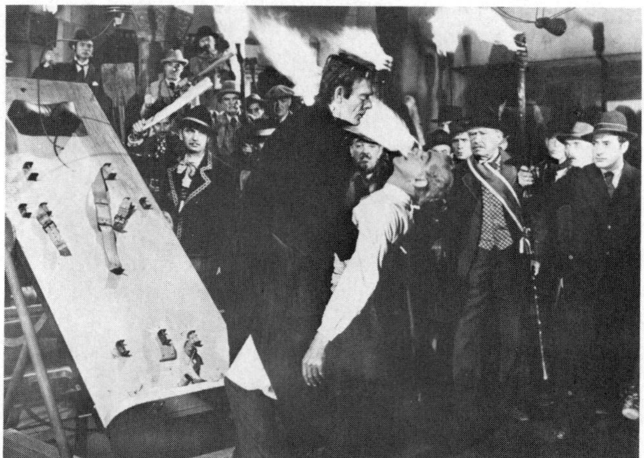

The watery climax of *Frankenstein Meets the Wolf Man* pleased Curt Siodmak. The great flood which rampaged through the castle ruins and washed away the battling horrors seemed to the screenwriter to be a definitive way of ridding the world of the Monster and the Wolf Man. Siodmak certainly did not envy the writer who got the job of bringing the creatures back to life again.

Ironically, Siodmak got the job! A year after the release of *Frankenstein Meets the Wolf Man,* Universal assigned Siodmak to concoct a super horror epic, a big parade of favorite Universal goblins. Not only were the waterlogged Monster and Wolf Man to be revived, but also Dracula (who had not stirred at Universal since the original 1931 film) and the Mummy (who, in the swathed form of Lon Chaney, had most recently waddled into a backlot swamp, lugging "reincarnated love" Ramsay Ames in *The Mummy's Ghost*).

Universal was desperate.

At Universal, the prevailing idea of horror was a werewolf chasing a girl in a nightgown up a tree.[191]

Mark Robson, director.

By 1944, Universal was fighting almost maniacally to preserve its reputation as Hollywood's No. 1 horror studio. Certainly, in 1943, there had been little or no real competition. Columbia, which had produced Karloff's *"Mad Doctor"* series of 1939–42, presented Bela Lugosi in *Return of the Vampire,* (due to Universal's copyright of the name Dracula, the bloodsucker was named Armand Tesla). Poor Monogram was still purveying pictures like *The Ape Man,* in which "B" starlet Louise Currie sashayed about in her high heels, pelting a hirsute Lugosi with a whip and waving her hands as an ape tears him asunder. And bottom-of-the-pile Producers Releasing Corporation unleashed such drek as *Dead Men Walk,* with George Zucco in the dual role of a doctor and a vampire, and Dwight Frye scuttling and squealing as his final movie hunchback.

However, the top horror films of this period were not issuing from the gates of Universal. They came from RKO, where producer Val Lewton and his young, gifted talent force (directors Jacques Tourneur, Robert Wise and Mark Robson and writer DeWitt Bodeen) were revolutionizing the terror genre with subtle, imaginative, masterfully crafted nightmare tales. Lewton's first production, 1942's *Cat People,* had saved RKO from bankruptcy with an international gross of $4 million. Now, such Lewton chillers as 1943's *I Walked with a Zombie* (which Curt Siodmak scripted with Ardel Wray) and *The Seventh Victim* were reaping critical applause and upstaging the Universal products at the box office.

RKO's success was Universal's poison, and there was much gnashing of teeth on Lankershim Boulevard. Intimidated by the literacy and sensitivity of Lewton's talent force, Universal decided the time had come for a true battle for horror supremacy. One of the studio's first strategems was to host a dinner party on the lot, showing off to the press such terror attractions as Karloff, (who had finally returned to Hollywood after his *Arsenic and Old Lace* tour), Lugosi, Chaney, George Zucco and, of course, ace screamer Evelyn Ankers.

The soiree almost became a total shambles. The ever-erratic Chaney, seated near Miss Ankers and her husband, actor Richard Denning, began amusing himself by insulting his frequent co-star's spouse. Denning, realizing Chaney was "in his cups," politely ignored him, until Chaney demanded, "How come you're in the Navy and still in Los Angeles?" Noting Lon's 4-F status, Denning (who was soon to begin submarine duty) replied, "It's a lot better than not being in the service at all during wartime," which inspired Chaney to wipe some of his green pistachio ice cream on Denning's dress blues. Seconds later, Chaney's face was pistachio green, courtesy of Denning's dessert dish. "With all that green dripping from his face, he looked as if he were back in makeup for one of his monster characters,"[192] remembers Miss Ankers of Chaney, who was preparing to hurl his hot coffee at Denning when Miss Ankers intervened, much to the disappointment of the wide-eyed press.

The Topper of 'Em All . . . From the company that gave you them all . . . !

Universal trade ad for *House of Frankenstein.*

Things were more peaceful in the Universal executive building, where Boris Karloff signed a two-picture starring contract—at triple the price he was receiving before his *Arsenic and Old Lace* triumph. To accommodate Karloff, producer George Waggner dusted off the old chestnut *The Climax,* had Curt Siodmak revamp the story, reopened the old Paris Opera set on soundstage 28 where he had produced his 1943 remake of *Phantom of the Opera,* and added Technicolor and Susanna Foster. Paul Malvern, veteran "B" western producer who was enjoying new prestige following the success of his Maria Montez/Jon Hall Technicolor *Ali Baba and the 40 Thieves,* was entrusted with the other Karloff project, envisioned as the ultimate in Universal horror.

The original title was *The Devil's Brood.* As things evolved, Curt Siodmak wrote only the story

The midnight horror show: Peter Coe, J. Carrol Naish, Lionel Atwill, Sig Rumann, Anne Gwynne.

for the film, which cleverly presented the various ghouls via a traveling Chamber of Horrors, pirated by mad Dr. Gustav Niemann and his pathetic, psychotic hunchbacked assistant. Edward T. Lowe wrote the actual screenplay. The men conservatively decided to drop the mummy "Kharis," that shuffling one-eyed ragbag whom Chaney had been playing with loud protests against the makeup.

Presented to Karloff was the pivotal role of the crazed Niemann; though the actor was willing to return to the Frankenstein series, he was not about to break his vow never to play the Monster again. By no means charmed by the film's *raison d'etre* of parading and destroying favorite box office nightmares, Karloff gentlemanly strove to find something nice to say:

> Horror implies abhorrence, aversion and repugnance. Terror makes your hair stand on end. I don't play roles that are revolting or repulsive. Nor is . . . my new picture revolting or repulsive, though it is certainly destined to take the curl out of anyone's hair.[193]

Karloff also revealed that daughter Sara Jane had been to see only two movies: Disney's *Dumbo* and *Bambi.*

Sharing star-billing with Karloff was Chaney, who, as demonstrated in his dinner party gaffe, was becoming increasingly difficult. He believed that he was at least partially vindicated in his misbehavior. The studio had promised him his father's role in the remake of *Phantom of the Opera,* and then signed Claude Rains for the part. Still, Chaney was happy with this new picture. He was pleased to play his "baby," the Wolf Man, for a third time, and he was proud that the script fashioned for him a love affair. Chaney had not yet given up his campaign to become a screen heart throb.

Originally, Universal announced that Bela Lugosi would don the cape of Dracula (no problem for wardrobe, as Lugosi owned and cherished several such capes). Lugosi very much wanted the part; he had frothed (and rightly so) when the studio starred Chaney in 1943's *Son of Dracula,* unleashing the pudgiest vampire in cinema memory. However, the aging Lugosi sadly saw himself

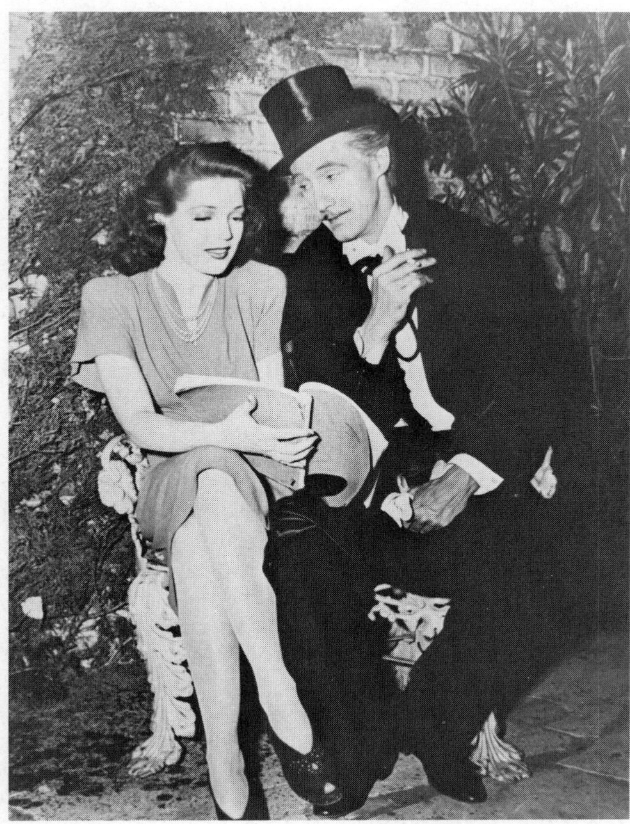

Anne Gwynne and John Carradine look cozy as they relax between scenes of *House of Frankenstein*.

passed over by Universal for reasons ranging from the actor's poverty row commitments and his poor health to the studio's lingering displeasure over his *Frankenstein Meets the Wolf Man* performance.

So Universal awarded the role of the Count to John Carradine, now so infamous a Hollywood villain that while riding in a movie star parade, he was booed and pelted with trash along the two-mile route. Laureled for his performances in such John Ford classics as *The Prisoner of Shark Island* (as vicious Sgt. Rankin), 1939's *Stagecoach* (as the mysterious gambler Hatfield), and 1940's *The Grapes of Wrath* (unforgettable as the martyr Casy), the cadaverous Carradine, 38, had also reigned from 1936–42 as the skunk supreme of 20th Century-Fox, where, as Bob Ford in 1939's *Jesse James*, he committed his worst atrocity—shooting Tyrone Power in the back. Now freelancing at $3,500 per week, Carradine was the producer/director/star and sole owner of his own Shakespearean repertory company, touring the West Coast as Hamlet, Shylock, and (alternately) Othello and Iago. He gallantly financed the company via such films as Monogram's *Voodoo Man* (as Lugosi's idiot helper, leering at the female zombies) and Universal's *The Mummy's Ghost* (as a high priest of Karnak, brewing tana leaves for the crumbling Kharis). Still eccentric, Carradine was then one of the most picturesque inhabitants of the legendary "Garden of Allah," where he resided with his "Ophelia," voluptuously blonde Sonia Sorel. Allah survivors still remember the night that Carradine announced (after some excellent Scotch) that he was the Christ, and would prove it by walking across the swimming pool. His neighbors left their villas, congregated poolside and made bets as to whether or not Carradine was truly divine. He was not.

Also signed for the "sensation" and promised special billing in the bargain, was J. Carrol Naish. Like Carradine, the 47-year-old Naish (who, for all his expertise at playing Indians, Mexicans and Italians, was actually of Irish ancestry), was one of Hollywood's best paid and busiest character men. His credits ranged from low budget abortions such as *The Monster Maker* (which he had just finished at PRC) to Columbia's epic *Sahara* (for which he had just won an Academy Award nomination as the self-sacrificing Italian soldier)* and Columbia's 1943 *Batman* serial, in which he played super-Oriental villain, Dr. Daka. A soft-spoken, retiring and very conscientious actor, Naish prepared for his role of the warped hunchback Daniel by finding a hunchbacked derelict in a grimy Los Angeles boarding house and spending time with him to observe his mannerisms. Since being sought out as a model for a part in a horror picture was no compliment, Naish rewarded the hunchback for his services: "I paid a month's rent for the hunchback in a clean, moderate class hotel," Naish told director Erle C. Kenton, "and advised him to keep on taking baths."[194]

Excellent players filled the supporting ranks. Lionel Atwill, who in April of 1943 publicly wept with joy when absolved of his perjury conviction in a court appeal, had returned to work with a vengeance as "The Scarab" in Republic's *Captain America* serial. The irrepressible "Pinky," now seriously romancing a 27-year-old radio producer/singer named Paula Pruter, happily accepted the cameo role of Inspector Arnz. George Zucco, that superb British screen menace of the bald pate and funereal voice, made his only Frankenstein film appearance as Professor Bruno Lampini, original charlatan of the Chamber of Horrors. The lovely Anne Gwynne, Universal's "TNT girl" ("trim, neat, terrific"), who scarcely received time to adjust her garter belt between Universal potboilers, was cast

*Naish lost in the 1943 supporting actor race to Charles Coburn of *The More the Merrier.* In 1945, the official year of release of *House of Frankenstein,* Naish was again a Best Supporting Actor nominee for Paramount's *A Medal for Benny,* losing to James Dunn of *A Tree Grows in Brooklyn.*

Glenn Strange (1899–1973).

as Rita, Dracula's intended victim. Already a survivor of such studio melodramas as 1940's *Black Friday,* 1941's *The Black Cat* and 1944's *Weird Woman,* the copper-haired Miss Gwynne was the lot's No. 2 horror girl, never really anxious to try harder than her good friend Evelyn Ankers. And, for the doomed Ilonka, Larry Talbot's gypsy romance, Universal signed the vivacious, pleasingly plump teenage starlet Elena Verdugo.

But what of the Monster?

Boo! I became the Monster![195]

Glenn Strange

During the 1931 Christmas season, Glenn Strange, 32-year-old boxer, wrestler, rodeo performer and movie stunt man/bit player, went with his brother Virgil to see *Frankenstein* in El Paso, Texas. As they left the theater, Virgil turned to his brother and said, "You know they can't build a guy up like that and make him breathe again. But where the hell did they ever find a guy that looked like *that?*"[196]

Glenn Strange had just worked with the "guy" in Columbia's *The Guilty Generation.* And, although the six-feet-four, 218-pound "Peewee" (as he was called by his pals) devoted his major energies over the next 12 years to his family, nightclub brawls, comic books, and scores of "B" westerns, screen horror seemed to loom in his destiny. In Universal's original 1936 *Flash Gordon* serial, Strange had played three parts: a robot of Ming the Merciless, a soldier of the Emperor, and a reptilian creature ("The Gocko" of the comics) that snared Flash in lobster-like pincers. In PRC's execrable *The Mad Monster* of 1942, Strange was the title terror, a hairy horror who, save for the fangs, was a dead ringer for Gabby Hayes. He had played a bit in *The Mummy's Tomb,* and was featured in PRC's *The Monster Maker.*

Strange had no idea that Universal was seeking a new actor to play the Monster the morning he reported to Jack Pierce's studio to receive a facial scar. Nor was he aware that fellow western heavy Lane Chandler had already made a test for the part. While Strange reclined in the makeup chair, Pierce suddenly excused himself, called Paul Malvern on the telephone and told the producer that he had found the Monster.

Truly, Strange was just what Universal wanted. He was big, he was strong, he was prunefaced, he required no muscle padding, and he wouldn't need a double. The 44-year old Strange was also in no position to demand the high salaries and lofty billing already promised Karloff, Chaney, Naish and Carradine. After a run-through in makeup for Pierce and Malvern, Glenn Strange became the fourth actor to play Universal's Frankenstein Monster.

Comedian Ole Olsen and Glenn Strange enjoy one of Strange's comic books.

On April Fool's Day 1944, George Waggner completed shooting of *The Climax.* With Karloff now free, Erle C. Kenton turned full energy to the shooting of *The Devil's Brood.*

A movie monster can get the wits scared out of him, the same as humans. He can get cold and hungry and tired. He can be insulted, and have his feelings hurt because people don't want to be in his company.[197]

Glenn Strange

The Devil's Brood was a happy set. John Carradine now and then treated the company to his recitations of Shakespeare. Lon Chaney, who loved to cook, sometimes prepared a lavish lunch in his dressing room for his co-stars. However, for Glenn Strange, there were many rude awakenings as he took on the role of the Monster. There was, of course, the three-and-a-half-hour makeup adventure each day with Jack Pierce, and its side effects:

> When I had the Monster makeup on, I used to have trouble seeing because the Monster's eyelids hung over my eyes. The makeup made my face raw, and lots of times I felt like I had water on the brain. You see, the skull cap I wore was so tight, it wouldn't let the perspiration out. So, after a couple of hours on the set, I could shake my head and the water would rattle around inside the skull cap.[198]

Strange discovered that playing a Monster created social repercussions, too:

> I wasn't allowed in the studio commissary. I guess they didn't want me turning the stomachs of the stars and starlets. They brought me my lunch in a paper sack and I had to eat it where nobody would see me![199]

As Strange adapted to these indelicacies, he was fortunate in the fact that the Monster was comatose for most of the film. Once Strange reached the soundstage each day, he usually had little more to do than to lay prostrate and look ugly. Yet even this posed its dangers, and Strange would wince whenever he recalled how the glass case (in which Niemann supposedly thawed the Monster's frozen tissues with steam) very nearly became his coffin:

> The prop men pumped vapor into the box to make it look like steam. But I couldn't breathe, on account of the prop steam, so they put long rubber hoses in my nose so I could get air.
>
> I was scared even before they put me in that thing. I told them, "Now don't strap me down, cause if anything goes wrong, I want to *get out quick*!"[200]

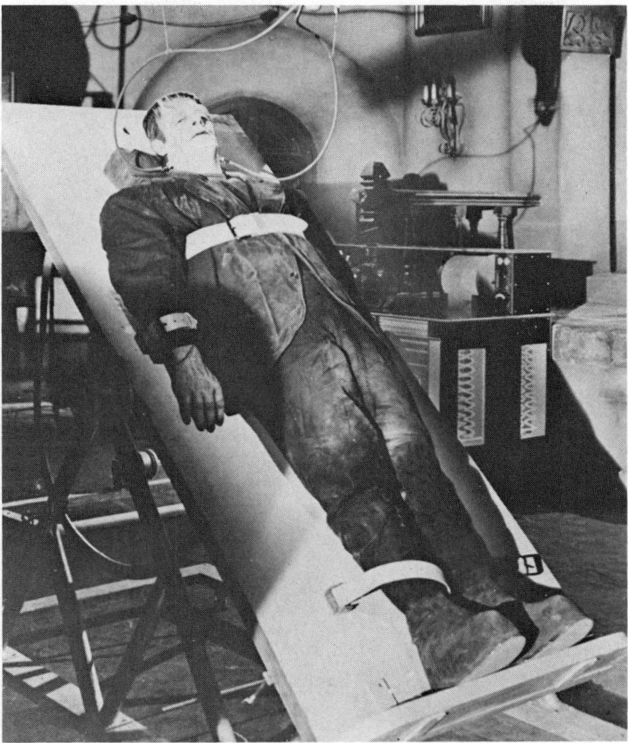

Glenn Strange as the Monster.

Sympathetic, the prop crew installed a panic button inside the case. If Strange thought himself in danger, he could push this button and a red light would flash. Unfortunately, nobody was told to keep an eye on the light.

> Sure enough, something went wrong. The hoses were so long, I couldn't breathe out the bad air and I was starting to suffocate. I laid on the panic button they gave me to push if anything happened, and that red cue light was flashing like Fourth of July. Believe me, I almost died before somebody saw the light and got me out of there.[201]

When Strange finally arose in the climax, more near-disasters awaited him. While carrying Karloff's double under his arm, Strange almost fell down 40 steep castle steps when an overly excited extra among the pursuing villagers threw his heavy torch and hit Strange in the back. Strange also was almost seriously burned (the hair of Karloff's double was singed) when the back lot swamp exploded into flames more violently than the special effects crew had planned, causing Strange to galumph much faster than he was directed into the safety of the quicksands.

Actually, the worst accident on the film did not victimize Strange; it was, to his great regret, caused by him. For the scene where the Monster

Lon Chaney and Elena Verdugo take a break outside the sound stage.

threw Daniel through the window, the prop crew had placed plush mattresses behind the set upon which Naish could comfortably land. "As I mentioned, it was hard for me to see with the Monster makeup on,"[202] said Strange, who misjudged his aim. The little actor crashed through the breakaway window, missed the mattresses completely, and landed smack on the cement soundstage floor. Fortunately, the large padded "hunchback" that Naish was wearing under his costume cushioned his fall sufficiently to prevent serious injury.

Still, for all the misadventures, Strange loved the engagement. For, in playing the Monster, he had the help of Karloff himself, whom Strange later saluted as " . . . the greatest man in show business."[203] Though Karloff was ill at the time with serious back trouble, drinking a quart of milk a day and nibbling crackers to try to gain weight, he was happy to help:

> I'd never have been the Monster I was if it hadn't been for Boris Karloff. I remember, for instance, that he was sick during some of the filming. He had finished his scenes and could have gone home, but he stayed on and worked with me. He showed me how to make the Monster's moves properly, and how to do the walk that makes the Monster so frightening. . . .[204]

Vivacious Elena Verdugo had the unusual experience of working for the first time upon soil that once belonged to her forefathers . . .

from the *House of Frankenstein* pressbook.

Was it fun to be the leading lady in a monster rally? Very much so, according to Elena Verdugo. There was a special irony in all her performances at Universal City, a locale owned by her ancestors. As the charming actress told me:

> It's true. Much of North Hollywood, Studio City, Burbank and Universal City was the original Spanish land grant to Jose Maria Verdugo, a soldier in the Spanish army. I once got a laugh when I reminded an irritating director at Universal that he was standing on my property!
>
> I was not under contract to Universal. The main condition for it had been for me to lose weight, and I rebelled. But I played more pictures for them than did many of the studio's contract players, and *House of Frankenstein* was my debut there.[205]

Although she was only 19 at the time, Miss Verdugo was already an experienced performer:

> I was a local L.A. girl, and had been a dancer from age 5. Movies were work, not glamour. Almost all of my family were in some area of film or music locally. My mother usually took me to the set, and then I went home to my family and my old neighborhood.

It was Miss Verdugo's talent as a dancer, as well as her beauty and dramatic energy, that won her the role of the gypsy dancer Ilonka, who sacrifices her life to release Larry Talbot from the curse of lycanthropy. Universal, however, could not accept a blonde gypsy girl:

> As Ilonka, I used a brunette wig. In fact, I had to wear a wig in several pictures until I escaped those "gypsy" roles and played Lou Costello's girl in *Little Giant* (1946). Sometimes dye was used instead of a wig. An industry joke was that I was Hollywood's only light-at-the-roots brunette!

Miss Verdugo cherished the opportunity to work in the picture with such professionals:

> Working with Boris Karloff, I had an intense awareness that I was working with a "great." He was a serious actor, but never unkind. Lon Chaney was a lovely, friendly man. I remember often sitting and chatting with him. I had met J. Carrol Naish on the set of my first picture,

Karloff gives starlet Elena Verdugo a present, while director Erle C. Kenton (center) smiles, Lon Chaney looms, and Paul Malvern approves.

> *Down Argentine Way* (20th Century-Fox, 1940), when I was 15. He loved working. I simply loved him. He helped, he supported, he gave so much. I'd see Glenn Strange in the makeup department every A.M. Glenn was dear, and Jack Pierce, his makeup man, was a genius.

Acting with so many seasoned veterans, Miss Verdugo soon discovered that she too was expected to be a "trouper." Her gypsy dance, which comprises over a minute-and-a-half of screen time, was entirely her own creation:

> I had to choreograph the gypsy dance carefully myself. It was difficult, because at the last moment I learned that it was to be done on a slope that had not even been cleared of rocks.

Still, the actress enjoyed herself—though there was one wig-raising experience:

> For the horror films at Universal, they used to have professional screamers on the sets. For the scene in which the Wolf Man attacked me, they called one of those "screamers" to our stage. This was one of the show's first shots, and I hadn't seen Lon in his makeup. Well, when the Wolf Man jumped out at me, I was so scared and screamed so wildly that they cancelled the professional screamer!
>
> All in all, I enjoyed making the picture very much. I was a still-growing teenage girl, and *all* of those fine actors were kind, considerate, and made me feel a part of everything.

Elena Verdugo would win her greatest popularity on television as the star of *Meet Millie,* the CBS comedy series that ran from 1952–56. Most recently, she appeared as Nurse Consuelo Lopez on ABC's *Marcus Welby, M.D.* which kept her busy at Universal from 1969–76. As she remembers:

> During my early years at the studio, Universal was a small, close family. There was much USO activity, service men visited the lot—it was a happy place. Then I returned after all those years, and discovered that Universal had become a factory.

Here's to a son to the house of Frankenstein!

Toast of old Baron Frankenstein (Frederick Kerr) in 1931's *Frankenstein.*

Although shooting of *The Devil's Brood* "wrapped" on May 8, 1944, the film became bogged in a studio backlog and would wait seven months before playing its first engagements. In the meantime, Hans J. Salter again contributed a splendid score, dominated by gypsy themes, and the title was changed to the more commercial *House of Frankenstein.* On December 14, 1944, Universal previewed what it heralded as "The Greatest Shock Show the Screen Has Ever Seen!" in the studio projection room, and the next day,

The Wolf Man strikes: Chaney and Verdugo.

Glenn Strange carries Karloff's double into a studio quagmire.

the film opened at New York City's horror salon, The Rialto. Most Manhattan critics made mincemeat of the mayhem:

> *New York Herald-Tribune:* . . . The plot stumbles along endlessly in its top-heavy attempt to carry on its shoulders too many of yesterday's nightmares . . . When Dracula raises his arms and flies away as a little bat, the strongest possible reaction is "Quick Henry, the flit." And when Dr. Niemann restores the Monster to life in a laboratory maze of dynamos . . . the effect is little short of ludicrous . . . the *House of Frankenstein* is only a little more terrifying than the house that Jack built.[206]

On December 22, 1944, *House of Frankenstein* opened at Hollywood's 956-seat Hawaii Theatre, supported on a double bill by *The Mummy's Curse.* The *Hollywood Citizen-News* gave a studio-delighting endorsement:

> . . . *House of Frankenstein* is a thriller deluxe. In this Universal horror extravaganza, Director Erle C. Kenton has gathered together Boris Karloff, Lon Chaney, John Carradine, J. Carrol Naish, and Glenn Strange, a master group of terror specialists who can't be equalled in a fancy nightmare . . . excitement mounts to a high pitch, as the principals get tangled in assorted complications—all thrill-packed and spine-tickling. It's a film guaranteed to provide an acute case of jitters. . . .[207]

House of Frankenstein officially entered national release in February 1945. Business was good, bolstered in many theaters by a studio-concocted "Hiss the Villain" contest. "All theatre-goers like to 'hiss' the villain," noted the exhibitors' pressbook. "Instead of only *one* villain to hiss, *House of Frankenstein* has *five* . . . Set up a regulation ballot-box in your lobby. Carry this banner copy across the top: 'Hiss The Villain Contest . . . Vote for the Horror Character You Hate the Most!' . . ."

There was never an official tally as to who won the lion's share of the hate votes. However, as evidenced by the snorts and giggles that sounded in theaters as the Monster moronically waded into the quicksand, Frankenstein's Monster had become easier to laugh at than to hate.

The Monster became a clumsy automaton . . . Where Karloff's Monster was a nightmare with its sunken, shadowed cheeks, thin, cruel lips, and hate-blazing eyes, the later Monster had chubby cheeks and dead eyes and the face of a mindless somnambulist rather than a vibrantly living, evil creature. Karloff's Monster was a being of deadly cunning; the beast of Lugosi and Strange seemed to have lost all power of thought . . .[208]

from *Horror!*, by Drake Douglas.

House of Frankenstein survives today as a slick, fun, horror mini-epic; it has action (including the exciting chase of the mounted gendarmes after Dracula's coach through back lot fields, stream and woods), some mood (particularly in the very impressive ice cavern sequence), and some directorial style (e.g., Kenton's treatment of Chaney's first transformation from man to beast, panning the human footprints that change into paw prints just before a long shot shows the Wolf Man loping madly into the woods). Yet, despite such virtues, its beautiful score and its grand cast, the film has never succeeded in transcending its ignoble purpose: to cram together as many horrors as 70 minutes would allow. Nor has it ever been forgiven by the more discriminating terror film aficionados for taking another giant step in the degradation of Frankenstein's Monster.

For many years, fans have chastised Strange for playing the Monster like a zapped-out, moronic goon—and there's no denying that this is exactly what he suggests. Yet it should be noted in his defense that this unsophisticated actor was merely playing the script's conception of the character. Despite the rather dense face, with its glazed, dead eyes and its saggy dewlaps, Strange *does* manage to suggest superhuman strength, as when he scoopes up Daniel like a stuffed toy and throws him through the castle window.* There is, too, one very clever touch to his performance. When Strange's Monster awakes after 100,000 megavolts and sees Daniel, he laughs at him—obviously amused by the little hunchback's deformity. It is a cruel, ironic touch, one more suggestive of James Whale than Erle C. Kenton. However, for most of his limited footage, the Monster could have been played by a dummy (and, for a few moments in the recharging scene, he was!). The fact that Strange's Monster is mired at the bottom of the film's closing credits seems a punishment for his outrageously stupid gaffe of plodding into the quicksand, despite Karloff's raspy warnings—a buffoonery grossly unworthy of the screen's greatest Monster.

As for the other players, Karloff is a fine ringmaster for the circus of terrors, flashing his eyes and milking such dialogue as "The undying Monster—the triumphant climax of Frankenstein's genius!" Chaney again possesses that strange magnetism as the cursed Talbot, while Atwill, Zucco and Sig Rumann (as the Burgomaster of Reigelburg) all bring color, however briefly, to the film. Elena Verdugo has great spirit and zest as Ilonka, while Anne Gwynne, as Dracula's desired femme, brings a very sensual quality to her vampire-induced trance.

A special laurel must be awarded John Carradine for his lascivious Count Dracula. With his suavely cocked top hat, continental charm and sepulchrally seductive tones, Carradine's Dracula is an alluring incubus, with touches of the romantic and the lustful which would later flourish in Universal's 1979 *Dracula* with Frank Langella. However, the film's top performance is J. Carrol Naish's pathetic Daniel. When, heartsick over Miss Verdugo, Naish cries at the Monster, "She hates me because I'm an ugly hunchback! If it wasn't for you, I'd have Talbot's body!" and begins whipping the creature with a strap, the superb actor brings true pathos and a juicy slice of Freud to the hokum.

The profits of *House of Frankenstein* abetted Universal in achieving a 1945 fiscal profit of $4 million. The studio convinced itself that the film had recouped Universal's status as the most successful producer of screen horror. But it wasn't to be. Leaving Universal, Karloff signed a star contract with Val Lewton's outfit at RKO, where he so chillingly portrayed *The Body Snatcher,* directed by Robert Wise. In May of 1945, that superb melodrama (featuring Lugosi and double-billed with RKOs *The Brighton Strangler*) opened at Hollywood's Hawaii Theatre (where *House of Frankenstein* had played five months earlier) and shattered all first-week attendance records. *The Body Snatcher* also placed on James Agee's Best of 1945 list and caused Universal to realize bitterly that all of its gruesome stock company *en masse* was no match for clever imagination, masterful story-telling and true talent.

*The scream, incidentally, that accompanies Naish's fall from the castle roof is the same scream that Karloff unleashed in *Son of Frankenstein* when he discovered the slain Ygor! So impressed was Universal by Karloff's howl that the studio re-recorded it and added the scream to the sound effects library. It was utilized on the soundtrack of several films, including the Sherlock Holmes mystery *The Spider Woman* (1944).

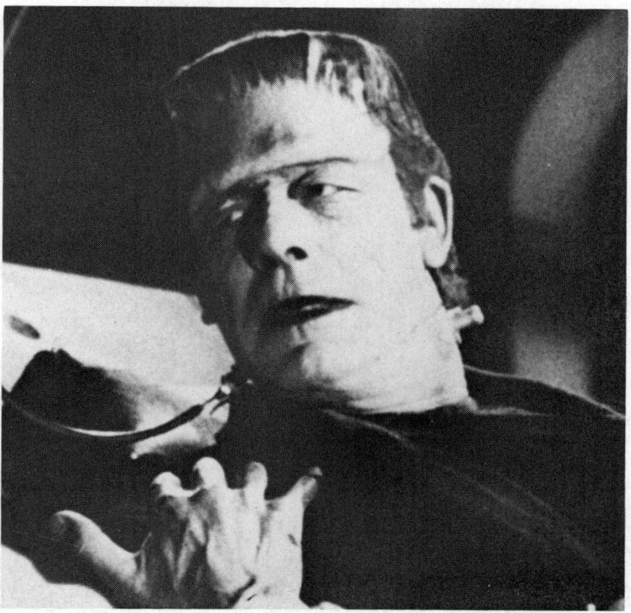

The Strange Monster.

While Karloff, whose triumph as *The Body Snatcher* established him as a major cinema character star welcome in every genre, never had too much to say about *House of Frankenstein,* his true feelings about it are hinted by his praise for Lewton as "the man who rescued me from the living dead and restored my soul."[209]

And, as for Karloff's feelings on Strange's Monster:

> Well, he wasn't as lucky as I was. I got the cream of it, being the first. I know I wished him lots of luck . . . hoping it would do as much for him as it did for me, but. . . .[210]

House of Dracula poster.

House of Dracula (1945)

Producer, Paul Malvern; *Executive Producer,* Joe Gershenson; *Director,* Erle C. Kenton; *Screenplay,* Edward T. Lowe; *Photography,* George Robinson; *Film Editor,* Russell Schoengarth; *Art Direction,* John B. Goodman and Martin Obzina; *Sound Director,* Bernard B. Brown; *Technician,* Jess Moulin; *Set Decorations,* Russell A. Gausman and Arthur D. Leddy; *Gowns,* Vera West; *Makeup Artist,* Jack P. Pierce; *Hair Stylist,* Carmen Dirigo; *Special Photography Effects,* John P. Fulton; *Musical Director,* Edgar Fairchild; *Assistant Director,* Ralph Slosser.

Completed, Universal City, California, October 25, 1945; Previewed at studio, November 28, 1945. Running Time: 67 minutes.

HOUSE OF DRACULA— SYNOPSIS

In her bedroom in the old castle on the craggy seacoast of Visaria, blonde Miliza Morelle is tossing with strange, perverse dreams. Outside her French windows, a large bat hovers in the night and, in a strange flurry, is transformed into a tall, skeletal man in flowing cape and top hat, who gazes lustfully at Miliza . . .

Downstairs, the stranger enters the study of Dr. Franz Edelmann, the brilliant scientist renowned for his near-miraculous cures of supposedly hopeless cases. As his cat squeals at the sight of the tall visitor, Edelmann awakes. The stranger introduces himself as Baron Latos and asks Edelmann to escort him to the gloomy old armor room of the castle where the scientist sees a large coffin with an infamous talisman.

"The Dracula crest!" exclaims Dr. Edelmann.

"Yes, doctor. I am Count Dracula. You see before you a man who's lived for centuries, kept alive by the blood of innocent people. That's why I've come to you—to seek release from a curse of misery and horror, against which I'm powerless to fight alone. You could effect a cure?"

"It would be a challenge to medical science," muses Edelmann.

"Accept that challenge, doctor, but decide quickly," says Dracula, looking toward the great window. "The dawn . . . "

Edelmann agrees to treat Dracula, unaware that the vampire's true goal lies in the bedroom above, still plagued by nightmares.

The next day Edelmann begins work on developing an antitoxic for Dracula's blood. Assisting him is Nina, a lovely brunette nurse afflicted with a hunched back. Edelmann plans to reward Nina's dedication to his experiments by repairing her deformity via a bone-softening extract culled from an exotic plant known as the Clavaria Formosa, grown in the doctor's laboratory under tropical conditions. Meanwhile that evening, Dracula arrives for a consultation with Edelmann, and sees the doctor's other assistant, Miliza.

"Baron Latos!" smiles the surprised woman.

"Miss Morelle! You left Schoenheim just as we were becoming acquainted. Now that 'chance' has brought us together again, I hope to see you quite often. . . ."

Edelmann gives Dracula his diagnosis. An examination of his blood has revealed the presence of a hitherto unknown parasite. The scientist hopes that a pure culture of the parasite injected into Dracula's bloodstream, will destroy itself. And Dracula agrees to his first transfusion.

The moon had not yet risen that night when a drawn stranger arrives at the castle begging for an immediate audience with Edelmann. "If you'll just give him my name . . . Talbot, Lawrence Talbot . . . then he'll understand." Miliza promises that the scientist will see him as soon as the transfusion is over. "There isn't time," raves Talbot, and he races into the night.

Later that evening, the telephone rings at the castle. It proves to be Inspector Holtz, asking the doctor to come at once to the town in regard to a stranger in the jail. As Edelmann and Miliza arrive, they see a crowd milling about the station,

The Players

Lawrence Talbot	Lon Chaney
Count Dracula	John Carradine
Miliza	Martha O'Driscoll
Inspector Holtz	Lionel Atwill
Dr. Franz Edelmann	Onslow Stevens
The Monster	Glenn Strange
Nina	Jane Adams
Ziegfried	Ludwig Stossel
Steinmuhl	Skelton Knaggs
Brahms	Joseph E. Bernard
Villager	Dick Dickinson
Gendarmes	Fred Cordova
	Carey Harrison
Villager	Harry Lamont
Johannes	Gregory Muradian
Mother	Beatrice Gray

with Steinmuhl, the ugly village idiot, in the fore.

"If I find the person who started the rumor we have a crazy man here," barks Holtz at the mob, "I'll lock him up!"

"As a matter of fact, doctor, we have!" admits Holtz to Edelmann in the privacy of the jailhouse. "He came here a little while ago and demanded that I put him in a cell—to keep him from committing murder! Decent sort of chap otherwise, name of *Talbot.*"

John Carradine as Dracula.

"Doctor," pleads Talbot, "have you ever heard of the pentagram—the mark of the beast? When the full moon rises, I turn into a werewolf, with only one desire in my mind—to kill!"

As Edelmann tries to convince Talbot that his lycanthropy is only in his mind, the prisoner suddenly peers into the moonlight that filters through his cell window. Suddenly, as Edelmann, Holtz and Miliza watch in horror, Talbot licks and snarls as his face and hands metamorphose into those of a terrible beast, one that leaps at the cell bars, lunging and stretching his claws at the trio of onlookers.

The next morning, Holtz brings Talbot to the castle. "Do you think he can help me?" the lycanthrope asks Miliza, who feels a strange sympathy and attraction toward the haunted Talbot. "He's done some wonderful things," encourages the nurse, and Edelmann offers his diagnosis. He has found, he says, pressure upon certain parts of Talbot's brain which, along with Talbot's belief in his lycanthropy, brings about just that change when the moon is full.

"During the period in which your reasoning processes give way to self-hypnosis, the glands which govern your metabolism get out of control—like a steam engine without a balance wheel. When this happens, the glands generate an abnormal supply of certain hormones," which, implies the doctor, are responsible for the physical transformation.

Edelmann fears the risk of a surgical operation to enlarge the cranial cavity, but there may be an alternative. In the laboratory, the scientist shows Talbot the Clavaria Formosa plants from which he can extract a substance that can soften any hard substance composed of calcium phosphate—

Onslow Stevens and Lon Chaney.

such as the skull. Edelmann hopes to enlarge Talbot's cranial cavity to relieve the pressure.

"You can do that now?" asks Talbot, who receives a sad pause in response. *"Can you?"*

Edelmann admits he cannot. It will take some time to produce the mold in sufficient quantities, and he suggests that Talbot confine himself again that night when the moon will be full again.

"No, doctor. No. I can't go through that again!" Talbot races from the castle and to the cliffs above the sea. For a moment he stares at the raging waters far below, then hurls himself into the sea.

That night, in the moonlight, the villagers gather on the cliffs erecting for Edelmann a crane by which he might lower himself to the Devil's Cave far below, where he hopes the sea has washed Talbot. The scientist meticulously times his actions to the last minute; if he arrives after Talbot changes back into human form, he fears the man will try to kill himself again; if he arrives too early, while Talbot is still a beast, he fears for his own life.

Edelmann ventures into the darkness of the cave. Suddenly a wild snarl sounds and the Wolf Man wrestles the scientist to the cave floor. However, seconds before the creature rips into Edelmann's throat, the moon sets and the beast changes back into a man.

Edelmann tells the despairing Talbot that he had wanted to die, but that he will live because, "God in His divine workings, has led you to the very thing which makes help possible." The temperature and humidity in the cave were ideal for growing the spore-producing plants needed for Talbot's cure. Before the next full moon, there should be enough for the process.

Exploring farther into the cavern, the men soon make a startling discovery. There, in the mud, is the Frankenstein Monster, cradling the skeleton of the Dr. Niemann whom he had carried into the quicksand years before. "He's still alive!" Talbot exclaims of his old enemy. "He's indestructible," replies Edelmann. "Frankenstein's creation is man's challenge to the laws of life and death!" Finally, the two men discover an old room—history had mentioned an old torture chamber in the castle—with an entrance to the castle proper, an ideal place for a new laboratory to produce the Clavaria Formosa.

Fascinated by the Monster, Edelmann exhumes him from the mud and brings the comatose creature to the castle laboratory, determined to revive him. Talbot and Nina protest. "Think what you're doing, doctor!" says Nina. "To bring him back again . . . would unleash worse than murder upon humanity. . . . Man's responsibility is to his fellow man!" These words convince Edelmann, and he turns off the electrical machinery. "Frankenstein's Monster must never wreak havoc again," says the scientist.

Night falls, and Miliza, in the great hall, is playing "Moonlight Sonata" on the piano as the Count enters. As he gazes at her, suddenly the music changes to a wild, demonic tune. "I've never heard this music before, yet I'm playing it!"

"You're creating it—for *me,*" replies Dracula.

"It frightens me!"

"It's beautiful! It's the music of the world from which I come."

"It makes me see strange things—people who are dead—yet they're alive. . . ."

Dracula advances on Miliza, but before he can caress her, a strange impulse causes her to lift a little necklace crucifix from her bodice. Dracula whirls away and the music returns to the "Moonlight Sonata."

Nevertheless, Dracula hovers about the castle that night. When Nina returns from the new laboratory in the cave, she sees Miliza in a passionate trance, standing next to him before a mirror.

"I couldn't see his reflection!" gasps Nina to Edelmann, who rushes into action. He tells her that if anything happens to him, that she is to go to the old armor room in the basement and burn what she finds there.

Outside in the garden, Dracula has succeeded in persuading Miliza to drop her cross. Edelmann appears and cooly asks Dracula back into the castle for another transfusion. Dracula suavely agrees, but as the scientist loses consciousness during the process, the vampire rises from the operating table, takes the vial of parasitic blood and shoots

The Dream Sequence: Glenn Strange and Onslow Stevens.

it into Edelmann's bloodstream.

Transformed into a bat, Dracula flies into the bedroom, where Miliza, in a negligee with her hair down, awaits her undead bridegroom. Nina runs to Talbot's room for help, and Talbot breaks into Miliza's room, just as Edelmann lunges through another door, waving a cross at the vampire. Dracula races to the armor room to the sanctuary of his coffin, and Edelmann follows, dragging the coffin into the light of the dawn, which reduces Dracula to a skeleton. At the same time, Miliza suddenly breaks from her trance and looks warmly at Talbot.

Not long afterwards, Edelmann begins to feel the presence of Dracula's blood in his veins. Late one evening, as his cat runs in terror, Edelmann watches his reflection in the mirror become hideous and degenerate—and then vanish. He collapses into a wild, perverse dream, one in which Dracula rises from the dead, and the Monster rampages through the village and Nina, no longer deformed, now seductively beautiful, walks to him . . . .

Awakening, Edelmann runs to the laboratory and begins recharging the Monster. However, the spell passes, and the doctor confesses his illness to Nina. He wants to operate on her immediately, but the nurse unselfishly insists that Edelmann operate on Talbot instead. The next day, Edelmann enlarges Talbot's cranial cavity, and orders his nurses to devote all their energies to extracting enough spores for him to perform his operation on Nina as soon as possible. Talbot waits until the next full moon appears, his fears soothed by Miliza. She tells the man with whom she is falling in love that he will soon see the night as a time of peace and beauty.

"Until that time comes," answers Talbot, "I'll live a thousand hopes—and die a thousand times."

Meanwhile, Edelmann enters another horrible spell of bestiality. He sneaks out into the night and leaps upon the coach of his servant Ziegfried, who orders his horses to race faster and faster as Edelmann's face leers at him in the darkness. "Your hands are trembling, Ziegfried . . . You're afraid of me . . . you're afraid I'm going to *kill* you. . . ." Seconds later, Edelmann pounces on Ziegfried, and rips out his throat.

The runaway coach careens into the village, dumping Edelmann into the streets. The villagers pour from their homes, and the mob chases the murderer through the town and up the hills and through the cemetery before the madman escapes over the walls of Edelmann's castle. As the scientist tumbles to the grounds, Larry Talbot is watching from his window.

Minutes later, Inspector Holtz arrives and demands to see Talbot. Edelmann, having returned to normal, escorts the Inspector to Talbot's room, but insists that Talbot is guiltless, claiming his recent medical care makes any physical exertion out of the question. Later that night, Talbot comes to Edelmann's room, tells him that he is aware he murdered Ziegfried and that he wants to help the doctor if he possibly can. Edelmann confides to Talbot the horror of what has befallen him since he feels that the former lycanthrope will understand as others would not. He begs Talbot to say nothing to Holtz at this time in order to give him "time to do for Nina what I've done for you. After that, this evil thing must be destroyed. You have my word that it will be, my boy. But if I'm unable—*you* must do it for me."

The next night, the full moon is about to rise. Edelmann, Miliza and Nina all encourage Talbot, who walks alone on the estate grounds to confront the rising of the moon. Soon the moon looms over the horizon, and Talbot impulsively raises his hand against his face to block its light. However, he soon realizes that there will be no change—that his curse of lycanthropy is gone—and he stands tall, staring at the moon which so terrified him for so many years.

"Doctor, it's wonderful!" rejoices Nina, who turns to find Edelmann has gone. From the laboratory comes the terrible sound of humming electricity. Nina enters the laboratory and sees Edelmann, madly controlling the machinery, rasping at the revived Monster, "I'll make you strong . . . stronger than you've ever been . . . the strength of a hundred men . . . !

"No, Dr. Edelmann," wails Nina. "No! You promised!"

Edelmann spins around and leers at the little hunchback. "You're spying on me . . . you shouldn't have come here . . . I don't like people who see what they're not supposed to see . . . ." Grabbing Nina by the throat, he wrenches the life out of the girl and hurls her crooked body into the cave laboratory below.

Down in the village, Steinmuhl has learned that a medical emblem of Edelmann's was found in the hand of his dead brother Ziegfried. He leads a mob of townspeople to the estate, while Holtz, alerted of this discovery, marches to the castle with two gendarmes. When Nina's scream is heard, Talbot, Miliza and the police run into the laboratory and see the crazed Edelmann and the risen Monster. The police attack, and the Monster pummels them as Edelmann throws Holtz into an electrical dynamo that explodes and roasts the life out of the Inspector.

Reluctantly, Talbot fires two bullets into the man who saved his life and, seconds before death, Edelmann's face shows a sign of peace.

The Monster, outraged that his friend has been slain, goes mad. He lunges for Talbot, who dodges behind a towering shelf of highly combustible chemicals which topples. The castle explodes into flames. "Get out!" shouts Talbot to the villagers who have stormed the castle, "the Frankenstein Monster!" As they run in terror, and Talbot clutches his lovely Miliza, the Monster galumphs about in the flames, finally falling under a massive beam and perishing in the inferno.

HOUSE OF DRACULA— PRODUCTION HISTORY

One picture as ludicrously bad as this one probably will merely make audiences laugh. Another one might arouse monster anger in a whole theatre full of people and send them on a bloodthirsty quest for Universal overlords' necks to bite.[211]

New York World-Telegram review of *House of Frankenstein*, December, 1944

"Universal's Super-Sequel to Record-Wrecking *House of Frankenstein* . . . The Same BIG *Sell* . . . Geared to Even BIGGER Grosses!" trumpeted the loud trade ads for *House of Dracula.* The sensational verbiage was fooling no one. From the opening credits (featuring a re-recording of the theme from *Son of Frankenstein*) to its fiery finale (tacked on from the climax of *The Ghost of Frankenstein*), the last serious chapter of the once-great Frankenstein series croaked an ugly and pervading death rattle.

Fifteen-year-old Ronald Chaney (second from left) and his seventeen-year-old brother Lon (right) visit dad on the set. John Carradine and Martha O'Driscoll join the fun.

The year 1945 was an unusual one for Universal City. Not a single studio release placed on the top moneymaker movie list of mid-1944 to mid-1945. Yet business was booming as Universal tried to wring every last drop of blood from its most reliable profit-makers. Deanna Durbin sang "Danny Boy" in *Because of Him* and tried playing a femme fatale in the mystery *Lady on a Train,* while her young studio counterpart Gloria Jean trilled in *Easy to Look At* and *I Remember April.* Lou Costello posed as a female basketball star in *Here Come the Co-Eds* and reprised (again) "Who's on First?" with ever-sardonic Abbott in *The Naughty Nineties.* Maria Montez and Jon Hall posed in the lush Technicolor of *Sudan,* The Andrews Sisters jived in *Her Lonely Night,* Olsen and Johnson were silly in *See My Lawyer* and Rathbone and Bruce were sagacious in three Sherlock Holmes adventures, *The House of Fear, The Woman in Green* and *Pursuit to Algiers.* Ironically, even as the studio plodded along, buoyed by the reputations and followings of its stars, rumors began circulating of a major upcoming studio shakedown that would put many veteran Universal attractions out to pasture. As such, if there was any more box office gold to be mined via the Frankenstein series, it would have to be mined soon.

Hence came a reunion for many of the *House of Frankenstein* talents. Again, producer Paul Malvern and executive producer Joe Gershenson mounted the "B" production, returning Erle C.

Jane Adams shows John Carradine a sweater she is knitting for her overseas husband.

Kenton to his director's post, putting Edward T. Lowe back to work on a new script (which made no attempt to explain the resurrections of Dracula and the Wolf Man, and, for a new surprise, placed Visaria on a seacoast) and re-engaged many of the same players.

By this time, top-billed Lon Chaney had purchased 1,300 acres in El Dorado County, christening the estate "Lennie's Ranch." Now sporting a moustache (an interesting affectation for a lycanthrope), Chaney had surrendered hopes of a studio build-up as a romantic lead, and was content just to remain on contract, the loss of which he desperately feared. Consequently, 1945 audiences had already seen Chaney plod through two putrid "Inner Sanctum" bores, *The Frozen Ghost* (which proved the Universal swan song for pregnant Evelyn Ankers) and *Strange Confession*. He had also found himself playing the buffoon for Abbott and Costello in their *Here Come the Co-Eds*.

"If this goes over," John Carradine had vowed of his Shakespearean company, "I'm through with Hollywood *forever*!"[212] It had gone over, and Carradine now had glorious dreams of devoting himself to the classical theater with his new bride, Sonia.* Still, Universal's offer to return to the cape and opera hat of Dracula was lucrative enough for Carradine to stay in Hollywood a bit longer and shear his shoulder-length "Buffalo Bill" hair-style that was attracting stares on Hollywood Boulevard.

Glenn Strange was of course happy to return to the Monster part. His playing of Frankenstein's creation had placed him in a casting twilight zone in Hollywood; having averaged a dozen screen performances per year prior to *House of Frankenstein*, Strange had, since its release, played in only a single western, Universal's *Renegades of the Rio Grande* (1945). While his playing of the screen's most infamous Monster might have elevated him beyond the status of a run-of-the-mill "B" western heavy, it clearly had not established him as an in-demand character actor either.

For the film's pivotal role of Dr. Franz Edelmann, Universal cast the excellent but unheralded (and hence reasonably priced) character actor Onslow Stevens. No stranger to Universal City (he had played in such serials as 1934's *Radio Patrol* and *The Vanishing Shadow*), Stevens faced the challenge of carrying the film as the brilliant, religious scientist transformed into a Jekyll/Hyde

*She would bear him three boys, including Keith, who would win the Oscar for his song "I'm Easy" in the 1975 film *Nashville*.

Lionel Atwill, fatally ill with bronchial cancer, poses for the still photographer.

beast by the blood of Dracula. The studio's lovely blonde contractee Martha O'Driscoll as Miliza had to sacrifice some feminine pride by wearing spinachy-green pancake makeup (which photographed deathly white) for her seduction scene with Dracula, but it was Universal's brunette starlet Jane "Poni" Adams who won the prize for lack of female vanity by accepting the role of the hunchbacked nurse, Nina.

However, the most dramatic personal situation was that of Lionel Atwill. On July 7, 1944, he had taken his fourth bride, Paula Pruter, in Las Vegas, and during production of *House of Dracula,* on October 14, 1945 the 60-year-old actor became the proud father of a baby, Lionel. The infant was both a comfort and a heartache for Atwill who was now fatally ill with bronchial cancer. As Atwill reported for night shooting on the old back lot village set, parading authoritatively as Inspector Holtz, nobody in the crowd of extras could have suspected that the veteran actor had only months left to live.

In late summer of 1945, *House of Dracula* began shooting.

Economy was the cry as *House of Dracula* began filming. For close shots of Edelmann's abode, for instance, the old *Tower of London* (1939) castle was used. Also the yak hair that comprised Chaney's Wolf Man makeup had run dangerously low—the studio had not received a shipment of yak hair, via Central Asia, since before the war—and Jack Pierce discovered that, with judicious application, he had just enough yak left to glue on Chaney for two brief appearances in the werewolf makeup. Furthermore, a nightmare sequence, obviously inspired by the famous De Sadesque dream of MGM's 1941 *Dr. Jekyll and Mr. Hyde,* was padded with *Bride of Frankenstein* footage of Karloff running through the village and overturning the Bishop statue. This augmented the specially filmed scenes of Strange, Carradine, Stevens, Miss Adams (sans hump) and company. Earlier horror themes created by Hans Salter, Frank Skinner and Charles Previn were pirated for *House of Dracula* by musical director Edgar Fairchild. The hodgepodge finale was ludicrous. Chaney, bellowing "Get out! The Frankenstein Monster!" literally is shown running away from himself (and Eddie Parker) as the Monster in *The Ghost of Frankenstein,* an economy measure that saved the special effects crew the time and expense of fanning a fire.

Therefore, Strange, aside from stomping about a bit in the nightmare sequence and lumbering around the castle set before the substitution of *The Ghost . . .* footage, had virtually nothing to do but lay on the operating table, pose for publicity stills and immerse himself in the prop "quicksand" for his opening scene. As Strange remembered of the mud:

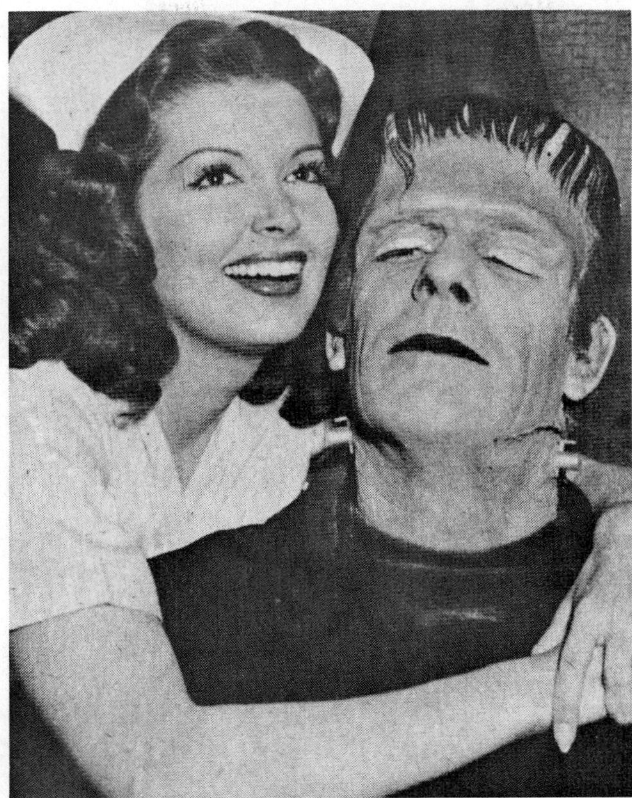

Jane Adams gives Glenn Strange a hug.

> . . . I was in there all day long and that stuff was cold! . . . Chaney came down with a fifth and I think I got most of it. He poured it down me and it warmed me up some. They finished shooting and I went up to the dressing room. Of course they had a nice fire up there. They took the makeup off and by the time I got about half undressed I was so looped I could hardly get up. . . .[213]

. . . Frankenstein's little boy doesn't die easily. And, unfortunately, neither does this type of cinematic nightmare.[214]

New York Times review of *House of Dracula*

On Thursday, October 15, 1945, *House of Dracula* was completed, and on Wednesday, November 28, Universal previewed the film at the studio. *The Hollywood Reporter* was impressed:

> Universal holds another congress of its whole array of indestructible monsters. . . . It is a mighty good show they put up, the realms of

Director Erle C. Kenton (center) explains the workings of a "camera distortion screen" to John Carradine and camera crewman Frank Heisler (right).

> pseudo-science interestingly invaded. . . . Box office expectancies should match, possibly even better, the hit grosses of . . . *House of Frankenstein* . . . the greatest burden of acting is asked of Onslow Stevens as Dr. Edelmann. He performs his chores to excellent effects. . . .[215]

Variety also liked the film, (" . . .upholds traditions of company's past offerings in this field"),[216] with special praise for Stevens' "outstanding" performance. However, when the film braved New York City, critics were awaiting the December 21, 1945 Rialto opening with axes sharpened. The *New York Daily News* for instance:

> While there's always the possibility that *House of Dracula* may have been an attempt to write a few debits in Universal's income tax blank, I'm afraid it was a cold-blooded experiment to determine audience saturation point. At any rate, vampires, werewolves, and monsters are definitely not at their best in wholesale competition, and unless the bunching up means there'd be a couple less pictures of this ilk, there's no apparent advantage. . . .[217]

On February 6, 1946, *House of Dracula* opened in Los Angeles at the Guild, United Artist, Vogue and Fox Wilshire Theaters—but not as a solo attraction. Universal's "Epic of Unbelievable Thrills" was booked as the bottom half of a double bill, playing second banana to Universal's *The Daltons Ride Again.*

House of Dracula closed the Universal Frankenstein saga. It was, in many ways, also the end of an era—by the time the film had played its early engagements, Universal had dumped a deeply bitter Chaney from the contract roster. *House of Dracula* co-stars Martha O'Driscoll and Jane Adams were also dropped. And, despite a $4.6 million profit for 1946, there were pink slips for most of Universal's stalwarts: The Andrews Sisters, Susanna Foster, Gloria Jean, Peggy Ryan, Turhan Bey, David Bruce, Olsen and Johnson, Robert Paige and June Vincent. On October 1, 1946, the studio officially merged with International Pictures and became Universal-International. In its dedication to "high quality pictures," Universal City cavalierly announced its intention to cancel any present and future production of horror films, serials and "B" westerns, the very entertainment that had built so many soundstages for the studio. Only Deanna Durbin, Abbott and Costello, Maria Montez, Yvonne de Carlo, Ella Raines, Andy Devine and a handful of other players survived on the studio payroll.

Sadly, Lionel Atwill, long a favorite on the Universal lot, died before his fate there could be decided. The dying Atwill had gallantly reported to the lot in early 1946 to sport his monocle and a panama hat as Sir Eric Hazarias, the villain of the serial *The Lost City of the Jungle.* After Atwill had completed most of his scenes,* his bravado finally failed him, and on the evening of the Monday after Easter, April 22, 1946, respiratory failure killed the 61-year-old actor at his notorious hideaway at 13515 D'Este Drive in the Pacific Palisades. His wife Paula, who was at his bedside when he died, and baby son Lionel, inherited the bulk of the actor's $250,000 estate.

. . . Tighter scripted than the previous potpourri, Edward T. Lowe intertwining the devil's brood where Curt Siodmak had opted for episodes, the film created an excellent new character in the Jekyll/Hyde fiend of Onslow Stevens. Yet it missed something: sincerity perhaps? love perhaps? Karloff perhaps?[218]

Denis Gifford, *A Pictorial History of Horror Movies*

House of Dracula has aged nicely; Kenton's well-paced direction, George Robinson's low-key photography, the sets and special effects make for a handsome production, and there are some memorable sequences. Especially good are Carradine's seduction of Miss O'Driscoll as she plays "Moonlight Sonata," and another of those chases that veteran western producer Malvern so dearly loved, and which Kenton enlivens with shadows and very energetic leaps by Stevens' double, Carey Loftin. The performances are generally colorful;

* Universal hired George Sorel, photographed from the sides and the back, to complete them.

Carradine, less sensual and more hammy than in *House of Frankenstein,* is still suavely menacing, while Chaney appears alternately drawn and powerful. There are nice cameos by Ludwig Stossel as Siegfried (Stossel would go on to play Einstein in MGM's *The Beginning or the End* and later would become the "Little Old Winemaker" of television commercials), and Skelton Knaggs as Steinmuhl, the village creep (Knaggs was an English grotesque with a face to match his name). Stevens, of course, as Edelmann, is excellent, and his leering face as he rides with Stossel on the wagon gives the film its one genuinely frightening moment.

Yet, for its assets, *House of Dracula* is an unabashed bastardization, the weakest chapter of the series and a pathetically tawdry finish to a once-grand cinema saga. Since *Abbott and Costello Meet Frankenstein* must be taken on its own farcical terms and not as a part of the classic Frankenstein legend, *House of Dracula* is the saga's final act—and a wretched one indeed. The one happy blessing of the film is its liberation of Chaney's Talbot from his curse of lycanthropy. This blessing is unsatisfyingly counterbalanced by the pathetic demises of Stevens' Edelmann and Jane Adams' Nina. Both have managed to make the audience care about them in the film, and it seems unfair to have Chaney escape clutching the lovely Miss O'Driscoll while both Stevens and Adams are ruthlessly destroyed. It is especially frustrating to the audience to witness such scriptwriter callousness toward Miss Adams. After the young actress consented to wear that hump, it seems overly sadistic to have her strangled in the finale, her deformed body rolling over the laboratory floor and into a pit with a most unlady-like tumble!

Most miserable of all, however, is Strange's Monster. After spending the film lying in muck and strapped to a table, Strange finally gets one real chance to act when, realizing that his power-restorer Edelmann is dead, he looks up at Chaney in a close-up full of hatred. Apparently Strange's intent was to look horrifying. Instead he looks bilious. Once again, the Monster is a dolt, stumbling into a shelf of combustible chemicals; while both surviving principals and a gaggle of extras easily escape the ensuing flames, the awkward, shuffling Monster becomes the only living thing to perish.

What had happened to Frankenstein's Monster? The Monster, with his magnificent eyes and those pleading hands and the cries of fear and loneliness, had produced such a profound effect in 1931, becoming so many things to so many people. He was the cinema's most terrifying horror, haunting adult nightmares, scaring children from visiting their attics or cellars; he was also a heartbreaking creation, scorned and bewildered, and of special appeal to many Depression-era moviegoers who

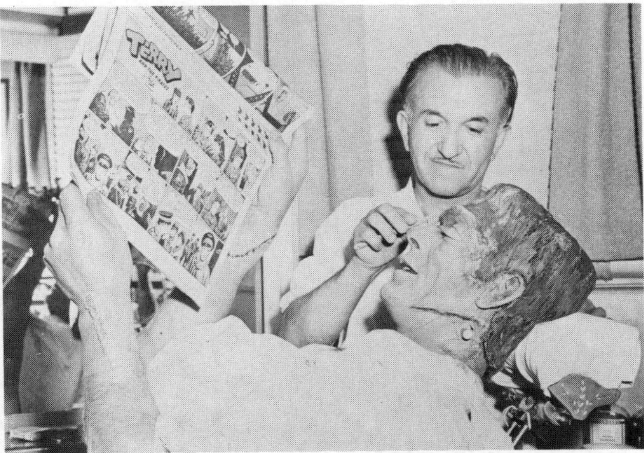

Glenn Strange enjoys the comics while Jack Pierce adds finishing touches to his makeup.

themselves felt forsaken by their dreams or country or even God. For a moment, he had become an almost blasphemous yet strangely moving Christ symbol, and for some, the Monster was one of Hollywood's most bizarre sex symbols—an insight that would cause Karloff to laugh, but one he never dismissed. (" . . . The sexuality was there in every stride he took, every motion of his arms and hands," said the actor.)[219] By 1939, the Monster, via Karloff's exquisite pantomime and love for the creature, was still the cinema's most fascinating horror, hence the success of *Son of Frankenstein.*

However, different actors, different producers and directors, and a different world finally combined forces to mock the "dear old Monster." Sadly, Chaney, Lugosi and Strange, all effective actors in their own ways, never really understood that there was more to the Monster than four hours of makeup, 13-pound boots, a shuffling walk and a paycheck. Nor did Universal executives later recognize in the Monster more than an infamous spook, a profit-rolling goblin who, via script department black magic and Jack Pierce's wizardry, could stalk across movie screens, luring adults who craved horrors other than War Department telegrams, flag-draped coffins, and fiances who lost limbs and faces, or children anxious to cheer and scream and toss popcorn at a screen filled with a doomed-to-destruction Monster.

So, with *House of Dracula,* Universal's Frankenstein Monster hit bottom. Burned, blown up, boiled alive, burned again, battered by flood, gulped by quicksand, and now roasted once more, he had toppled from a cinema sensation to the bottom half of a double bill. A rest was long overdue. At Universal, the Monster would rise once more, but only in the context that a post-war world, after degenerative sequels and the atomic bomb, would accept—a comic butt.

Abbott and Costello Meet Frankenstein poster.

Abbott and Costello Meet Frankenstein (1948)

Producer, Robert Arthur; *Director,* Charles T. Barton; *Original Screenplay,* Robert Lees, Frederic I. Rinaldo and John Grant; *Director of Photography,* Charles Van Enger; *Art Direction,* Bernard Herzbrun and Hilyard Brown; *Film Editor,* Frank Gross; *Sound,* Leslie I. Carey and Robert Pritchard; *Set Decorations,* Russell A. Gausman and Oliver Emert; *Orchestrations,* David Tamkin; *Gowns,* Grace Houston; *Hair Stylist,* Carmen Dirigo; *Makeup,* Bud Westmore; *Special Photography,* David S. Horsley and Jerome H. Ash; *Assitant Director,* Joseph E. Kenny; *Music,* Frank Skinner.

Completed, Universal City, California, March 20, 1948; Previewed, Forum Theatre, Los Angeles, June 25, 1948. Running Time: 82 minutes.

ABBOTT AND COSTELLO MEET FRANKENSTEIN—SYNOPSIS

The moon is slowly rising behind the tower of Big Ben, which chimes ominously through the ghostly fog of London. In a hotel room, a tall, husky man paces the floor, waiting for the overseas operator to complete his call to a baggage station in La Mirada, Florida.

Finally, a voice—the high, excitable voice of chubby baggage clerk Wilbur Grey—answers.

"Hello," says Lawrence Talbot. "Do you have two crates addressed to the McDougal House of Horrors? . . . Now listen closely. I'm flying out of here at dawn. Under no circumstances are you to deliver those crates until I arrive! Understand? Under . . ."

Talbot's voice breaks away. Over the phone comes a strange, throaty growl . . .

"Mr. McDougal," says Wilbur, assuming that is the caller's identity, "will you stop gargling your throat? . . . You're awful silly to call me all the way from London just to have your dog talk to me! . . . Great conversation. The guy growls like a wolf!"

Wilbur hangs up. And, in the London hotel room, the Wolf Man madly rips his claws into the furniture.

On the other side of the baggage desk is the apoplectic face of Mr. McDougal himself, who angrily orders Wilbur to bring him the two crates. McDougal turns to a tall, sinuous brunette beside him, and informs her of the crates' contents—the coffin and remains of Count Dracula, and the body of the Frankenstein Monster! A European exhibitor has strangely picked McDougal's name out of the air, and the proprietor relishes the business prospects. "Guess that combination's enough to scare the pants—er, I mean, the shirt right off your back, ain't it?" guffaws McDougal to the brunette.

"I don't scare easily," replies Dr. Sandra Mornay, who now informs Wilbur, her little heartthrob, that their date will have to be cancelled for that night. She seductively assures him, however, of another rendezvous. "Boy," gushes Wilbur, much to the disgust of his partner, Chick Young, "I'm floating on a cloud of love!"

That night, Chick and Wilbur deliver the ominous crates to McDougal's spook house. The electrical storm that crashes outside does nothing to soothe the nerves of the cowardly Wilbur, who shivers as he regards the guillotine and the leering wax figures. The storm soon knocks out the power, and, by candlelight, Wilbur uncrates Dracula's coffin, and reads the accompanying Dracula legend, which tells how Dracula sleeps in his casket, but rises every night . . .

Wilbur hears the coffin lid creak. "Chick!" screams Wilbur, telling his partner he heard a creak.

"That's the wind!" snaps Chick.

"It should get oiled," replies Wilbur.

Chick tends to other business again while Wilbur continues reading the legend, relating how Dracula can turn into a bat and soar about the countryside. . . .

Wilbur turns to see a hand slide from beneath the coffin lid. Again, Chick returns at the sound of Wilbur's scream.

" . . . Listen, Wilbur. I know there's no such a

The Players

Chick	Bud Abbott
Wilbur	Lou Costello
Lawrence Talbot	Lon Chaney
Count Dracula	Bela Lugosi
Frankenstein's Monster	Glenn Strange
Dr. Sandra Mornay	Lenore Aubert
Joan Raymond	Jane Randolph
Mr. McDougal	Frank Ferguson
Dr. Stevens	Charles Bradstreet
Bits	
Mr. Harris	Howard Negley
Man	Joe Kirk
Man in Armor	Clarence Straight
Photographer	Harry Brown
Woman at Baggage Counter	Helen Spring
Man	George Barton
Man	Carl Sklover
Sergeant	Paul Stader
Man	Joe Walls
and	
The Invisible Man	Vincent Price

person as Dracula. You know there's no such a person as Dracula . . . "

"But does Dracula know it?" asks Wilbur.

Chick leaves. Wilbur reads on, learning how Dracula keeps himself alive by drinking the blood of the living . . .

The candle atop the coffin lid begins to slide. And, finally, the tall, imperious figure of Count Dracula rises from the coffin, posing in the shadows as a wax statue when Chick rushes back at Wilbur's screams.

". . . That's the bunk!" shouts Chick about the legend.

"That's what I'm trying to tell ya!" cries Wilbur, regarding the coffin. "That's his bunk!"

Chick shows Wilbur that the coffin is empty. Together they begin uncrating the box containing the Frankenstein Monster, a creature who, according to his legend card, was assembled by Frankenstein from old dead bodies and brought to life via electricity. Under the excelsior, Wilbur sees the grotesque head of the Monster, leaps back, bumps into the guillotine and decapitates a dummy.

McDougal arrives with the insurance investigator. As Chick goes to greet them, Dracula reappears from the shadows and places Wilbur in a trance. The vampire approaches the Monster, and vitalizes him.

"Master," acknowledges the Monster.

Breaking out of his crate, the Monster rises, sees Wilbur, and recoils in fright.

"Don't be afraid," speaks Dracula to his giant slave. "He won't hurt you. Come!"

McDougal and the insurance investigator arrive to find the "exhibits," insured for $20,000, gone. Chick and Wilbur (who snaps out of his trance) spend the night in jail.

A great bat flies about an ancient castle that looms over the craggy rocks and surf of a little is-

Lou Costello, Bud Abbott, Glenn Strange, Bela Lugosi, and Lon Chaney.

land off the Florida coast. Moments later, Count Dracula calls at the door.

"My dear Count," purrs the black-clad Dr. Mornay. "It's so good to see you again."

Dracula informs his Sandra that his alias is now "Dr. Lahos." He doesn't wish to frighten Sandra's handsome young technical assistant, Dr. Stevens, who has been asking too many questions. Sandra wraps herself in a mink and goes with Dracula outside to see the Monster.

"Nervous, my dear?" asks Dracula as Sandra examines the ill, weakened Monster.

"This is risky business," she replies.

"Not as risky as those curious operations of yours which so intrigued the European police," vollies Dracula. "Yet, much more profitable. Restore the Monster for me, and you shall have anything you wish."

Sandra has been studying Dr. Henry Frankenstein's *The Secrets of Life and Death* (with its addenda from Wolf and Ludwig Frankenstein) and is confident regarding the operation Dracula wishes her to perform. "And about the brain," says the vampire. "I don't want to repeat Frankenstein's mistake and revive a vicious, unmanageable brute. This time, the Monster must have no will of his own—no fiendish intellect to oppose his master."

There, Sandra believes, she can exceed the Count's greatest wishes. The new brain she has chosen is " . . . so simple, so pliable, he will obey you like a trained dog!" In fact, Sandra has a date with Wilbur in two days to attend a masquerade ball, but she smiles that she's sure her little round beau would prefer a quiet evening at home . . . .

Meanwhile, Wilbur and Chick have been bailed out of jail. They return to their hotel, where there is a new resident across the hall—Larry Talbot, who spoke with Wilbur from London. Talbot tells the men of Dracula's dream to revive the Monster, but soon stops—for the moon is about to rise. He begs Wilbur to lock him in his room. "Remember!" orders the frantic Talbot, "No matter what you hear or what happens, *don't let me out*!"

However, Talbot has left his bag, and Wilbur returns it to his room moments later. He's unaware, as he writes Talbot a note and steals a piece of fruit, that he has come very close to being ripped to pieces by the lurking Wolf Man.

The next morning, Chick and Wilbur have two callers: Sandra, who reminds Wilbur of their date, and a blonde named Joan Raymond, who reveals that she bailed them out of jail. Joan, who is actually an insurance investigator, pretends to be madly in love with Wilbur, hoping to employ her feminine wiles to persuade Wilbur to reveal what happened to the exhibits. Hence, Wilbur miraculously finds himself with two dates for the ball.

Glenn Strange, Lenore Aubert, and Bela Lugosi.

Recovering from this unexpected fortune, Wilbur suddenly realizes that Talbot is still locked in his room. Chick and Wilbur open the door, and find the room and furniture a shambles. Talbot relates the tragic story of how, years before, he was bitten by a werewolf. "Ever since, when the full moon rises, I turn into a wolf myself."

Wilbur is sympathetic, and tells Talbot not to worry: "I'm sort of a 'wolf' myself!"

Talbot is in no mood for jokes. "You have seen the living dead!" he tells Wilbur, and insists that Dracula and the Monster must be destroyed—and that, together, he and Chick and Wilbur must find them. Wilbur begs off. He has two dates.

"But you and I," says Talbot, "have a date with destiny!"

"Let Chick go with Destiny" pleads Wilbur.

That night, Wilbur and Joan and the dateless Chick arrive at the castle to pick up Sandra for the ball. While waiting, the telephone rings, and Wilbur answers it. It's Talbot. He has learned that electrical equipment of the variety needed to revive the Monster has been delivered to the very castle where Wilbur is—the very house of Dracula! Wilbur makes a mad dash to leave, but Chick, hoping to prove to Wilbur once and for all that no such horrors as Dracula and the Monster exist, forces him to join in a search through the castle. Naturally, Wilbur, penetrating secret passageways and the gloomy old cellar with a misty inlet and pier, manages to sit on the very lap of the Monster and stare into the face of Dracula, while Chick never sees them at all.

Back in the great hall, "Dr. Lahos" appears, dapper in a long robe, and warms to Wilbur. "I must say, my dear," says "Lahos" to Sandra, "I approve *very highly* of your choice. What we need today is young blood and brains."

The charm of Lahos helps Wilbur overlook the doctor's resemblance to Dracula. "Young people," smiles the vampire, perusing the young group which now includes the suspicious Professor Stevens. "Making the most of life—while it lasts." He asks that the young professor accompany the group to the masquerade, and Stevens, attracted by Joan, agrees.

Sandra, however, suddenly develops a bad headache and refuses to go. In her boudoir, she tells the scowling Count that a check of Joan's purse has revealed her to be an insurance investigator. Sandra also thinks that Stevens is asking too many questions, and she fears what Wilbur might have seen in the cellar.

"I must warn you, my dear Sandra," intones Dracula, "I am accustomed to having my orders obeyed—especially by women with a price on their head!"

Sandra is not scared. She returns to Dracula *The Secrets of Life and Death* and refuses to operate, believing her will to be as strong as the vampire's.

It is not.

"Look into my eyes," orders Dracula. "Look . . . deeper. Tell me what you see . . . " Sandra sees in his eyes a large bat, and as she falls under his hypnosis, Dracula passionately sinks his teeth into her jugular vein.

At the masquerade ball, strange things begin to happen. Dracula arrives with a strangely staring Sandra. Talbot confronts the vampire and accuses him of truly being Count Dracula; Dracula suavely suggests that Talbot consult his physician. As the Count invites Joan to dance with him, hoping to place the investigator under his control, Sandra asks the wide-eyed Wilbur to take her for a walk.

"I want to be the only one in your life," sighs Sandra to Wilbur on a bench in the forest. "I want to be a part of you. I want to be in your blood . . . You're so full of life, so round, so firm . . . "

"So fully packed," concludes Wilbur, "and I want to stay that way!" He accidentally pricks himself. Blood appears. Sandra stares hungrily at it.

"Look into my eyes," she demands. " . . . Look! Deeper . . . deeper . . . " Wilbur sees the images of bats.

"Don't you know what's going to happen now?" asks Sandra.

"I'll bite," answers Wilbur.

"Oh no," replies a passionate Sandra. "I will."

The sudden cries of Chick and Talbot scare Sandra away. Joan has disappeared. Meanwhile, the moon rises, and Talbot is transformed into the beast. Again he creeps up behind Wilbur, who, believing it to be Chick in his wolf costume, kicks him in the rump, bops him on the nose and somehow manages to escape. The Wolf Man, however, does find a victim that night—McDougal, who survives badly cut, his jugular vein within just half an inch of being severed. Believing that it was Chick (in his masquerade costume) who attacked him, McDougal accuses Chick of attempted murder. Chick manages to escape and hide in the forest; Dracula manages to imprison Joan and Wilbur back on his island castle.

The night arrives for the operation. Wilbur finds himself in a stock-like device. All day, his pleas for help from the Monster (sleeping in his increasingly weakened condition) and Sandra (corpse-like by day now that she is a bride of Dracula) have received no response. As night falls, Sandra rises to inform him that he will no longer be short and plump, but big and strong . . . no longer mortal, but immortal . . . for his brain will be placed in the skull of the Monster, whom Wilbur has chummily nicknamed "Junior."

While Wilbur reacts to the news with hoots and screams, Professor Stevens confronts Dracula with his crimes. Sandra stealthily sneaks up behind the professor and knocks him unconscious. Now Dracula orders the operation to begin, and the Monster and Wilbur are each strapped to an operating table. "Frankie," cries Wilbur, "I'm telling ya,' it's a bad deal. I've had this brain for 30 years and it hasn't worked right yet!"

However, as the electrical equipment begins blazing, shooting strengthening electricity into the Monster's veins, Chick and Talbot break into the castle to rescue the captives. Talbot bends over Wilbur's body to free him and then looks up, agonized, at the window. There is a full moon. . . .

In the laboratory, Dracula hears Wilbur screaming and sees the Wolf Man snarling. As the beast lunges madly at the vampire, pursuing him on a wild chase through the castle, the Monster, now filled with electrical potency, rises from the table! He grabs the wicked Sandra, lifts her into the air and hurls the woman through the great skylight. As she plummets to her death, the Monster whirls on Chick and Wilbur!

While the Monster pursues the baggage clerks, Dracula is hurling bric-a-brac at the Wolf Man, who chases the Count onto a balcony high above the surf. As the vampire tries to escape by changing into a bat, the lycanthrope grasps it in his claws, tumbles over the railing, and falls, shredding the winged mammal as he plunges to the water and rocks below. With the vampire's death, Joan suddenly comes out of her trance, and looks into the rescuing face of the revived Professor Stevens.

Strange, Costello, and Aubert.

Still the Monster stalks, tearing down an iron gate as he chases Chick and Wilbur across the estate grounds. McDougal* and his posse arrive to see the missing "exhibit" pursuing the clerks to the edge of a pier, where Chick and Wilbur take refuge in a rowboat as the Monster hurls barrels at them. Professor Stevens arrives and, filling buckets with gasoline, sets the pier ablaze. Flames envelop the Monster, who gropes through the fire as the pier collapses and topples into the water.

Out in the rowboat, Chick and Wilbur rejoice. " . . . there's nobody to frighten us anymore," claims Chick, oblivious to the cigarette that seems to be dangling in mid-air behind him and Wilbur.

"Oh, that's too bad," announces a voice. "I was hoping to get in on the excitement. . . . Allow me to introduce myself. I'm the Invisible Man!" As the Invisible One merrily laughs, Chick and Wilbur dive out of the rowboat and splash into the water.

*Apparently, Talbot's Wolf Man wounded McDougal's throat with his claws rather than his teeth, since McDougal is not a lycanthrope himself as the film concludes.

ABBOTT AND COSTELLO MEET FRANKENSTEIN— PRODUCTION HISTORY

Ride High With U-I.

Universal-International Slogan, 1948

In its first year of operation, Universal-International almost went bankrupt. While "U-I" honored its pledge of "artistic" productions via such 1947 films as *A Double Life* (for which Ronald Colman won an Oscar) and the British J. Arthur Rank imports, *Black Narcissus* and *Great Expectations*, the post-war public preferred fare a la *The Egg and I*, the Claudette Colbert/Fred MacMurray comedy whose $5.75 million gross saved the studio from an early doom.

Such an irony pained William Goetz. Now in charge of production since Universal merged with his International Pictures, the erudite Goetz was

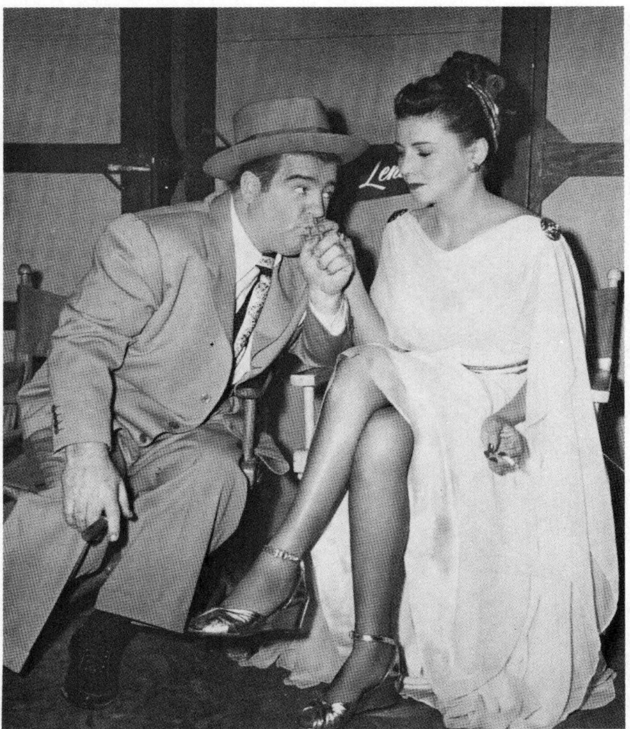

Costello and Aubert.

best noted in Hollywood for two reasons: his magnificent art collection and his marriage to Louis B. Mayer's daughter Edie.* Goetz had done his best to scour from the lot the horse-hugging cowboys, the wiggling harem girls and the ever-amok monsters who had given the studio, in his opinion, so "tacky" an image. Nevertheless, as Goetz surveyed his near-bankrupt empire as New Years 1948 arrived, there were many vestiges of the old regime. The "show boat" was afloat on a back lot lake for *River Lady,* and the Wild West town ready for *Black Bart,* both vehicles for the shapely "survivor" Yvonne de Carlo. Deanna Durbin, entering her 12th year as a Universal attraction, was rehearsing such songs as "Oh! Say Can You See" and "Close as Pages in a Book" for her new extravaganza, *Up in Central Park.*

Goetz accepted such artifacts; good business was, after all, good business. However, there was one sight on the lot left from the earlier reign that caused Goetz to wince—the giant, deluxe dressing room trailers of Abbott and Costello.

Bud: You know, strange as it may seem, they give ballplayers peculiar names nowadays. On the St. Louis team, Who's on first, What's on second, I Don't Know is on third.

Lou: That's what I want to find out. I want you to tell me the names of the fellows on the St. Louis team.

Bud: I'm telling you. Who's on first, What's on second, I Don't Know is on third. . . .

"Who's on First?" routine of Abbott and Costello.

Ever since the February 1941 release of *Buck Privates,* a comedy musical slapped together by Universal for a very modest $180,000 that grossed more than $10 million, Bud Abbott and Lou Costello were acknowledged as show business legends—and the most powerful stars at Universal. The team had formed in Minskey's Burlesque in 1937 and leapt into the movies' No. 1 box office spot in 1942. The pair reaped $150,000 per picture plus 10 percent of the profits; earned an additional $20,000 per week via their NBC Thursday night radio show; and raised $80 million worth of war bonds. Each lived in opulent splendor in the San Fernando Valley (Bud in a 17-room mansion at 4504 Woodley Avenue, Lou in a gadget-filled domain at 4121 Longridge Avenue); and fought bitterly. In 1945, the team almost split, their differences climaxing when Bud hired a maid that Lou had fired from his own house. Indeed, the popularity and success of the team is all the more incredible when one reviews the tragedies of the comics' private lives. Bud suffered from severe epilepsy, an affliction he blamed for a serious drinking problem; Lou almost died of rheumatic heart disease in 1943, the same year that his son Butch, 2 days short of his first birthday, fell into the pool and drowned. (His Mother was on the telephone and his Dad was at a radio show rehearsal.)

Fated to become Abbott and Costello's favorite and busiest director (on nine pictures) was Charles Barton, the top comedy director at Universal City from 1945 to 1952. "They were great days . . . Oh, God, it was wonderful!"[221] recalled the small, very pleasant former vaudevillian/prop man/actor, when he spoke with me in his Toluca Lake house near Universal:

> We had a great relationship. You hear a lot of things about little Lou—and he was a little terror! He was a very hot-headed little Italian, and he'd have tantrums you wouldn't believe—*really* wouldn't believe. A lot of people showed fear, and that's what he loved, so he'd walk all over them. But for some reason, with me, and I don't know why in the hell it was, we got along even better than brothers. Things that I'd like him to do in a picture, he would at least try—some-

*Mayer, who had invested in 20th Century-Fox Studios to give his son-in-law his first important post, later came to loathe "the son of a bitch"[220] and bitterly cut Edie from his will because of her loyalty to Goetz.

thing he *wouldn't* do with many other directors—and that showed that he had confidence in me. We became very good friends. We were very close.

Bud was a quiet man. A very heavy drinker, due to his epilepsy. 4 P.M. was the end of the day for Bud, because fear came into his mind, and he started hitting the bottle. He'd tell you beforehand, "You better get it all before 4." It was a horrible sight to see one of those epileptic fits. Oh God, it would just break your heart. Lou would hit him so hard in the pit of the stomach (Lou had been a fighter at one time), and that snapped Bud out of it, for some reason. Then Lou would grab him, and we'd take him over in the dressing room. Bud was a very faithful man, and he loved Lou. They had so many fights—I can't tell you how many they had—and Bud was very hurt one time when Lou wanted more money and wanted to change the team's billing to "Costello & Abbott."* But he never turned against Lou. In his last years, Lou tried to work without Bud—but he knew damn well he couldn't.

By 1948, it appeared that Abbott and Costello were on the wane. They hadn't placed in the Top Ten box office list since 1944; MGM, where they had an outside contract, had dropped its option for more films; Camel Cigarettes dropped their radio show in 1947. Although both their 1947 films, *Buck Privates Come Home* and *The Wistful Widow of Wagon Gap* (each directed by Barton) had performed big business, the team no longer qualified as a "sensation."

Goetz was pleased. "Bill Goetz and his partner, Leo Spitz, wanted nothing to do with Abbott and Costello," said Barton. "Oh God almighty! Bud and Lou were making millions for them, and they didn't want any part of the boys." Goetz and Spitz found their comedy not funny, their epic poker games that stalled productions irresponsible, their ribald practical jokes (e.g., once giving a leading lady on her birthday a suitcase filled with Kotex) disgusting. In fact, there were rumors that Abbott and Costello were not long for Universal, but then . . .

You don't think I'll do that crap, do you? My 5-year-old daughter can write something better than that![222]

Lou Costello after reading the script of *The Brain of Frankenstein*.

---

*This battle, which waged in 1942, did not change the billing but it did change the salary. Thereafter, Lou received 60 percent of the team's earnings, Bud 40 percent.

Director Charles Barton lights the cigarette of Lenore Aubert on the Universal back lot.

The brainstorm of resurrecting Frankenstein's Monster, Count Dracula and the Wolf Man (as well as, originally, Kharis the Mummy, Dracula's son Alucard, and The Invisible Man) belonged to producer Robert Arthur, formerly a writer and associate producer of MGM musicals. Veteran Abbott and Costello writers Frederic Rinaldo and Robert Lees (as well as their long-time gag man John Grant) accepted the challenge of pounding out a script. Cut from the final draft were poor Kharis (as he had been in *House of Frankenstein*) and Alucard (read it backwards). Reserved for a gag ending was the Invisible One. In the plot, the Wolf Man became the hero, the Monster became Dracula's slave, and Dracula (fearing that the Monster might someday turn on its master) was the seeker of a harmless, simple, silly and puerile brain to pop into the Monster's square cranium.

The obvious donor would have none of it. Lou Costello read the script, took a big puff on his cigar, and refused to play it. Barton explains:

> If you go over the picture, you'll see it's not quite the typical Abbott and Costello vehicle. It didn't have too many stand-up routines in it. My first film with the boys, *The Time of Their Lives* (1946), was in the same vein, and Lou didn't want to do that one at all either. He just wanted to stand up and do routines.

Producer Arthur still had faith in the project—so much so that he offered Lou a $50,000 advance on his percentage if he would do the picture. Ever in debt and hungry for cash, Lou agreed. Costello also was pleased when the title of the project was

Bela Lugosi and Glenn Strange find something to laugh about on the set.

changed to the less awesome *Abbott and Costello Meet Frankenstein.*

Still, the vision of a movie house marquee reading *Abbott and Costello Meet Frankenstein* was just too much for William Goetz. He wouldn't even look at the script. Meeting with Arthur on the eve of production, Goetz offered his only words of encouragement:

> Good luck—and God bless you.[223]

JEEPERS! The Creepers are after Bud and Lou!
Poster copy for *Abbott and Costello Meet Frankenstein*

For most of the "Horror Men," the new Frankenstein film was a blessing. Fate's face had not beamed too brightly on most of these actors since the second wave of cinema horror had dehydrated at the close of World War II.

Boris Karloff, the happy exception, was now a top-priced character star, welcome in everything from musical comedy (Goldwyn's 1947 *The Secret Life of Walter Mitty*) to historical spectacle (DeMille's 1947 *Unconquered*). His affection for the Monster remained strong, as it would for the rest of his life, and he refused to play the role, especially under such farcical conditions. Hence, the studio recalled Glenn Strange. Since *House of Dracula,* Strange had played in only a handful of films: Monogram's *Beauty and the Bandit* (1946), Eagle-Lion's *Frontier Fighters* (1947), Universal's *Brute Force* (1947) and the most recent Abbott and Costello feature, *The Wistful Widow of Wagon Gap* (also 1947). Receiving the script, Strange discovered that the Monster now had dialogue—"Master" and "Yes, Master."

The Wolf Man, as ever, was Lon Chaney's "baby," and it was a heavier, aged Chaney who returned to the studio that had dropped him two years before. In the interim, he had returned to the stage, touring in a national company of *Born Yesterday* and reprising Lennie in a Laguna Beach, California revival for *Of Mice and Men.* There had been some films, too, such as Paramount's Bob Hope-Dorothy Lamour comedy *My Favorite Brunette,* featuring Chaney as a moronic heavy. "It haunts me," Chaney groaned. "I get a call to play a dumb guy and the director tells me not to be Lennie. But he's never happy until I play the part like Lennie, and then he doesn't know why he likes it!"[224]

Most happily, the film finally returned Bela Lugosi to the screen as Dracula.* The Hungarian had not worked in a Hollywood studio since the spring 1946, when he labored on poverty row in a color "B" called *Scared to Death.* He too had returned to the stage, having toured summer stock theaters in 1947 in yet another revival of *Dracula.* Added to Lugosi's career problems was now a very tragic personal one: narcotics. A medical gaffe in 1944 had addicted Lugosi to the needle, and the expense and strain of the addiction was cruelly sapping the actor's health and fortune. Vacating the "Dracula House," the Lugosi family now lived south of Los Angeles at Lake Elsinore, where Bela junior was attending the Naval and Military school. "We had a home right by the beautiful lake," Lillian told me, "with 150 feet of private lake front—and we loved it."[225] Lugosi returned to Hollywood and boarded with Hungarian friends as work began on the picture.

Charmingly rounding out the cast were two ladies: brunette Lenore Aubert, the alluring Yugoslavian actress, who portrayed Dracula's sexy accomplice, Dr. Sandra Mornay; and blonde Jane Randolph of Val Lewton's *Cat People* and *The Curse of the Cat People,* as Joan Raymond, insurance investigator who seeks the missing horror

*One story, well-circulated by a former agent of Lugosi, claims that Universal had signed Ian Keith to play Dracula in *Abbott and Costello Meet Frankenstein.* With shooting scheduled to start on February 14, 1948, the agent (according to his story) stormed into the studio president's office five days before the shooting began, reminded him that Lugosi had been paid only $3,500 for his work in the original *Dracula,* and claimed that the studio "owed" Lugosi the part, allegedly persuading the front office to drop Keith and sign Lugosi.

Actually, Lugosi had been cast as Dracula as early as January 26, 1948, the date that the news of his casting appeared in the *Los Angeles Times.* This is a full two weeks before the enterprising agent's supposed coup. (This agent, incidentally, is the same man who claimed to have Lugosi's *Frankenstein* test reel for sale.)

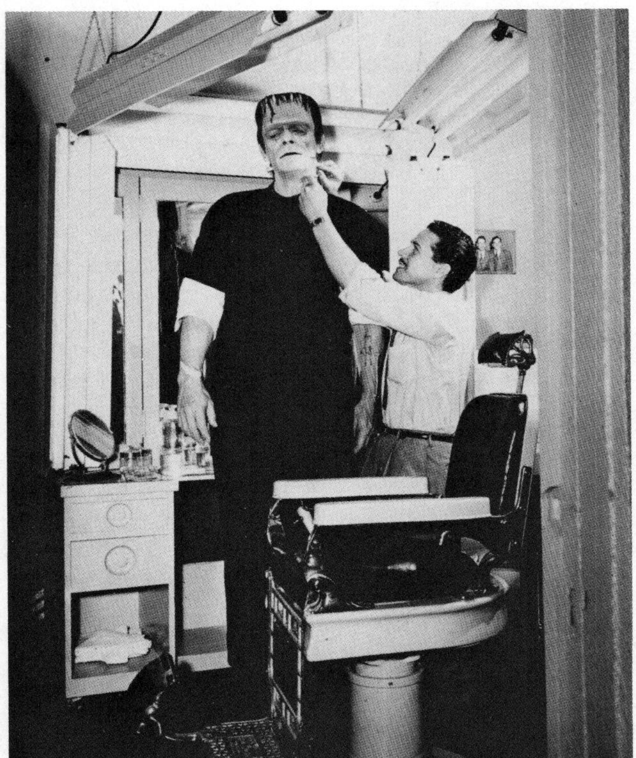

Makeup man Jack Kevan refines Strange's makeup.

"exhibits." Behind the camera was Charles Van Enger, who was cinematographer of the Lon Chaney, Sr. classics *The Hunchback of Notre Dame* and *The Phantom of the Opera*.

On February 14, 1948, the 17th anniversary of the New York premiere of *Dracula*, Bela Lugosi returned to Universal City for *Abbott and Costello Meet Frankenstein*.

All three of the "monsters" were the nicest. The *real* monsters were Abbott and Costello![226]

Charles Barton

Production of *Abbott and Costello Meet Frankenstein* did not begin under particularly merry circumstances. As Barton remembers:

> Bud and Lou had quite a chip on their shoulders about doing it, and they'd fight me like hell. But I stood my ground with them, and so did Bob Arthur. Still, Bud and Lou went home several times during shooting, and stayed there for six days or so!
>
> Our budget was very cheap—maybe $1 million, not very much for that time. The only thing that really cost us money was when the boys got on their high horse and wouldn't show up. Another trick they loved to pull was to sit over on the side of the set and play cards for three days. Three days! And for big, big money!
>
> Yet, during all these problems, we never had any trouble with Lon or Bela or Glenn. The "monsters" were as sweet as little babies. Isn't that wonderful? God, they were great!

Certainly the monsters had never been so comfortable. For when Chaney, Lugosi and Strange reported to makeup, Jack P. Pierce was no longer there to greet them with his formal "Good morning." Universal-International, decreeing the 58-year-old Pierce too old and his painstaking techniques obsolete, had dropped him from the studio after 20 years of service. The new head of the makeup department was young Bud Westmore, assisted by Jack Kevan (who tended to Strange's makeup) and Emile LaVigne (who tended to Chaney's). They created horrors out of the same material that filled the brassieres of many Hollywood starlets—foam rubber. The makeup for the Monster* and the Wolf Man† was created mostly from this material, and Chaney and Strange required only a single hour each morning in the makeup chair before reporting to the set. Much of Strange's makeup, in fact, was now a rubber mask (silvery in color, rather than the corpse-like blue-green of the previous seven films) and it was a picture of this mask that ironically accompanied more than one of Boris Karloff's obituaries in 1969! As for Lugosi, Westmore clearly thought that the 65-year-old actor was too old to play Dracula, and applied heavy powder to his face, heavy rouge to his lips, and a dark dye to his graying hair. Though very obvious, these cosmetics brought a strangely proper touch to Lugosi's Dracula, underscoring the vanity of the ancient Count who would so gleefully indulge himself on young Miss Aubert's neck in the course of the film.

Barton has very pleasant memories of all the film's villains:

> Lon Chaney I had known for a long, long time. I had directed him in a picture called *Rose Bowl*

*Westmore fashioned some modifications in the Monster's makeup. In addition to the silver cast of the face, the forehead scar became more jagged, the neck bolts were raised a bit, and the hair was longer and combed back at the sides.

†The Wolf Man's on-camera metamorphosis from man to wolf was still an ordeal for Chaney, as LaVigne applied eight or nine separate makeups during a work day that lasted from 8 A.M. to midnight. As Al Taylor and Sue Roy reported in their book *Making a Monster:* "The days were long and weary, and Lon Chaney, Jr., at times had a little too much to drink. LaVigne found that he didn't exactly relish putting glue all over a man Chaney's size when he was a little high."[227]

A proud Bela Lugosi introduces co-star Lenore Aubert (right) to his wife Lillian and Bela junior on the set.

at Paramount in '36. I had also known Lon senior—a pretty nice guy. Lon junior was as gentle as a little lamb (now I'm talking about with *me*). He was so kind—he'd do anything. He was really cooperative. Of course, he had that drinking problem . . . oh God, *awful*. By late afternoon, he didn't know where he was. He had the problem all through his life, even when he was very young. I don't know why. I guess *he* knew.

Bela Lugosi? He was a hell of a good actor. He was very helpful to Lon, and to me, and to everybody. Particularly that wonderful, beautiful girl, Lenore Aubert. I remember in the scene where Lugosi told her "Look into my eyes" how he tried to help her look as if she were really hypnotized. It was a hard scene to do, and damn, he worked with her like a real pro. He was a lovely, lovely guy.

As for Glenn Strange—how he would laugh! Do you remember that pantomime scene, where Lou sat in the chair on the Monster's lap, and he got his hands mixed up with the Monster's? Well, Lou didn't want to do that. I had worked with John Grant on that bit and when Lou read it, he said "What the hell is this?" I said, "Well, if you just listen and try it, you'll find out that it is *beautiful*." At first Lou didn't understand it, but finally he did get very enthusiastic. He just loved it. Well, we began shooting the scene, and right in the middle of it, Glenn started to laugh. And by God, he couldn't stop! So Lou got mad at him. I'll never forget that. Lou said, "Damnit Glenn, you're trying to do that just to make it worse for me!" Glenn said, "No, of course not. I don't know what the hell it is about you, but even on the back of your head I can see what's going on!"

As Bud and Lou settled into the picture, it became a very wild, fun set. Strange later recalled the film as ". . . one of the most enjoyable pictures I ever worked on,"[228] and he, Chaney and Lugosi* enjoyed the antics. "They had to put up with a lot—like pie fights," said Barton. "We always had to have pies ready on the set, in case Bud and Lou suddenly wanted to throw pies. The pie bill on a picture like that was $3,800 to $4,800!" Sometimes Chaney joined the pie battles, though Lugosi, as Barton recalls was "afraid" of this particular extracurricular activity and Strange's heavy

* Lillian Lugosi Donlevy, who visited the set with Bela junior, denies the perennial story that her ex-husband was offended and distraught by Abbott and Costello's raucous behavior.

Glenn Strange clowns with Ann Blyth, costumed for *Mr. Peabody and the Mermaid*.

rubber eyelids handicapped him so he wasn't a fair target. Neither Bela nor Glenn had to worry about being hit. "Bud and Lou had great respect for these people," remembers Barton. "The boys had their own tantrums, but they still had respect for them. They were professionals and Bud and Lou knew it."

Even outside the soundstage, mayhem became the tone. One day, Miss Aubert, wrapped in her mink, put a leash on Strange and, joined by Bud, Lou, and Chaney (in his full werewolf regalia), took "Junior" (as Lou called the Monster) for a stroll around the lot—to the open-mouthed stares of the tourists. On another occasion, Strange lunched with Ann Blyth, working on a neighboring soundstage in *Mr. Peabody and the Mermaid*—with hysterical results. As Strange reminisced:

> . . . We were just minding our own business, having our lunch outside a soundstage, when it happened. Like me, Ann had to keep on her makeup until the day's shooting was over. Naturally, she couldn't walk around with her feet covered with a mermaid's body, so they had fixed up a little cart for her to lie in.
>
> Well, this tourist suddenly came around the corner and saw us. She took one look at the crazy sight of a Monster and mermaid eating lunch together, let out a screech, and hit me in the face with her purse! Then she ran off screaming bloody murder, leaving me with my lunch all over my face and costume![229]

By the time the cast played the wild climax, with Bud and Lou and the horrors all chasing each other around the castle, all varieties of raucous play were going on. Lou, who had come to enjoy Strange's problem of breaking up, pelted his co-star with ad-libs that reduced the Monster time and again to guffaws. In the scene where the team pushed against a door to blockade the rampaging Monster, Lou purposefully disregarded his marker—the result being Strange's fist crashing through the balsa wood door and smashing right into Lou's head. Barton so enjoyed Lou's reaction that the "accident" remained in the release print.

However, once again one of those serious accidents that plagued the Frankenstein series arose, almost causing a temporary production shutdown. For the scene where the Monster hurls Dr. Mornay to her deserved end through a window, the crew attached an invisible wire to the rather ample Miss Aubert to help Strange lift her and to help ease her fall onto the cushion-covered platform out of camera range. There was a foul-up with the wire. When Strange tossed the actress through the window, she suddenly swung back into camera range, kicking and screaming like a spastic Peter Pan. Strange gallantly lunged to catch her, fell and broke his foot.

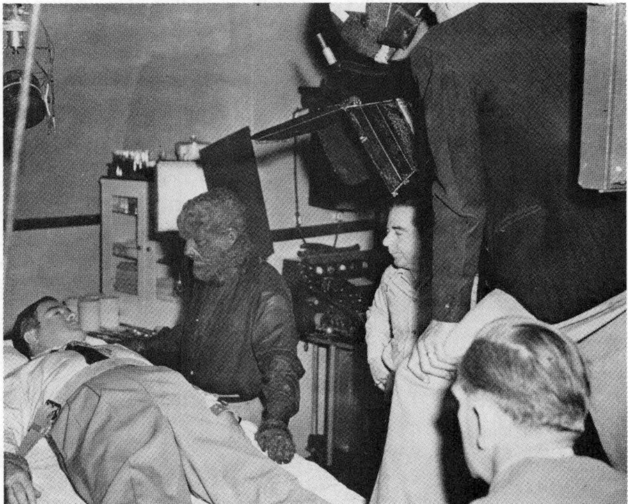

Lou Costello and Lon Chaney wait while director Charles Barton (on profile) supervises a camera setup.

As Strange's injury was treated, the company expected to lose three days of shooting, until Lon Chaney learned of the accident. As Barton remembers:

> Lon said, "I'll put the makeup on. *I'll* do it." He had done it before, and that was a hell of a job to put that makeup on and everything. No quarrels . . . just as happy as he could be to do it.

So, for that one shot, Chaney donned the makeup and costume and threw a stunt girl through the re-assembled window. Shortly afterwards, a grateful Strange, in foot cast, completed his scenes, including the ripping down of an iron gate on the back lot.

For the final scene, a mechanical dummy of the Monster marched through the flames on a back lot lake pier, and Vincent Price, who had played the title role in Universal's 1940 *The Invisible Man Returns*, supplied the voice of the Invisible Man who sent the comedy team jumping into the lake for the fadeout laugh.

On Saturday, March 20, 1948, shooting of *Abbott and Costello Meet Frankenstein* was completed.

None of the front office bigwigs ever even visited our set. They wouldn't even tell us after the picture was finished if it was good or bad. They didn't know or care for comedy. They just wanted to get the picture out as soon as possible so it could make several million for them.

Charles Barton

Post-shooting production began immediately on the film. Frank Skinner (who had scored *Son of*

Frankenstein and had joined Charles Previn and Hans Salter in scoring *The Wolf Man*) composed an ominously exciting and original score. Universal's long-time special effects magician John P. Fulton had been dropped by Universal in the same purge that had exiled Pierce from the lot, and young David Horsley and Jerome Ash tackled the special visual effects, including the bats that could be seen in the seductive staring eyes of Lugosi and Miss Aubert, and the quite unconvincing animation that transformed Lugosi's Dracula into a prop room bat. A special treat was the pre-credit animation sequence, in which the Monster scares the skeletons of Abbot and Costello. The comic skeletons collide into one another, and their flying bones spell the film's title.

Tragically, before the film was released, one of the stars almost died. On the night of April 22, 1948, Lon Chaney, following a serious fight with his wife, swallowed 40 sleeping pills. One of his sons found him unconscious in the truck, and the actor was rushed to Van Nuys Receiving Hospital, where he was listed as being in critical condition. Fortunately, he soon rallied, was moved to St. Joseph Hospital in Burbank, and reconciled with his very distraught wife Patsy.

On Friday, June 25, 1948, *Abbott and Costello Meet Frankenstein* previewed at Los Angeles' 1,766-seat Forum Theatre. On Monday morning, the trade papers were rejoicing:

> *The Hollywood Reporter:* . . . a crazy giddy show that combines chills and laughs in one zany sequence after the other . . . Robert Arthur's production spells out showmanship right down the line, and Charles T. Barton's direction keeps things moving at a lively, vigorous pace . . . Lon Chaney, as the Wolf Man, and Bela Lugosi, playing his old role of Count Dracula, make excellent foils, as does Glenn Strange in the spot of the Monster . . . Charles Van Enger's camera work helps establish the eerie mood . . .[230]
>
> *Variety:* Combination of horror and slapstick should pay off brilliantly . . . Chaney, Lugosi, Strange, and Lenore Aubert as Lugosi's sinister assistant are right in the groove for the numbskullduggeries . . . Bud Abbott and Lou Costello work like beavers from some hefty yocks. Producer Robert Arthur and director Charles T. Barton can chalk it up as one of the best for the comedians. . . .[231]

Lou Costello, meanwhile, had remained convinced that the film wasn't funny. It wasn't *The Hollywood Reporter* or *Variety* that changed his mind—it was his mother. After the premiere, she turned to her son, smiled, and said, "It's the best one you've ever done."[232] Only then would Lou accept the fact that *Abbott and Costello Meet Frankenstein* was a top comedy.

Shortly afterward, on July 24, 1948, Universal-International opened the film at Los Angeles' United Artists, Guild, Ritz, Iris and Studio City theaters. The result was a phenomenon. Philip K. Scheuer, critic for the *Los Angeles Times,* braved a matinee at the Ritz, a happening he described as ". . . a bedlam which had soon communicated itself from shadows to spectators, most of them in their teens or younger. They shrieked with that fusion of terror and glee which only a motion picture of this sort can inspire . . . I wouldn't have missed the show—the one going on around me, anyhow—for anything."[233] However, *Abbott and Costello Meet Frankenstein* caused lines to form not only at the kiddie matinees, but for the adult-favored evening performances as well. As the very discriminating Mr. Scheuer noted, ". . . The film has been put together with enormous ingenuity. Its comic inventiveness seldom falters, yet it never seriously violates the tradition of the three celebrated creatures who are its antagonists."[234]

On July 28, 1948, *Abbott and Costello Meet Frankenstein* opened at New York City's Loew's Criterion Theatre. The engagement began during an air conditioning engineers' strike, and the majority of the Manhattan critics so cavalierly panned the film that *The Hollywood Reporter* ran an editorial panning the Manhattan critics! Nevertheless, the sweltering Criterion was soon enjoying sell-out business, with most of the delighted audiences siding with the New York *Star* critic Cecelia Ager:

> . . . It's heart-warming to see all our favorite monsters once more . . . It's kind of like a class reunion . . . everybody connected with this nostalgic travesty of horror movies deserves credit . . . they have made *Abbott and Costello Meet Frankenstein* a broad, friendly comedy, good to see. It's real American folklore; look at it that way.[235]

Abbott and Costello Meet Frankenstein became the most successful film of the series since *Frankenstein* 17 years before. The movie made Hollywood's top moneymaker list of 1947–48, and joined U-I'S *Naked City* and *Tap Roots* (which featured Karloff as a noble Indian) as one of the studio's "Big 3" grossers of the year 1948—a year in which the front office's pretensions resulted in a fiscal loss of $3.2 million. The studio shrewdly augmented the film's appeal by dispatching Lugosi with his cape and Strange with his mask, boots and costume to certain key cities, where they appeared "Live On Stage" in conjunction with the movie. Strange delighted the audiences by stepping out in front of the curtain after the act and giving a little speech that always ended:

Boris Karloff delighting the Universal publicity department at Loew's Criterion Theatre, New York City.

". . . If I made a good Monster, the credit goes to one of the nicest guys I know—Boris Karloff."[236]

Karloff, incidentally, did not completely escape the clutches of *Abbott and Costello Meet Frankenstein.* So eager was Universal to associate Karloff with the film that the studio offered to pay his New York hotel bill if he would simply pose outside Loew's Criterion for publicity shots. Karloff agreed—"as long as I don't have to see the movie!"[237]

I never understood Lou. I never knew why he broke us up so suddenly.[238]

Bud Abbott

The wonderful success of *Abbott and Costello Meet Frankenstein* catapulted the team back into the 1948 Top Ten box office list, where they would remain through 1951. The team now faced another seven years at Universal City, destined, like the "Ma and Pa Kettle" and the "Francis the Talking Mule" series, to keep the studio solvent and win the revenue necessary for its big budget, egg-laying dramas. Noting how profitably Lou Costello quivered, Universal launched the team through a whole new series of high jinx with bogey men, the first being 1949's *Abbott and Costello Meet the Killer, Boris Karloff.* The star who had refused to spoof his Monster had no qualms about spoofing himself. "Karloff was great—one hell of a guy, boy," remembered Barton, who directed this one too. "Bud and Lou loved him." Following in decreasing quality and profits came *Abbott and Costello Meet the Invisible Man* (Arthur Franz sharing the title spot), 1953's *Abbott and Costello Meet Dr. Jekyll and Mr. Hyde* (with Karloff again) and, their last for Universal, 1955's *Abbott and Costello Meet the Mummy* (with none other than Eddie Parker as the bandaged one). Sadly overexposed by the regurgitations of their famous routines on television's *The Colgate Comedy Hour* and the syndicated *The Abbott and Costello Show,* they would make just one more film together, UA's 1956 *Dance With Me, Henry* (directed by Barton) before the climactic blow-up came. The eruption took place in Las Vegas at Christmas 1956, while the team was playing in a revue called "Miltown Revisited." Between shows, the shrewd casino proprietors plied the heavy-gambling Bud with liquor to help him feel lucky. When Bud went on stage later that night, he couldn't remember his lines and didn't know where he was. Lou pushed him off the stage and refused ever to work with Bud again after that engagement.

When Lou Costello died at age 52 of a heart attack on March 3, 1959, following two sad years of limited success as a "single," Charles Barton wasn't surprised:

> Not too long before, I had a bad experience with Lou in Catalina. The two of us had gone away on his boat, and he got an attack. I called the hospital, and they sent a sea plane over for him. He was in bad shape.
>
> Now Bud was on vacation on a yacht, and he heard that call I made to the hospital. Whether he had picked it up on the radio, or whatever, I'll never know. But he got a plane from the isthmus and came right to the hospital so he could see Lou. Bud was a very loyal man.

Fifteen years of poor health, near-poverty and merciless harassment from the Internal Revenue Service for delinquent income tax remained for Bud Abbott. Not long before the end, the Nostalgia Book Club ran a notice that Bud was heartsick for letters from people who had loved him as children, and supplied an address from which such letters could be forwarded. On April 24, 1974, Bud Abbott died of cancer at age 78 in his Woodland Hills house, which was subsequently sold to appease new tax claims.

"Bud and Lou were a great pair," said Charles Barton, "and the end for the two of them was tragic—really sad."

Costello, Abbott, Strange, Lugosi, and Chaney.

I used to enjoy horror films when there was thought and sympathy involved. Then they became comedies. Abbott and Costello ruined the horror films: they made buffoons out of the monsters. . . .[239]

Lon Chaney, Jr.

As suggested by Chaney's lament, there are many who perceive *Abbott and Costello Meet Frankenstein* as the absolute and final degradation of the once great horror characters. However, there are many others who realize that the film was really a blessing: an affectionate, polished spoof which allowed audiences to bid a legitimately merry goodbye to creatures who, because of the changing world and the abuse of the studio, had themselves become quite laughable.

First of all, it must be noted that *Abbott and Costello Meet Frankenstein* is a beautifully mounted, splendidly atmospheric comedy thriller. Director Barton mixed his vigorous, slick comedy style that served the comedy team so well with a surprising flair for melodrama that allowed the three villains to play their parts Gothically straight. Reviewers (and there were quite a few) who hoped to see Dracula take a pratfall or the Monster get hit by a pie were disappointed (the New York *Herald-Tribune* complained, "Universal has designed this film as though it didn't want to make too much fun of its own wax museum . . . ").[240] Of course, it was the blending of the straight horror with the slick comedy that made the film work so delightfully. Aside from the Monster recoiling in fear when he first sees Lou Costello, Barton had the three horror stars play their traditional characters with affection and respect.

Not surprisingly, the film's top performance is Bela Lugosi's powdered but proud Count Dracula. What a joy it is to see that neither drugs, age, nor Hollywood's neglect could diminish the lustre of this actor in his classic delineation! When Lugosi flamboyantly waves his hands as he hypnotizes Costello, suavely swirls his cape, and seductively demands of Miss Aubert, "Look into my eyes," Lugosi *is* Count Dracula, radiant in a role for which he is clearly destined never to be forgotten.

Lon Chaney is free to win sympathy as the woeful lycanthrope. His eyes, so agonized as Talbot, still gleam with bloodlust through the sponge-rubber Wolf Man mask, and he's privileged here to play the film's most truly frightening moment. After being transformed into a werewolf in his London room, Chaney claws a plush chair and the stuffing flies wildly into the air to a burst of Skinner's grand score.

And, as for Strange's Monster, although he knocks down a door, rips down a gate and throws the villainess through a window, he has in his mask and demeanor a queer pathos. As Ms. Ager wrote of the Monster in her New York *Star* review, ". . . his look of lonely sadness is almost unbearable now. Always a sympathetic character, his obvious need for affection makes him positively lovable here . . ."[241] The poor Monster appears ready to tolerate anything—be he sheepishly murmuring "Yes, Master" as Dracula's goonish slave, or sitting stoically stonefaced as Costello

Strange and Costello.

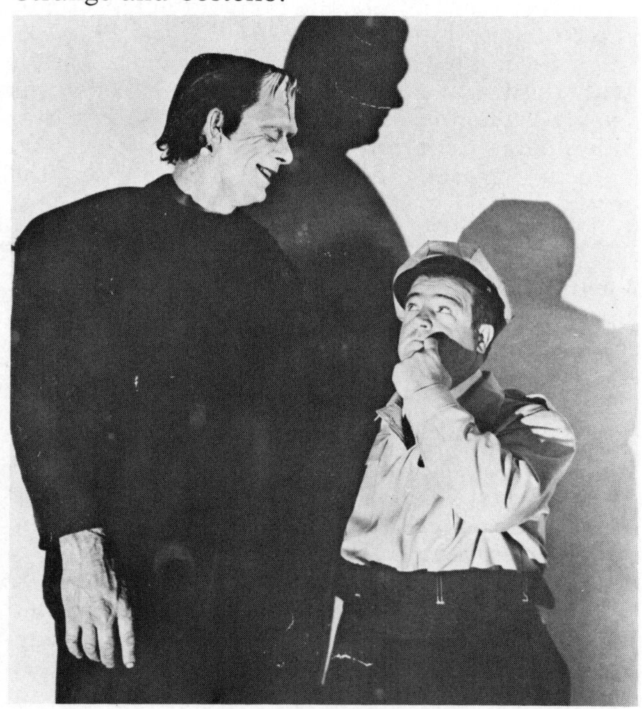

calls him "Junior" in a mocking falsetto voice. It is as if the many revivals and resurrections have been just too much to take for this once-awesome creature, and he's now perfectly willing to give the comics and the audience a good time, perhaps dreaming of a true rest as he stalks with dignity through the flames that consign him to his obligatory doom.

It would have been difficult for a 1931 audience to believe that a roly-poly comic could sit in the lap of Frankenstein's Monster, play "handsies," and live to hoot about it. It would have been difficult for a 1941 audience to accept the vicious Wolf Man lunging after a five-feet-five, 200-pound clown in a tiny hotel room and a dense forest, and allowing him to escape his claws both times. But this was 1948. While these veteran screen ogres might have genuinely scared the children, they were almost old friends to the adults who had lived with them through a world Depression and war. The Depression was vanquished, the war was won, and the three cinema bogey men were now nostalgia. The Monster, Dracula and the Wolf Man were like a nightmare that had caused one to wake up screaming, something to be remembered with some respect, but basically something to be laughed away and forgotten in the light of a new day.

So it was Abbot and Costello who were fated to help audiences laugh away, with respect, the Wolf Man, Count Dracula, and the Frankenstein Monster. This was a new day, one with new horrors of radiation mutants and atomic destruction. In the nightmares spawned by these obscenities, Frankenstein's Monster could only be welcomed as an old friend.

Dracula's impressively dank cellar: Abbott and Costello with Lugosi and Strange.

Bela Lugosi posing and smiling for reporters after his commitment for drug addiction (April 1955). He weighed only 125 lbs. when this picture was taken.

Denouement

There's a curse . . . The curse of Frankenstein!
from *The Ghost of Frankenstein*

When *Abbott and Costello Meet Frankenstein* completed production in the spring 1948, Universal's Frankenstein saga had survived several of its celebrated talents: Colin Clive, Dwight Frye, Lionel Atwill and *Frankenstein Meets the Wolf Man* director Roy William Neill (who died in London on December 14, 1946, at age 59 of a reported cerebral hemorrhage). For some veterans of the series, a new, more rewarding career began, but others were doomed to play out their lives in the Frankenstein shadow—and many, strangely enough, faced unhappy and tragic deaths.

On the evening of August 16, 1956, a heart attack killed 73-year-old Bela Lugosi in the bedroom of his Hollywood apartment at 5620 Harold Way. Death was a mercy. Aside from a temporarily encouraging tour of *Dracula* in England in 1951, the actor had suffered through final years marked by putrid movies (e.g., 1952's *Bela Lugosi Meets a Brooklyn Gorilla),* humiliating personal appearance horror shows, and a heartbreaking 1953 divorce. ("Maybe I shouldn't have done that to him," Lillian Lugosi Donlevy emotionally told me. "He just couldn't stand being by himself."[242]) Parted from his wife of 20 years and his son, Lugosi turned more and more to the needle from which Lillian had weaned him before the divorce, and the spring of 1955 presented the world with Lugosi's grotesquely publicized self-incarceration as a drug addict at Metropolitan State Hospital in Norwalk, California. (". . . My body grew hot, then cold. I tried to eat the bed sheets, my pyjamas. My heart beat madly. . . .")[243]

Lugosi courageously triumphed over his addiction, but he could not overcome Hollywood's apathy—or his bitterness over *Frankenstein.* There was a special irony in his last two film roles—a mute butler in *The Black Sleep* (1956), an all-star chiller with Rathbone, Chaney and Carradine, and a mute ghoul in the disastrous *Plan 9 From Outer Space.* It was as if the scorned Monster was wagging a mocking finger at the actor who once was so proud of his speaking voice, yet now was too ill to learn and speak dialogue.

"He was just terrified of death . . . " said Hope Lininger Lugosi, the actor's 40-year-old widow who had married him in 1955 after years of sending him passionate fan letters, and who would share his $2,900 estate with Bela junior. ". . . I did my best to comfort him, but you might as well save your breath with people like that. They're still going to be afraid of death."[244] Besides his nightmares about dying, Lugosi truly had nightmares about *Frankenstein* and Boris Karloff. Three nights before Lugosi's death, his wife awoke to find her spouse stumbling about the dark bedroom. Lugosi insisted that Karloff was in the living room—and that he had to spruce up to go in to see him.

On August 18, 1956, Bela Lugosi was buried according to his last wishes—in his Dracula cape. Today, many horror buffs make the pilgrimage to Inglewood's Holy Cross Cemetery, where, not far from the grave of Bing Crosby, there is a small marker:

BELA LUGOSI
Beloved Father
1882–1956

"Poor Bela," lamented Boris Karloff in his later years. "He was worth a lot more than he got."[245] Indeed he was.

The following year, Death claimed another famous artist of the Frankenstein saga in bizarre and sordid fashion.

Early in the afternoon of May 29, 1957, a maid named Anna Ryan discovered the fully dressed corpse of 63-year-old James Whale, with an ugly gash on the forehead, floating face up in the pool behind his villa at 788 S. Amalfi Drive in the Pacific Palisades. Nearby was Whale's final painting—the unfinished oil portrait of a naked beach boy. After sounding a scream worthy of a horror heroine, Ms. Ryan ran to the telephone—but did not notify the police. She called the young gas station worker who shared Whale's house, and George Lovett, Whale's business manager. The two men

James Whale (circa 1955).

raced to the house, pulled the body from the water, and then called Fire Department rescuers and the police.

The result was an old-fashioned, sensational, Hollywood murder scandal. "Even the newspaper accounts of the time were mysterious and full of innuendo," screenwriter-historian DeWitt Bodeen told me. "A drunken orgy did take place at Whale's house the night before his body was found. There's very little doubt of that, and there may have been drugs. There have been insinuations that Whale was a dead man before his body was thrown into the pool. All this could be true; he had a curious coterie of 'friends.'"[246] The coroner ruled the death of the man who directed *Frankenstein* and *Bride of Frankenstein* a "possible drowning," and accounts of the demise vary wildly. Some claim that Whale suffered a stroke while swimming (a ridiculous theory, as he was fully clothed); others insist he fell into the pool and struck his head on the bottom; another suggests suicide. The most popular version in Hollywood circles (and the one Kenneth Anger related in the 1965 edition of his famous "underground" expose, *Hollywood Babylon*), was that Whale had his "head bashed in," very possibly by the homosexual friend whose portrait Whale was in the midst of painting.

The grotesque tableau which Anna Ryan beheld on May 29, 1957 was a sickly poetic finale to the sad, mysterious life of James Whale. The great director had passed the last 16 years of his life in elegantly bitter exile from the studios. There had been two major comeback attempts. In 1944, Whale directed a stage thriller, *Hand in Glove,* at the Pasadena Playhouse; he went with the play to Broadway, where it opened at the Playhouse Theatre on December 4, 1944 and ran only 40 performances. Then, in 1949, Whale directed a 41-minute version of William Saroyan's one-act play *Hello, Out There,* a part of a multi-story feature. Producer Huntington Hartford disliked the performance of his wife, Marjorie Steele and scrapped the movie. Whale spent most of his remaining days painting, visiting European art galleries, drinking heavily and hosting those gay "orgies" which might have been the background for his tragic death. Whale had suffered at least one stroke before the fatal "accident."

It wasn't until June 6, 1957, that the Chapel of the Pacific at Santa Monica's Woodlawn Cemetery cremated Whale's body. His estate totalled almost $600,000, and "The James Whale Co.," a real estate and investment firm he founded with George Lovett, prospered for a long time after Whale's death.

At the time of his death, Whale was toying with the idea of designing scenery for a fantasy operetta, based on the works of Ray Bradbury and Max Beerbohm, which Charles Laughton hoped to produce on Broadway as a showcase for Elsa Lanchester. "Charles and I hadn't seen him for years," Miss Lanchester told me. "We were trying to persuade him to 'return to life,' so to speak, as he had dropped out of life so entirely. So brilliant . . . so bitter."[247]

Shortly after midnight, on January 20, 1960, Eddie Parker, the Monster's double of *The Ghost of Frankenstein* and *Frankenstein Meets the Wolf Man,* died of a heart attack at his home at 4236 Sherman Oaks Avenue. He was 59. During his tenure at the studio, Parker deservedly won the title of "The Universal Monster." In addition to doubling Chaney and Lugosi as the Monster, he is credited with doubling Chaney as Kharis of *The Mummy's Tomb, The Mummy's Ghost* and *The Mummy's Curse,* and cavorting for Karloff behind a Westmore rubber mask in 1953's *Abbott and Costello Meet Dr. Jekyll and Mr. Hyde.* Ironically, one of Parker's later jobs was doubling a very frail Lugosi in the low budget *Bride of the Monster,* in which his substitution for Lugosi in the action sequences is all too obvious. His final job came as a stunt performer on *The Jack Benny Show.*

On August 6, 1964, 71-year-old Sir Cedric Hardwicke, "Ludwig" of *The Ghost of Frankenstein,* died of emphysema in New York University Medical Center. Though the patrician actor had enjoyed many cinema successes (e.g., Hitchcock's 1947 *Rope*, Olivier's 1956 *Richard III*, DeMille's 1956 *The Ten Commandments*) and numerous Broadway hits (such as *Antigone* with Katharine Cornell in 1946 and *Caesar and Cleopatra* with Lilli Palmer in 1949), his last years were full of financial woes, illness and a great fear of dying in an actors' home. At the time of his death, he was believed to be "alimony poor" after a 1961 divorce from his second wife, actress Mary Scott (he was 68 at the time, she was 32); the Actors' Relief Fund had to pay for his cremation. Bitterly regretting the years he gave to Hollywood, Hardwicke wrote in his 1961 memoir, *A Victorian in Orbit:* "On the whole, Hollywood gave me more, much more, than I was able to return. I thought it would be a wonderful place to live in. What I did not appreciate was that there was very little in the place for me to live for."[248]

Dr. Frankenstein's "first son" also found things difficult in his last years. On July 21, 1967, 75-year-old Basil Rathbone died of a heart attack in his apartment at 135 Central Park West in New York City. Tiring of his stardom as Sherlock Holmes in the Universal film series and the MBS Network radio program, Rathbone deserted Hollywood in 1946 ("It was a simple question of survival—Holmes or Rathbone")[249] to return to his first love, the theater. He became the winner of a 1948 Antoinette Perry "Tony" Award as Best Dramatic Actor for his performance of Dr. Sloper in *The Heiress*, and performed much acclaimed television work (including a wonderful Scrooge in the Christmas 1956 musical special "The Stingiest Man in Town"). At times Rathbone returned to Hollywood for such films as John Ford's 1958 *The Last Hurrah*. Sadly, saving money had never been one of Rathbone's talents (his wife Ouida had been one of the most extravagant spenders and party hostesses of Hollywood's Golden Age), and by the 1960s, the splendid actor was madly scrambling to maintain solvency, touring in his one-man show, *An Evening with Basil Rathbone*, and playing in such cinema rot as 1966's *The Ghost in the Invisible Bikini* and (his last), 1967's *Hillbillys in a Haunted House*. Rathbone's widow rapidly spent the $15,000 estate left to her and lived her last years (she died in 1974 at the age of 88) aided by the charity of her surviving friends from the old Hollywood aristocracy. "I wish to be buried beside my wife," Rathbone wrote in his will, "so close that, if it were possible, we might hold each other's hand. . . . I wish to be buried above ground, as I look upon death as a gateway to an ascension and an elevation—not a descent."[250]

Route 66 TV shot: Martin Milner, Lon Chaney, Boris Karloff, George Maharis, and Peter Lorre.

"The Makeup is copyrighted by Universal," said Boris Karloff of his Monster to *The New York Times* in 1968, "which is very funny, when you think that the man who did it now sits in a valley in California, retired, and not getting a penny from it."[251] After being dropped by Universal, Jack P. Pierce freelanced (he had made up Glenn Strange as Atlas, the bearded giant of Monogram's 1949 *Master Minds*) and worked on such television programs as *You Are There, Fireside Theatre*, and *Mr. Ed.* However it was his reputation as Universal's Monster Maker that won him his greatest fame and caused him his deepest bitterness. In his last years, bedridden with arthritis, living in a small apartment at 4547 Colbath Avenue in Sherman Oaks, Pierce painfully felt the injustice of Universal's gluttony for royalties from Monster rubber masks, plastic models, toys and games, while he himself received no compensation beyond a modest pension. On the afternoon of July 19, 1968, the 79-year-old Pierce died of uremia at Burbank's St. Joseph Hospital, and 23 mourners (only three of them makeup men) joined his widow Blanche at the funeral service at the Wee Kirk o' the Heather of Forest Lawn, Glendale on July 23. "Hollywood bid farewell by staying

Boris Karloff, as villainess Mother Muffin, relaxes with Stefanie Powers and friend between scenes of "The Mother Muffin Affair" episode of NBC's *The Girl From U.N.C.L.E.* (1966).

away," wrote Frank Taylor in the *Los Angeles Times*, "but it might be that Jack Pierce didn't want to see them anyway."[252] Boris Karloff, at home in England when he learned of Pierce's death, mourned and sent a beautiful floral wreath in sympathy and tribute to the man he always praised as "a genius."

"I'm sure I'd be marvelous as Little Lord Fauntleroy, but I'm quite sure I'm altogether alone in that belief!"[253] laughed Boris Karloff in 1968. On February 2, 1969, respiratory problems took the life of the seemingly inconquerable 81-year-old at King Edward VII Hospital in Midhurst, England. The actor's last two decades were joyous. There were Broadway hits (Mr. Darling/Captain Hook to Jean Arthur's *Peter Pan*, 1950–51, Bishop Cauchon to Julie Harris's Joan of Arc in *The Lark*, 1955–56). And there was television (everything from singing "Mama Look a'Boo Boo" on *The Dinah Shore Show* in 1957 to four teleseries of his own: ABC's *Boris Karloff Presents* (1949), England's *Col. March of Scotland Yard* (1952–54), NBC's *Thriller* (1960–62) and England's *Out of This World* (1962). In addition there were classical recordings, radio (including a 12-year stint as a daily reader of *Reader's Digest* material), summer stock, and, of course, films (ranging from the regrettable 1958 *Frankenstein 1970* to the fun farces, 1963's *The Raven* and 1964's *The Comedy of Terrors*). Near the end, Karloff had to cope with half a lung, crippling arthritis and a tired heart; yet, with a lovely country cottage near the sea in his beloved England, money wisely invested in savings and stocks, and his fifth, very caring wife Evelyn (whom he wed in April, 1946, the day after his divorce from Dorothy) ever at his side, Karloff determined to die "with my boots, and my greasepaint on."[254] A whole new generation came to love the grand old actor who capered in drag as Mother Muffin on *The Girl From U.N.C.L.E.* (1966), lovingly narrated Dr. Seuss's "How the Grinch Stole Christmas" (1966) and played that superb performance in Peter Bogdanovich's *Targets* (1968).

Only four people attended the private services for Boris Karloff at the Guildford Crematorium in England on February 5, 1969, while the international press published front-page obituaries. The Garden of Remembrance buried the actor's ashes, and St. Paul's Convent Garden (England's "Actors' Church") features a memorial plaque, with the following words from Andrew Marvell's "Upon Cromwell's Return from Ireland:"

He Nothing Common Did or Mean
Upon That Memorable Scene

Karloff gave Frankenstein's Monster a classic cinema interpretation; the Monster in turn rewarded him with a full and rich career and a faithful following. "God bless the old boy" Karloff would affectionately say. "Without him I would have been nowhere."[255]

On the afternoon of July 12, 1973, 67-year-old Lon Chaney, Jr., died of a heart attack at his home, 207 Calle de Ansa, in San Clemente, California. "They don't know how to make good horror films in Hollywood anymore," opined Chaney not long before the fatal attack. "Boy, they really need me!"[256] The actor had prospered through the 1950s with solid dramatic performances in such films as 1952's *High Noon* (the old lawman), 1955's *Not as a Stranger* (Robert Mitchum's drunken father), and 1958's *The Defiant Ones* ("Big Sam"); he also worked steadily on television, including the 1956–57 syndicated series *Hawkeye and The Last of the Mohicans,* in which he played an Indian with the outrageous name of Chingachgook. However, by the 1960s, Chaney's long-standing alcoholic bouts had almost overtaken him. In Sweden to star in the teleseries *13 Demon Street* in 1961, Chaney drank from a fifth in open view of his co-workers, defying director Curt Siodmak to command him to stop. With this dissipation came a sad career slump, though he was good as

An ailing Lon Chaney, Jr. in *Dracula vs. Frankenstein* (1971).

the doomed bartender of *Welcome to Hard Times* (1967). He was soon playing in dismal exploiters such as *Cannibal Orgy* and, hitting bottom, *Dracula vs. Frankenstein,* in which the bloated, clearly degenerating Chaney stumbled about as a mute zombie.

By 1969, Chaney junior was suffering from the same disease which had killed Chaney senior—throat cancer. The cobalt treatments proved devastating, and his recovery was wracked by a merciless series of illnesses: gout, beriberi, liver trouble, heart trouble, arthritis of the back and hips, cataracts, and hepatitis. Near the end, the agonized Chaney resorted to acupuncture to relieve his misery.

Still, Chaney, afraid to be known as a "has-been" and needing money, met his end with bravado. He began work on his memoirs, hunted backing for a comeback vehicle he had written for himself called *Gila Man,* and at the time of his death, was studying the role of Jonathan for a stock revival in Ohio of *Arsenic and Old Lace,* which he hoped to play with the aid of a special throat microphone. Death intervened. Chaney left explicit instructions that his demise was to receive no publicity whatsoever, and his widow Patsy never divulged the fact that his body had been donated to the University of Southern California School of Medicine as an anatomical specimen.

Seventy days after Chaney's death, on the evening of September 20, 1973, 74-year-old Glenn Strange died of lung cancer at St. Joseph Hospital in Burbank. "The Lord's been good to me," said Strange late in his life. "I've been lucky to have worked with so many grand people in this business."[257] In the early days of television, Strange had played another famous heavy, Butch Caven-

Boris Karloff and Glenn Strange (1966).

dish, the desperado whose gang slaughtered all but one of a platoon of Texas Rangers—the one survivor becoming "The Lone Ranger."* In the late 1950s, Strange took time out from films (such as 1957's *Gunfire at Indian Gap*) and television (an estimated 500 appearances) to don a black mask and a clown suit and to perch atop the 150-foot KTLA radio mast in Hollywood, defying viewers to guess his identity. For ten days, from noon to midnight, Strange took his bizarre post, and the television station received 50,000 letters, 80 percent guessing the mystery man to be Karloff, 15 percent guessing Chaney. In 1963, Strange wore a Don Post Monster mask and played the creature in a color amateur serial entitled *The Adventures of the Spirit,* directed by Donald F. Glut. Strange also made gag appearances as the Monster on several television variety shows of the 1950s.

Strange's happiest engagement, however, came in 1962 when he joined the cast of CBS's *Gunsmoke* as Sam, the bartender of the Long Branch Saloon. Between seasons, he toured rodeos, performing with such *Gunsmoke* friends as Ken Curtis and Milburn Stone. "The *Gunsmoke* cast is the closest family of performers ever to do a television show," said the program's producer John Mantley when Strange died. "Glenn was one of the nicest men the Lord ever made. . . . He was a marvelous professional."[258] Mantley delivered the eulogy at Strange's funeral at the Church of the Hills, Forest Lawn in Hollywood Hills on September 24, 1973. The last actor to play the Monster in Universal's *Frankenstein* series was dead.

On December 21, 1975, Rowland V. Lee, director of *Son of Frankenstein,* died of a heart attack in Palm Desert, California. After directing UA's *Captain Kidd* (1945), starring Charles Laughton, Lee announced his retirement from movie-making. ("The fun had gone out of the picture business entirely. People were coming into the business who had been making safety pins!")[259] He retired to his huge ranch in the San Fernando Valley to raise cattle and alfalfa, and later converted a section of the ranch that overlooked the Chatsworth reservoir to a film location which he rented to various studios. He came out of retirement to produce and write the screenplay for *The Big Fisherman* (1959), based on the Lloyd C. Douglas religious novel; it was only a mild success and Lee promptly returned to retirement. In 1972 he sold the ranch and moved to a house in Palm Desert. The 84-year-old Lee had just completed writing a mystery screenplay called *The Belt* at the time of his fatal attack.

On May 16, 1979, 78-year-old Robert Florey died at Santa Monica Hospital after a lengthy illness. His defeat at the manicured hands of James Whale on *Frankenstein* proved no handicap to Florey's career. He directed such acclaimed films as Paramount's *Hollywood Boulevard* (1936), Warner's *God is my Co-Pilot* (1945), and, perhaps his most famous credit, co-directed *Monsieur Verdoux* (1947) with his long-time associate Charles Chaplin. In 1950 the French Legion of Honor knighted Florey for his contributions to the cinema. Florey also became a pioneer in television direction, and in 1953 won the Directors Guild of America award for the *Four Star Playhouse* episode entitled "The Last Voyage," starring Charles Boyer. On May 18, 1979, graveside services were held at Forest Lawn of the Hollywood Hills. His wife of 39 years, Virginia Dabney, survived him.

Carl Laemmle, Jr., who began Universal's classic saga of Frankenstein during that fateful haircut in 1931, died of a stroke late in the afternoon of September 24, 1979 at the age of 71. It was the 40th anniversary of the death of Carl Laemmle, Sr. Rarely has anyone endured so terribly total a downfall as did the sensitive little man who produced such legendary films as *All Quiet on the Western Front, Bride of Frankenstein* and *Show Boat.* Junior never produced another picture after the Universal coup of 1936, never married, and had been an invalid since 1963, suffering from

*Strange's Cavendish would repeat the atrocity yearly on the anniversary show.

multiple sclerosis. Cruelly forgotten by Hollywood, the still-wealthy Laemmle followed the racetrack news and annually invited old friends to his lavish New Year's Eve party—an event which, in the final years, took on the morbid hue of Norma Desmond's "Happy New Year" bash of *Sunset Boulevard.* He refused offers to write his memoirs, and the few who managed to enter the old mansion at 1641 Tower Grove Drive in Beverly Hills brought back sad reports of a senile, lonely "vegetable." On September 26, 1979, the Home of Peace Cemetery Chapel in Whittier was the site of funeral services, just as it had been for Laemmle senior four decades before. Junior was interred at the Laemmle Family Mausoleum. He was survived by a niece, a nephew, and many cousins.

On January 28, 1980, Erle C. Kenton, director of *The Ghost of Frankenstein, House of Frankenstein* and *House of Dracula,* died at the age of 83 at Glendale Memorial Hospital. He had retired from feature film direction after 1950's *One Too Many,* and devoted his time to such teleseries as *Racket Squad, Public Defender,* and *The Texan.*

The survivors? There are precious few left. Mae Clarke, Elizabeth of *Frankenstein,* was at last report living alone in Panorama City, north of Hollywood. All three of her marriages ended in divorce; none produced any children. In October of 1953, Miss Clarke made unhappy headlines when she was given a 20-day suspended sentence for failing to report $43 she had earned while receiving unemployment compensation from the State of California. After some years of television work and movie bits, the one-time Queen of Universal has recently spent her time painting, coaching young drama students, and recording books for the blind. Elsa Lanchester, of *Bride of Frankenstein,* still lives in the Hollywood Hills house she has occupied since 1949, acts occasionally, and tends wildflowers. Both Miss Clarke and Miss Lanchester returned to Universal City at Halloween time 1979 to receive "Golden Scroll Awards" from the Academy of Science Fiction Fantasy and Horror Films for their respective Frankenstein performances.* Josephine Hutchinson, Elsa von Frankenstein of *Son of Frankenstein,* lives on Manhattan's East Side in a lovely old penthouse decorated with sensitive paintings by her late husband, actor/artist Staats Cotsworth. Evelyn Ankers, Elsa Frankenstein of *The Ghost of Frankenstein,* is long and happily retired, and a delighted grandmother. She vows she will never act again, and lives blissfully in a condominium in Maui, Hawaii, where husband Richard Denning had played the Governor in CBS's long-running teleseries *Hawaii 5-0.* The Dennings adore Hawaii, where they experience, in Evelyn's words, ". . . a life more like we think God intended us to live: quiet, clean, healthy, but most of all peaceful—away from the man-made rat race!"[260] Elena Verdugo, Ilonka of *House of Frankenstein,* is also happily retired, lives in North Hollywood and is married to Dr. Charles Rosewall, chief psychiatrist of the Los Angeles County Department of Mental Health. She is an accomplished painter, and is considering returning to the cinema in 20 years as, in her own words, "America's Margaret Rutherford."[261]

George Waggner, producer of *The Ghost of Frankenstein* and *Frankenstein Meets the Wolf Man,* presently resides at the Motion Picture Country House and Lodge in Woodland Hills, where he has been quite ill. Curt Siodmak, who wrote the screenplay for *Frankenstein Meets the Wolf Man* and the story for *House of Frankenstein,* lives on his large ranch in Three Rivers, California, and recently completed a horror stage musical entitled *Song of Frankenstein.* And Charles Barton, director of *Abbott and Costello Meet Frankenstein,* later became a popular director for Walt Disney (such films as *Toby Tyler* and such series as *Zorro* and *Spin and Marty*), and recently moved from his Santa Monica beach house to Toluca Lake, just north of the Universal lot.

Today, Universal City is the third large tourist attraction in the world (trailing behind only the Disneylands of California and Florida). Four million people a year (often 27,000 a day) board the "Glamour Trams," enjoying a five-hour ride past such sights as the New York street from *Kojack,* and "Bruce," the mechanical shark from *Jaws;* surviving such near-calamities as a collapsing bridge and the parting of the Red Sea; and visiting the huge Entertainment Center. Among the various shows there (stunt men, animals, screen tests, and such), a recent addition is "Castle Dracula," an elaborately decaying haunted house populated by such vintage Universal attractions as The Mummy, the Wolf Man, the Phantom of the Opera, and, of course, Frankenstein's Monster. Appropriately enough, "Castle Dracula" has become the most popular attraction on the tour.

Far less heralded is the old European village on the back lot. It is the village where, 50 years ago, the mob lit torches and marched into the hills in search of the Monster. One can imagine what ghosts return to that old, forsaken set each evening after the last "Glamour Tram" putters away—and one can only wonder what those ghosts think of the incredible lasting popularity of the most beloved horror film series ever created.

*Other Golden Scroll Award winners that day: Ralph Bellamy for *The Wolf Man,* Gloria Stuart for *The Invisible Man,* John Agar for *Revenge of the Creature,* and Christopher Lee for *Horror of Dracula.*

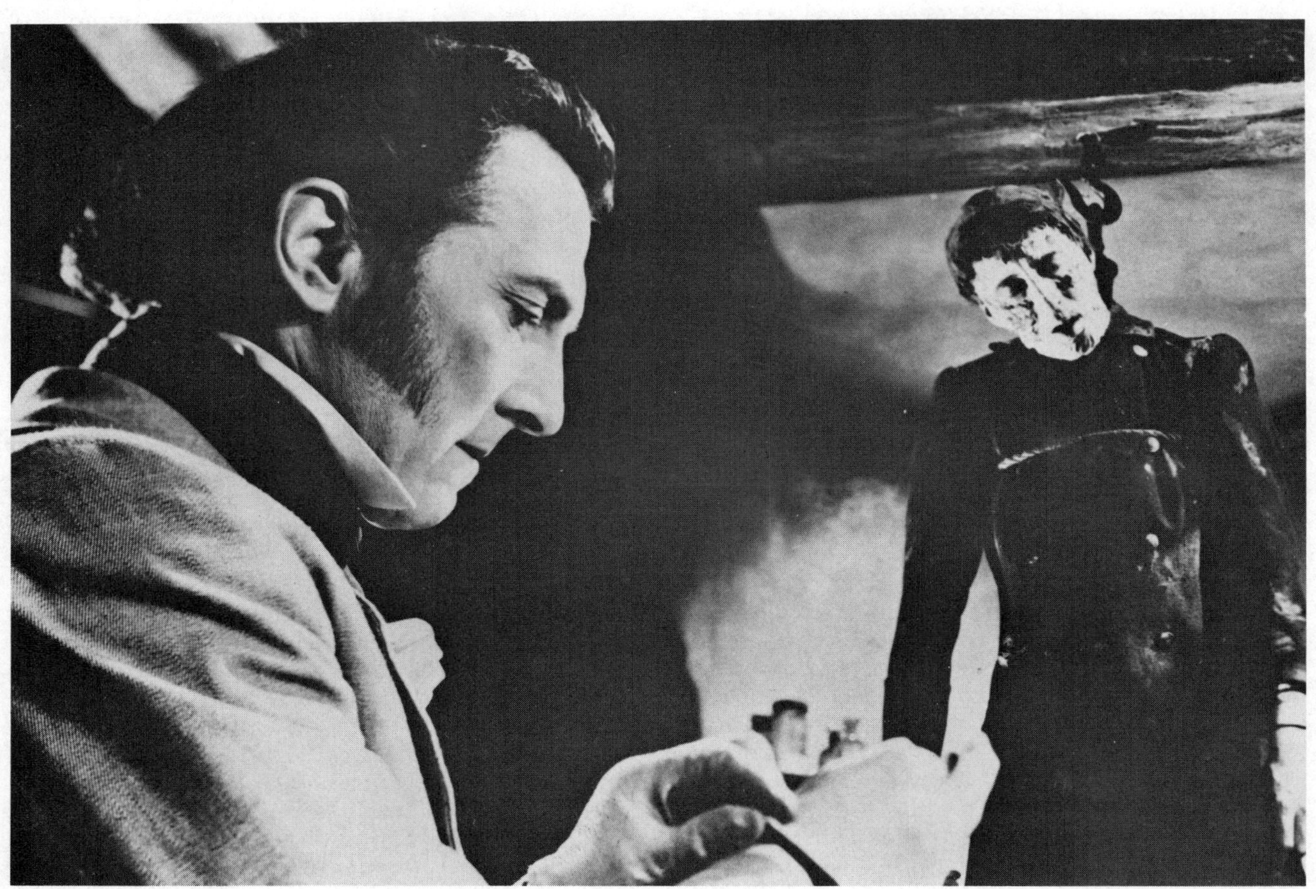

The Curse of Frankenstein (1957): Peter Cushing, Christopher Lee.

Further Frankensteins

If the Monster appeared to be sadly blasé as he stumbled about the flaming pier in *Abbott and Costello Meet Frankenstein,* he had good reason. Even if Universal was content to let the Monster rest on the bottom of a back lot lake, it was only a matter of time before other studios invoked his ominous name and horrific reputation to lure audiences and profits. Over the past three decades, Mary Shelley's Monster has inspired scores of films, yet none has won the revered status of "classic"—and none has escaped the shadow cast by Universal's saga. While this book is, of course, primarily concerned with the original series, an examination of some of the later efforts can perhaps put the Universal saga into clearer perspective.

In 1957, the biggest money-making movie in England was *The Curse of Frankenstein,* produced by Hammer Films. The shocker brought to the fore two hitherto-unknown actors: 43-year-old Peter Cushing (as Dr. Victor Frankenstein) and 35-year-old Christopher Lee (as the Creature*). There was at least one major pre-natal problem: Universal's protective guardianship of its copyrighted Monster makeup. Terence Fisher, a journeyman "B" film director who also won an identity via this film, refused to acknowledge this as a handicap: "We wanted the monster to fit Chris Lee's melancholy personality. We wanted a thing which looked like some wandering forlorn minstrel of monstrosity, a thing of shreds and patches, but in flesh and blood and organs."[262] Not everyone was impressed with makeup man Philip W.N. Leakey's results. Lee himself felt his Creature looked like "a circus clown,"[263] while a popular observation at the time likened Lee's Creature to "Jerry Lewis with acne." (Lee would find a far more satisfying role the following year in Hammer's *Horror of Dracula,* wherein his lustful Count won him terror genre superstardom.)

In the United States, Warner Bros. released *The Curse of Frankenstein* in May of 1957. It was a huge commercial success, though by no means a critical one. The ample footage of blood and guts, lovingly captured in Eastmancolor, nauseated many, and the strokes of sadism (e.g., half the Creature's face is shot away in mid-film) left little room for the poetry of Whale's *Frankenstein.* Director Fisher later refused to compare his version with Whale's:

> I wouldn't dream of comparing them! . . . Please. His was made some time ago. He did what he considered best. Everybody's right is to express themselves in the way they want . . . His was probably a greater achievement in that it was the first one . . .[264]

Audiences themselves had a chance to compare when *Shock Theatre* caused a television sensation in the fall of 1957. The popularity of the old Universal horrors, as well as the receipts of the Hammer films, inspired the British studio to become the new purveyor of celluloid mayhem. Along with a new *Dracula* series, and remakes of *The Mummy* (1959) and *The Phantom of the Opera* (1962), they began their own Frankenstein saga, and since Lee's Creature had dissolved in an acid bath, Cushing's Frankenstein became the recurrent character. In 1958's *The Revenge of Frankenstein,* Cushing escaped the guillotine to assemble a new creature (played by Michael Gwynn). In 1964's *The Evil of Frankenstein,* Cushing found the body of the Creature (now somewhat resembling the Universal conception and played by an Australian wrestler with the none-too-horrifying name of Kiwi Kingston) caught in a glacier (shades of *Frankenstein Meets the Wolf Man* and *House of Frankenstein*). An evil hypnotist sent the Monster on another rampage, and an exploding laboratory resolved the plot. The exotic *Frankenstein Created Woman* (1967) saw Cushing revived by electrical energy; he soon brought back to life a drowned, voluptuous blonde (Susan Denberg), instilled into her the soul of her guillotined boyfriend, and unleashed a wild vengeance spree. Hammer achieved perhaps its most sadistic film in 1969's *Frankenstein Must Be Destroyed,* despite the fact that no Monster was present. Instead, Cushing performed brain surgery by drilling into a skull with a brace and bit, with the accompaniment of splashed blood and grisly sound effects. *Horror of Frankenstein* in 1970 was virtually a remake of *The Curse*

*The Monster was referred to as the Creature out of fear of another possible copyright entanglement with Universal.

David Prowse, fated to wear the guise of Darth Vader in *Star Wars,* shown here in *Frankenstein and the Monster from Hell* (1974).

of Frankenstein, with Ralph Bates stepping in for Peter Cushing as Frankenstein, and David Prowse (destined to play Darth Vader in *Star Wars* and *The Empire Strikes Back*) as the Monster; 1974's *Frankenstein and the Monster from Hell* retained Prowse as the Monster and restored Cushing to the role of Frankenstein. Fisher directed all of the films of the series, save for *The Evil of* . . . (directed by Freddie Francis) and *Horror of* . . . (directed by Jimmy Sangster, who had worked on the script of the original Hammer entry).

Hammer has succeeded in winning its own cult of disciples over the past 20 years. Cushing, a splendid actor, has played Frankenstein with impeccable flair; Fisher (who died June 18, 1980, at age 76) was not without a certain romantic style as a director; the laboratory sequences, filmed in color with bubbling beakers and spectacular electrical effects, are far more elaborate than Kenneth Strickfaden's sets—just as the physical endowments of Hammer's leading ladies are more elaborately showcased than those of Universal's ankle-strapped ingenues. However, the Hammer Frankenstein series has been severely handicapped by the unrelenting accent on blood and gore, and the absence of a consistent, and effective Monster. In his book *A Pictorial History of Horror Movies,* English critic Denis Gifford shows an incisive lack of bias when he writes of the British studio, "In quantity Hammer films are fast approaching Universal, but in quality they have yet to reach Monogram."[265]

While Hammer was busy, the low budget studios have also churned out their variations on the Frankenstein theme. The 1957 release of American-International's *I Was a Teenage Frankenstein,* was memorable mainly because of the exasperation of Frankenstein (Whit Bissell) toward his pubescent monstrosity (Gary Conway): "I know you have a civil tongue in your head! I sewed it there myself!" In 1958, Allied Artists released *Frankenstein 1970,* with the box office bonus of starring Boris Karloff. ". . . I don't mind playing in another Frankenstein film," said Karloff, who for the first time actually joined the Frankenstein family as Dr. Victor von Frankenstein, "because I have a sentimental attachment and a sorrow for the things done to the poor Monster in the other pictures which I didn't appear in . . . I feel I owe him a debt of gratitude and affection . . ."[266] Karloff's affection, admirable as it was, was misplaced in this opus, wherein the actor, as a disfigured Nazi victim, revived the Monster via the ever-popular 1950s' touch of an atomic device. The climax—the Monster's unbandaged face revealing the image of a young Karloff—did provide a poetic (albeit senseless) denouement to the hokum. Astor's 1958 *Frankenstein's Daughter* was a total disaster, in which young Oliver Frankenstein (Donald Murphy), failing to persuade a girlfriend (Sally Todd) to sacrifice her purity on Hollywood's Mulholland Drive, drove over her in his convertible and used her mangled head to complete a female monster (played by an unbilled male). In 1965 theaters (and drive-ins) featured both Vernon's *Frankenstein Meets the Space Monster* (. . . "a monstrous mess," reported the *New York Herald-Tribune*) and Embassy's *Jesse James Meets Frankenstein's Daughter* (directed by William Beaudine, veteran of Monogram horrors of the 1940s). Embassy followed in 1967 with the "animagic" feature *Mad Monster Party,* with Karloff supplying the voice of the puppet "Baron von Frankenstein." Then too, there were many foreign

Boris Karloff, out of makeup, smiles with his wife Evelyn and his daughter Sara Jane on the set of *Frankenstein 1970* (1958).

productions: Mexico produced 1963's *El Infierno del Frankenstein* and 1964's *El Testamento del Frankenstein;* Japan's Soho Productions created 1965's *Furankenshutaen Tai Baragon* (*Frankenstein Conquers the World*), with the Monster wrestling with and munching on a variety of rubber creatures; and Spain released in 1972 *La Marcha del Hombre Lobo* (also known as *Frankenstein's Bloody Terror*), which boasted 3-D, but had no Monster (a foreword claiming that the Frankensteins had all become werewolves).

Perhaps the saddest of these quickie fiascos was slapped together in 1969: Independent-International's *Dracula vs. Frankenstein.* Amazingly, the idea to pit the infamous vampire (miserably played in fangs and an Afro by Zander Vorkov) against the Monster (played by seven-feet-four, clay-covered John Bloom) came only after the original film, *The Blood Seekers,* proved too brief and ludicrous for distribution. The most miserable ingredients of this travesty (which featured in mid-film Russ Tamblyn, a motorcycle gang and a rape) were J. Carrol Naish and Lon Chaney, the co-stars of *House of Frankenstein,* respectively as Dr. Durea (who, in the new footage, was revealed to be Dr. Frankenstein) and Groton, a Lennie-like Zombie. The sight of Naish, confined to a wheelchair and coping with thick glasses and what appear to be ill-fitting dentures, and Chaney, grossly overweight and without dialogue (due to his throat cancer), is almost too much to bear for any fan who fondly remembers the men in their prime. The film was reportedly no treat for the stars either. Naish was deeply upset by the *ad hoc* nature of the low-budget mess, and bitterly demanded a set chair with his name on it and an aide to assist him in and out of the car each day; Chaney ignored the indelicacies via his usual method, toting a flask filled with "iced tea." The film, with laboratory equipment supplied by Kenneth Strickfaden himself, was finally released in 1971, and received limited bookings under a menagerie of horrid titles, including *Blood Freaks, Satan's Blood Freaks,* and *Blood of Frankenstein.*

Late in 1974, just when it appeared that the name Frankenstein would be associated forevermore with cheap exploitation features, 20th Century-Fox released one of the most successful films of the decade: Mel Brooks' *Young Frankenstein.* In satirizing the Universal classics, director Brooks took an approach very similar to the one so seriously executed in 1931:

> The concept is a larger-than-life presentation. It has to do with man's dream of becoming God. One aspect of it is the outrage of man in God's defeating him. It's also about womb-envy, and the mob's ignorance and fear of genius. So it becomes a very Promethean work.
>
> The look and feel is German Expressionism. It's a salute to James Whale and the wonderful directors of the past, and that beautiful black-and-white look . . . I want it to be a spectacular and rich (visually and philosophically) entertainment that would house the comedy. It should be funny, thrilling, moving and touching. There should be cheers at the end if we've done the right thing, and I think we have. . . .[267]

Indeed they did. The script, by Gene Wilder and Brooks, resembled *Son of Frankenstein* most of all, with young Dr. Frederick Frankenstein ("That's Franken*steen*," insists the doctor, sensitive about his ancestry) forsaking teaching, returning to the legendary castle, and meeting a host of charmingly lampooned characters. Igor (pronounced I-gor) was played by Marty Feldman as a hunchback with a moving hump; Inspector Kemp (Kenneth Mars), the village constable, has a wooden arm (*a la* Atwill's Inspector Krogh) thanks to an early encounter with the Monster, and wears a monocle over his eyepatch; and an original character, Frau Blucher (Cloris Leachman), old Frankenstein's mistress, is a formidable crone whose very name causes any horse in the area to whinny. With original Kenneth Strickfaden equipment, Frankenstein soon vitalizes a Monster (bald-domed Peter Boyle, in a William Tuttle-designed makeup complete with a zipper in his neck), and Brooks proceeds to spoof gleefully and lovingly some of the original series' most famous episodes. The Monster meets and plays with a little girl (they take a seesaw ride, and the Monster inadvertently catapults the child into the air, through a window, and into her bed); he meets an old hermit (Gene Hackman), who plays "Ave Maria" on a phonograph and performs a repertoire of blind jokes, including pouring soup into the Monster's lap and lighting Boyle's thumb instead of his cigar.

Brooks does not confine himself to the Frankenstein saga in his spoofing. One of the film's most hilarious episodes parodies *The Walking Dead* by Warner Bros. (1936). Wilder's Frankenstein decides to introduce the Monster to the world as a song and dance man, and then joins the tuxedoed Monster in a rendition of "Puttin' on the Ritz." In the Warner's film, Edmund Gwenn, having brought Karloff back to life from the electric chair, decorously introduces him to an assemblage as a pianist. And the Brooks scene's climax (the Monster goes berserk when the press begins taking flash pictures) is, of course, a take-off on that famous moment from RKO's 1933 *King Kong.*

Young Frankenstein even gave the Monster something he never had before—a happy ending. By the picture's close, the Monster's brain has been stimulated, he is successful in business, and he has thawed and wed Frankenstein's frigid fi-

Peter Boyle and Kenneth Mars in *Young Frankenstein* (1974).

ancée Elizabeth (Madeline Kahn), who greets her husband in the boudoir in a negligee and wig—the hair piece being a frizzy, gray-streaked replica of Elsa Lanchester's famous coiffure of *Bride of Frankenstein.* It is a tribute to Universal's Frankenstein series (especially the first three films) that this luxuriant satire has come closer than any other Frankenstein film of the past three decades to meriting accolades as a "classic."

Unfortunately, there followed in 1974 a spoof of the Hammer series—*Andy Warhol's Frankenstein,* a French-Italian production directed by Paul Morrissey (Warhol's director of such "cult" pieces as *Trash* and *Heat*) and originally titled *Flesh for Frankenstein.* Here, charm was totally lacking; instead, audiences beheld an orgy of blood, globs and guts, all dumped into their laps via 3-D, and the sight of Frankenstein (Udo Kier) mounting his female monster. Amazingly, this nauseating film attracted such large and curious crowds that it now resides on *Variety*'s "All-Time Rental Champs" list with a gross of $4.7 million, despite the fact that it is already largely and mercifully forgotten.

Television, too, has taken stabs at the Frankenstein story. Already mentioned was the episode of "Frankenstein," starring Lon Chaney, Jr., as a bald, scarred Monster, telecast live in 1952 on ABC's series *Tales of Tomorrow.* In 1958, Hammer joined with Screen Gems to produce a pilot for a series entitled *Tales of Frankenstein.* The pilot episode, "The Face in the Tombstone Mirror," was directed by Curt Siodmak, and starred Anton Diffring as Frankenstein and Don Megowan as the Monster (resembling the Jack Pierce makeup, but with no electrodes). The series never sold.

The Munsters premiered on CBS September 24, 1964. The horror/comedy series was filmed at Universal. Fred Gwynne, as Herman Munster, was made up daily to suggest Karloff's original (the favorite joke of Universal employees who saw Gwynne in his guise was "Working today, Fred?"); Yvonne de Carlo was his ghoulish spouse Lily; Butch Patrick was their widow-peaked son Eddie;

and Al Lewis was Grandpa, Lily's 378-year-old mad scientist/vampire father. There was also a niece, Marilyn (played by Beverly Owen and later Pat Priest), a knockout blonde for whom the Munsters felt deep sympathy. The series ran for two seasons, spawned the 1966 feature film *Munster Go Home,* and is still popular in syndication. Gwynne, who saved his salary and residual payments, can now afford to indulge his dramatic ambitions in classical theater and Broadway (he played Big Daddy in a 1974 New York revival of *Cat on a Hot Tin Roof*); his co-star and friend Lewis, however, now tours the dinner theater circuit and bitterly calls *The Munsters* "the greatest mistake of my professional life."[268]

The *ABC Wide World of Entertainment* telecast a version of *Frankenstein,* January 16 and 17, 1972, with Robert Foxworth in the title role, Susan Strasberg as Elizabeth, and Bo Svenson as the Monster—a blond, jovial creature reminiscent of Lennie in Steinbeck's *Of Mice and Men.* Far more elaborate was Universal's NBC special "Frankenstein: the True Story," a 180-minute mini-epic filmed at Pinewood Studios in England under the direction of Jack Smight and telecast in two parts on November 30 and December 1, 1973. There was an all-star cast: Leonard Whiting (Romeo of Zeffirelli's 1968 *Romeo and Juliet*) as Frankenstein, Michael Sarrazin as Adam, his Monster (originally beautiful, later oozingly awful); James Mason as Dr. Polidori (presented here very much in the style of Ernest Thesiger's Pretorius in *Bride of Frankenstein*); and David McCallum as Dr. Clerval, whose experiments inspire Frankenstein's creation. The acting honors went to the beautiful Jane Seymour, who played the Monster's intended mate, Prima, a vain, precious creation who wears a necklace to conceal the stitches that join her head to her body. In an unforgettable scene that must rank as one of prime-time television's most sadistic moments, Sarrazin's frustrated Monster crashes a ball where Prima is the adored femme, causes his scornful mate to explode into violent hisses, exposes her scarred neck to the shocked guests, and then pulls off her head (not shown) and tosses it at the feet of Mason's cringing Polidori. This ambitious film, not completely successful nor by any means truly representative of Shelley's story, does have many Gothic flourishes to recommend it, and ends with a distinctly Romantic touch: Frankenstein and the Monster perish in an avalanche, entombed together for all time.

The most intriguing Frankenstein film of recent years was not "a horror movie," but *The Spirit of the Beehive,* a Spanish film directed by Victor Erice, which opened in New York in 1976 after winning European film festival honors. *The Spirit of the Beehive* takes place in 1940 in a little European village, where a travelling film exhibitor shows the townspeople the James Whale—Boris Karloff *Frankenstein.* A lonely, sensitive little girl (played by Ana Torrent) falls in love with the hapless Monster, and when her teasing sister tells her he is really alive, Ana begins a solitary search for the Monster through the countryside. It is a beautiful film, with a very special appeal to anyone who ever was moved by the lonely bewilderment of Karloff's Frankenstein Monster.

The Munsters (CBS, 1964).

There have been, of course, many other films and television adaptations internationally, as well as stage productions (notably by "The Living Theatre" in Europe in 1965 and the United States in 1966). And, as this book neared completion, a new stage production of *Frankenstein* made theater history—of a sort. Victor Gialanella's *Frankenstein,* based both on Mary Shelley's novel and the classic films, was scheduled to open at the Palace Theatre in New York on December 18, 1980. It was the most expensive straight play in Broadway history, boasting a $1.25 million budget, and featured one of the actors who rejected the Monster role half-a-century ago: John Carradine (as the blind hermit). The trouble-plagued production had its opening delayed twice, ran for 29 preview performances, finally opened on January 4, 1981, received withering reviews—and closed after one performance. *Frankenstein* won a place in theater annals as the most expensive flop in Broadway history, with a loss of $2 million. Said producer Terry Allen Kramer: "The curse of Frankenstein was visible the whole time."

David Dukes and Keith Jochim in the ill-fated stage version of *Frankenstein* (1981).

Biographical Appendix

This appendix includes brief biographies for 23 of the more celebrated veterans of Universal's *Frankenstein* series. There has been no attempt to be complete in listing credits; what follows is a sampling of the work of these artists.

Key to Studio Abbreviations:

AA	Allied Artists
A-I	American-International
BV	Buena Vista
Col.	Columbia
FBO	Film Booking Offices
FN	First National
I-I	Independent-International
Maj.	Majestic
MGM	Metro-Goldwyn-Mayer
Mon.	Monogram
Par.	Paramount
PDC	Producers Distributing Corporation
PRC	Producers Releasing Corporation
Rep.	Republic
RKO	RKO Radio
TCF	20th Century-Fox
U	Universal
UA	United Artists
WB	Warner Brothers

In cases where vital statistics information varied with reference sources, the author checked birth certificates and/or death certificates, if available, and is grateful to the State of California Department of Health Services for assistance in this matter.

ANKERS, Evelyn, actress; Elsa Frankenstein in *The Ghost of Frankenstein;* b. Valparaíso, Chile (to English parents) Aug. 17, 1918; e. Latymer and Godolphyn schools, London, and Royal Academy of Dramatic Art, London; m. 1942, actor Richard Denning, daughter: Diana Dee; now retired and residing in Maui, Hawaii.

Theater: Made stage bow in *The Daughter of Dolores,* (Colombia, South America, 1928); played on London stage in *Bats in the Belfry* (1937); played on Broadway stage as the screaming maid of *Ladies in Retirement* (1940), which she reprised in Los Angeles (1940).

Films: Made film debut in England in *Belles of St. Mary's* (MGM, 1936), and played in such British films as *Rembrandt* (UA, 1936), *Wings of the Morning* (Fox-British, 1937) and *The Villiers-Diamond* (Fox-British, 1938). After aborted contract with 20th Century Fox, signed with Universal, where she became "Queen of the Horrors" via such films as *The Wolf Man* (1941), *Captive Wild Woman, The Mad Ghoul, Son of Dracula* (all 1943), *The Invisible Man's Revenge* (1944), et al; also fine as a farceur (*All by Myself,* 1943) and a villainess (*Weird Woman,* 1944). Left Universal, 1944, freelanced in such fare as *Black Beauty* (TCF, 1946), *Tarzan's Magic Fountain* (RKO, 1949), and *The Texan Meets Calamity Jane* (as the latter, Col., 1950). Most recent film appearance in *No Greater Love* (1960), a Lutheran Church sponsored featurette.

Radio: Starred in her own musical program, "The Evelyn Ankers Hour" (Buenos Aires, 1939).

Television: Guest-starred on *Calvacade of America* (ABC, 1953), *General Electric Theatre* (CBS, 1953), *Screen Directors Playhouse* (NBC, 1955), *20th Century-Fox Hour* (CBS, 1956), and *Cheyenne* (ABC, 1958).

ATWILL, Lionel, actor; Inspector Krogh in *Son of Frankenstein,* Dr. Theodor Bohmer in *The Ghost of Frankenstein,* the Mayor in *Frankenstein Meets the Wolf Man,* Inspector Arnz in *House of Frankenstein,* Inspector Holtz in *House of Dracula;* b. Lionel Alfred William Atwill, March 1, 1885, Croydon, England; e. private tutors and Mercer School, London; original vocation: architecture; m. (1) 1913, actress Phyllis Relph, son: John, div. 1919, (2) 1920, actress Elsie Mackay div. 1928, (3) 1930, Louise Cromwell Stotesbury MacArthur, div. 1943, (4) 1944, Mary Paula Pruter, son: Lionel; d. April 22, 1946, at home, 13515 D'Este Drive, Pacific Palisades, Calif., (respiratory failure due to bronchial cancer), cremated April 25, 1946, Pierce Bros. Mortuary, Santa Monica, Calif.

Theater: Made London stage bow as a footman in *The Walls of Jericho* (1905). Toured English provinces and Australia in works of Shakespeare, Shaw, Ibsen, et al. Scored London success in *Milestones* (1912), followed by *The Little Minister* and *Years of Discretion.* Came to U.S., 1915, as leading man to Lillie Langtry in *Mrs. Thompson* and *Ashes;* made Broadway debut in title role of *The Lodger* (1917). Enjoyed many New York triumphs, including *Eve's Daughter* (with Billie Burke, 1918), *Deburau* (1920), *The Outsider* (with Katharine Cornell, 1924), *Caesar and Cleopatra* (with Helen Hayes, 1925), *Fioretta* (with Fannie Brice, 1929), *The Silent Witness* (last on Broadway, 1931); directed such New York plays as *A Kiss of Importance* (1930). After long Hollywood stay, returned to stage, summer 1943, in stock editions of *The Play's the Thing, The Outsider,* and *My Dear Children.*

Films: Made cinema debut in *Eve's Daughter* (Par., 1918) reprising stage role of the *Man-Siren*, and played in such other New York-made silents as *Lionel Atwill in The Actor's Advice to his Son* (Fox short, 1928). Arrived in Hollywood in 1932, re-creating stage role in *The Silent Witness* (Fox, 1932); proceeded to become one of Hollywood's greatest heavies via such films as *Doctor X* (WB, 1932), *The Vampire Bat* (Maj., 1933), *Mystery of the Wax Museum* (mad, wax-faced Ivan Igor, WB, 1933), *The Song of Songs* (lecherous Baron von Merzbach, Par., 1933), *The Devil is a Woman* (Dietrich's "puppet" Pasqual, Par., 1935), *Captain Blood* (lash-cracking Col. Bishop, WB., 1935), *The Three Musketeers* (de Rochefort, TCF, 1939), and many more. Busy at Universal in early 1940s in films like *Man Made Monster* (leering Dr. Rigas, 1941), *The Mad Doctor of Market Street* (title role, 1942), *Pardon My Sarong* (menacing Abbott and Costello, 1942), *Sherlock Holmes and the Secret Weapon* (Moriarty, 1942), etc., and the serials *Junior G-Men of the Air* (1942), *Raiders of Ghost City* (1944), and *The Lost City of the Jungle* (final screen work, 1946); also noteworthy as "The Scarab" in Rep.'s *Captain America* serial (1943).

Radio: Performed several dramatic broadcasts, including "Deburau" (WGY, New York, 1928).

BARTON, Charles T., director of *Abbott and Costello Meet Frankenstein;* b. May 25, 1902, near San Francisco, Calif.; married, no children; d. December 5, 1981.

Films: Entered the movie industry (following acting experience in stock and vaudeville) in silent comedies. Soon became a prop man for James Cruze, later for William Wellman, with whom he worked on many films, including *Wings* (1927); later became assistant director of the Wellman Company. Became a contract director at Paramount, 1934–38 (1934's *Wagon Wheels*, 1935's *The Last Outpost*, 1936's *Rose Bowl*, many others); Columbia, 1939–44 (1940's *Island of Doomed Men*, 1942's *Shut My Big Mouth*, 1943's *Reveille with Beverly*, many others). Joined Universal City, 1945, where he directed Abbott and Costello in six films: *The Time of Their Lives* (1946), *Buck Privates Come Home* (1947), *The Wistful Widow of Wagon Gap* (1947), *Abbott and Costello Meet Frankenstein* (1948), *Mexican Hayride* (1948), and *Abbott and Costello Meet the Killer, Boris Karloff* (1949). Also directed the team at Eagle-Lion (*The Noose Hangs High*, which he also produced, 1948) and at UA (1949's *Africa Screams*, 1956's *Dance With Me Henry*). Directed such Universal stars as Peggy Ryan (*Men in Her Diary*, of which he was also associate producer, 1945), Dan Duryea (*White Tie and Tails*, 1946), Yvonne de Carlo (*Buccaneer's Girl*, 1950), Donald O'Connor (*The Milkman*, 1950), Marjorie Main and Percy Kilbride (*Ma and Pa Kettle at the Fair*, last for U., 1952); for Walt Disney, *The Shaggy Dog* (BV, 1959) and *Toby Tyler* (BV, 1960).

As an actor, appeared in William Wellman's *Beau Geste* (as the cowboy McMonigal, Par., 1939).

Television: Has directed episodes of many situation comedies, including *The Amos and Andy Show* (CBS), *Dennis the Menace* (CBS), *Hazel* (NBC), *McHale's Navy* (ABC), *Petticoat Junction* (CBS), *Family Affair* (CBS), more; and for Walt Disney, directed such teleseries as *Zorro* (ABC, 1957–59), *Spin and Marty* (for *The Mickey Mouse Club*), more.

CARRADINE, John, actor; a hunter in *Bride of Frankenstein*, Count Dracula in *House of Frankenstein* and *House of Dracula;* b. Richmond Reed Carradine, Feb. 5, 1906, New York City; e. Christ Church School in Kingston, N.Y., Episcopal Academy in Philadelphia and Graphic Arts School, New York; original vocation: portrait and marine artist; m. (1) 1935, Ardanelle McCool Cosner, sons: Bruce and John (AKA David), div. 1944, (2) 1945, actress-artist Sonia Sorel, sons: Christopher, Keith and Robert, div. 1955, (3) 1957, Doris Rich, two stepsons, widowed 1971, (4) 1975, Emily Cisneros; now resides in Oxnard, Calif.

Theater: Made professional stage bow at St. Charles Theater, New Orleans, in *Camille* (1925), subsequently joining a New Orleans Shakespearean company. After arrival in Hollywood, 1928, acted on Los Angeles stage in many plays, e.g. *Window Panes* (1929) and *Richard III* (title role, 1930); appeared often during 1930s at the Pasadena Playhouse, including the 1935 pageant of Shakespeare's historical plays; played King Louis XI in *The Vagabond King*, San Francisco and Los Angeles, 1941 and 42. Created own Shakespearean Company, 1943, playing Hamlet, Shylock, and alternately Othello and Iago in Los Angeles, San Francisco, Seattle, etc.; played in stock productions of such plays as *My Dear Children* (1945) and *Arsenic and Old Lace* (Jonathan, 1946). Made Broadway bow in *The Duchess of Malfi* (1946), followed by such plays as *Galileo* (1947), *The Madwoman of Chaillot* (1948), *The Time of Your Life* (1955), *A Funny Thing Happened on the Way to the Forum* (1962). Toured stock, colleges, etc., in scores of plays, including *Tobacco Road, The Winslow Boy, J.B., A Man for All Seasons, Long Day's Journey into Night, Oliver!, Paint Your Wagon*, many more; returned to Broadway (January 1981) in a new stage version of *Frankenstein*.

Films: First entered movies as a scenic designer for C.B. DeMille, 1928. Made movie debut in *Tol'able David* (Col., 1930) under name of Peter Richmond, later billed as John Peter Richmond in bits in such films as *The Sign of the Cross* (Par., 1932), *The Invisible Man* (U., 1933) and *The Black Cat* (U., 1934). Changed moniker to John Carradine in 1935 and soon won hisses as Sgt. Rankin of John Ford's *The Prisoner of Shark Island* (TCF, 1936); thereafter prospered as a Fox contract player and a member of Ford's "stock company"; in such vintage films as *Captains Courageous* (Long Jack, MGM, 1937), *Of Human Hearts* (Lincoln, MGM, 1938), *Jesse James* (Bob Ford, TCF, 1939), *Stagecoach* (gambler Hatfield, UA, 1939), *Drums Along the Mohawk* (the Tory Caldwell, TCF, 1939), *The Grapes of Wrath* (Casy the preacher, TCF, 1940), many others. Departed Fox, 1942, and acted in such films as *Captive Wild Woman* (U., 1943), *Hitler's Madman* (as Nazi Heydrich, MGM, 1943), *Voodoo Man* (Mon., 1944), *The Mummy's Ghost* (U., 1944), et al. After a stay in East for stage work, returned to Hollywood in 1954, credits ranging from such movies as *The Ten Commandments* (Par., 1956), *Around the World in 80 Days* (Todd-UA, 1956), *The Last Hurrah* (Col., 1958), *The Man Who Shot Liberty Valance* (Col., 1962), *Everything You Always Wanted to Know About Sex But Were Afraid to Ask* (UA, 1972), *The Shootist* (Par., 1976), et al, to low-budget rot such as *Vampire Hookers* (Caprican Three, 1978).

Radio: Guest-starred on many radio programs, such as *The Charlie McCarthy Show* (NBC, 1942).

Television: Has guest-starred on many shows, including *Lights Out* (NBC, 1950), *Suspense* (CBS, 1953), *Gunsmoke* (CBS, 1955), *The Red Skelton Show* (CBS, 1956), *Cheyenne* (ABC, 1957), *DuPont Show of the Month* (CBS, 1957), *Wagon Train* (NBC, 1958), *The Twilight Zone* (CBS, 1960), *Bonanza* (NBC, 1961), *Thriller* (NBC, 1961), *Alfred Hitchcock Theatre* (NBC, 1965), *The Girl From U.N.C.L.E.* (NBC, 1966), *Daniel Boone* (NBC, 1968), *Night Gallery* (NBC, 1971), *Kung Fu* (ABC, 1972), *Hollywood Television Theatre* (PBS, 1974), *Greatest Heroes of the Bible* (NBC mini-series, 1978), many more. Appeared recurrently on the series *My Friend Irma* (CBS, 1952), *The Munsters* (CBS, 1965) and *Branded* (NBC, 1965). Acted in many telefeatures, e.g., "The Night Strangler" (ABC, 1973), "The Stowaway to the Moon" (CBS, 1975), "Death at Love House" (ABC, 1976), more.

Miscellaneous: Exhibited nationally his works of sculpture, early 1940s.

CHANEY, Lon, Jr., actor; The Monster in *The Ghost of Frankenstein,* Lawrence Talbot (Wolf Man) in *Frankenstein Meets the Wolf Man, House of Frankenstein, House of Dracula* and *Abbott and Costello Meet Frankenstein;* b. Creighton Tull Chaney, February 10, 1906, Oklahoma City; e. Hollywood High School, Commercial Experts Training Institute of Los Angeles; original vocation: plumber; m. (1) Dorothy Hinckley, sons: Lon and Ronald, divorced, (2) 1937, model Patricia Beck; d. July 12, 1973, at home, 207 Calle de Ansa, San Clemente, Calif., (cardiac failure), body donated to University of California School of Medicine as anatomical specimen.

Theater: Entered show business at age three in a trapeze act with his father, Lon Chaney (1883–1930). Appeared as Lennie in the West Coast production of Steinbeck's *Of Mice and Men* (1939); toured as Harry Brock in national company of *Born Yesterday* (1946); reprised Lennie in stock productions, 1947 and 1966.

Films: Made film debut as an RKO contract player, dancing in the chorus of *Girl Crazy* (1932), billed as Creighton Chaney. Went on to play heroes (*The Last Frontier,* RKO 1932 serial), villains (*Scarlet River,* 1933), singing collegiates (*Girl O'My Dreams,* Mon., 1934), et al, as well as working as stuntman, bit player and extra. Changed billing to Lon Chaney, Jr., 1935. Left RKO, freelancing in such fare as *Undersea Kingdom* (Rep. serial, 1936), *Rose Bowl* (Par., 1936) and *Cheyenne Rides Again* (Victory, 1937); signed 20th Century-Fox pact 1937, wasted in bits in *Midnight Taxi* (1937), *Alexander's Ragtime Band* (1938), *Jesse James* (1939), etc.

Won "overnight stardom" as Lennie in the Los Angeles production of *Of Mice and Men,* repeating performance in the film version (Roach-UA, 1939); starred in *One Million B.C.* (Roach-UA, 1940) before signing a Universal contract, commencing with *Man Made Monster* (1941); became the Universal's top horror man via *The Wolf Man* (1941); other horror roles of the era include Dracula (*Son of Dracula,* 1943), The Mummy (*The Mummy's Tomb,* 1942, *The Mummy's Ghost* and *The Mummy's Curse,* 1944), and the "Inner Sanctum" series (*Calling Dr. Death,* 1943, *Weird Woman,* 1944, *Pillow of Death,* 1946, et al). Also used by the studio in exotica (*Cobra Woman,* 1944), westerns (*Frontier Badmen,* 1943), comedies (*Here Come the Co-eds,* 1945), propaganda (*Follow the Boys,* 1944) and serials (*Overland Mail,* 1942).

Dropped by Universal in 1946. Played in films such as *My Favorite Brunette* (Par., 1947) and *The Counterfeiters* (TCF, 1948); appeared throughout the 1950s in films like *High Noon* (old lawman, UA, 1952), *Not as a Stranger* (drunken father, UA, 1955), and *The Defiant Ones* ("Big Sam," UA, 1958), as well as horror films (*The Black Sleep,* UA, 1956, *The Cyclops,* AA, 1957, *The Alligator People,* TCF, 1959 etc). Active through 1960s in horror movies (*The Haunted Palace,* A-I, 1963), westerns, (*Black Spurs,* Par., 1965, *Welcome to Hard Times,* MGM, 1967); ended feature film career in lurid low budgeters such as *Dracula Vs. Frankenstein* (I-I, 1971) and finally *The Female Bunch* (Dalia, 1971).

Television: Appeared as Chingachgook in the Canadian-filmed "Hawkeye and the Last of the Mohicans" (syndicated, 1956–57); starred in Sweden-filmed horror series *13 Demon Street* (1959). Made many guest appearances e.g., *The Colgate Comedy Hour* (as the Monster with Abbott and Costello, NBC, 1951), *Tales of Tomorrow* ("Frankenstein," ABC, 1952), *Calvacade Theatre* (ABC, 1955), *Rawhide* (CBS, 1959), *Bat Masterson* (NBC, 1960), *Wagon Train* (NBC, 1961), *Route 66* ("Lizard's Leg and Owlet's Wing" episode with Karloff and Lorre, 1962), *Have Gun Will Travel* (CBS, 1963), *Pistols and Petticoats* (CBS, 1966), *The Monkees* (NBC, 1966), *What's New* (NET, 1969), *The Tonight Show* (NBC, 1969), many others.

Radio: Made assorted guest appearances on radio programs, including *Inner Sanctum* (Blue Network, 1941).

Miscellaneous: Recorded "The Monster's Holiday" (45 rpm record for the TAR label, mid-1960s); was working on several book projects, including *A Century of Chaneys,* a biography of Chaney senior, and his own autobiography at the time of his death. None were completed.

CLIVE, Colin, actor; Dr. Henry Frankenstein in *Frankenstein* and *Bride of Frankenstein;* b. Colin Clive-Greig, Jan. 20, 1900, St. Malo, France (to English parents); e. Stonyhurst College, Sandhurst Royal Military Academy, Royal Academy of Dramatic Art, London; m. 1929, French actress-mimic-playwright Jeanne de Casalis, later estranged; d. June 25, 1937, Cedars of Lebanon Hospital, Hollywood, Calif., (pulmonary tuberculosis), cremated June 29, 1937, Rosedale Crematory, Hollywood, Calif.

Theater: Made London bow in *The Eclipse* (1919). Toured in many plays and acted three seasons with the Hull Repertory Company. Appeared in the chorus of West End musicals, and as Steve in *Show Boat* (1928); won stardom as the doomed Captain Stanhope of *Journey's End* (1929); later appeared on London stage in such plays as an all-star *Hamlet* (as Laertes, 1930) and *A Crime at Blossoms* (1931). Made Broadway debut in *Overture* (1930), followed by *Eight Bells* (1933), *The Lake* (Katharine Hepburn's leading man, 1933), and *Libel!* (1935). Played on the Hollywood stage in a revival of *Journey's End* (1934).

Films: Made film debut as Stanhope in Hollywood version of *Journey's End* (Tiffany, 1930). Thereafter played in such English films as *Lily Christine* (Par., 1932), such Hollywood films as *Christopher Strong* (Katharine Hepburn's married lover, RKO, 1933), *Jane Eyre* (as Rochester, Mon., 1934), *One More River* (Diana Wynyard's sadistic spouse, U., 1934), *Mad Love* (knife-craving Orlac, MGM, 1935), *History is Made at Night* (Jean Arthur's madly jealous husband, UA, 1937), *The Woman I Love* (last, as LaFayette Escadrille Captain, RKO, 1937), et al.

Radio: Mr. Clive made several dramatic radio broadcasts, including the *Campbell's Soup* version of "The Woman I Love" (April, 1937).

FRYE, Dwight, actor; Fritz of *Frankenstein,* Karl in *Bride of Frankenstein,* villager in *Son of Frankenstein* (footage deleted), village agitator in *The Ghost of Frankenstein,* Rudi in *Frankenstein Meets the Wolf Man;* b. Dwight I. Fry, Feb. 22, 1899, Salina, Kansas; e. Denver, Colorado; m. 1928, actress Laurette Bullivant, son: Dwight Jr.; d. Nov. 7, 1943, Hollywood Receiving Hospital, Calif., (heart attack); interred Forest Lawn Memorial Park, Glendale, Calif., Nov. 10, 1943.

Theater: Made stage bow in the O.D. Woodward stock company, Denver. Toured in vaudeville show *Magic Glasses* and musical comedy *La La Lucille.* After stock work in Michigan and Massachusetts, made Broadway debut in *The Plot Thickens* (1922); won acclaim in New York stage in farce, tragedy and musical comedy, in such plays as *Six Characters in Search of an Author,* (1922), *Sitting Pretty* (1924), *Puppets* (1925), *A Man's Man* (1925), *The Devil in the Cheese* (1926), *Mima* (1928), *Keeper of the Keys* (1933), *Queer People* (last on Broadway, 1934). Played in West Coast companies of such plays as *Rope's End* (1930), *The Criminal at Large* (1933), *The Pursuit of Happiness* (1934), *Her Majesty the Widow* (1934), *Night Must Fall* (1937), and *Dracula* (with Lugosi and Van Sloan, 1940).

Films: First appeared in films as a wedding extra in New York-made silent *The Night Bird* (U., 1928). Made Hollywood film debut in *Doorway to Hell* (as thug, WB, 1930). Film sampling: *Dracula* (Renfield, U., 1931), *The Maltese Falcon* (psycho Wilmer, WB, 1931), *The Vampire Bat* (village lunatic Herman, Maj., 1933), *The Invisible Man* (Reporter, U., 1933), *The Crime of Dr. Crespi* (von Stroheim's nemesis, Rep., 1935), *The Great Impersonation* (Monster of the Black Bog, U., 1935), *The Road Back* (Villager, U., 1937), *The Shadow* (Twistbacked horse handler, Col., 1937), *Adventure in Sahara* ("The Jackal," Col., 1938), *The Man in the Iron Mask* (foppish valet, UA, 1939), *The People vs. Dr. Kildare* (jury foreman, MGM, 1941) *Dead Men Walk* (hunchbacked Zolarr, PRC, 1943), *Dangerous Blondes* (gangster, last film, Col., 1943). Also appeared in the fifth chapter of the serial *Drums of Fu Manchu* (museum curator, Rep., 1940). Had signed to play Secretary of War Newton Baker in *Wilson* (TCF, 1944) just before his death; replaced by Reginald Sheffield.

HARDWICKE, Sir Cedric, actor; Dr. Ludwig Frankenstein in *The Ghost of Frankenstein;* b. Cedric Webster Hardwicke, Feb. 19, 1893, Lye, England; e. Bridgeworth Grammar School in Shropshire, Royal Academy of Dramatic Art, London; served in British Army, 1914–21, attaining the rank of captain, British Expeditionary Force, France; m. (1) 1928, actress Helena Pickard, son: Edward, div. 1948, (2) 1950, actress Mary Scott, son: Michael, div. 1961; knighted in 1934 for outstanding performances on London stage. d. Aug. 6, 1964, New York University Medical Center (emphysema) cremated, ashes sent to England.

Theater: First seriously acted at age 12, staging and starring in *The Tempest* and *The Merchant of Venice* in his home. Trained with the Frank Benson Company (touring South Africa and Rhodesia), the "Old Vic," and the Birmingham Repertory Co., where he triumphed as Captain Shotover in Shaw's *Heartbreak House.* Scored in London in such Shavian roles as Caesar of *Caesar and Cleopatra,* the burglar of *Too True to be Good,* and King Magnus of *The Apple Cart,* as well as Cap'n Andy of *Show Boat* (1928), Mr. Barrett of *The Barretts of Wimpole Street* (1930) and Dr. Haggett of *The Late Christopher Bean* (1933). Later returned to the British stage in such plays as *Tovarich* (1936) and *Yellow Sands* (for British USO, 1946), also directing such plays as *Ambassador Extraordinaire* (1948).

Made Broadway debut in *Promise* (1936), later enjoying such New York successes as *The Amazing Dr. Clitterhouse* (1937), *Shadow and Substance* (1938), *Candida* and *Antigone* (in repertory with Katharine Cornell, 1946), *Caesar and Cleopatra* (1949), *A Majority of One* (1959), and (last on Broadway) *Too True to be Good* (1963). Also directed Broadway productions, e.g., *Pygmalion* (with Gertrude Lawrence and Raymond Massey, 1945), and toured the U.S. and England, 1952, in *Don Juan in Hell* (with Laughton, Agnes Moorehead and Charles Boyer).

Films: Made professional acting debut in British film *Riches and Rogues* (c. 1911). Appeared in such British films as *Dreyfus* (title role, Col.-British, 1931) and *The Ghoul* (with Karloff, Gaumont-British, 1933); made Hollywood film bow in *Les Miserables* (as the Bishop, UA, 1935); followed by *Things to Come* (Korda-UA, 1936), *King Solomon's Mines* (Gaumont-British, 1937), *On Borrowed Time* (favorite film role as Mr. Brink, AKA Death, MGM, 1939), *Stanley and Livingstone* (the latter, TCF, 1939), *The Hunchback of Notre Dame* (the wicked Justice, RKO, 1939), *Victory* (evil Mr. Jones, Par., 1940), *The Moon is Down* (TCF, 1943), *The Lodger* (TCF, 1944), *Lured* (UA-Stromberg, 1947), *I Remember Mama* (RKO,

1948), *Rope* (WB-Transatlantic, 1948), *A Connecticut Yankee in King Arthur's Court* (King Arthur, Par., 1949), *The Winslow Boy* (Eagle-Lion, 1950), *The Desert Fox* (TCF, 1951), *Richard III* (Lopert, 1956), *The Ten Commandments* (Par. 1956), *Around the World in Eighty Days* (Todd-UA, 1956), *Baby Face Nelson* (UA, 1957), *Five Weeks in a Balloon* (TCF-Irwin Allen, 1962), *The Pumpkin Eater* (Romulus-Col., 1964, his last), 50 others.

Radio: Made many dramatic guest visits to radio, including the CBS Summer Shakespeare Festival (1937), and starred in the series *Bulldog Drummond* (Mutual Network, 1953).

Television: Made many guest appearances on many shows, including *Schlitz Playhouse of Stars* (CBS, 1952), *Suspense* (CBS, 1953), *Motorola TV Hour* (ABC, 1953), *Climax* ("Dr. Jekyll and Mr. Hyde" episode, CBS, 1955), *Playhouse 90* (CBS, 1957), *Matinee Theatre* (NBC, 1957), *Alfred Hitchcock Presents* (CBS, 1957), *U.S. Steel Hour* (CBS, 1960), *Twilight Zone* (CBS, 1963), *Outer Limits* (ABC, 1964), many more, and was a regular on the series *Mrs. G. Goes to College* (CBS, 1961–62).

Miscellaneous: Lectured on Drama at Cambridge, 1936. Wrote his autobiography, *Let's Pretend: Recollections and Reflections of a Lucky Actor* (1932), which he re-wrote (with James Brough) as *A Victorian in Orbit* (Doubleday, 1961).

KARLOFF, Boris, actor; The Monster in *Frankenstein, Bride of Frankenstein,* and *Son of Frankenstein,* Dr. Gustav Niemann in *House of Frankenstein;* b. William Henry Pratt, Nov. 23, 1887, Dulwich, England; e. Merchant Taylors' School, Uppingham School, King's College of the University of London; original vocations: farmer, lumberjack; m. (1) c. 1912, actress Olive de Wilton, divorced, (2) 1920, musician Montana Laurena Williams, divorced, (3) 1924, actress-artist-dancer Helen Vivian Soule, div. 1928, (4) 1930, Dorothy Stine, daughter: Sara Jane, div. 1946, (5) 1946, Evelyn Hope Helmore; d. Feb. 2, 1969, King Edward VII Hospital, Midhurst, England (respiratory failure), cremated, Feb. 5, 1969, Guildford Crematorium, England.

Theater: Made stage bow at age nine as the Demon King of *Cinderella* in Enfield parish Christmas play, 1896; after diplomatic training, was "exiled" to Canada, arriving May 17, 1909. Made professional debut with The Jean Russell Players, Kamloops, British Columbia, as Hoffman the banker of *The Devil* (1910); later toured Canada and northern U.S. with The Harry St. Clair Players in such plays as *Way Down East, East Lynne, Charley's Aunt,* etc., performing in 106 plays in 53 weeks. Later toured U.S. with such troupes as The Billie Bennett Company and The Maude Amber Players; acted on the Los Angeles and San Francisco stages, late 1920s, in such plays as *The Idiot, Hotel Imperial, Kongo, Window Panes,* and, in 1930, *The Criminal Code* (as Galloway); toured vaudeville, 1938, performing Poe's *The Tell Tale Heart.* Made Broadway bow, January 1941, in *Arsenic and Old Lace,* playing mad Jonathan Brewster for one and one-half years in New York City, 66 weeks on tour, and in G.I. version, Pacific Islands (1945). Appeared on Los Angeles stage, 1946, in *On Borrowed Time;* returned to Broadway in *The Linden Tree* (1948), *The Shop at Sly Corner* (1949), *Peter Pan* (as Mr. Darling and Captain Hook, 1950), in which he also toured, and *The Lark* (as Cauchon, 1955); toured summer stock, 1960, in *On Borrowed Time.*

Films: Entered films, Hollywood, 1919.* First credited appearance in *His Majesty the American* (UA, 1919). Soon seen as a villain in such fare as *The Courage of Marge O'Doone* (as Tavish, a baby kidnaper, Vitagraph, 1920), *The Çave Girl* (Baptiste, a wicked half-breed, FN, 1922), *Lady Robin Hood* (lascivious Spaniard Cabraza, FBO, 1925), *The Bells* (sinister mesmerist, Chadwick, 1926), *The Nickle Hopper* (leering lecher, Pathe-Roach three-reeler, 1926), *The Phantom of the North* (as Jules Gregg, French-Canadian murderer, Giltmore, 1929), many more. Also played in many serials: *The Masked Raider* (Arrow, 1919), *Perils of the Wind* (U., 1925), *Vultures of the Sea* (Mascot, 1928), more.

Reprised stage role of Galloway in *The Criminal Code* (Col., 1931). Roles followed like dope-pushing Cokey Joe of *Young Donovan's Kid* (RKO, 1931), evil convict of French version of Laurel and Hardy's *Pardon Us* (Roach-MGM, 1931), and the pervert Isopod of *Five Star Final* (WB, 1931). After triumph in *Frankenstein,* won a Universal star contract and created a gallery of classic performances: Morgan of *The Old Dark House* (U., 1932), Im-Ho-Tep of *The Mummy* (U., 1932), Fu Manchu of *The Mask of Fu Manchu* (MGM, 1932), Sanders of *The Lost Patrol* (RKO, 1934), Hjalmar Poelzig of *The Black Cat* (U., 1934), twin Counts of *The Black Room* (Col., 1935), Janos Rukh of *The Invisible Ray* (U., 1936), John Ellmann of *The Walking Dead* (WB, 1936), et al. Played Mr. Wong series (*Mr. Wong, Detective,* etc.) at Monogram, "Mad Doctor" series (*The Man They Could not Hang,* etc.) at Columbia. After *Arsenic and Old Lace* success, returned to Hollywood, notably as star of celebrated trio of Val Lewton RKO chillers, *The Body Snatcher* (1945), *Isle of the Dead* (1945), and *Bedlam* (1946). Remained a popular character star in films for more than two more decades in such films as *The Secret Life of Walter Mitty* (Goldwyn-UA, 1947), *Unconquered* (DeMille-Par., 1947), *Tap Roots* (U., 1948), *Abbott and Costello Meet Dr. Jekyll and Mr. Hyde* (U., 1953), *Frankenstein 1970* (AA, 1958), *The Raven* (A-I, 1963), *Comedy of Terrors* (A-I, 1963), *The Venetian Affair* (MGM, 1967), *Targets* (superb as old terror star Byron Orlok, Par., 1968), many more. Ended movie career (after more than 150 films) in four co-productions of Mexico's Azteca Studios and Hollywood's Columbia Studios, *The Fear Chamber, The Snake People, House of Evil* and *The Incredible Invasion,* all shot in five weeks in Hollywood, spring 1968, all released posthumously.

Radio: Made many guest performances, including *The Charlie McCarthy Show* (NBC, Jan. 1938), *Lights Out* (five special visits, NBC, March–April 1938). *Kay Kyser's Kolloge of Musical Knowledge* (with Lugosi and Lorre,

* Karloff denied the rumor that he appeared in *The Dumb Girl of Portici* (U, 1916), noted in some reference works as his first movie credit.

NBC, September 1940), *Inner Sanctum* (many shows, Blue Network, 1941–42), *Information Please* (NBC, 1942), etc. Was host of a short-lived revival of *Lights Out* (Mutual, 1947), and *Starring Boris Karloff* (ABC, 1949). Was disc jockey of radio show for children, New York, 1949 and early 1950s; and from 1956 to 1968, taped daily spot for the *Readers Digest* syndicated program.

Television: Starred in four series: *Starring Boris Karloff* (ABC, 1949, also on radio), *Col. March of Scotland Yard* (British-syndicated, 1952–54), *Thriller* (NBC, 1960–62) and *Out of this World* (British-BBC, 1962). Made TV debut on "Chevrolet on Broadway" (NBC, 1949). More than 75 guest spots including *Columbia Workshop* (as Don Quixote, CBS, 1952), *Suspense* (as Rasputin, CBS, 1953), *Best of Broadway* (Jonathan in *Arsenic and Old Lace,* CBS, 1955), *Donald O'Connor* (singing and dancing English music hall songs, NBC, 1955), *$64,000 Question* (winning $16,000 in category of children's stories, CBS, 1956), *Hallmark Hall of Fame* (Cauchon in *The Lark,* NBC, 1957), *Shirley Temple Storybook* (Father Knickerbocker of "The Legend of Sleepy Hollow," NBC, 1958), *DuPont Show of the Month* (Billy Bones in *Treasure Island,* CBS, 1960), *Hallmark Hall of Fame* (Jonathan in *Arsenic and Old Lace,* NBC, 1962), *Route 66* (masquerading as the Monster, with Chaney and Lorre, CBS, 1962), *Shindig* (singing "The Monster Mash," ABC, 1965), *The Girl from U.N.C.L.E.* (as Mother Muffin, NBC, 1966), "How the Grinch Stole Christmas" (narrator and voice of Grinch in this cartoon special, CBS, 1966 and repeated annually), *The Red Skelton Show* (CBS, 1968), *The Jonathan Winters Show* (CBS, 1968), *The Name of the Game* ("The White Birch" episode, NBC, 1968), many others.

Miscellaneous: Made recordings ("Peter and the Wolf," works of Kipling, etc.). Did commercials for such products as Schaeffer Pens (1966), Volkswagen (1967) and A-1 Steak Sauce (1968). Edited several anthologies of terror tales and poems: *Tales of Terror* (World Pub., 1943), *And the Darkness Falls* (World, 1946), and *The Boris Karloff Horror Anthology* (Souvenier, 1965).

KENTON, Erle C., director of *The Ghost of Frankenstein, House of Frankenstein,* and *House of Dracula;* b. Aug. 1, 1896, Norboro, Mo.; m. Claire, stepson: Alfred Fournier; d. Jan. 28, 1980, Glendale Memorial Hospital, Calif.

Films: Kenton began as a writer for Mack Sennett in 1914 and later directed for Sennett. His first documented feature directing credit, *A Small Town Idol* (Associated Producers, 1921). After working for Warners, Pathe, PDC, etc., joined Columbia, 1928–31 (1928's *Nothing to Wear,* 1929's *The Song of Love,* 1931's *Lover Come Back,* and 10 more). Contracted with Paramount, 1932–34, directing *Island of Lost Souls* (with Laughton and Lugosi, 1932), *You're Telling Me* (with W.C. Fields, 1934), and five more. Rejoined Columbia, 1934–37, directing *The Best Man Wins* (with Lugosi, 1935), *The Devil's Squadron* (1936) and seven more. At RKO, 1939–41 (1939's *Everything's on Ice* and three more). Joined Universal, 1941–46, as a highly competent director of comedy (1942's *Pardon My Sarong* and *Who Done It?,* and 1943's *It Ain't Hay,* all with Abbott and Costello), mystery (1942's *Frisco Lil,* 1946's *The Cat Creeps*), musical comedy (1943's *Always a Bridesmaid,* with the Andrews Sisters), adventure (1942's *North to the Klondike,* with Ankers and Chaney), as well as the three Monster sagas; later directed *Bob and Sally* (Social Guidance, 1948), and *One Too Many* (Hallmark, 1950).

Television: Directed such teleseries as *Racket Squad* (Syndicated, 1950, CBS, 1951–53); *Public Defender* (CBS, 1954); and *The Texan* (CBS, 1958–59; ABC, 1960–62).

LAEMMLE, Carl, Jr., producer of *Frankenstein* and *Bride of Frankenstein;* b. April 28, 1908, Chicago, Illinois; e. The Clark School, New York; served in U.S. Army Signal Corps in World War II; d. Sept. 24, 1979 at home, 1641 Tower Grove Drive, Beverly Hills, Calif., (stroke), entombed in the Laemmle Family Crypt, Home of Peace Memorial Park, Los Angeles, Sept. 26, 1979.

Began his career by writing, casting and supervising the Universal Junior Jewell series, *The Collegians* (1926–29). Was "associate producer" on such Universal films as *Broadway* (1929). Received post of General Manager in Charge of Production of Universal City, April 28, 1929, as a 21st birthday present from his father, Universal founder Carl Laemmle, Sr.; from 1929 to 1936, supervised the production of many films, including *All Quiet on the Western Front* (1930, won Best Picture Academy Award), *The King of Jazz* (1930), *Dracula, Waterloo Bridge, Strictly Dishonorable* (all 1931), *Murders in the Rue Morgue, Back Street, The Old Dark House, Air Mail, The Mummy* (all 1932), *The Invisible Man* (1933), *The Black Cat, Little Man What Now?,* (both 1934), *The Man Who Reclaimed his Head, The Good Fairy, Night Life of the Gods, The Werewolf of London* (all 1935), *Show Boat* (1936) and others.

"Resigned" the General Manager's post after Laemmle senior's sale of Universal, in April 1936. Joined MGM as an associate producer, May 1937; resigned following autumn, having produced no films.

LANCHESTER, Elsa, actress; Mary Shelley and the Monster's Mate in *Bride of Frankenstein;* b. Elizabeth Lanchester Sullivan, Oct. 28, 1902, London; e. Kettle School in London and Isadora Duncan's Dance Academy in France; m. 1929, actor Charles Laughton, widowed 1962; present residence: Hollywood Hills, Calif.

Theater: First worked as a dance instructor, founding London's The Classical Dancing Club at age 11. Later established The Children's Theatre in London (1918) and was a co-founder and performer at the theatrical nightclub, The Cave of Harmony (1921–28). Made London West End bow in *Thirty Minutes in a Street* (1922), followed by such plays as *The Insect Play* (1923), *The Pool* (1927), *The Outskirts* (1929), *Ten Nights in a Barroom* (1930), and *Payment Deferred* (1931), as well as such revues as *Riverside Nights* and *Midnight Frolics* (both 1926). Acted with Laughton at London's "Old Vic," 1933–34, in Shakespeare's *Henry VIII, Measure for Measure* and *The Tempest* (as Ariel), as well as *The Importance of Being Earnest, Love for Love* and *The Cherry Orchard.* Played Peter Pan to Laughton's Captain Hook in London, Christmas 1936; starred in *The Party* (directed by and co-starring Laughton) in London, 1958.

Made Broadway debut in *Payment Deferred* with Laughton (1931), later playing on the Broadway stage in *They Walk Alone* (1941). Was diseuse-in-residence of The Turnabout Puppet Theatre, Los Angeles, 1941–56; and toured nightclubs, colleges, etc., throughout the 1950s in her one-woman musical show, eventually docking at Broadway's 41st Street Theatre under the title *Elsa Lanchester—Herself* (1961).

Films: Made London film bow in *One of the Best* (Gainsborough, 1927); starred in three short silent comedies written for her especially by H.G. Wells: *Bluebottles, The Tonic* and *Daydreams* with Laughton performing in the first and third productions (all 1928). Won international laurels as Anne of Cleves in *The Private Life of Henry VIII* (London-Korda, 1933), for which Laughton won the Academy Award. Made Hollywood film debut in *David Copperfield* (MGM, 1935), followed by such films as *Naughty Marietta* (MGM, 1935), *Rembrandt* as Hendrickje Stoffels (London-Korda, 1936), as missionary Martha Jones in *The Beachcomber* (AKA *Vessel of Wrath,* Mayflower-Par., 1938), *Ladies in Retirement* (Col., 1941), *Lassie Come Home* (MGM, 1943), *The Spiral Staircase* (RKO, 1946), *The Razor's Edge* (TCF, 1946), *The Big Clock* with Laughton (Par., 1948), *Come to the Stable,* gaining an Academy nomination as artist (TCF, 1949), *The Inspector General* (WB, 1949), *Androcles and the Lion* (RKO, 1952), as the bearded lady in *Three Ring Circus* (Par., 1954), *Witness for the Prosecution* with Laughton, gaining an Academy nomination for her portrayal of the nurse (UA, 1957), as Aunt Queenie the witch in *Bell, Book and Candle* (Col., 1958), *Mary Poppins* (BV, 1964), *That Darn Cat* (BV, 1965), *Blackbeard's Ghost* (BV, 1968), *Willard* (Cinerama, 1971), *Terror in the Wax Museum* (Cinerama, 1973), *Arnold* (Cinerama, 1974), as Dame Jessica Marbles in *Murder by Death* (Col., 1976), and many others.

Radio: Made numerous guest visits to radio programs, including C.B. DeMille's *Lux Radio Theatre* in "The Sidewalks of London" with Laughton (NBC, 1940).

Television: Appeared as a regular on *The John Forsythe Show* (NBC, 1965–66), in the telefeature "In Name Only" (ABC, 1969). Has guest-starred on many programs, including *Studio One* (CBS, 1953), *Ford Theatre* (NBC, 1955), *I Love Lucy* (CBS, 1956), *Shirley Temple's Story Book* (NBC, 1958), *Wanted Dead or Alive* (CBS, 1960), *Burke's Law* (ABC, 1963), *Alfred Hitchcock Theatre* (NBC, 1964), *The Man from U.N.C.L.E.* (NBC, 1965), *World of Disney* (NBC, 1969), *It Takes a Thief* (ABC, 1969), *Night Gallery* (NBC, 1972), and more.

Miscellaneous: Has recorded musical albums, e.g., "Elsa Lanchester: Bawdy Cockney Songs" (Everest Records); wrote the book *Charles Laughton and I* (Harcourt Brace, 1938); and served as "research consultant" and author of Introduction for Charles Higham's *Charles Laughton: An Intimate Biography* (Doubleday, 1976).

LEE, Rowland V., producer and director of *Son of Frankenstein;* b. Sept. 6, 1891, Findlay, Ohio; e. Columbia University, New York; served in the U.S. Infantry, France, World War I; m. Eleanor; d. Dec. 21, 1975, at home in Palm Desert, Calif., (heart attack).

Films: Began career as a stage actor in stock and New York City. After temporarily forsaking the stage for Wall Street, returned to theater and began film career in 1916 as actor with Thomas Ince in Hollywood. First documented directing credit, *Cupid's Brand* (Arrow, 1921). Joined Fox Studios, 1922–26, directing 1925's *The Man Without a Country,* 1926's *The Outsider,* many more. Joined Paramount, 1927–30 directing *The First Kiss* (1928), *The Wolf of Wall Street* (his first "talkie," 1929), *The Mysterious Dr. Fu Manchu* (1929), many others. Won special acclaim via *Zoo in Budapest* (also co-scripted, Fox, 1933), later directing such films as *I Am Suzanne* (also co-authored, Fox, 1934), *Count of Monte Cristo* (also co-scripted, UA, 1934), *Cardinal Richelieu* (UA, 1935), *The Three Musketeers* (UA, 1935), *Love From a Stranger* (UA, 1937), *The Toast of New York* (RKO, 1937). Joined Universal City, 1938, producing and directing *Service De Luxe* (1938), *The Sun Never Sets* (1939), and *Tower of London* (with Rathbone and Karloff, 1939), as well as the third in the Monster saga. Went on to direct *The Son of Monte Cristo* (UA, 1940), *Powder Town* (RKO, 1942), *The Bridge of San Luis Rey* (UA, 1944) and *Captain Kidd* (UA, 1945).

After over a decade of retirement, produced and co-scripted *The Big Fisherman* (Centurion-BV, 1959).

LUGOSI, Bela, actor; Ygor in *Son of Frankenstein* and *The Ghost of Frankenstein,* The Monster in *Frankenstein Meets the Wolf Man,* Count Dracula in *Abbott and Costello Meet Frankenstein;* b. Bela Ferenc Dezso Blasko, Oct. 20, 1882, Lugos, Hungary; e. Hungarian State Superior Gymnasium in Lugos and Academy of Performing Arts in Budapest; original vocation: mine laborer; m. (1) 1917, Ilona Szmik, div. 1920, (2) 1921, actress Ilona von Montagh, div. 1924, (3) 1929, Beatrice Woodruff Weeks, div. 1929, (4) 1933, Lillian Arch, son: Bela Jr., div. 1953, (5) 1955, Hope Lininger; served as second lieutenant and captain of 43rd Infantry Regiment, Hungary, during World War I; d. Aug. 16, 1956 at home, 5620 Harold Way, Hollywood, Calif., (heart attack), interred Holy Cross Cemetery, Inglewood, Calif., Aug. 18, 1956.

Theater: Made stage bow at age of nine, writing, producing, and starring in plays he presented for free in an empty warehouse in Lugos. First documented professional appearance, as Count Konigsegg in National Actors' Company production of *Ocskay Brigaderos,* in Deva, Transylvania, Aug. 24, 1902. Later played with such troupes as the Franz Joseph Repertory Theatre and the Szeged Repertory Theatre (where he won bravos as Romeo); joined the Hungarian Theatre, 1911, acting such roles as Vronsky in *Anna Karenina;* from 1913 to 1919, was member of Hungary's famed National Theatre, playing more than 80 roles, including Achilles of *Caesar and Cleopatra,* Valere of *Tartuffe,* Jesus Christ of *The Passion,* Lodovico of *Othello,* Laertes of *Hamlet,* Demetrius of *A Midsummer Night's Dream,* Jacques of

As You Like It, and Tybalt of *Romeo and Juliet.* Arrived in U.S. in 1921 and created his own Hungarian repertory company in New York, producing and starring in such plays as *Bluebeard, The Tragedy of Man,* and *Fata Morgana.* Made Broadway debut, Dec. 20, 1922 as Fernando, the apache pirate of *The Red Poppy;* after appearing on Chicago stage in *The Werewolf* (1924), acted on Broadway in plays *Arabesque* (1925), *Open House* (1925), and *The Devil in the Cheese* (1926). Opened Oct. 5, 1927, Fulton Theatre, New York, in title role of *Dracula,* and toured widely in role, 1928–30. After Hollywood sojourn, made final Broadway appearance in Earl Carroll's show *Murder at the Vanities* (1933). Starred as Jonathan Brewster in a national company of *Arsenic and Old Lace* (1943); acted in plays in Los Angeles (*Murdered Alive,* 1932, *Devil's Paradise,* 1956), San Francisco (*Tovarich,* 1937, *No Traveler Returns,* 1945), Montreal (*The Devil Also Dreams,* 1950), and London (*Dracula,* 1951). Toured vaudeville in scenes from *Dracula* (1933, '44, '45, '47) and in Ed Sullivan's *Stardust Calvacade* revue (1940); toured summer stock in *Dracula* (1947) and *Arsenic and Old Lace* (1948, '50); and starred in several revivals-tours of *Dracula* (1940, '43, more).

Films: Entered Hungarian films in 1917 under name of Arisztid Olt; first documented film, *Alarcosbal* (*Masked Ball,* 1917); soon returned to usual stage name and played in *Casanova* (1918), *Lulu* (1918), and others. Acted in German cinema, 1919–20, in such films as *Der Januskopf: Eine Tragodie am Rande der Wirklichkeit* (*The Head of Janus: A Tragedy on the Border of Reality,* 1920, based on *Dr. Jekyll and Mr. Hyde,* with Lugosi as the doctor's butler), and *Lederstrumpf* (*Leatherstocking,* 1920, based on James Fenimore Cooper's tales, with Lugosi as Chingachgook). Made U.S. film debut in *The Silent Command* (as the evil spy Hisston, Fox, 1923), and played in such other New York-filmed silents as *The Midnight Girl* (wealthy roue Nicholas Harmon, Chadwick, 1925). On tour with *Dracula* in Los Angeles, Lugosi made Hollywood movie bow in *How to Handle Women* (bodyguard, U., 1928), and proceeded to play in such films as *The Thirteenth Chair* (Inspector Delzante, MGM, 1929) and *Renegades* (sadistic Arab chieftan, Fox, 1930); in wake of *Dracula* (U., 1931) gave grandly flamboyant performances in many famed shockers: *Murders in the Rue Morgue* (Dr. Mirakle, U., 1932), *White Zombie* (Murder Legendre, Halperin, 1932), *Chandu the Magician* (Roxor, Fox, 1932), *The Island of Lost Souls* (The Sayer of the Law, Par. 1932), *The Black Cat* (Dr. Vitus Werdegast, U., 1934), *Mark of the Vampire* (Count Mora, MGM, 1935), *The Raven* (Dr. Richard Vollin, U., 1935), *The Phantom Ship* (AKA *The Mystery of Marie Celeste,* British-Hammer, 1936), others. Also fine as comic heavy (General Nicholas Branovsky Petronovich of Paramount's 1933 all-star *International House*), bizarre hero (title role in Principal's 1934 serial *The Return of Chandu*), red herring (Degar of Columbia's 1933 *Night of Terror*), and "straight" character (Garbo's Commissar in MGM's 1939 *Ninotchka*). By early 1940s was playing leads at Monogram (e.g., *The Ape Man,* 1943) PRC (*The Devil Bat,* 1941), and Columbia (*Return of the Vampire,* 1943) while in supporting roles at Universal (e.g., as Bela the gypsy lycanthrope of 1941's *The Wolf Man*) and RKO (e.g., as Joseph, Karloff's dim-witted victim of 1945's *The Body Snatcher*). In 1950s, appeared in *Old Mother Riley Meets the Vampire* (British-Realart, 1952), followed by sad rot: *Bela Lugosi Meets a Brooklyn Gorilla* (Realart, 1952), *Glen or Glenda?* (sex exploitation film, Banner, 1953), and *The Bride of the Monster* (pathetically grand as Dr. Eric Vornoff, Banner, 1956). After drug addiction cure, made "comeback" as mute servant Casimir in *The Black Sleep* (Camden, 1956). Final movie role: The Ghoul Man of *Plan 9 From Outer Space* (unfinished at time of his death, scenes completed by a double; Reynolds, 1959).

Also appeared in serials *The Whispering Shadow* (Mascot, 1933), *Shadow of Chinatown* (Victory, 1936), *S.O.S. Coast Guard* (Rep., 1937), and *The Phantom Creeps* (U., 1939).

Radio: Made various guest visits to radio programs, e.g., *Suspense* (CBS, early 1940s), and was host and star of his own syndicated program, *Mystery House* (mid-1940s).

Television: Performed some TV guest star work, e.g., *The Red Skelton Show* (CBS, October, 1953).

Miscellaneous: Visited movie houses, 1949–52, in personal appearance horror show act; starred in *The Bela Lugosi Review,* Silver Slipper Saloon, Las Vegas, 1954.

MASSEY, Ilona, actress-singer; Baroness Elsa Frankenstein in *Frankenstein Meets the Wolf Man;* b. Ilona Hajmassy,* June 16, 1910, Budapest, Hungary; m. (1) 1935, Nicholas Szavozd, div. 1935, (2) 1941, actor Alan Curtis, div. 1942, (3) 1952, Charles Walker, div. 1955, (4) 1955, Air Force General Donald S. Dawson; d. Aug. 20, 1974, in the Naval Hospital, Bethesda, Md., after a "three-month illness."

Theater: After work as apprentice dressmaker, made stage bow in chorus of The Budapest Musical Comedy House; auditioned successfully for the Vienna Folks Opera, making operatic debut in *Tosca;* won contract with the Vienna State Opera, where she was a leading diva, 1934–36; made Broadway bow in *Ziegfeld Follies,* 1943; toured summer stock, early 1950s in *Tonight or Never* and *Angel;* performed concert tour of South Africa, 1960.

Films: Made film debut in Austrian movie, *Knox Und Die Lustigen Vagabunden* (1935), followed by another Austrian opus, *Der Himmel Auf Erden* (1935). Came to MGM Studios, Hollywood, as a discovery of L.B. Mayer, 1936, singing gloriously in *Rosalie* (1937) and *Balalaika* (1939), both with Nelson Eddy; later films include *New Wine* (UA, 1941), *International Lady* (UA, 1941), *Invisible Agent* (U., 1942), *Holiday in Mexico* (MGM, 1946), *Northwest Outpost* (with Eddy again, *Rep., 1947*), *The Plunderers* (Rep., 1948), *Love Happy* (with The Marx Brothers and Marilyn Monroe, UA, 1950), *Jet Over the Atlantic* (Inter-Continent, 1959).

Television: Guest-starred on such programs as *Studio One* (CBS, 1950), *Faith Baldwin Playhouse* (ABC, 1951),

*The English translation of "Hajmassy" is "garlic."

Curtain Call (NBC, 1952), etc. Starred in her own short-lived series, *Rendezvous* (ABC, February–March, 1952), and *The Ilona Massey Show* (DuMont, 1954–55).

NEILL, Roy William, director of *Frankenstein Meets the Wolf Man;* b. Roland de Gostrie, 1887, Ireland's Dublin Harbor on his father's ship; e. Saint Mary's College, Moraga Valley; war correspondent in the Chinese Civil War, 1911; m. Elizabeth, daughters: Patricia and Barbara; d. Dec. 14, 1946 in London, England, (cerebral hemorrhage), interred, England.

Theater: First worked as an actor in San Francisco in 1911; later toured the Orient and Europe as a thespian; became a stage manager for David Belasco and the manager-director of the Alcazar Theatre, San Francisco.

Films: Began as a director for Thomas Ince, Hollywood, 1915; first directing credit, *A Corner in Colleens* (in which he also acted, Vitagraph, 1916). After work for Paramount, Pathe, FBO, etc., joined the Fox lot, 1925–27, directing such films as *Black Paradise* (1926), *The Arizona Wildcat* (1927), more. Later signed with Columbia, 1930–36, directing *The Circus Queen Murder* (1933), *The Black Room* (with Karloff, 1935), *The Lone Wolf Returns* (1936), many others; directed *Dr. Syn* for General Film Distributors, 1937. After 1938–39 stint at Warners, joined Universal in 1942, devoting most of his expertise to the Basil Rathbone-Nigel Bruce *Sherlock Holmes* films, directing *Sherlock Holmes and the Secret Weapon* (1942), *Sherlock Holmes in Washington* (1943), producing and directing the subsequent 9 films of the series (ending with *Dressed to Kill*, 1946).* Also at Universal, directed *Madame Spy* (1942), *Eyes of the Underworld* (1943), *Rhythm of the Islands* (1943), *Gypsy Wildcat* (1944), and his last which he also co-produced, *Black Angel* (1946).

Also co-scripted the films *Murder Will Out* (WB, 1939), *Hoots Mon* (WB, 1939) and *His Brother's Keeper* (WB, 1939); and worked (uncredited) on the scripts of the *Sherlock Holmes* series.

PARKER, Edwin "Eddie," bit player-stuntman; double for Lon Chaney as The Monster in *The Ghost of Frankenstein* and for Bela Lugosi as The Monster in *Frankenstein Meets the Wolf Man;* b. Dec. 12, 1900, Minnesota; m. Bess; d. Jan. 20, 1960, at home, 4236 Sherman Oaks Avenue, Sherman Oaks, Calif., (heart attack), interred Calvary Cemetery, Los Angeles, Jan. 23, 1960.

Films: Entered movies in 1925 as stuntman; performed stunts and/or played bits in such features as *Lucky Texan* (Mon., 1934), *Our Relations* (MGM-Roach, 1936), *The Spoilers* (U., 1942), *The Body Snatcher* (RKO, 1945), *The Enchanted Cottage* (RKO, 1945), *Mighty Joe Young* (RKO, 1949), *The Strange Door* (U., 1951), *Rear Window* (Par., 1954), *Tarantula* (as disfigured scientist, U., 1955), *The Mole People* (U., 1956), *Around the World in 80 Days* (UA, 1956), *Bride of the Monster* (doubling Lugosi, Banner, 1956), *Monster on the Campus* (as ape-man, U., 1958), *Curse of the Undead* (U., 1959), *Spartacus* (his last, U., 1960), and many others. Also busy in such serials as *Flash Gordon* (U., 1936), *Flash Gordon's Trip to Mars* (U., 1938), *Buck Rogers* (U., 1939), *Flash Gordon Conquers the Universe* (U., 1940), *The Masked Marvel* (Rep., 1943), *The Tiger Woman* (Rep., 1944), *Haunted Harbor* (Rep., 1944), *Son of Zorro* (Rep., 1947), *King of the Rocket Men* (Rep., 1949), *Batman and Robin* (Col., 1949), many more. Became known as "The Universal Monster," doubling Chaney (1942's *The Mummy's Tomb*, 1944's *The Mummy's Ghost* and *The Mummy's Curse*), Karloff (1953's *Abbott and Costello Meet Dr. Jekyll and Mr. Hyde*), as well as playing the mummy in *Abbott and Costello Meet the Mummy* (1955) and the Metaluna Mutant in *This Island Earth* (1955).

Television: Performed bits and stunts on many programs; last professional job was as stuntman on *The Jack Benny Show* (CBS).

PIERCE, Jack P., makeup artist; creator of makeup and chief makeup artist for *Frankenstein, Bride of Frankenstein, Son of Frankenstein, The Ghost of Frankenstein, Frankenstein Meets the Wolf Man, House of Frankenstein* and *House of Dracula;* b. May 5, 1889, Greece; original vocation; baseball shortstop; m. Blanche Craven; d. July 19, 1968, St. Joseph Hospital, Burbank, Calif., (uremia), interred Forest Lawn Memorial Park, Glendale, Calif., July 23, 1968.

Films: Came to California in 1910 after success as semi-pro shortstop with the Logan Square team, Chicago, and tried out for the Coast League, but failed because he was too light. To survive, took job as nickelodeon projectionist; later, became theater manager for Harry Culver, and associate to Young Deer, noted redskin producer of the K.B. film studio. Joined Universal in 1914 as actor and assistant cameraman. Later drifted into makeup work for Jackie Coogan and Jesse Lasky; after his touted transformation of Jacques Lerner into ape in Fox's *The Monkey Talks* (1926), rejoined Universal as chief of studio's makeup department.

Won fame as the designer and applier of Karloff's Monster makeup of *Frankenstein;* created all of Universal's horror makeups, 1926–47, including The Mummy (his favorite achievement), the Wolf Man (both Henry Hull's lycanthrope of 1935's *The Werewolf of London* and the later Lon Chaney beast), Paula the Ape Woman (Acquanetta of 1943's *Captive Wild Woman* and 1944's *Jungle Woman*, Vicky Lane of 1945's *Jungle Captive*). Also excelled at creating character makeup (e.g., Frye as Fritz, Lugosi as Ygor, Karloff as Satanic high priest of *The Black Cat*), as well as performing more conventional glamourizing tasks.

Dropped by Universal in 1947. Freelanced in feature films, including *Master Minds* (Mon., 1949), creating for Glenn Strange the bearded guise for the giant Atlas.

Television: Worked on such teleseries as *Fireside Theatre* (NBC, 1949–55), *You Are There* (CBS, 1953–57) and *Mr. Ed* (syndicated, 1960–61, CBS, 1961–66).

*The only film of Universal's Holmes series that Neill did not direct was the first, *Sherlock Holmes and the Voice of Terror*, which was directed by John Rawlins.

RATHBONE, Basil, actor; Dr. Wolf von Frankenstein in *Son of Frankenstein;* b. Phillip St. John Basil Rathbone, June 13, 1892, Johannesburg, South Africa (to English parents); e. Repton School, London; original vocation: insurance clerk; served with British Army in World War I as a second lieutenant of the Liverpool Scottish Regiment (receiving the Military Cross for service in France, 1918); m. (1) 1914, actress Ethel Marion Foreman, son: Rodion, div. 1926, (2) 1926, writer Ouida Bergere, adopted daughter: Cynthia; d. July 21, 1967, at home, 135 Central Park West, New York (heart attack).

Theater: Made professional stage bow as Hortensio in *The Taming of the Shrew* with Shakespearean company of his cousin Frank Benson, Ipswich, 1911; joined Benson's Stratford-Upon-Avon Shakespearean players, 1912. Made London West End bow in *The Sin of David* (1914); later enjoyed great successes in *Romeo and Juliet* (as Romeo, 1919), *Peter Ibbetson* (title role, 1920), *Othello* (as Iago, 1921), and *Diplomacy* (1933).

Made Broadway debut in *The Czarina* (1922); later New York City credits include *The Swan* (1923), *The Command to Love* (1927), *Judas* (co-author and actor of title role, 1929), *The Devil Passes* (1932), and others. Was leading man to Katharine Cornell in repertory tour of *Romeo and Juliet, Candida,* and *The Barretts of Wimpole Street* 1933–34, reprising Romeo on Broadway in 1934. After Hollywood sojourn, returned to New York in such plays as *The Heiress* (winning a 1948 Tony Award for his Dr. Sloper), *Julius Caesar* (1950), *Sherlock Holmes* (1953) and *J.B.* (1959). Headed national company of *J.B.* (1959–60), toured summer stock in such plays as *The Winslow Boy* (1955) and *Witness for the Prosecution* (1957), and toured widely in his one-man show, *An Evening with Basil Rathbone.*

Films: Entered films in the British feature *The Fruitful Vine* (Stoll, 1921); U.S. film debut, *Trouping with Ellen* (PDC, 1924); "talkie" debut, *The Last of Mrs. Cheyney* (MGM, 1929). After filling voids between stage roles with films like *Loyalties* (British-Associated, 1933), signed with MGM and soon became the cinema's most polished villain in films such as *David Copperfield* (Mr. Murdstone, MGM, 1935), *Anna Karenina* (Karenin, MGM, 1935), *A Tale of Two Cities* (St. Evermonde, MGM, 1935), *Captain Blood* (Levasseur, WB, 1935), *Romeo and Juliet* (Academy nomination for his Tybalt, MGM, 1936), *The Adventures of Robin Hood* (Sir Guy of Gisbourne, WB, 1938), *If I Were King* (Academy nomination for his Louis XI, Par., 1938), *Tower of London* (Richard III, U., 1939) *The Mark of Zorro* (Captain Pasquale, TCF, 1940). First played Sherlock Holmes in *The Hound of the Baskervilles* (TCF, 1939), followed by *The Adventures of Sherlock Holmes* (TCF, 1939) and the 12 entries of the Universal Holmes series from 1942 to 1946. After return to New York in 1946, occasionally visited Hollywood for feature films, e.g. *Ichabod and Mr. Toad* (voice of the latter, Disney-RKO, 1949), *We're No Angels* (Par., 1955), *The Black Sleep* (UA, 1956), *The Last Hurrah* (Col., 1958), *The Magic Sword* (UA, 1962), *The Comedy of Terrors* (A.I., 1963), et al. Sadly ended career in such fare as *Ghost in the Invisible Bikini* (A-I, 1966) and his last, *Hillbillys in a Haunted House* (Woolner Bros., 1967).

Radio: Starred in 275 broadcasts of the *Sherlock Holmes* radio show Blue Network (1939–43), Mutual Network (1943–46); starred in the series *Scotland Yard* (Mutual, 1947). Made several visits to DeMille's NBC *Lux Radio Theatre* ("A Doll's House" with Joan Crawford in 1938, "Wuthering Heights" with Ida Lupino in 1940, "The Phantom of the Opera" with Susanna Foster in 1943, and more). Guest-starred on numerous other programs.

Television: Guest-starred on such shows as *NBC Showcase* ("Sherlock Holmes," 1950), *Suspense* ("Dr. Jekyll and Mr. Hyde," CBS, 1951), *Motorola Television Hour* (ABC, 1953), *World of Disney* ("The Reluctant Dragon," ABC, 1955), *Alcoa Hour* (Scrooge in the musical "The Stingiest Man in Town," NBC, 1956), *U.S. Steel Hour* (CBS, 1957), *DuPont Show of the Month* ("Aladdin," CBS, 1958), *Dr. Kildare,* (NBC, 1965), many more.

Miscellaneous: Performed in commercials for such companies as Gillette; made recordings of the works of Poe, the Sherlock Holmes tales, etc. Wrote his memoirs, *In and Out of Character* (Doubleday, 1962).

SIODMAK, Curt, screenwriter; author of screenplay for *Frankenstein Meets the Wolf Man* and story for *House of Frankenstein.* b. Kurt Siodmak, Aug. 10, 1902, Dresden, Germany; e. University of Zurich; Ph.D. in Mathematics, 1932; original vocations: engineer, newspaper reporter, novelist; m. son Geoffrey; now resides in Three Rivers, Calif.

Relative in Motion Pictures: brother, Robert Siodmak (1900–1973), director of such films as *Son of Dracula* (U., 1943), *The Suspect* (U., 1945), *The Spiral Staircase* (RKO, 1946), *The Killers* (U., 1946), *The Crimson Pirate* (WB, 1952), many others.

Films: Began writing screenplays for UFA in Germany, 1930; scripted *F.P.1. Does Not Answer* (1933), based on his novel; later worked in France (*La Crise est Finie,* 1935) and England (*Transatlantic Tunnel,* Gaumont-British, 1935); came to Hollywood, 1937, and began work at Paramount (*Her Jungle Love,* 1938); at Universal, contributed to the scripts of many famous horror/fantasy films: *The Invisible Man Returns, Black Friday* (both 1940), *The Invisible Woman, The Wolf Man* (both 1941), *Invisible Agent* (1942), *Son of Dracula* (1943), *The Climax* (1944); also busy at Universal with such films as *Frisco Sal* (1945); in demand too at such studios as Monogram (*The Ape,* 1940) and RKO (Val Lewton's *I Walked with a Zombie,* 1943); later scripted such films as *The Beast with Five Fingers* (WB, 1946), *Berlin Express* (RKO, 1948), *Tarzan's Magic Fountain* (RKO, 1949), *Four Days Leave* (Film Classics, 1950), many more.

Later became a director, working on the scripts of all his films: *Bride of the Gorilla* (Realart, 1951), *The Magnetic Monster* (UA, 1953), *Curucu, Beast of the Amazon* (U., 1956), *Love Slaves of the Amazon* (U., 1957, also producer), *The Devil's Messenger* (with Herbert L. Strock, Herts-Lion, 1962), *Ski Fever* (AA, 1969).

Television: Has written teleplays for many shows, and created the series "#13 Demon Street," filmed in Sweden (1959).

Novels: Mr. Siodmak is the author of the classic *Donovan's Brain* (1943), as well as such novels as *The Third Ear, City in the Sky,* others.

STRANGE, Glenn, actor; Frankenstein's Monster in *House of Frankenstein, House of Dracula* and *Abbott and Costello Meet Frankenstein;* b. George Glenn Strange, Aug. 16, 1899, Carlsbad, New Mexico; original vocation: cowboy; m. Min Thompson, daughter: Janine; d. Sept. 20, 1973, St. Joseph Hospital, Burbank, Calif., (lung cancer), interred Forest Lawn Memorial Park, Hollywood Hills, Calif., Sept. 24, 1973.

Before Films: First "performed" as a fiddle player at cowboy dances at age 12; while punching cattle, became a professional heavyweight boxer; performed on radio in El Paso, 1928, and toured the rodeo circuit as a broncobuster; "discovered" by Hoot Gibson, who hired him for his own rodeo and brought him to Hollywood.

Films: Entered movies as stuntman, 1929; quickly became an actor and scowled in scores of "B" westerns, usually as a heavy, supporting such other stars as John Wayne (*New Frontier,* Rep., 1935), William Boyd (*In Old Mexico,* Par., 1938), Roy Rogers (*Rough Riders Roundup,* Rep., 1939), Gene Autry (*Blue Montana Skies,* Rep., 1939), Tex Ritter (*Rhythm of the Rio Grande,* Mon., 1940), Buster Crabbe (*Billy the Kid Wanted,* PRC, 1941), Hoot Gibson (*Wild Horse Stampede,* Mon, 1943), many others. Also acted in such serials as *Hurricane Express* (Mascot, 1932), *Flash Gordon* (U., 1936), *The Lone Ranger Rides Again* (Rep., 1939) and *Riders of Death Valley* (U., 1941). Unknowingly prepared for his Monster role in such films as *The Mad Monster* (title role, PRC, 1942), *The Mummy's Tomb* (U., 1942), and *The Monster Maker* (PRC, 1944).

Following his three outings as the Monster, played Atlas in *Master Minds* (Mon., 1949), then returned to predominately western fare: *Red Badge of Courage* (MGM, 1951), *The Great Sioux Uprising* (U., 1953), *The Road to Denver* (Rep., 1955), *Quantrill's Raiders* (AA, 1958), others.

Tested unsuccessfully for the title roles in *Tarzan the Ape Man* (MGM, 1932) and *The Creature from the Black Lagoon* (U., 1954).

Television: Appeared (by his own estimation) on more than 500 television shows; memorable as wicked Butch Cavendish, adversary of *The Lone Ranger* (ABC, 1949, and annually on special anniversary show), and, from 1962 to his death, as Sam Noonan, bartender of the Long Branch Saloon, on *Gunsmoke* (CBS).

THESIGER, Ernest, actor; Dr. Septimus Pretorius in *Bride of Frankenstein;* b. Jan. 15, 1879, London; original vocation: artist (work displayed in a gallery on Bond Street, London); m. Janette Mary Fernie Ranken; awarded the Order of Commander of the British Empire, June 1960; d. January 14, 1961, in his London home.

Theater: Made stage bow at St. James Theater, London, 1909; played in Greek tragedy, Shakespeare, musical comedy, and revues; London successes include *The Scarlet Lady* (1926), *Excelsior* (1928), *The Devil* (1930), *Saint Joan* (1936), *The Country Wife* (1936), *Madame Bovary* (1937), *In Good King Charles's Golden Days* (1939), *Big Ben* (1939).

Made New York debut as Cosmo Penny in *The Devil Passes* (1932); later appeared on Broadway in *A Sleeping Clergyman* (1934), *As You Like It* (with K. Hepburn, 1950), *The Country Wife* (1957).

Played Polonius (his favorite role) in a British company of *Hamlet* that played Moscow, 1956.

Films: Played in over 50 features; British productions include *The Real Thing at Last* (1916), *The Bachelor's Club* (1921), *Weekend Wives* (1928), *The Ghoul* (with Karloff and Hardwicke, 1933), *The Man Who Could Work Miracles* (1936), *The Lamp Still Burns* (1943), *Henry V* (as Duke of Berri, directed by Olivier, 1945), *Caesar and Cleopatra* (as Theodotus, 1946), *The Winslow Boy* (1948), *The Man in the White Suit* (1951), *An Alligator Named Daisy* (1955), *Sons and Lovers* (1960), many more. Hollywood films include *The Old Dark House* (as Horace Femm, U., 1932), *The Robe* (as Tiberius, TCF, 1953): final film, England's *Invitation to Murder* (posthumously released, 1963).

Miscellaneous: Was an accomplished "crochet king," and wrote a book on the subject, *Adventures in Embroidery.*

WHALE, James, director of *Frankenstein* and *Bride of Frankenstein;* b. July 22, 1893, Dudley, England; e. public schools in Dudley and art academy in London; served in World War I as a second lieutenant, Seventh Worcester Infantry Regiment, France; original vocation: cartoonist for the London *Bystander;* d. May 29, 1957, at home, 788 S. Amalfi Drive, Pacific Palisades, Calif., (possible drowning), cremated, Chapel of the Pacific, Woodlawn Cemetery, Santa Monica, Calif., June 6, 1957.

Theater: First acted in plays presented by fellow prisoners of P.O.W. camp, Holzminden, Germany; made professional bow as a supernumerary in *The Famous Historie of the Knight of the Burning Pestle,* Birmingham Repertory Theater, Aug. 30, 1919; acted with Shakespeare's Stratford-On-Avon Theater Company, Manchester, Sir Nigel Playfair's Repertory Company, Liverpool, and various provincial theaters, designing sets and directing as well; acted on the London stage in such plays as *A Comedy of Good and Evil* (as "Gas" Jones, 1925) and *A Man with Red Hair* (winning praise as Charles Laughton's mad son, 1928); also busy in London as a stage manager (e.g., the 1926 revue *Riverside Nights*), set and costume designer, and director; directed and designed the set of *Journey's End* for the London Stage Society (December 1928), and restaged it for the West End opening (January 1929) to great acclaim; also directed companies of *Journey's End* in New York and Chicago (1929). Directed *Badger's Green* (London, 1930), *One Two Three* (New York, 1930), *Hand in Glove* (Pasadena Playhouse, Calif., 1944 and New York, 1944) and *Pagan in the Parlor* (Bath, England, 1951); as well as staging several World War II charity shows in Los Angeles.

Films: Arrived in Hollywood in 1929 and was engaged as dialogue director of *The Love Doctor* (Par., 1929) and *Hell's Angels* (Howard Hughes/UA, 1930); directed *Journey's End* (Tiffany-Gainsborough, 1930), winning international praise and a contract with Universal. There he directed *Waterloo Bridge* (1931), *Impatient Maiden* (1932), *The Old Dark House* (1932), *The Kiss Before the Mirror* (1933), *The Invisible Man* (1933), *By Candlelight* (1934), *One More River* (1934), *Remember Last Night?* (1935), *Show Boat* (1936), *The Road Back* (also produced, 1937), *Sinners in Paradise* (1938), *Wives Under Suspicion* (1938), and *Green Hell* (1940), as well as the first two Frankenstein sagas. Also directed *The Great Garrick* (also produced, WB, 1937), *Port of Seven Seas* (MGM, 1938), *The Man in the Iron Mask* (UA, 1939), and *They Dare Not Love*, which was completed by Charles Vidor after Whale quit (Col., 1941). Directed 41-minute version of Saroyan's *Hello Out There* (Huntington Hartford Productions, 1949), but it was never released.

MORE VETERANS OF UNIVERSAL'S FRANKENSTEIN SERIES

ABBOTT, Bud (William), comic-actor; Chick of *Abbott and Costello Meet Frankenstein;* b. Oct. 2, 1895, Asbury Park, New Jersey; d. April 24, 1974, Woodland Hills, Calif:, (cancer).

BELLAMY, Ralph, actor; Erik Ernst in *The Ghost of Frankenstein;* b. June 17, 1904, Chicago, Illinois.

BELMORE, Lionel, actor; Burgomaster Vogel of *Frankenstein*, Emil Lang in *Son of Frankenstein*, Councillor in *The Ghost of Frankenstein;* b. 1867, England; d. Jan. 30, 1953, Woodland Hills, Calif.

BOLES, John, actor; Victor Moritz of *Frankenstein;* b. Oct. 27, 1895, Greenville, Texas; d. Feb. 27, 1969, San Angelo, Texas, (heart attack).

CLARKE, Mae (Violet Mary Klotz), actress; Elizabeth in *Frankenstein;* b. Aug. 16, 1907, Philadelphia, Pennsylvania.

CLIVE, Edward E., actor; Burgomaster in *Bride of Frankenstein;* b. circa 1880, Monmouthshire, England; d. June 6, 1940, North Hollywood, Calif.

COSTELLO, Lou (Louis Francis Cristillo), comic-actor; Wilbur in *Abbott and Costello Meet Frankenstein;* b. March 6, 1906, Paterson, New Jersey; d. March 3, 1959, Los Angeles, Calif., (heart attack).

EDESON, Arthur, cameraman of *Frankenstein;* b. Oct. 24, 1891, New York City; d. Feb. 14, 1970.

FLOREY, Robert, original adaptor and director for *Frankenstein;* b. Sept. 14, 1900, Paris, France; d. May 16, 1979, Los Angeles, Calif.

GORDON, Gavin, actor; Lord Byron in *Bride of Frankenstein;* b. April 7, 1901, Chicora, Mississippi; d. Nov. 18, 1970, London, England, (heart attack).

GWYNNE, Anne, actress; Rita Hussman in *House of Frankenstein;* b. Dec. 10, 1918, Waco, Texas.

HEGGIE, O.P., actor; the Hermit in *Bride of Frankenstein;* b. Sept. 17, 1879, Angaston, South Australia; d. Feb. 7, 1936, Los Angeles, Calif., (pneumonia).

HOBSON, Valerie, actress; Elizabeth in *Bride of Frankenstein;* b. April 14, 1917, Larne, Ireland.

HUTCHINSON, Josephine, actress; Elsa von Frankenstein in *Frankenstein;* b. Oct. 12, 1903, Seattle, Washington.

KERR, Frederick (Frederick Grinham Keen), actor; Baron Frankenstein in *Frankenstein;* b. Oct. 11, 1858, London, England; d. May 2, 1933, London, England.

KNAGGS, Skelton, actor; Steinmuhl in *House of Dracula;* b. June 27, 1911, England; d. April 30, 1955, Los Angeles, Calif., (cirrhosis of the liver).

KNOWLES, Patric, actor; Dr. Frank Mannering in *Frankenstein Meets the Wolf Man;* b. Nov. 11, 1911, England.

LAEMMLE, Carl, Sr., founder of Universal Studios and "presenter" of *Frankenstein* and *Bride of Frankenstein;* b. Jan. 17, 1867, Laupheim, Bavaria, Germany; d. Sept. 24, 1939, Los Angeles, Calif., (heart attack).

MARK, Michael, actor; Ludwig of *Frankenstein*, Ewald Neumuller in *Son of Frankenstein*, Councillor in *The Ghost of Frankenstein*, Strauss in *House of Frankenstein;* b. March 15, 1889, Russia; d. Feb. 3, 1975, Woodland Hills, Calif.

NAISH, J. Carrol (Joseph Carrol Patrick Naish), actor; Daniel in *House of Frankenstein;* b. Jan. 21, 1897, New York City; d. Jan. 24, 1973, La Jolla, Calif., (heart attack).

O'CONNOR, Una, actress; Minnie in *Bride of Frankenstein;* b. Oct. 23, 1880, Belfast, Ireland; d. Feb. 4, 1959, New York City.

O'DRISCOLL, Martha, actress; Miliza Morelle in *House of Dracula;* b. March 4, 1922, Tulsa, Oklahoma.

OUSPENSKAYA, Maria, actress; Maleva in *Frankenstein Meets the Wolf Man;* b. July 29, 1876, Tula, Russia; d. Dec. 3, 1949, Los Angeles, Calif. (stroke and burns sustained because of smoking in bed).

SALTER, Hans J., composer-arranger; arranger of musical score for *Son of Frankenstein*, composer-arranger of scores for *The Ghost of Frankenstein, Frankenstein Meets the Wolf Man* and *House of Frankenstein;* b. 1896, Vienna, Austria.

STEVENS, Onslow (Onslow Ford Stevenson), actor; Dr. Franz Edelmann in *House of Dracula;* b. March 29, 1902, Los Angeles, Calif.; d. Jan. 5, 1977, Van Nuys, Calif.

VAN SICKEL, Dale, actor-stuntman; Monster (cameo gag appearance) in *Hellzapoppin;* b. 1906; d. Jan. 25, 1976.

VAN SLOAN, Edward (Edward Van Sloun), actor; Dr. Waldman in *Frankenstein;* b. Nov. 1, 1881, San Francisco, Calif.; d. March 6, 1964, San Francisco, Calif.

VERDUGO, Elena, actress; Ilonka in *House of Frankenstein;* b. April 20, 1925, Paso Robles, Calif.

WAGGNER, George, producer of *The Ghost of Frankenstein* and *Frankenstein Meets the Wolf Man;* b. September 7, 1894, New York City.

WALTON, Douglas (J. Douglas Duder), actor; Percy Shelley in *Bride of Frankenstein;* b. Woodstock, Toronto, Canada; d. Nov. 15, 1961, New York City.

WAXMAN, Franz (Franz Wachsmann), composer; composer of musical score for *Bride of Frankenstein;* b. Dec. 24, 1906, Koenigshutte, Upper Silesia, Germany; d. Feb. 24, 1967 (cancer).

ZUCCO, George, actor; Professor Bruno Lampini in *House of Frankenstein;* b. Jan. 11, 1886, Manchester, England; d. May 28, 1960, South San Gabriel, Calif.

NOTES

1. Mary Shelley, "Introduction to 1831 edition of *Frankenstein,*" in Mary Shelley's *Frankenstein* (New York: Bantam Books, Inc., 1967), p. xv.
2. Arthur Lennig, *The Count: The Life and Films of Bela "Dracula" Lugosi* (New York: G.P. Putnam's Sons, 1974), p. 71.
3. Robert Cremer, *The Man Behind the Cape* (Chicago: Harry Regnery Co., 1976), p. 116.
4. Al Taylor, "The Forgotten Frankenstein," *Fangoria No. 2,* p. 40.
5. Shelley, *op. cit.*
6. Radu Florescu, *In Search of Frankenstein* (Boston: New York Graphic Society Ltd., 1975), p. 165.
7. Denis Gifford, *A Pictorial History of Horror Movies* (London: The Hamlyn Publishing Group Ltd., 1973), p. 41.
8. *Ibid.,* p. 10.
9. Robert Florey, *Hollywood: d'hier et d'aujourd'hui* (Paris: 1948).
10. Taylor, *op. cit.*
11. Shelley, *op. cit.,* p. 42.
12. "Interview with Jack Pierce," *Monster Mania,* October 1966.
13. Mike Parry and Harry Nadler, "*CoF* interviews Boris Karloff," *Castle of Frankenstein* No. 9, (New Jersey, Gothic Publishing Co., 1966), pp. 10, 12.
14. "Interview with Jack Pierce," *op. cit.*
15. "Great Horror Figure Dies," *Famous Monsters of Filmland* No. 31 (New York: Warren Publishing Co., 1964), p. 50.
16. Taylor, *op cit.*
17. Lennig, *op. cit.,* p. 115.
18. Joseph Moncure March, "Letter," *Look* (New York) March 23, 1954.
19. "James Whale and Frankenstein," *The New York Times,* December 20, 1931, p. 4x.
20. Lillian Lugosi Donlevy, interviewed by Gregory William Mank (Culver City, Ca., July 31, 1976).
21. *Ibid.*
22. "Interview with Jack Pierce," *op. cit.*
23. Tom Hutchinson, *Horror and Fantasy in the Movies,* (New York: Crescent Books, 1974), p. 32.
24. John Carradine, interviewed on Channel 17, Philadelphia, Pa. (Philadelphia, 1976).
25. "Love That Monster," *TV Guide* (Radnor, Pa.: Triangle Publications, Inc., January 11, 1958).
26. Cynthia Lindsay, *Dear Boris,* (New York: Alfred A. Knopf, 1975), p. 54.
27. Denis Gifford, *Karloff—The Man, the Monster, the Movies,* (New York: Curtis Publishers, 1973), p. 19.
28. "Being a Monster is Really a Game," *TV Guide* (Radnor, Pa., Triangle Publications, Inc., October 15, 1960).
29. "James Whale and Frankenstein," *op. cit.*
30. Lindsay, *op. cit.*
31. Donlevy, *op. cit.*
32. Ken Beale, "Boris Karloff, Master of Horror," *Castle of Frankenstein Monster Annual* (New Jersey: Gothic Publishing Co., 1966), p. 58.
33. Donlevy, *op. cit.*
34. Sara Jane Karloff Brodsack, interviewed by Gregory William Mank (Yucaipa, Ca., June 18, 1975).
35. Peter J. Jarman, "The House at the End of the World," in *The Frankenscience Monster,* ed. by Forrest J. Ackerman (New York: Ace Publishing Corp., 1969), p. 161.
36. Donlevy, *op. cit.*
37. David Manners, interviewed by Gregory William Mank (Pacific Palisades, Ca., July 30, 1976).
38. "James Whale and Frankenstein," *op. cit.*
39. "Clive of Frankenstein," *The New York Times,* November 15, 1931, p. 6x.
40. Art Ronnie, "Frankenstein Revisited," *Southland Sunday* magazine (Long Beach, Ca.), December 5, 1971.
41. David Ragan, *Who's Who in Hollywood* (New York: Arlington House, 1976), p. 84.
42. *Ibid.*
43. "James Whale and Frankenstein," *op cit.*
44. Ronnie, *op. cit.*
45. "Great Horror Figure Dies," *Famous Monsters of Filmland, op. cit.,* p. 43.
46. "James Whale and Frankenstein," *op. cit.*
47. "Oh You Beautiful Monster," *The New York Times,* January 29, 1939, p. 4x.
48. "Frankenstein Finished," *The New York Times,* October 11, 1931.
49. *Ibid.*
50. Gifford, *Karloff: The Man . . .,* p. 46.
51. "Oh You Beautiful Monster," *op. cit.*
52. Parry and Nadler, *op. cit.,* p. 12.
53. "Oh You Beautiful Monster," *op. cit.*
54. Denis Gifford, *Movie Monsters,* (New York: E.P. Dutton & Co. Inc., 1969), p. 12.
55. Beale, *op. cit.,* p. 58.
56. Gifford, *Karloff: The Man . . .,* p. 45.

57. Frank Taylor, "Jack Pierce: the Man the Frankenstein Monster Made," *Los Angeles Times Calendar,* August 11, 1968, p. 9.
58. Arlene and Howard Eisenberg, "Memoirs of a Monster," *The Saturday Evening Post,* November 3, 1962.
59. Ronnie, *op. cit.*
60. Peter Underwood, *Karloff* (New York: Drake Publishers, Inc., 1972), p. 66.
61. *Variety,* September 8, 1931.
62. Calvin Thomas Beck, *Heroes of the Horrors,* (New York: MacMillan Publishing Co., 1975), p. 116.
63. Gifford, *Karloff: The Man . . .,* p. 44.
64. Ronnie, *op. cit.*
65. "Clive of Frankenstein," *op. cit.*
66. Ronnie, *op. cit.*
67. "James Whale and Frankenstein," *op. cit.*
68. Forrest J. Ackerman, "The Bride of Dr. Frankenstein," *Famous Monsters of Filmland* #100 (New York: Warren Publishing Co., 1973), p. 66.
69. Eisenburg, "Memoirs of a Monster," *op. cit.*
70. Ronnie, *op. cit.*
71. Parry and Nadler, *op. cit.,* p. 12.
72. Ackerman, "The Bride of Dr. Frankenstein," p. 66.
73. Hutchinson, *op. cit.,* p. 42.
74. Parry and Nadler, *op. cit.,* p. 12.
75. Curtis Harrington, "Boris Karloff: His Reign of Terror," in *Close-Ups,* ed. by Danny Peary (New York: Workman, Publishing Co., 1978), p. 331.
76. Ronnie, *op. cit.*
77. "Great Horror Figure Dies," *op. cit.,* p. 50.
78. "Son of Frankenstein Review," *Motion Picture Herald,* January 21, 1939.
79. Leo Meehan, "Frankenstein review," *Motion Picture Herald,* November 14, 1931.
80. "James Whale and Frankenstein," *op. cit.*
81. "Frankenstein," *Variety,* December 8, 1931.
82. Mordaunt Hall, "Frankenstein," *The New York Times,* December 5, 1931.
83. Favius Friedman, *Great Horror Movies,* (New York: Scholastic Book Services, 1974), p. 12.
84. Boris Karloff, "The Hollywood Horror Man," in *The Hollywood Nightmare,* ed. by Peter Haining, (New York: Taplinger Publishing Co., 1971), p. 137.
85. Gifford, *Karloff: The Man . . .,* pp. 46–47.
86. Eisenberg, "Memoirs of a Monster," *op. cit.*
87. "James Whale and Frankenstein," *op. cit.*
88. Eisenberg, "Memoirs of a Monster," *op. cit.*
89. Drake Douglas, *Horror!,* (New York: The MacMillan Publishing Co., 1966), pp. 109, 113.
90. Gifford, *Karloff: The Man . . .,* p. 48.
91. Gifford, *Movie Monsters,* p. 12.
92. Brodsack, *op. cit.*
93. Eisenberg, "Memoirs of a Monster," *op. cit.*
94. Shelley, *Frankenstein,* p. 131.
95. Brodsack, *op. cit.*
96. Irene Thirer, "Director James Whale Here En Route to Europe," *New York Post,* June, 1936.
97. Eisenberg, "Memoirs of a Monster," *op. cit.*
98. Personal letter from DeWitt Bodeen to Gregory William Mank (January 14, 1978).
99. James T. Coughlin, "Dwight Frye," in *The Real Stars,* ed. by Leonard Maltin (New York: Popular Library, 1979), p. 180.
100. "Interview with John Carradine," *Castle of Frankenstein* (New Jersey: Gothic Publishing Co.).
101. William Saroyan, "Phyllis Brooks: B Movie Standout," in *Close-Ups,* ed. by Danny Peary (New York: Workman Publishing Co., 1978), p. 221.
102. Elsa Lanchester, interviewed by Gregory William Mank (Hollywood, Ca., June 10, 1979).
103. Florian Roberts, "Elsa Lanchester," *Films in Review* (New York: National Board of Review of Motion Pictures, Inc., August/September 1976), p. 385.
104. Eisenberg, "Memoirs of a Monster," *op. cit.*
105. Jonah Maurice Ruddy, "The Dulwich Horror," in *The Frankenscience Monster,* ed. by Forrest J. Ackerman (New York: Ace Publishing Corp., 1969), p. 36.
106. Parry and Nadler, *op. cit.,* p. 12.
107. John W. Waxman's album notes for *Sunset Boulevard: the Classic Film Scores of Franz Waxman* (RCA Records).
108. Page Cook, "Franz Waxman," *Films in Review,* (New York: National Board of Review of Motion Pictures, Inc., August/September, 1968).
109. *Ibid.*
110. "A New Frankenstein Film," *The Hollywood Reporter,* April 6, 1935.
111. Frank S. Nugent, "Bride of Frankenstein," *The New York Times,* May 11, 1935.
112. "Bride of Frankenstein," *Variety,* May 15, 1935.
113. Trade Paper poster quoted by Denis Gifford in *A Pictorial History . . .,* p. 104.
114. "Bride of Frankenstein," *Kinematograph Weekly,* (England) June 6, 1935.
115. Gifford, *A Pictorial History . . .,* p. 115.
116. David Zierold, *The Moguls* (New York: Coward–McCann, 1969), p. 117.
117. William G. Obbagy, "Bela Lugosi," in *Horrors of the Screen #3* (New York: Alexander Soma Enterprises, 1964), p. 9.
118. "Basil Rathbone Obituary," *The New York Times,* July 22, 1967.
119. Beale, *op. cit.,* p. 58.
120. Donlevy, *op. cit.*
121. "Oh You Beautiful Monster," *op. cit.,* p. 4x.
122. Faith Service, "He's the *Mental* Lon Chaney!", *Motion Picture* magazine, July 1933.
123. Josephine Hutchinson, interviewed by Gregory William Mank (New York, August 17, 1978).
124. *Ibid.*
125. Beck, *op. cit.,* p. 150.
126. Donlevy, *op. cit.*
127. Jarman, *op. cit.,* p. 161.
128. Preston Neal Jones, "The Ghost of Hans J. Salter," *Cinefantastique* Vol. 7, No. 2, p. 14.
129. "Son of Frankenstein review," *Motion Picture Herald, op. cit.*
130. "Son of Frankenstein review," *The Hollywood Reporter,* January 1939.
131. "Son of Frankenstein review," *New York Daily Mirror,* January 1939.
132. "Son of Frankenstein review," *The Cinema* (England) February 22, 1939.
133. Women's University Club review of Son of Frankenstein from the file of the Academy of Motion Picture Arts and Sciences, (Beverly Hills, Ca.)
134. Hy Gardner, "Broadway Newsreel," *The Brooklyn*

Eagle, April 5, 1939.
135. Brodsack, *op. cit.*
136. Gifford, *Karloff: The Man . . .,* p. 233.
137. Cremer, *op. cit.,* p. 189.
138. *Ibid.*
139. Donlevy, *op. cit.*
140. Paul M. Jensen, *Boris Karloff and his Films,* (Cranbury, New Jersey: A.S. Barnes, 1974), p. 115.
141. Donald F. Glut, *The Frankenstein Legend,* (Scarecrow Press, 1973), p. 142.
142. Robert Bloch, "Dr. Psycho and Mr. Stein," in *The Frankenscience Monster,* ed. by Forrest J. Ackerman (New York: Ace Publishing Corp., 1969), p. 55.
143. Beck, *op. cit.,* p. 152.
144. Jarman, *op. cit.,* p. 162.
145. Lon Chaney, Jr., interviewed on NBC's *Tonight Show* (October 8, 1969).
146. "An Interview with Lon Chaney, Jr.," *Castle of Frankenstein* No. 10 (New Jersey: Gothic Publishing Co.).
147. Sir Cedric Hardwicke and James Brough, *A Victorian in Orbit,* (Garden City, New York: Doubleday & Company, Inc., 1961).
148. *Ibid.*
149. Service, *op. cit.*
150. Florabel Muir, "They Wouldn't Believe Him," *New York Sunday News,* September 13, 1942.
151. Doug McClelland, "Evelyn Ankers, Queen of the Horrors," *Film Fan Monthly* No. 88, p. 5.
152. *The Ghost of Frankenstein* pressbook, p. 4.
153. Universal Publicity Release, (January, 1942).
154. Gifford, *A Pictorial History . . .,* pp. 136, 139.
155. Personal letter from Curt Siodmak to Gregory William Mank (April 18, 1980).
156. "Interview with Jack Pierce," *op. cit.*
157. *Ibid.*
158. Reginald LeBorg, "Lon Chaney Jr.: A Man Living in a Shadow," in *Close-Ups,* ed. by Danny Peary (New York: Workman, Publishing Co., 1978), p. 339.
159. Universal Publicity Release, (January 1942).
160. Universal Publicity Release, (January 1942).
161. "An Interview with Ralph Bellamy," *Film Fan Monthly* No. 111.
162. *The Ghost of Frankenstein* pressbook, p. 4.
163. Evelyn Ankers, "The 'B' and I," introduction to *The Golden Age of "B" Movies* by Doug McClelland (Charter House, 1978), pp. 7, 8.
164. "The Ghost of Frankenstein review" *The Hollywood Reporter,* March 2, 1942.
165. "The Ghost of Frankenstein review," *Motion Picture Herald,* March 7, 1942.
166. Bosley Crowther, "The Ghost of Frankenstein review," *The New York Times,* April 4, 1942.
167. William K. Everson, *Classics of the Horror Film,* (Secaucus, New Jersey: Citadel Press, 1974), p. 51.
168. *Frankenstein Meets the Wolf Man* pressbook, p. 5.
169. Curt Siodmak, interviewed by Gregory William Mank (Three Rivers, Ca., July 1, 1980).
170. *Ibid.*
171. Donlevy, *op. cit.*
172. James Miller, "Interview with Ilona Massey," *Varulven* magazine No. 4.
173. Muir, *op. cit.*
174. LeBorg, *op. cit.*
175. Miller, *op. cit.*
176. *Ibid.*
177. Gifford, *A Pictorial History . . .,* p. 136.
178. *Ibid.*
179. Donlevy, *op. cit.*
180. Obbagy, *op. cit.*
181. Jones, "The Ghost of Hans J. Salter," p. 12.
182. *Ibid.* p. 16.
183. "Frankenstein Meets the Wolf Man," *Movie Story* magazine, March, 1943.
184. *Ibid.*
185. "Frankenstein Meets the Wolf Man review," *Variety,* February 19, 1943.
186. "Frankenstein Meets the Wolf Man review," *The Hollywood Reporter,* February 19, 1943.
187. Bosley Crowther, "Frankenstein Meets the Wolf Man review," *The New York Times,* March 6, 1943.
188. Florescu, *op. cit.,* p. 198.
189. Gifford, *A Pictorial History . . .,* p. 141.
190. Gifford, *Karloff: The Man . . .,* p. 56.
191. Joel E. Siegel, *Val Lewton: The Reality of Terror* (New York: The Viking Press, 1973), p. 71.
192. Ankers, *op. cit.*
193. *House of Frankenstein* pressbook, p. 4.
194. *Ibid.,* p. 5.
195. Jack Jones, "A Strange Interview," *The Monster Times* No. 21.
196. Glut, *op. cit.,* p. 168.
197. "My Life As a Monster!" *Mad Monsters Magazine* No. 4.
198. *Ibid.*
199. *Ibid.*
200. *Ibid.*
201. *Ibid.*
202. *Ibid.*
203. Forrest J. Ackerman, "The Lone Stranger," *Famous Monsters of Filmland* No. 105, (Warren Publishing Co.).
204. "My Life As a Monster!" *op. cit.*
205. Personal letter from Elena Verdugo to Gregory William Mank, (October 15, 1979).
206. "House of Frankenstein review," *New York Herald–Tribune,* December 16, 1944.
207. "House of Frankenstein review," *The Hollywood Citizen-News,* December 23, 1944.
208. Douglas, *op. cit.*
209. Siegel, *op. cit.,* p. 72.
210. Parry and Nadler, *op. cit.,* p. 14.
211. "House of Frankenstein review," *New York World-Telegram,* December 1944.
212. "Carradine's Hamlet," *Time,* November, 1943.
213. Glut, *op. cit.,* p. 176.
214. "House of Dracula review," *The New York Times,* December 22, 1945.
215. "House of Dracula review," *The Hollywood Reporter,* November 29, 1945.
216. "House of Dracula review," *Variety,* November 29, 1945.
217. Dorothy Masters, "House of Dracula review," *New York Daily News,* December 22, 1945.
218. Gifford, *A Pictorial History . . .,* p. 144.
219. "Frankenstein's Monster . . . Created by a Girl," in *Out of This World* Vol. I, ed. by Perrott Phillips, (New York: Phoebus Publishing Co., 1978), p. 30.

220. Bosley Crowther, *Hollywood Rajah* (New York: Dell Publishing Co., 1960), p. 340.
221. Charles Barton, interviewed by Gregory William Mank (Toluca Lake, Ca., October 7, 1979).
222. Bob Thomas, *Bud and Lou* (Philadelphia, J.B. Lippincott, Co., 1977), p. 154.
223. *Ibid.*, p. 155.
224. James Robert Parish and Michael R. Pitts, "Lon Chaney Jr. 1906–1973," *Films In Review*, New York National Board of Review of Motion Pictures, Inc. November, 1973.
225. Donlevy, *op. cit.*
226. Barton, *op. cit.*
227. Al Taylor and Sue Roy, *Making a Monster,* (New York: Crown Publishers, Inc., 1980), p. 82.
228. Unidentified clipping.
229. "My Life As a Monster!" *op. cit.*
230. "Abbott & Costello Meet Frankenstein review," *The Hollywood Reporter,* June 28, 1948.
231. "Abbott & Costello Meet Frankenstein review," *Variety,* June 28, 1948.
232. Jim Mulholland, *The Abbott & Costello Book* (New York: Popular Library).
233. Philip K. Scheuer, "Abbott & Costello Meet Frankenstein review," *Los Angeles Times,* July 26, 1948.
234. *Ibid.*
235. Cecelia Ager, "Abbott & Costello Meet Frankenstein review," *New York Star.*
236. Glut, *op. cit.*, p. 168.
237. Bill Warren, "Fascinating Karloff Facts," in *The Frankenscience Monster,* ed. by Forrest J. Ackerman (New York: Ace Publishing Corp., 1969), p. 159.
238. Thomas, *op. cit.*, p. 200.
239. Gifford, *A Pictorial History . . .*, p. 208.
240. "Abbott & Costello Meet Frankenstein review," *New York Herald–Tribune.*
241. Ager, *op. cit.*
242. Donlevy, *op. cit.*
243. Lennig, *op. cit.*, p. 310.
244. Barry Brown, "Lugosi's Tragic Addiction," *Castle of Frankenstein* No. 10 (New Jersey: Gothic Publishing Co.), p. 10.
245. Jarman, *op. cit.*, p. 161.
246. Personal letter from DeWitt Bodeen to Gregory William Mank, (November 10, 1978).
247. Lanchester, *op. cit.*
248. Hardwicke and Brough, *op. cit.*, p. 217.
249. "Basil Rathbone Obituary," *op. cit.*
250. Michael B. Druxman, *Basil Rathbone: His Life and his Films* (Cranbury, New Jersey: A.S. Barnes, 1975), p. 105.
251. Mark Shivas, "Karloff, Still Eager to Scare Us Witless," *The New York Times,* April 14, 1968.
252. Taylor, "Jack Pierce: the Man the Frankenstein Monster Made," *op. cit.*
253. Shivas, *op. cit.*
254. Robert C. Roman, "Boris Karloff," *Films In Review,* (New York National Board of Review of Motion Pictures, Inc. August/September 1964).
255. Lindsay, *op. cit.*, p. 60.
256. Parish and Pitts, *op. cit.*, p. 538.
257. Jones, "A Strange Interview," *op. cit.*
258. Joan Zyda, "Glenn Strange Dies . . .," *Los Angeles Times,* September 22, 1973).
259. John Brosnan, *The Horror People,* (New York: St. Martin's Press, 1976), p. 275.
260. McClelland, *op. cit.*, p. 8.
261. Verdugo, *op. cit.*
262. "Terence Fisher interview," *Films and Filming* magazine, July, 1964.
263. Glut, *op. cit.*, p. 191.
264. Harry Ringel, "Terence Fisher Underlining," *Cinefantastique,* Vol. 4, No. 3, p. 126.
265. Gifford, *A Pictorial History . . .*, p. 208.
266. Richard Bojarski and Kenneth Beale, *The Films of Boris Karloff,* (Secaucus, New Jersey: Citadel Press, 1974), p. 33.
267. Dale Winogura, "Young Frankenstein," *Cinefantastique,* Vol. 3, No. 4, p. 46.
268. Richard Lamparski, *Whatever Became Of. . ?* (New York: Bantam Books, 1977), p. 180.